50 -10

READINGS IN
CORRECTIONAL CASEWORK
AND COUNSELING

READINGS IN CORRECTIONAL CASEWORK AND COUNSELING

Edited by
EDWARD E. PEOPLES
Administration of Justice Department
San Jose State University

Goodyear Publishing Company, Inc.
Santa Monica, California

Library of Congress Cataloging in Publication Data

Main entry under title:

Readings in correctional casework and counseling.

    1. Corrections—Addresses, essays, lectures.
2. Rehabilitation of criminals—Addresses, essays,
lectures. 3. Crime and criminals—Addresses, essays,
lectures. I. Peoples, Edward E.
HV9275.R4   364.6   74-21275
ISBN 0-87620-190-7

Current Printing (last digit):
10 9 8 7 6 5 4 3

ISBN: 0-87620-190-7
Library of Congress Catalog Card Number: 74-21275

Y-1907-8

Printed in the United States of America

Dedicated to my wife, Corinne,
for joining me to share of life,
as we two become.

Contents

Preface

The primary goal of corrections has always been the protection of society. Few would question the validity of the goal itself; however, in recent years many have questioned the means of achieving it. As a result, the nature and scope of corrections have been going through a process of redefinition. Traditionally, the very term *corrections* has been associated in the public mind (and in the more narrow professional minds as well) with institutions, places where offenders are contained until they are "corrected"—prisons or correctional facilities, and reform or training schools.

Since the mid-1960s, there has been increasing disillusionment with the rehabilitative effectiveness of institutions and with the social protection they allegedly provide. Not only has the evidence justified this disillusionment; it has shown that the dehumanizing effects of incarceration actually mitigate against society's receiving the protection that it demands. Consequently, the thrust of the "new corrections" has been back to the community; it minimized institutional commitments and established community-based treatment programs as a more effective alternative. Obviously, community treatment is not a new concept. Probation and parole have been used as alternatives to incarceration for many years but with an orientation of traditional corrections. Probation was viewed as a privilege granted the offender in lieu of incarceration; a chance to prove himself worthy to remain in the community. Parole, the early return of an offender to the community from an institution in lieu of having him serve his full term, was a tentative chance to prove himself worthy after having paid his debt to society. In both "treatment" situations, the classical theory of free will predominated, and the full responsibility for behavior change rested with the offender. His adjustment in society was to be immediate and complete.

Casework did not mean to work *with* clients but to have clients literally *under* supervision. Counseling was not a dialogue between agent and offender, but rather a monologue delivered by the agent in which he told the offender what was wrong with him and what was expected of him. Beyond this, the caseworker assumed a reactive posture, providing surveillance, so that if and when the offender deviated from these expectations the agent could respond to enforce the social and legal norms. The purpose of casework was to insure social protection through conformity, and the function of counseling was to superimpose society's prevailing standards on those of the individual. This purpose was particularly true in juvenile corrections, where the court allegedly intervened "on behalf of" the youth.

The effectiveness of this traditional community treatment was impossible to measure, but oftentimes it was as questionable as that of the institution. Nevertheless, the scope of community treatment expanded to include halfway houses, juvenile ranches and camps, jail farms, foster homes, residential centers, and a whole array of other public and private programs. However, merely designating a correctional program as community based did not insure its success. As long as the needs of the client were determined by the caseworker, as long as counseling remained a monologue to demand conformity, and as long as enforcement was considered the primary method to insure protection for society, corrections criminalized offenders in the community more often than it treated them.

With the thrust of the new corrections, the role of the caseworker has taken on a whole new dimension and a new working philosophy has changed the nature of community treatment. Basic to this philosophy is the belief that society's protection is best assured through casework intervention strategies which facilitate the offender's efforts to achieve self-direction and a meaningful existence within the boundaries of legal behavior. Social protection is still a primary goal, but real and lasting protection is achieved only as a by-product of the offender's personal growth and enrichment, and his personal satisfaction from legal behavior. The only other choice is neutralization forever; we have been that route before, and failed.

The enforcement role of the caseworker has not been replaced, necessarily, for many professionals believe that enforcement is inherent in the nature of any socialization or resocialization process. However, the caseworker has a new dimension as a pro-active treatment facilitator. Treatment is not used here in the traditional meaning of the word. The caseworker does not cure his clients, because they are not sick. He does not *fix* his clients, because they are not *broken*.

Nevertheless, the caseworker does have a responsibility to his client and to society to facilitate changes in his client's life and life style to the extent needed. He also has the responsibility not to attempt changes when they are not needed. And the determination of "needed" is mutually arrived at *by the agent and the client*.

The caseworker of today does not supervise the lives of offenders; rather, they participate with him in their own correction. It is a collaborative process, facilitated by the agent, which blends the needs of the client with those of society. It is a process in which both agent and client share some responsibility for direction and outcome, yet one in which they also have divided and individual responsibilities.

Ultimately, the offender is responsible for his own behavior; within the alternatives available to him, he does make choices. The caseworkers' responsibility is to expand the range of alternatives; to maximize the offender's real freedom to choose; and to aid him in developing the requisite personal skills for self-direction and fulfillment. It may also involve changing the environment, rather than the individual.

To reiterate, *the offender is not a sick person in need of a cure,* but often his behavior is inappropriate; it is out of tune with the legal and social, and, frequently, with his own personal expectations. All of us could live in better harmony with ourselves, with each other, and with our social and legal environment, and come closer to a full realization of our potential as human beings. Correctional counselors work with a specific clientele group, defined by law as offenders, in a growth process that gives meaning to their lives, on their terms, and that benefits society. I emphasize "that benefits society," because that is still the goal of corrections, still the function of the pro-active counselor. It just happens that the working ingredients of the "new corrections" philosophy benefits the client as well.

In his pro-active role, the correctional caseworker needs to develop a repertoire of counseling strategies, and must be able to call into play a multitude of intervention skills. This book introduces a variety of theoretical counseling models and applies them to correctional casework in the hope of providing a framework of understanding around which those strategies and skills can be developed. The content is limited to counseling for behavior change.

The book is designed to serve as a college text for courses in administration of justice, corrections, criminology, counseling, social work, and related programs. Secondarily, it provides counseling agencies with a source book for training personnel in client counseling. In both instances, the material is for students and professionals in the field who are, or intend to become, responsible for casework with juvenile or adult offenders in community-based programs. Under certain conditions the material is appropriate for an institutional setting; however, the focus here is the community.

The selection and sequence of the readings came from my years of observing that new personnel are almost totally unable to perform effectively in the caseworker role. Colleges have not prepared them to cope with the experiential realities of the job, let alone give them counseling skills. And, for many, the lack of agency resources has perpetuated a pall of casework dysfunctionalism created by this absence. Hopefully, this book can make some contribution toward filling that preparation gap.

The material in each section is linked together by a common purpose and direction. The readings follow one from another to guide developmental preparation in a logical manner. Part I presents theories of personal and social development that explain criminality and delinquency. Part II shows how those theories have been, and are now, applied in corrections; reviews the current trends in examining the cause and treatment of antisocial behavior; and discusses some of the practical aspects of the environment in which casework is conducted. Part III focuses on two of the most vital elements in counseling: the style and attitude of the caseworker and the dynamics of the worker-client relationship.

When the reader has a grasp of the theoretical assumptions upon which counseling is based, has made the transition from theory to application, and has formed a perception of his own role in the correctional process, he can proceed to acquire and utilize a variety of specific counseling strategies that are the real essence of constructive casework. Strategies in current use, both nationally and internationally, are presented in the remaining portions of the book.

Part IV introduces the offender classification and treatment models that primarily serve in one-to-one counseling and facilitate the application of individualized strategies and programs. In Part V, group-counseling models are examined, and some of the distinctions between group and individual counseling are noted.

Whether the caseworker decides on group, family, or individual counseling depends on the nature of the case, his own skills and level of comfort within the various counseling environments. One word of caution is offered to the reader entering the field of correctional counseling. Sometimes the best treatment is no treatment at all. Develop the skills to facilitate behavior change when it is needed, learn to accept behavior that does not need to be changed, and develop the wisdom to recognize the difference.

I am indebted to many people for my own professional development in the field of corrections. However, no one deserves my gratitude more than the offender himself. For without his contribution, the correctional system could not have colonized as it has; and both you and I would have no choice but to spend our efforts cultivating our own gardens.

I

CAUSAL THEORIES OF CRIME AND DELINQUENCY

INTRODUCTION

The value of theories which attempt to explain the causes of criminal and delinquent behavior is often debated. These debates usually focus on two major issues: 1) the general usefulness of theories in developing counseling strategies, and 2) if theories are useful, which of the many causal theories provides the most accurate basis for counseling?

The first issue can be addressed by stating several obvious, but often overlooked, facts. An individual's approach to counseling others is determined by the general assumptions he makes about human nature and the specific theory of personality that he holds. Without a set of guiding theoretical principles, the caseworker's intervention strategies become little more than a process of "muddling-through." This latter approach can be observed when casual rap sessions pass for on-going group counseling, and when the effectiveness of individual counseling is measured by the number of client contacts per month.

Theories provide a framework for understanding behavior, a guide for planning and implementing counseling strategies, and a basis for evaluating the outcome of casework. Theories can also be destructive in counseling if the caseworker is rigidly locked into using one theory to explain all deviant behavior. It is as dangerous not to question one's theories as it is not to have any.

So we come to choosing the most accurate or most appropriate theory. Admittedly, the debate has never been resolved, and perhaps it never should be. From a humanistic view, the fact that differing theories exist is a healthy sign; it recognizes that man is unique and that the forces interacting in his development are complex.

The purpose of understanding causal theories is not to seek absolutes, but to appreciate more fully the scope of the forces that produce

1

change and then to form a conceptual basis for utilizing their energies in guiding the change process. In the final analysis, choosing the most accurate theory, or theories, for counseling is a situational task determined by the nature and extent of the behavioral problem and by the goals of treatment.

In Part I, each theoretical model presents a different perspective on the nature and cause of antisocial behavior. The reader becomes familiar with the principal theoretical constructs upon which almost all correctional counseling is based, and does not need to choose one from among them.

In the first article, four psychological theories are detailed by Dr. Milton F. Shore. He reviews each theory, relates one to another, identifies their common elements, and suggests the need for a comprehensive psychological theory that will account for delinquent and criminal behavior.

Then C. G. Schoenfeld presents a psychoanalytic theory of juvenile delinquency. Taking a Freudian view of child development, Schoenfeld relates the cause of delinquent behavior to the formation of a weak superego resulting from lax or inconsistent parental discipline. At a time when permissiveness and the expression "do your own thing" are popular in our society, Schoenfeld calls for more strict parental controls and a social climate that emphasizes normative behavior.

Traditional psychoanalysis, according to Schoenfeld, is not an effective therapeutic solution to delinquency. Rather, a combination of group therapy (peer pressure), family discipline, and a restructuring of environmental influences may provide the adequate inner and outer controls necessary to change delinquent behavior.

In the third reading, Professor C. R. Jeffery offers a unique perspective on how people learn to become criminals. He reformulates the long-established sociological theory of differential association in the light of current psychological research.

Sutherland's theory of differential association states that an individual learns criminal behavior by associating with criminals, and law-abiding behavior by associating with noncriminals. This theory has been popular for many years; while Professor Jeffery believes that it is basically sound, he feels that it is an oversimplification of what is now known to be a more complex phenomenon. By integrating Sutherland's concepts with the operant behavior theory of psychology, Jeffery formulates a learning theory which accounts for both the social and the personal forces that maintain criminal behavior.

Jeffery explains that, as the criminal operates on his environment, his behavior is either reinforced or extinguished by its consequences. Criminality, then, is the result of a relationship between the individual and his environment, and Jeffery suggests how to apply learning theory to control criminal behavior.

1

Psychological Theories of the Causes of Antisocial Behavior

MILTON F. SHORE

Chief, Clinical Research and Program Evaluation Section, Mental
Health Study Center, National Institute of Mental Health, U.S.
Department of Health, Education, and Welfare

Supervising Psychologist, Worcester (Mass.) Youth Guidance Center,
1957–62; Chief Psychologist, Newton Project, Judge Baker Guidance
Center, Boston, Mass., 1962–64

A.B., 1949, Harvard College; M.A., 1950, Ph.D., 1955, Boston
University

This paper attempts to review, organize, and evaluate the many
theories that have been developed to explain the roots of antisocial behavior from a psychological perspective. Four general
categories are suggested—biopsychological theories, developmental theories, psychodynamic theories, and social psychological theories. Common elements in the theories are extracted
and suggestions are made for future research.

The need for a theory that can explain the causes of criminal and delinquent behavior is threefold: first, it helps organize the known data;
second, it assists in setting directions for further exploration and research; and third, it aids in planning intervention programs oriented
toward preventing antisocial behavior.

But evolving an adequate theory of the origins of antisocial behavior is extremely complex, largely because of the difficulty in accurately defining what is antisocial. Antisocial behavior is not a diagnostic
category or unitary symptom, but a socially defined phenomenon
closely tied to cultural values and often dependent on the interpretation given a behavior pattern by those agencies responsible for the reg-
ulation of social interaction. In certain communities, for example, the

Reprinted, with permission of the National Council on Crime and Delinquency, from
Crime and Delinquency, October 1971, pp. 456–468.

Adapted from a position paper written for the President's Commission on Law Enforcement and Administration of Justice in 1966.

tolerance for deviance is lower and certain behavior may be labeled antisocial which, in another context, would not be considered deviant at all.

However, despite the cultural and social aspects of antisocial behavior, there are individuals who, given the best social opportunities, still are violent and aggressive, while others under poor social conditions do not reveal delinquent or criminal behavior. Therefore, aside from the need to understand and explain the social and cultural forces that foster criminal behavior, there is need for a theory of individual behavior that can account for individual differences and the ways in which individuals interpret and respond to social forces.

From a psychological perspective, the problem in the control of antisocial behavior can be conceived of as the question of how control over behavior is developed so that, under ordinary circumstances, antisocial behavior will not take place.[1] What are the relevant influences within the person and within his environment that foster the development of inner behavior controls? What are the relevant variables for understanding the development of inner controls (conscience, identification, self-image, etc.)? What are the factors essential for the adequate functioning of these controls?

This paper is a review of the theories dealing with the psychological aspects of delinquent and criminal behavior. It attempts to categorize and organize the large number of psychological theories, determine their assumptions, relate them to one another, and derive the common psychological elements that need to be considered when any intervention program is planned. It is not a critical analysis or a comprehensive literature review. It aims to meet the need in the field for a broad look at the various theories so that a comprehensive theory may develop in the near future.

BIOPSYCHOLOGICAL THEORIES

Historically, the development of psychiatry and psychology from the nineteenth century's biological and medical traditions led to many early efforts to explain most antisocial behavior in biological terms. These explanations take two forms: those based on the genetic transmission of antisocial traits from generation to generation ("bad seed"),[2] and those that sought to relate criminal behavior to structural constitutional characteristics such as mental capacity, neural organization, and body type. Both these approaches—the genetic and the constitutional —attempt to tie psychological characteristics, such as the motor orientation, inability to delay, and low frustration tolerance, to biological roots.

One of the first attempts to correlate body structure to criminal behavior was made by Lombroso,[3] who stated that the biological structure of the criminal was biologically atavistic and that ideal social conditions had only a limited effect on criminals, for these persons could not restrain their antisocial behavior. This was confirmed, he believed, by the histological structure of the cortex.

Sheldon,[4] although he did not attribute inferior evolutionary status to the offender, related delinquent behavior to body build. The body build, he believed, was highly correlated with an inborn substratum of basic psychological traits ("temperament") which caused the person to respond in a particular way to environmental stimulation.

The interest in the biological structure and mechanisms underlying the criminal personality was continued in the work of Cleckley,[5] who believed the psychopathic personality had biological roots. Some support for his view has come from those who have found a greater number of signs of neurological disorder (tremors, exaggerated reflexes, tics, etc.) in psychopaths,[6] as well as greater physiological responsiveness to environmental changes and many more early diseases that might have damaged the brain.

At present there is great concern with the chromosomal XYY syndrome, which is believed to be associated with hypermasculinity and poor control of aggression.

The biopsychological theories address themselves to certain known facts. There is no doubt that the antisocial behavior of certain individuals has sometimes been found to be impermeable to change by current techniques and that certain individuals have required external control within an institutional setting. Also known is that certain individuals under drugs of various kinds (e.g., alcohol) show a marked breakdown in behavioral controls. Certain neurological phenomena have also been directly related to motor control.[7] All these facts suggest that one factor that must be considered in evaluating the causes of antisocial behavior in an individual is his neurological and biochemical structure.

However, research has shown that the biological structure of the person, although contributing to lack of control under certain stimulating conditions, is in no way a prerequisite for that loss of control, nor is it often the major element in determining the antisocial dimension of the behavior.[8]

If the future directions in the field are in any way related to those of the past, many traits and tendencies which are believed to be biological in origin will most likely be found to be closely tied to experiences, perhaps to events occurring in infancy, a fact that could account for the problems in reversibility and change. For example, the current work on imprinting, where a particular event occurring during a critical period in biological maturation results in certain behavior,[9] is significant in this regard.

Recently, a close tie between experience and neurological organization has been found.[10] If certain experiences do not occur at certain ages, adequate neurological development does not take place.

These discoveries have begun to narrow the link between maturation and experience and to highlight the close ties between the two. It augurs well for eventual breakthroughs in the understanding of biological factors related to the development of behavioral controls.

DEVELOPMENTAL THEORIES

Cognitive Development

The ability to control motor activity, to delay fulfillment of wishes and desires, to use guilt to regulate behavior, and to experience the pangs of conscience after transgression does not occur at birth but develops in a sequential order from the interaction of the maturative processes and the environment. For example, the young child who takes something belonging to another child is regarded as having an insufficient understanding of the situation and therefore is not considered to have committed an antisocial act. It is assumed that only at a certain age does awareness of the consequences of an action arise. (The concept of "legal age" implies that only at a certain chronological age can the person be assumed to understand the consequences of an act and therefore take responsibility for what he has done.) The study of the development of the understanding of morality (moral judgment) was initiated by Piaget,[11] who saw moral values as having two stages, moral realism and moral relativism. From a literal, inflexible interpretation of rules and blind obedience to a higher external authority, the child progresses to an understanding, at about age eight, of the situational and motivational elements of an act and to internalized rules.

Kohlberg[12] has studied the stages of moral development in greater detail than Piaget. True understanding of morality and justice, he believes, does not develop until adolescence.

Developmental theories assume a sequence of formal stages in the development of moral understanding. The nature of this sequence is independent of sex, intelligence, culture, social group, and biological background. However, environmental factors can delay the transition from one stage to another.

There are two important questions about cognitive theories. First, what is the relationship between the understanding of morality (a cognitive function) and moral conduct (overt behavior)? Second, what are the necessary personal and environmental conditions for the adequate development of higher moral judgment?

Studies of the relationship between moral judgment and moral behavior often show low correlations between the two.[13] Investigators in behavior modification through rewards and punishments have shown that control over overt behavior is possible without concomitant cognitive changes or generalization to other situations.[14]

Cognitive theorists have also tended to ignore the affective components in antisocial behavior. Motivation plays a minor role in their studies and often appears to lower any correlation that might exist. However, the cognitive theorists have contributed two significant ideas to the understanding of behavioral control. They have delineated the stages in the development of controls so that one can determine how development is taking place. They have also shown why moral training and exposure to moral influences, as in Boy Scouts or religious training, are not, in themselves, adequate for developing an understanding of morality but are effective only if a certain level of conceptualization has been reached.

Socialization

The largest group of studies on the origins of antisocial behavior deals with socialization experiences. These studies have attempted to identify the nature and the quality of the experiences necessary for the adequate development of internal controls.

Role of Frustration. A major attempt to explain the social origins of aggressive behavior was the frustration-aggression hypothesis of Dollard and Miller.[15] This hypothesis has been criticized as incomplete.[16] However, there is little doubt that, although reactions to frustration may vary, under certain conditions—such as the social reinforcement of violence—aggression is a most likely response. Thus it is necessary to specify more clearly those elements or types of frustration that would lead to aggressive behavior, since even under certain stimulating conditions aggression does not always result. For example, deprivation or broken attachments may be more significant as a precursor to aggression than physical immobility at a young age.

Role of Family Structure and Early Family Experiences. The significant role of the family as the primary agent for socialization of the child cannot be denied. But what elements in family structure and functioning are essential to accomplish this socialization adequately? What factors result in inadequate socialization producing delinquent or criminal behavior?

Many years ago, attempts to determine the most important factors in early experience related delinquency to discrete general categories of rejection, parental neglect, working mothers, and broken homes. These attempts, which represent a relatively simple effort to conceptualize the area, have been found to be too general and simplistic. Recently, efforts have been made to define the complex subtle aspects of family interaction and family breakdown which are believed to be of particular significance in predisposing an individual to antisocial behavior.

1. Broken homes.   McCord, McCord, and Zola[17] reported that the roots of criminal behavior lie deep in early family experiences, so that only the most intensive measures, applied early in life, can ever offer hope of eradicating them. While they stated that cohesive homes produced fewer criminals, they contended that the influence of broken homes per se has been overstressed. A quarrelsome and neglectful home, whether or not it was broken, was found to be even more conducive to criminality. Toby's work[18] was consistent with these findings. Conflicts, tensions, and attitudes preceding the actual breakdown of the family are the most important factors, he felt. But the influence of those factors depends on the age of the child. Pre-adolescents are more affected by family breakdowns than adolescents.

McCord, McCord, and Thurber[19] added another element to those listed above—namely, mothers who are working. That is, an unstable family plus a working mother shows a high correlation with delinquent behavior.

A major contribution of recent work has been to challenge the stereotype that families must have a certain specific structure with the parents playing certain specific roles. The final breakup of a family may indeed be a healthy sign if the forces that are mobilized as a result try to lead to the resolution of problems rather than their perpetuation. Likewise, mothers who choose to work may be able to better deal with their children than if they felt an obligation to remain at home seething with boredom, frustration, and guilt.

2. Influence of father.   Andry[20] has suggested that the role of father —specifically, the physical or psychological absence of the father—has been underemphasized as an etiological factor in criminal behavior. Mischel[21] agrees, pointing out that absence of the father is highly correlated with the demand for immediate gratification (a feature found in severe delinquents) in eight- and nine-year-olds. This relationship was not present, however, in older children (eleven to fourteen years of age).

In an effort to determine what might be the reasons behind the high correlation between social class, absence of the father, and delinquency, Kvaraceus[22] concluded that aggressive behavior in lower-class male adolescents results from role anxiety. The anxiety over one's sexual role is derived from the unstable and derogatory father image presented in the home by the absence of the father or through continual devaluation of adult males by lower-class adult females.

McCord, McCord, and Zola[23] found that although the father's personality had an important bearing on antisocial behavior, it was an oversimplification to see the father and his role as the sole irreversible determining factor in delinquency. They felt that the effects of paternal neglect could be overcome if there was strong maternal love or consistent love-oriented discipline. Thus, even if the father was a criminal, maternal love and consistent discipline tended to prevent a son from identifying with the antisocial paternal model.

3. *Separation and loss.* Bowlby[24] suggested still another aspect of early family experience as significant in setting the stage for later antisocial behavior. A large number of separation experiences in early life which deprived the child of a stable close attachment to one mothering person, he felt, could lead to the development of certain basic attitudes and reactions to people which are identical to those found in delinquents and criminals. He sees this tie to a maternal figure as rooted in early biological needs.

McCord, McCord, and Zola[25] confirmed the importance of maternal love in the early years. Maternal love, even if complicated by an over-protective attitude, by anxiety, or by neurosis, was found to lead to low rates of crime. Maternal passivity, on the other hand, was significantly related to criminal behavior.

4. *Other familial influences.* McCord, McCord, and Zola[26] found that boys in the middle of the birth order, especially if viewed by their parents as troublemakers, tended to be antisocial.

Discipline and Family Climate. Many investigators have attempted to describe the elements of parent-child relationships most closely related to the development of antisocial behavior in an individual. One of the most obvious is discipline; it is usually believed that disciplinary measures within a family lead to the development of self-discipline.

Glueck and Glueck[27] listed discipline by the father, supervision by the mother, affection from each, and cohesiveness of the family as the factors most important for predicting future delinquent behavior (they form the items of the Glueck Prediction Scale). McCord and McCord,[28] in their review of the Cambridge-Somerville Youth Study, found that consistent discipline, either punitive or love-oriented, tended to prevent criminality, while erratic punitive punishment was correlated with every type of crime except traffic violations.

The work of Sears et al.[29] sums up the findings of many studies: Discipline is necessary in child rearing, but parents of highly aggressive children have consistently been found to be more aggressive, less warm, and more inconsistent in their disciplinary techniques.

An attempt to determine the origins of the authoritarian personality[30] found that harsh, threatening discipline during childhood, in which inflexible, black-and-white roles of dominance and submission were present, led not to a firmly internalized set of moral values but rather to a rigid, autocratic personality that was power-oriented and that viewed signs of weakness as dangerous.

The results of harsh discipline in child rearing are consistent with those found in experimental studies of punishment—namely, that punishment is effective in bringing about short-term conformity but does not lead to the internalization of moral values or behavioral control useful in other situations over long periods of time.

Out of these studies on discipline, three important elements emerge—consistency, intensity, and quality. Consistent discipline is more effective in producing internalization than either extreme permissiveness or lack of consistency. The more severe the punishment, the less the probability that internalization will later take place. With respect to quality, Aronfreed[31] has described two kinds of disciplinary activity. Verbal and physical attacks are sensitization techniques which make the child anticipate punishment from an external source. The opposite, which he calls induction, is where explanation and withdrawal of affection are used to try to correct the behavior. In this way independence of external factors is emphasized and the self-initiation aspects of control are in the forefront. Internalized control over behavior results.

Role of Learning and Identification. To explain why children who have been severely punished often show highly aggressive behavior, Bandura and Walters[32] proposed a theory of the social learning of deviant behavior. The violence that is reinforced in the culture and the violence to which a child is exposed during the period of his growth when imitation and identification are important cause him to model himself after the aggressor. The importance of an adult model with whom a child could identify was noted by Rohrer and Edmonson[33] in a study of a group of Negro youths in New Orleans. Significant adults were found to be extremely important in shaping the lower-class youth's behavior; if adults were not available, individuals joined gangs in what was believed to be an effort to supply role models and values of their own. Short and Strodtbeck[34] found that lower-class gang members had lower ego ideals than a control group of nongang members.

But identification is not a unitary process. Kohlberg[35] has suggested that there are two types of identification. In *personal identification* the person wishes to be like the parent. On the other hand, in *positional identification* family figures are seen as sources of power and the wish is to usurp the parents' sexual, authoritarian, or family roles. Research findings suggest that personal identification is related to moral learning, while positional identification is not. Personal identification clearly seems to be related to close contacts with a person whom one respects and trusts. Kohlberg sees a close tie between personal identification and the development of feelings of guilt. In identifying with another person, one assumes the role of that person in fantasy and becomes critical of transgressions, a first step in internalization and a prerequisite for experiencing guilt.

Role of the Community. Socialization occurs not only through the family but through other community institutions as well. The relationship between the community and the family has been investigated. Maccoby et al.[36] found that communities where delinquency was high were lacking in integration, with less concern expressed by people for one another. Lander's[37] work likewise indicated that the reason juvenile delinquency was concentrated in neighborhoods where there were lower-class residents is that these areas tend to be anomic: that is, there are no stable jobs, no long residences, and no networks of friends and relatives. When upper-class areas become anomic, the rate of crime would be expected to increase.

Short[38] suggests that the significant factor is that in lower-class urban environments, there is a breakdown of norms and a "general absence of any culture." Such a condition threatens the individual with loss of individual security and produces great psychological stress and strain resulting in personal breakdown and aberrations.

Leighton[39] felt that the frustration of sexual and aggressive impulses by socio-cultural forces was not the most important factor in precipitating antisocial behavior. Rather, the important factor was how socio-cultural disintegration produced noxious influences that then affected the achievement of love, recognition, spontaneity, and a sense of belonging to a moral order (feeling that one is right in what one does).

PSYCHODYNAMIC THEORIES

Psychodynamic theories of antisocial behavior have addressed themselves to the complex affective elements that are significant in personality development and in leading to an antisocial act. They focus on the motivational factors, the efforts to resolve conflicts, and the unconscious aspects of the various forces behind behavior. They emphasize that the nature of a particular antisocial act is, in itself, no indication of the personality structure of an individual (neurotic, psychotic, character problem, stress reaction, or normal in a delinquent subculture), but primarily represents a symptom (except in the delinquent subculture) whose primary purpose is an attempt to resolve the many intrapsychic tensions in the person. The dynamic theories stress the necessity for understanding the nature of the conflict and the many motivational causes of the anxieties that lead to antisocial behavior (such as the unconscious need for punishment or the desire to punish one's parents, to prove one's masculinity, or to deny one's needs for nurturance, etc.) before attempting to bring about change or planning any intervention program.

Early formulations of the psychodynamic theories focused primarily on the needs that were being gratified by the acting-out behavior.[40] Detailed analyses were made of drive arousal, frustration, and gratification. These were then related to early experiences with gratification during eating, bowel control, and sexual activity. These sources of gratification were seen not only as intrapsychic but as interpersonal as well. Johnson and Szurek,[41] for example, have shown how parents can unconsciously gain satisfaction from their children's antisocial behavior that they subtly provoke and perpetuate.

Recent formulations of psychodynamic theories have directed attention to those elements of the personality that screen, control, and direct the impulses as well as to the nature of the needs themselves. These functions (called functions of the ego) include the tolerance for frustration, the ability to delay gratification, the adequate functioning of guilt, the development of sublimations, and the evolution of self-esteem. Redl and Wineman[42] have described in some detail the ego distortions and ego defects in delinquents with severe character disorders. They elucidate the adaptive patterns of acting out where certain ego functions are well developed and serve the need for survival in an environment seen as unsatisfying and threatening.

Erikson[43] has taken these ideas a step further in his psychosocial concept of negative identity. Negative identity is defined as the ego's effort to derive stability and structure through integrating the past, present, and future into a role against society and its mores, a role seen by delinquents and criminals as preferable to the emptiness and helplessness experienced when one has no identity at all (identity diffuseness). The reinforcement of this negative identity by significant figures in the environment serves to perpetuate the antisocial behavior.[44]

The major contributions of dynamic theories lie in the highlighting of the affective elements of the personality. They are particularly valuable in pointing out the complex roots of antisocial behavior. They are also able to explain events not clearly explained by other theories, such as the differences between male and female delinquent behavior, the causes of delinquency in affluent middle-class families, and the reasons behind primitive acts of violence suddenly committed by socialized individuals.

SOCIAL-PSYCHOLOGICAL THEORIES

Social Forces and the Individual

Social psychologists have been primarily concerned with the antisocial individual within the context of the group. They have given special emphasis to the individual's need for involvement with groups of various kinds and to gang membership as a source of gratification. They attempt to identify the social forces that are influencing the individual's behavior in social and antisocial directions.

Cohen[45] suggested that working-class males were not equipped for middle-class competition. As a result, they tend to draw together and, through their sympathetic interaction, develop social systems of their own with their own standards and status. In this "delinquent subculture," virtue is seen as consisting of flouting and defying middle-class morality.

Short and Strodtbeck[46] posited a close association between school failures and joining a gang. They suggest that the school is rejected as an agent of socialization and the gang accepted because the family has not given the individual the necessary skills for coping with the middle-class educational structure. Conversely, those whose socialization confers verbal facility and achievement skills are better equipped to cope with the demands of school and other middle-class institutions.

Miller[47] felt that it was incorrect, however, to see gang membership as resulting primarily from a rejection of the majority culture. Rather it should be seen in terms of conformity to an in-group and the satisfactions obtained through conforming.

Gold[48] proposed a social-psychological theory involving many variables. He hypothesized that the higher the quality of recreational facilities in a community, the greater its attractiveness to the individual and the less the likelihood of delinquency and crime. However, the role of the father is of prime importance in communicating community values to family members. Thus, the father must be seen as a successful provider, as having status in the community, and as having influence over family decisions.

Role of Self-Image

Several investigations have tried to account for the nondelinquent and noncriminal within delinquent and criminal subcultures, with the hope that an understanding of these individuals might provide an explanation of vulnerability to delinquency. Reckless[49] found that most significant in this regard was the self-concept. An adequate self-concept served to protect the nondelinquent from the social and cultural pressures toward antisocial behavior. Clark,[50] in agreement, showed how, in Negroes, the loss of dignity and one's sense of self-worth leads to self-hatred and feelings of worthlessness, which in turn make the individual exceedingly susceptible to social pressures of all kinds, among them delinquency and crime.

Self-esteem continues to be seen as a significant variable in determining whether a person will be susceptible to delinquency. Bandura and Walters[51] found that children with low self-esteem more easily imitate the behavior of others. In line with their role-model theory, they suggested that criminal models would, therefore, have greater influence over these children. Sherif[52] concurred, finding that individuals who had their own personal standards were less influenced by the groups and group pressure.

Since self-image and self-esteem have been regarded as important elements in keeping a person from group influence and from delinquent behavior, Massimo and Shore[53] hypothesized that, in delinquents, changes in self-image should be highly correlated with decreases in antisocial behavior. Changes in self-image were brought about through a special program of comprehensive vocationally oriented psychotherapy.[54] This did, in fact, lead to a significant drop in delinquent behavior.

IMPLICATIONS

Research on the psychological elements believed to be related to criminal and delinquent behavior has arisen from a variety of theoretical frameworks. Addressing itself to finding the answers to certain phenomena, each theory attempted to broaden its scope by integrating the ideas of other theoretical frameworks. Five general comments can be made about these theories.

1. Many of the theories of etiology are based on correlations between certain events. Sometimes this has led to conclusions about causal relationships. Such etiological conclusions based on correlations cannot be made even on the basis of a high relationship between two or more factors.

2. Many studies of etiology are based on the recall and reporting of past experiences rather than on direct observation. Such recall has consistently been found to be of low reliability.

3. Many studies compare large groups of delinquents and/or criminals to a large nondelinquent population. The results from such studies of large groups can be applied only with extreme caution to the individual.

4. Many studies are *ex post facto*. Given a known group of antisocial individuals, such studies attempt to find factors which differentiate these individuals from nondelinquents. However, to determine whether these factors are indeed of etiological significance requires longitudinal studies, few of which have been made.

5. It is not clear why many of the factors considered to be of etiological significance lead specifically to antisocial behavior, since they are known to predispose individuals to other disturbances as well.

But despite the criticisms made of these studies, there are many areas of agreement among the psychological theorists:

1. Although the origins of antisocial behavior are very complex and although such behavior arises from many sources, plans for any program aimed at significantly reducing crime and delinquency should not ignore psychological elements. The important questions that need to be considered are as follows: What are the opportunities for the development of feelings of self-worth and self-esteem? What are the

opportunities to identify with someone who is respected, loved, and trusted? What are the chances to develop feelings that one has control and mastery over the environment? What are the elements that produce feelings of belonging to a group and social order? What are the aspects of the program that offer hope for the future?

2. Most of the theorists agree that the roots of antisocial behavior most often lie in early and extremely negative interpersonal experiences with important figures, such as parents. Large-scale programs can be successful only insofar as they can assist the parental figures in bringing about the intimate, intense, positive individual attachments necessary for growth and development. Programs for prevention must be aimed at improving the emotional climate of an individual's experience with important figures and assisting families and individuals during periods of stress and crisis.

3. Because there are a complex number of causes of criminal and delinquent behavior, there must be a variety of different services available to prevent antisocial behavior. Efforts should be made to identify those who are showing early signs of disturbance, as well as to help those already involved in antisocial activities. Programs will have to differ for males and females, different socio-economic groups, and groups that have special needs (such as those with neurological disorders).

4. At times it may be necessary to institutionalize an individual. However, the rehabilitative elements in such institutions should be derived from an understanding of the psychological needs that are related to the development of internalized behavioral controls. Such controls evolve only when respect and trust are present and where discipline is not geared toward humiliation and threats. Identification with a respected and socialized individual is a precondition for control over impulsive behavior.

5. Planned courses in building character and moral training do not in themselves result in moral behavior unless translated into significant personal relationships providing socialized role models whom the individual wishes to resemble and who he feels understand him. Individualized contacts should be encouraged and fostered in any program.

6. Psychological factors should not be separated from the social and cultural factors which serve to teach ways of satisfying particular personal needs. Violence within the society, as revealed in the mass media and other social institutions, presents delinquency and crime as a legitimate way of resolving personal frustrations and tensions. Those who have difficulties in controlling their primitive drives sometimes see this as a license to express their feelings directly in action.

7. No magical or simple answers for the eradication of antisocial activities can be given. Any program for crime prevention must be

comprehensive and multi-dimensional, and must incorporate several disciplines. No single factor has yet been found to be most decisive in preventing crime, nor is there any indication that any such factor will ever be found. But a review of the etiological aspects of criminal and delinquent behavior gives us some direction for planning and carrying out large-scale preventive programs that are broad in scope and that can be directed toward identifying and altering many of the influences destructive to the growth of the individual.

NOTES

[1] As has been shown in studies of behavior under extreme conditions, such as in concentration camps, every individual has a breaking point for control. Stealing, violence—even cannibalism—can result under conditions of severe deprivation.

[2] P. R. Newkirk, "Psychopathic Traits Are Inheritable," *Diseases of the Nervous System,* February 1957, pp. 52–54.

[3] C. Lombroso, *Crime, Its Causes and Remedies,* trans. by H. P. Horton (Boston: Little, Brown, 1912).

[4] W. H. Sheldon, *Varieties of Delinquent Youth: An Introduction to Constitutional Psychology* (New York: Harper, 1949).

[5] H. M. Cleckley, "Psychopathic States," in *American Handbook of Psychiatry,* ed. S. Arieti (New York: Basic Books, 1959), pp. 567–89.

[6] W. McCord and Joan McCord, *Psychopathy and Delinquency* (New York: Grune and Stratton, 1956).

[7] N. C. Kephart, *The Slow Learner in the Classroom* (Columbus, Ohio: C. E. Merrill, 1960).

[8] P. F. Briggs and R. D. Wirt, "Prediction," in *Juvenile Delinquency,* ed. H. C. Quay (Princeton, N.J.: D. Van Nostrand, 1965).

[9] W. Sluckin, *Imprinting and Early Learning* (Chicago, Ill.: Aldine, 1965).

[10] A. H. Riesen, "Stimulation as a Requirement for Growth and Function in Behavioral Development," in *Functions of Varied Experience,* eds. D. W. Fiske and S. R. Maddi (Homewood, Ill.: Dorsey Press, 1961).

[11] J. Piaget, *The Moral Judgment of the Child* (Glencoe, Ill.: Free Press, 1948).

[12] L. Kohlberg, "Moral Development and Identification," *Child Psychology: Yearbook of the National Society for the Study of Education* (Chicago: University of Chicago Press, 1963), pp. 277–333.

[13] R. Havighurst and H. Taba, *Adolescent Character and Personality* (New York: John Wiley, 1949).

[14] J. Aronfreed and A. Reber, "Internalized Behavioral Suppression and the Timing of Social Punishment," *Journal of Personality and Social Psychology,* January 1965, pp. 3–16.

[15] J. Dollard et al., *Frustration and Aggression* (New Haven, Conn.: Yale University Press, 1939).

[16] A. Bandura and R. H. Walters, "Aggression," *Child Psychology: Yearbook of the National Society for the Study of Education* (Chicago: University of Chicago Press, 1963), pp. 364–416.

[17] W. McCord, Joan McCord, and I. Zola, *Origins of Crime: A New Evaluation of the Cambridge-Somerville Youth Study* (New York: Columbia University Press, 1959).

[18] J. Toby, "The Differential Impact of Family Disorganization," *American Sociological Review,* October 1957, pp. 505–12.

[19] Joan McCord, W. McCord, and Emily Thurber, "The Effects of Maternal Employment on Lower Class Boys," *Journal of Abnormal and Social Psychology,* August 1963, pp. 177–82.

[20] R. G. Andry, *Delinquency and Parental Pathology* (London: Methuen, 1960).

[21] W. Mischel, "Father Absence and Delay of Gratification," *Journal of Abnormal and Social Psychology,* July 1961, pp. 116–24.

[22] W. C. Kvaraceus et al., *Delinquent Behavior: Culture and the Individual* (Washington, D.C.: National Education Association, 1959).

[23] McCord, McCord, and Zola, *Origins of Crime.*

[24] J. Bowlby, *Forty-four Juvenile Thieves: Their Characters and Home Life* (London: Baldiere, 1947).

[25] McCord, McCord, and Zola, *Origins of Crime.*

[26] Ibid.

[27] S. Glueck and E. Glueck, *Unravelling Juvenile Delinquency* (Cambridge, Mass.: Harvard University Press, 1950).

[28] McCord and McCord, *Psychopathy.*

[29] R. R. Sears, Eleanor E. Maccoby, and H. Levin, *Patterns of Child Rearing* (Evanston, Ill.: Row Peterson, 1957).

[30] T. W. Adorno, E. Frenkel-Brunswick, D. J. Levinson, and R. N. Sanford, *The Authoritarian Personality* (New York: Harper, 1950).

[31] J. Aronfreed, *Conduct and Conscience* (New York: Academic Press, 1968).

[32] A. Bandura and R. H. Walters, *Adolescent Aggression* (New York: Ronald Press, 1959).

[33] J. H. Rohrer and M. Edmonson, *The Eighth Generation* (New York: Harper, 1960).

[34] J. F. Short and F. L. Strodtbeck, *Group Process and Gang Delinquency* (Chicago: University of Chicago Press, 1965).

[35] L. Kohlberg, "Development of Moral Character and Moral Ideology," in *Review of Child Development Research,* eds. L. and M. Hoffman (New York: Russell Sage Foundation, 1964), pp. 383–433.

[36] Eleanor E. Maccoby, J. P. Johnson, and R. M. Church, "Community Integration and the Social Control of Juvenile Delinquency," *Journal of Social Issues,* 3 (1958): 38–51.

[37] B. Lander, *Towards an Understanding of Juvenile Delinquency* (New York: Columbia University Press, 1954).

[38] J. F. Short, "The Sociocultural Context of Delinquency," *Crime and Delinquency,* October 1960, pp. 365–75.

[39] D. C. Leighton, *The Character of Danger: Psychiatric Symptoms in Selected Communities* (New York: Basic Books, 1963).

[40] S. Freud, *Civilization and Its Discontents* (London: Hogarth Press, 1955 [originally published in 1930]); W. Healy and A. Bronner, *New Light on Delinquency and Its Treatment* (New Haven, Conn.: Yale University Press, 1936).

[41] Adelaide M. Johnson and S. A. Szurek, "The Genesis of Antisocial Acting Out in Children and Adults," *Psychoanalytic Quarterly,* July 1952, pp. 323–43.

[42] F. Redl and D. Wineman, *Controls from Within* (Glencoe, Ill.: Free Press, 1952).

[43] H. Erikson, *Childhood and Society* (New York: Norton, 1950).

[44] H. Erikson and K. T. Erikson, "The Confirmation of the Delinquent," *Chicago Review,* Winter 1957, pp. 15–23.

[45] A. K. Cohen, *Delinquent Boys: The Culture of the Gang* (New York: Free Press, 1955).

[46] Short and Strodtbeck, *Group Process.*

[47] W. B. Miller, "Lower Class Culture as a Generating Milieu of Gang Delinquency," *Journal of Social Issues,* 3 (1958): 5–19.

[48] M. Gold, *Status Forces in Delinquent Boys* (Ann Arbor, Mich.: University of Michigan Press, 1963).

[49] W. C. Reckless, S. Dinitz, and E. Murray, "Self Concept as an Insulator against Delinquency," *American Sociological Review,* December 1956, pp. 744–46; W. C. Reckless, S. Dinitz, and B. Kay, "The Self Concept in Potential Delinquency and Potential Nondelinquency," *American Sociological Review,* October 1957, pp. 566–70.

[50] K. B. Clark, "Color, Class, Personality, and Juvenile Delinquency," *Journal of Negro Education*, Summer 1959, pp. 240–51.

[51] A. Bandura and R. H. Walters, *Social Learning and Personality Development* (New York: Holt, Rinehart, and Winston, 1963).

[52] M. Sherif, "Group Influences upon the Formation of Social Norms and Attitudes," in *Basic Studies in Social Psychology*, eds. H. Proshansky and B. Seidenberg (New York: Holt, Rinehart, and Winston, 1965).

[53] J. L. Massimo and M. F. Shore, "The Effectiveness of a Comprehensive Vocationally Oriented Psychotherapeutic Program for Adolescent Delinquent Boys," *American Journal of Orthopsychiatry*, June 1963, pp. 634–42.

[54] J. L. Massimo and M. F. Shore, "Comprehensive Vocationally Oriented Psychotherapy: A New Treatment Technique for Lower Class Adolescent Delinquent Boys," *Psychiatry*, August 1967, pp. 229–36.

2

A Psychoanalytic Theory of Juvenile Delinquency

C. G. SCHOENFELD

Secretary-Treasurer, Schoenfeld and Sons, Inc., New York City
B.A., 1947, Yale University; LL.B., 1950, Harvard Law School; LL.M.
(Criminal Justice), 1971, New York University

This paper offers a psychoanalytic theory of juvenile delinquency, the essence of which is that juvenile delinquency (like other behavioral disturbances that tend to appear during puberty and adolescence) often reflects an inner struggle between a person's moral faculty—his superego—and the oral, anal, and phallic impulses of early childhood that are revived in him just before puberty. The view is advanced that juvenile delinquency may result not only when a person's superego is too strict or has criminal tendencies but more especially when it is too weak, defective, or incomplete to control properly these resurrected primitive, violent, and amoral—indeed, "criminalistic"—urges of infancy. In addition, some of the factors responsible for the improper formation of the superego (maternal deprivation, inconsistent discipline, etc.) are considered, as are ways of strengthening the superego through better methods of child rearing. Emphasis is on the need for better inner controls, as well as better outer or societal controls, to curb the growing incidence of juvenile delinquency.

To encourage psychoanalysts and sociologists to join in a concerted attack on juvenile delinquency—which in combination with youth crime is "the most serious single aspect" of today's growing crime problem[1]—this paper presents a psychoanalytic theory of juvenile delinquency that is implicit in Freudian-oriented writings concerning human development and that appears to be consistent with certain cur-

Reprinted, with permission of the National Council on Crime and Delinquency, from *Crime and Delinquency*, October 1971, pp. 469–480.

rent sociological theories regarding juvenile delinquency. Requiring brief mention first, however, are certain limitations inherent in the psychoanalytic theory to be considered.

To begin with, the insights that psychoanalytic psychology has to offer concerning juvenile delinquency pertain mainly to the characterological or psychological aspects of juvenile delinquency. Psychoanalysis has little to contribute to those aspects of juvenile delinquency that a biologist or a geneticist, for example, is likely to concern himself with. Hence, psychoanalytic psychology can offer, at best, only a partial or incomplete theory of juvenile delinquency—a fact that responsible psychoanalysts freely admit.[2] Indeed, since the psychoanalytic theory of juvenile delinquency to be presented will be limited mainly to a consideration of the relationship between man's moral faculty (what psychoanalysts call his "superego") and juvenile delinquency, this proposed theory will be partial or incomplete even in terms of the characterological or psychological aspects of juvenile delinquency.[3] Offering such an admittedly limited psychoanalytic theory of juvenile delinquency may well serve a very useful purpose, however, for if (as the noted psychoanalyst Edmund Bergler has insisted) man's moral faculty or superego is "the decisive part of the personality," the "real master of the personality,"[4] then this paper's concentration upon the role played by the superego vis-à-vis juvenile delinquency may well serve as a needed counterweight to psychoanalytic studies of juvenile delinquency that obscure or fail to emphasize sufficiently the role performed by the superego.[5] In fact, possibly because psychoanalysis developed largely in the context of attempts to cope not with juvenile delinquency or crime, but rather with neurotic (and sometimes psychotic) phobias, inhibitions, obsessions, compulsions, and the like, psychoanalytic studies of juvenile delinquency sometimes place undue emphasis upon certain psychoanalytic insights at the expense of psychoanalytic findings concerning delinquent behavior that would appear to be more general and more basic.[6]

LIFE STAGES

Implicit in Freudian-oriented writings regarding human development is the view that a child "enters the world as a criminal; i.e., socially not adjusted."[7]

> Side by side with loving attitudes and peaceful contentment, there are always to be found [in infants and young children] mental processes reminiscent of the most primitive aspects of savage life of an intensity that is only faintly mirrored later on by the distressing aspects of our international relations, including even the tortures and other atrocities. Violent and ruthless impulses of destruction (i.e., murder in adult language) follow on the inevitable minor privations of this

period. The jealousies, hatreds, and murderous impulses of which signs may be detected in childhood are, in fact, the weakened derivatives of a very sinister inheritance we bring to the world and which somehow has to be worked through and chastened in the painful conflicts and emotions of infancy.[8]

Psychoanalysts usually label the first year or year-and-a-half of life the "oral" stage of infancy. During this early period, the infant is thought to be beset by a variety of oral urges, including sadistic and cannibalistic wishes. Indeed, so pronounced are these desires when the infant begins to teethe that some psychoanalysts refer to the later half of the oral stage as the "oral-sadistic" or "cannibalistic" phase of infancy.[9]

The next stage of life identified by psychoanalysts is the so-called "anal" or "anal-sadistic" period, which lasts until a child is about three years of age. Typical of this period are characteristics that in an adult would be termed stubbornness, spitefulness, and cruelty. Indeed, many children of two and three years of age seem to be moved by a desire to hurt and destroy simply for the sake or "joy" of hurting and destroying:

> When a child tears off the legs and wings of butterflies and flies, kills or tortures birds or vents his rage for destruction on his playthings or articles in daily use, his elders excuse it on the ground of lack of capacity to feel for a different living creature, or his slight comprehension of the money value of things. But our observation teaches us something different. We hold that the child tortures animals, not because he does not understand that it adds to their suffering, but just because he wants to add to their sufferings, and small, defenseless beetles are the least dangerous of creatures.[10]

The anal or anal-sadistic stage is followed by the "phallic" period of early childhood. During this period (which continues until the age of about 5½), the child begins to direct strong erotic feelings toward the parent of the opposite sex and at times to experience powerful feelings of jealousy and hostility toward the parent of the same sex. Freud labeled this concatenation of parent-directed emotions (and the ideas associated with them) the "Oedipus complex," deriving the phrase from Sophocles' classic tragic drama *Oedipus Rex,* in which Oedipus kills his father, Laius, and marries his mother, Jocasta.

The Oedipus complex begins to disappear toward the end of the fifth year of life, in part because of the appearance at this time of internal prohibitions against incest and parricide—prohibitions that constitute the core of the superego.[11]

Man's moral faculty or superego (which includes what is ordinarily meant by the term "conscience," but which is in large part unconscious) does not exist at birth. Rather, it develops slowly and tentatively during the first few years of life, consisting at first largely of parental prohibitions that are alternatively internalized and externalized.[12] When a child reaches the age of six or so, however, he usually more or less permanently internalizes ("introjects") the image he has formed of his parents. This image becomes his superego, which then rules him from within as his parents once ruled him from without.

The formation of the superego heralds not only the disappearance of the Oedipus complex but also the beginning of what psychoanalysts call the "latency period." During this period (which begins at about the age of six and extends until puberty) the child's physical and psychosexual growth proceed extremely slowly. The latency period is generally marked, however, by the appearance of additions to the superego—particularly the so-called "reaction-formations" that inhibit contrary impulses.[13] Shame, for example, begins to hold exhibitionism in check; disgust helps to repel desires to touch and smell; and sympathy serves to dampen (and often block) aggressive and cruel wishes.[14] Indeed, by the onset of puberty, the superego has become a complex structure that performs a great number of functions, including setting moral and ethical standards, evaluating thoughts and actions (principally one's own) in light of these standards, granting rewards (for example, self-praise and self-love) for moral conduct, and demanding repentance and punishment (including unconscious self-torture) for unprincipled behavior.[15]

The upsets that mark puberty need hardly be detailed here, for they are as familiar as this morning's newspaper and today's television programs. Psychoanalysts have learned, however, that these upsets are not only a reaction to the physical and endocrinal changes of puberty but also a product of the revival just before puberty begins of long-dormant oral, anal, and phallic (especially Oedipal) impulses. More specifically, the behavioral disturbances of puberty are in large measure the product of an inner struggle between, on the one hand, these newly activated primitive, violent, amoral—and "criminal"—oral, anal, and phallic urges of infancy and, on the other hand, efforts by the superego (aided by the "I" of the personality—the ego) to reassert control over the revived infantile urges.[16]

In most cases, the struggle between the superego and the resurrected primitive wishes of infancy results in the so-called "normal" upsets of puberty—sudden enthusiasms and equally sudden depressions, bursts of rebelliousness and assertiveness coupled with periods of dependence and submissiveness, alternations between asceticism and self-indulgence, intellectualism and irrationality. All too often, however, the struggle between the superego and the resurrected desires of early childhood is reflected in the behavioral disturbances that psychoanalysts label "neuroses" and "psychoses" and—of particular significance here—in the antisocial behavior that the law labels "juvenile delinquency."[17]

One type of pubescent or adolescent who is likely to commit delinquent acts is the youth who has a superego with criminal tendencies (the sort of superego that may develop if, for example, a child is brought up by parents who lack respect for and fail to obey society's laws).[18] That is, if a youth's superego not only fails to oppose but is actually consistent with some of the antisocial childhood impulses resurrected in him at puberty (or with the pubescent or adolescent derivatives of these early wishes), it may actually encourage—rather than discourage—the youth to commit antisocial acts that express these childhood impulses.

Surprisingly, perhaps, delinquent behavior may also occur in just the opposite sort of case: for instance, when a pubescent youth's superego is unduly puritanical and opposes with undue vigor the antisocial urges revived in him at puberty. In such a case, the very presence of these primitive childhood wishes (and especially Oedipal desires) may so offend the superego as to cause it to engender considerable unconscious guilt.[19] And, paradoxically, in an effort to expiate this guilt the youth may actually commit crimes with the unconscious aim of being caught and punished.[20] Indeed, it is on this basis that one is able to understand why certain criminals make it so easy for the police to apprehend them—why, for example, some criminals, in effect, autograph their crimes with an invariable *modus operandi,* and why other criminals return to the scene of their crimes and into the arms of the waiting police.[21]

THE WEAK SUPEREGO

The essence of this paper's theory of juvenile delinquency, however, is that the vast majority of delinquent acts reflect the presence not of an unduly strict superego or of a superego with criminal tendencies but rather of a superego that is somehow so weak, defective, or incomplete that it proves unable to control properly the primitive and powerful urges of early childhood that are resurrected just before puberty, with the result that some of these antisocial urges (or their pubescent and adolescent derivatives) are expressed in delinquent behavior.[22]

A reasonably complete list of the reasons why a pubescent youth's superego may be too weak (or too defective or incomplete) to help him cope successfully with the revived antisocial wishes of early childhood—thus helping to prevent him from committing delinquent acts—has yet to be compiled. Nevertheless, psychoanalysts have identified *some* of the factors that appear to play a role in determining whether the superego of a pubescent or adolescent will be strong enough and complete enough to help him resist the antisocial impulses that inevitably beset him.

PARENTAL DEPRIVATION AND AFFECTION

Psychoanalysts have learned that the absence of the mother (or her surrogate) for a prolonged period during the first few years of a child's life may well have a devastating effect upon the child[23] and may certainly result in the formation of a superego that is seriously defective and incomplete—a superego that is unable to prevent his aggressive and hostile urges (which, incidentally, may be exacerbated by the mother's absence[24]) from finding expression in delinquent behavior. After all, the superego is essentially an internalized parent image; if a child's mother (or her surrogate) is absent for prolonged periods, it is almost inevitable that his internalized image of her will be incomplete and defective.

Like maternal deprivation, the absence of the father (or father substitute) during childhood is likely to be reflected in the formation of a defective and incomplete superego. Boys, especially, need a father figure to serve as a proper model of male behavior; and the absence of a father (or father substitute) in the home during the early years of a boy's life may well result in the boy's becoming a homosexual.[25] (The boy's superego would, among other things, presumably lack the completeness that the presence of a father in the home might have provided and that might have enabled the superego to prevent infantile homosexual urges resurrected at puberty from gaining ascendancy.[26]) Also, as psychoanalytically knowledgeable sociologists have stressed, boys brought up in a fatherless home may, in a desperate attempt to establish a male identity at puberty and during adolescence, repudiate the norms of good behavior (which these boys equate with femininity) and engage instead in delinquent behavior (erroneously regarded by these boys as normal male behavior).[27]

Like paternal and maternal deprivation, the lack of sufficient parental—particularly motherly—affection during childhood is likely to result in the development of a superego unable to control the antisocial impulses that appear during infancy and are revived just before puberty begins. A young child obeys his parents not only because of fear of punishment by them but also—and more especially—because of love for them and fear of losing their affection.[28] If the parents fail to show the child sufficient affection (including the indulgence, to some extent, of his dependency feelings[29]), he has, in a sense, that much less to lose if he disobeys them and is then punished by them by a withdrawal of their affection. Indeed, his having received too little parental affection may result not only in his failing to renounce his antisocial desires but also in his failing to internalize parental values contrary to and capable of opposing such antisocial desires.[30] As can be readily ascertained, these psychoanalytic insights find considerable support in sociological studies of patterns of affection within the family, studies which reveal that "affection is related to the child's internalization of parental values. . . . An affectionate parent-child relationship promotes the internalization of conventional values and thus insulates a child against delinquent behavior."[31]

LAX AND INCONSISTENT DISCIPLINE

Even more conducive to delinquent behavior, perhaps, than a lack of sufficient parental affection is the final factor to be considered here pertaining to the ability of the superego to withstand the onrush of resurrected infantile urges at puberty: lax and inconsistent discipline during early childhood[32] (a factor stressed by psychoanalysts and sociologists alike[33]). For one thing, lax discipline and the indulgence of the youngster's infantile wishes implicit in this laxity is, as psychoanalysts have learned, likely not to decrease but rather to increase the child's thirst for the primitive gratifications inherent in the infantile wishes[34]; and as the desire for these gratifications increases, the less able is the superego to resist this desire. In fact, if the need for the infantile urges of youngsters to find expression becomes too strong and insistent, they may well express themselves in delinquent behavior long before the advent of puberty; that is, during the latency period —or even earlier.

Paradoxically, sudden or unduly energetic attempts by parents to control the primitive urges of a child that they have previously tolerated or indulged may also have the effect of strengthening these urges (though they may temporarily disappear into "the unconscious"). As Kate Friedlander has put it: "Sudden repression of instinctive urges brings with it the danger of an unmodified and still antisocial impulse breaking through in later life against the wishes of the individual."[35] And if the child's discipline has, in general, been inconsistently and erratically conducted by his parents, then the probability that these and other forbidden infantile urges will escape effective control by his superego and express themselves in delinquent behavior is enhanced, for the child is all too likely to have a superego that is just as erratic and inconsistent as the discipline given him by his parents (in whose image his superego has presumably been formed). In short, the probability is that lax and erratic discipline not only will strengthen the primitive impulses of early childhood but also will result in the creation of a defective superego—a superego too erratic and inconsistent to prevent these impulses from finding expression in delinquent conduct, especially when they reappear during puberty and adolescence.

METHODS OF CHILD REARING

Perhaps the most obvious conclusion suggested by the material presented so far is that the more that can be learned concerning the formation and functioning of the superego, the greater is the likelihood of effecting a gradual reduction in juvenile delinquency. It would certainly prove useful, for example, for scholars to design a research program to discover methods of child rearing that would foster the development of a superego strong enough and healthy enough to withstand the onrush of the revived wishes of early childhood at puberty and during adolescence. Surely haphazard and part-time research by overworked psychoanalysts in private practice (which, unfortunately, is typical of how most psychoanalytic research has traditionally been and is still being accomplished) is no substitute for carefully planned, financed, staffed, and structured research projects designed to help resolve the problems regarding juvenile delinquency that psychoanalytic psychology is qualified to illuminate.

Even in the absence of such research, however, there appears to be no sufficient reason why educational programs should not be developed that would enable the public to benefit from whatever psychoanalytic discoveries have already been made concerning child rearing—and particularly from psychoanalytic discoveries regarding child-rearing methods that help to strengthen the superego so as to enable it to resist the antisocial wishes of infancy.[36] Those who plan these educational programs should keep in mind, however, that the persons most in need of enlightenment concerning methods of child rearing are the so-called "disadvantaged": persons in the lowest socioeconomic strata of society, who, unfortunately, are the least likely of the general public to attend seminars, lectures, or classes on child care, or to read articles (be they in scientific journals, in popular magazines, or even in newspapers) on the subject. Hence, creative thinking is needed to find methods of bringing psychoanalytic information on child care to the very segment of the population that is the most difficult to reach. One intriguing suggestion that has been advanced is that information regarding child raising be disseminated by the periodic showing on television of extremely short educational messages (much as brief—but dramatic and hard-hitting—messages are now shown on television to discourage smoking).

> There are a great many advantages that these parent-education-television messages would have. (1) The pre-selection that is involved when lengthy parent education messages (such as books, articles or lectures) are presented would be avoided. (2) If anything, the audience would have a disproportionate number of lower class people who would be the main target of concern. (3) The audience would be massive, and would include fathers as well as mothers, middle class people as well as lower class people; the message might therefore have more

impact because of such coverage. (4) The stigmatization involved in any attempt to select some special group that is in need of the message, such as mothers of predelinquents, would be avoided. (5) Information would be available on the characteristics of the audience watching at various times, so that messages could be scheduled at the most appropriate time.[37]

PSYCHOANALYSIS AS A THERAPEUTIC SYSTEM

Even though psychoanalytic discoveries may serve as the starting point for educational programs and research programs concerning the prevention of juvenile delinquency, by no means does it follow from this that psychoanalysis as *a system of therapy* is likely to prove successful vis-à-vis juvenile delinquency. The process of psychoanalysis is essentially an attempt to make conscious what is unconscious: an attempt to bring to the surface the primitive antisocial urges of early childhood, so that they may be examined carefully—and, it is hoped, either rejected or transmuted into socially useful strivings ("sublimated," to use the technical psychoanalytic term[38]). As a therapeutic method, psychoanalysis has proven effective mainly with intelligent, articulate, adult neurotics who are presumably capable (with the help of the psychoanalyst) of talking out—rather than having to act out—the infantile wishes that beset them (and that the psychoanalytic process has helped to raise to consciousness[39]). On the other hand, the typical juvenile delinquent is all too often an inarticulate and unintelligent adolescent who is more or less incapable of talking out the primitive antisocial infantile urges of infancy that assail him and who, instead, acts out these urges (or their pubescent or adolescent derivatives) in the form of delinquent behavior. To psychoanalyze such a juvenile delinquent—and in so doing to facilitate the entry into consciousness of even more of his primitive infantile wishes—would be, in effect, to compound his difficulties as well as the problems of the society in which he lives (a society that presumably seeks to lessen and to control his delinquent behavior).

Further (and perhaps more to the point), psychoanalysis is at best a tedious, highly technical, extraordinarily time-consuming, and extremely expensive procedure; and even if society had both the resources and the willingness to pay for the psychoanalysis of its delinquents, there would not be—either at present or in the foreseeable future—a sufficient number of trained psychoanalysts to begin to do the job properly. Thus even if psychoanalysis (or more accurately, a modified form of psychoanalysis) may, as some psychoanalysts believe, prove useful upon occasion in helping to minimize the delinquent behavior of juveniles,[40] the fact remains that, on both a theoretical and a practical level, psychoanalysis cannot be regarded as an appropriate form of therapy for juvenile delinquency.

GROUP THERAPY

This is not to say, however, that no form of psychological treatment is appropriate in regard to juvenile delinquency. If the analysis of juvenile delinquency presented in this paper is at all accurate, an appropriate form of psychological therapy appears to be one that would seek to strengthen and change the superego of a delinquent so as to enable it to resist the influence (especially at puberty and during adolescence) of the antisocial desires of infancy. Fortunately, certain psychological procedures (other than psychoanalysis itself) designed to change the superego have been developed since World War II; and, most important from a practical point of view, these procedures appear to work particularly well when employed with groups.[41] Though a detailed analysis of these procedures would certainly lead far beyond this paper's limits, it may prove useful here to note that when people act as members of certain groups (for instance, when juveniles act together and form a mob) they frequently tend to "regress"—that is, to revert to past and presumably long-outgrown behavioral reactions and patterns[42]; and when these people so regress, their superego is ordinarily far more susceptible to modification than usual—and may, in fact, be replaced to some extent (and sometimes almost completely) by the leader of the group.[43] It has been contended, for example, that one of the effects of the so-called "basic training" given to all new recruits in the armed forces is to induce a regression in them and thus increase the likelihood that their superegos will be replaced in part by the person who trains them.[44] In fact, the phenomenon of group regression, coupled with a resultant facilitation of changes in the superego of the members of the group, may help to explain why psychoanalytically oriented therapists who have worked with groups of juvenile delinquents have sometimes been able to report a measure of success.[45]

Despite the occasional successes of group therapy with juvenile delinquents, however, there can be no doubt that because of such matters as the scarcity of trained therapists, the unwillingness (or perhaps inability) of many delinquent youths to submit to therapy, and, indeed, the all-too-frequent ineffectiveness of psychological therapies with such youths, the psychological approach to juvenile delinquency—by itself—cannot begin to cope with the seemingly ever rising tide of juvenile crime. For effective action in regard to juvenile delinquency there must surely be (in addition to whatever psychological therapeutic measures prove successful) some environmental or social changes, some attempts to so structure the environment of the delinquent as to induce him to conform to accepted social norms.[46]

Determining what environmental or social changes are needed to help reduce juvenile delinquency would certainly seem to be a matter that lies far more within the competence of sociologists than psychoanalysts—and in addition, to be clearly beyond the scope of this paper. After all, this paper's essential purpose has been not to offer a comprehensive account of juvenile delinquency or a thorough-going remedial program concerning it, but rather to present a psychoanalytic theory concerning those facets of juvenile delinquency that psychoanalytic psychology seems best able to illuminate. Even so, it is certainly possible that the psychoanalytic material detailed in the preceding pages may well prove of value to those sociologists who seek to reduce juvenile delinquency by effecting environmental or social changes. As Kate Friedlander has contended, "An environmental change can have a remedial effect only if the alteration is based on the offender's needs in his particular psychological situation."[47]

Be this as it may, it is surely encouraging to learn that recent years have witnessed the appearance of new sociological theories concerning juvenile delinquency—so-called "control" or "containment" theories —which seem to provide a basis for combining psychoanalytic and sociological findings regarding juvenile delinquency. In brief, these theories suggest that the key to minimizing juvenile delinquency is the establishment of effective inner and outer controls over the behavior of juveniles, and they appear to recognize that whereas sociological findings are probably applicable to the establishment of outer controls over juvenile conduct, so psychoanalytic findings are likely to be relevant to the establishment of inner controls over such conduct.[48] Thus today's control or containment theories would appear to provide a mechanism for synthesizing sociological and psychoanalytic data: a means whereby sociologists and psychoanalysts can, if they wish, work together to reduce and control juvenile delinquency.

NOTES

[1] *Task Force Report: Juvenile Delinquency and Youth Crime* (Washington, D.C.: U.S. Government Printing Office, 1967), p. xi. The yearly increases in reported crimes in the United States are catalogued with doleful regularity in the FBI's *Uniform Crime Reports.*

[2] See, e.g., Kate Friedlander, *The Psychoanalytical Approach to Juvenile Delinquency* (London: International Universities Press, 1960), p. vii.

[3] A more complete psychoanalytic theory of juvenile delinquency would, for example, have to deal with the relationship between what psychoanalysts have labeled the "ego" (the "I" of the personality) and juvenile delinquency. For an excellent psychoanalytic study of the relationship between them, see Fritz Redl and David Wineman, *Children Who Hate* (Glencoe, Ill.: Free Press, 1951).

[4] Edmund Bergler, *The Superego* (New York: Grune and Stratton, 1952), pp. 7, 49.

[5] See the otherwise extremely useful collection of psychoanalytic studies of juvenile delinquency in *Searchlights on Delinquency*, ed. K. R. Eissler (New York: International Universities Press, 1949).

[6] One psychoanalytic insight regarding juvenile delinquency which many sociologists have criticized and which may have received undue emphasis in psychoanalytic papers on juvenile delinquency is the view that juvenile delinquency and crime are, in effect, deliberately fostered by society so as to provide society with scapegoats upon whom personal and social problems can be blamed. See, e.g., Ruth S. Eissler, "Scapegoats of Society," in

Eissler, *Searchlights*, pp. 288–305. This insight has recently been re-emphasized by Karl Menninger: "The inescapable conclusion is that society *wants* crime, *needs* crime, and gains definite satisfactions from the present mishandling of it! . . . Criminals . . . like scapegoats of old . . . bear the burdens of our displaced guilt and punishment." Karl Menninger, *The Crime of Punishment* (New York: Viking Press, 1968), p. 153.

[7] Franz Alexander and Hugo Staub, *The Criminal, the Judge, and the Public* (Glencoe, Ill.: Free Press, 1956), p. 30.

[8] Ernest Jones, *Hamlet and Oedipus* (Garden City, N.Y.: Doubleday, 1955), p. 85.

[9] See, e.g., Karl Abraham, "A Short Study of the Development of the Libido, Viewed in the Light of Mental Disorders," in *Selected Papers of Karl Abraham* (New York: Basic Books, 1953), 1: 418, 451, 496.

[10] Anna Freud, *Psychoanalysis for Teachers and Parents* (New York: Emerson Books, 1954), p. 55.

[11] Some psychoanalysts distinguish between the superego and the so-called "ego-ideal" (the standards of conduct toward which a person aspires). See, e.g., Samuel Novey, "The Role of the Superego and Ego-Ideal in Character Formation," in *Readings in Psychoanalytic Psychology*, ed. Morton Levitt (New York: Appleton-Century-Crofts, 1959), pp. 114, 119. For the purpose of this paper, the distinction is irrelevant.

[12] See Ernest Jones, "The Genesis of the Super-Ego," *Papers on Psychoanalysis* (London: Balliere, Tindall, and Cox, 1950), p. 149; J. C. Flugel, *Man, Morals and Society* (New York: Viking Press, 1961), pp. 115–17.

[13] Reaction-formations are classified by psychoanalysts as "ego-defenses"; see Anna Freud, *The Ego and the Mechanisms of Defense* (New York: International Universities Press, 1946), p. 51. Hence, technically, the reaction-formation described in the text may be part of the ego, rather than part of the superego. Yet even so, the superego would appear to supply the major impetus for the creation of the reaction-formations noted in the text. See Flugel, *Man, Morals and Society*, p. 70.

[14] A. A. Brill, *Lectures on Psychoanalytic Psychiatry* (New York: Knopf, 1946), p. 215.

[15] Charles Brenner, *An Elementary Textbook of Psychoanalysis* (Garden City, N.Y.: Doubleday, 1957), p. 125.

[16] See Freud, *Ego and Defense*, 149–89.

[17] See Herman Numberg, *Principles of Psychoanalysis* (New York: International Universities Press, 1955), and Nathan W. Ackerman, *The Psychodynamics of Family Life* (New York: Basic Books, 1959), pp. 207–46.

[18] See Paul Schilder, "Problems of Crime," in *Psychoanalysis Today*, ed. Sandor Lorand (New York: International Universities Press, 1944), pp. 342, 345–46.

[19] The ways in which the superego may engender guilt feelings—and the meaning and effect of these guilt feelings—are explored in detail in Sigmund Freud, *Civilization and Its Discontents* (London: Hogarth Press, 1930), pp. 105–22.

[20] See the comments on "criminals from a sense of guilt" in Sigmund Freud, "Some Character Types Met with in Psychoanalytic Work," in *Collected Papers* (London: Hogarth Press, 1956), 4: 342–44.

[21] See C. G. Schoenfeld, "Law and Unconscious Motivation," *Howard Law Journal*, Winter 1962, p. 15.

[22] Relevant here are Adelaide M. Johnson's "superego lacunae" theory presented in "Sanctions for Superego Lacunae of Adolescents," in Eissler, *Searchlights*, pp. 22–45. Also related to and consistent with the text are the sociological theories of Albert J. Reiss, Jr., set forth in "Delinquency as the Failure of Personal and Social Controls," *American Sociological Review*, 1951, pp. 196–207; and "Social Correlates of Psychological Types of Delinquency," *American Sociological Review*, 1952, pp. 710–18.

[23] The studies of John Bowlby, for example, reveal that when deprivation of maternal care is prolonged, "the child's development is almost always retarded—physically, intellectually, and socially." John Bowlby, *Child Care and the Growth of Love* (Harmondsworth, England: Penguin Books, 1953), p. 18. More dramatic, however, is a

study by Rene Spitz of a foundling home where children received impeccable medical and physical attention but no mothering. Spitz learned that "of a total of 88 children up to the age of 2½, 23 died"; the remainder of the children developed at an extraordinarily slow pace and became asocial, disturbed, and feeble-minded. Rene Spitz, "Hospitalism: An Inquiry into the Genesis of Psychiatric Conditions in Early Childhood," in *The Psychoanalytic Study of the Child* (New York: International University Press, 1945), 1: 54-74.

[24] Bowlby, *Child Care*, p. 27.

[25] See, e.g., Friedlander, *Psychoanalytic Approach*, p. 157.

[26] Psychoanalytic studies reveal that young children are beset not only by heterosexual urges but by homosexual urges as well. See, e.g., Sigmund Freud, "Analysis of a Phobia in a Five-Year-Old Boy," in *Collected Papers* (London: Hogarth Press, 1956), 3: 149-287.

[27] See Hyman Rodman and Paul Grams, "Juvenile Delinquency and the Family: A Review and Discussion," in *Task Force Report*, pp. 188, 192, 194.

[28] Friedlander, *Psychoanalytic Approach*, p. 36; Alexander and Staub, *Criminal, Judge, Public*, pp. 6-8.

[29] The existence of dependency feelings during childhood and the effects of indulging them are discussed in J. C. Flugel, *The Psycho-Analytic Study of the Family* (London: Hogarth Press, 1950).

[30] Aichhorn's seminal psychoanalytic report on juvenile delinquency, *Wayward Youth*, stresses these themes. "The great majority of children in need of retraining come into conflict with society because of an unsatisfied need for tenderness and love in their childhood." August Aichhorn, *Wayward Youth* (New York: Meridian Books, 1955), p. 115.

[31] Rodman and Grams, in *Task Force Report*, p. 200.

[32] "In my opinion this is the specific factor responsible for the development of antisocial character formation instead of neurotic disturbances. . . . Both Aichhorn . . . and Alexander . . . emphasize this constant alternation between frustration and gratification of early instinctive drives in the cases which they have fully investigated." Friedlander, *Psychoanalytic Approach*, p. 101.

[33] Pertinent sociological reports are listed in Rodman and Grams, in *Task Force Report*, pp. 198-99. Of special interest here are the data presented in Sheldon Glueck and Eleanor Glueck, *Unraveling Juvenile Delinquency* (New York: Commonwealth Fund, 1950).

[34] These gratifications, to use psychoanalytic terminology, are likely to serve as "fixation points." See Gerald S. Blum, *Psychoanalytic Theories of Personality* (New York: McGraw-Hill, 1953), pp. 49-50.

[35] Friedlander, *Psychoanalytic Approach*, p. 68.

[36] Admittedly, it might be wise to delay the development of these educational programs until further psychoanalytic data are amassed. Yet, as the great sociologist Edwin H. Sutherland once observed, "If practical programs wait until theoretical knowledge is complete, they will wait for eternity, for theoretical knowledge is increased most significantly in the efforts at social control." Edwin H. Sutherland, *Principles of Criminology*, ed. Donald R. Cressey, rev. ed. (Philadelphia: Lippincott, 1955), pp. 3-4.

[37] Rodman and Grams, in *Task Force Report*, p. 217.

[38] See Arthur P. Noyes, *Modern Clinical Psychiatry* (Philadelphia: Saunders, 1948), pp. 19-21.

[39] There is, of course, a plethora of articles and books concerning psychoanalysis as a therapeutic system. The "classic" article on the subject is Sigmund Freud's "Analysis Terminable and Interminable," in *Collected Papers* (London: Hogarth Press, 1956), 5: 316-57.

[40] See, e.g., Friedlander, *Psychoanalytic Approach*, pp. 207-19.

[41] "In hospitals, especially in rehabilitation centers, group psychotherapy has proved valuable in influencing not one, but a number of patients at the same time . . . by effecting changes in the superego. . . ." Ibid., p. 220.

[42] A particularly useful discussion of the concept of regression is to be found in Jacob A. Arlow and Charles Brenner, *Psychoanalytic Concepts and the Structural Theory* (New York: International Universities Press, 1964), pp. 56–83.

[43] See, e.g., Sigmund Freud, *Group Psychology and the Analysis of the Ego* (New York: Liveright, 1922), pp. 82, 102.

[44] Much the same point was made at the 1969 meeting of the American Orthopsychiatric Association in New York. *New York Times,* April 1, 1969.

[45] See, e.g., Aichhorn, *Wayward Youth,* pp. 111–43. As has been pointed out by S. R. Slavson (the great pioneer and theorist of group psychotherapy), "a large number of persons, and especially children, can be helped through groups only." S. R. Slavson, *The Practice of Group Therapy* (New York: International Universities Press, 1947), p. 22.

[46] Rodman and Grams, for example, insist that occupational deprivation underlies much juvenile delinquency, and they stress the importance of providing proper employment opportunities in programs designed to reduce juvenile delinquency in *Task Force Report,* p. 214.

[47] Friedlander, *Psychoanalytic Approach,* p. 237.

[48] A brief but authoritative résumé of control or containment theories is to be found in Walter C. Reckless, *The Crime Problem* (New York: Appleton-Century-Crofts, 1961), pp. 335-59.

3

Criminal Behavior and Learning Theory

C. R. JEFFERY

The author received his Ph.D. in sociology from Indiana University where he studied under the late Dr. Edwin H. Sutherland. He has held academic positions at Colby College, Southern Illinois University, and Arizona State University. He is currently affiliated with The Washington School of Psychiatry as a research associate, and with the New York University Law School as a visiting lecturer in criminology.

Dr. Jeffery was a senior fellow in the law and behavioral science program at the University of Chicago Law School, and a fellow in the institute on the administration of criminal justice sponsored by the Social Science Research Council at the University of Wisconsin. He is co-author of a book entitled Society and the Law, and he is now engaged in a research project in delinquency prevention and control, using principles derived from behavioral psychology.

* * *

DIFFERENTIAL ASSOCIATION

One of the most popular theories of criminal behavior, especially among sociologists and social psychologists, is the notion that criminal behavior is learned behavior. The theory of differential association, put forth by Edwin H. Sutherland[1], is a learning theory which formulates the process as one whereby criminal behavior is learned in association with those who have criminal attitudes and values, as compared to associations with those who have noncriminal attitudes and values.

Reprinted by special permission of the author and *Journal of Criminal Law, Criminology and Police Science*, Copyright © 1965 by Northwestern University School of Law, Vol. 56, No. 3.

Sutherland's theory is now over thirty years old, and there has been no major theoretical revision nor any empirical verification of the theory during its lifespan[2]. The purpose of this paper is to apply modern learning theory to differential association in order to place it in modern dress and to place it in a form which is empirically testable. The theory of differential association is not valid in its present form because, though it is basically sound in asserting that criminal behavior is learned, it does not make use of the learning principles which are now available as a result of experimental laboratory research. The principles were not available when Sutherland wrote, and it is therefore necessary to reappraise and reformulate his theory in terms of laboratory research carried on from 1940 to 1964.

OPERANT BEHAVIOR

Learning theory has revolved around the concept of conditioning, wherein behavior (responses) is related to the environment in which it occurs (stimuli). The Pavlovian type of classical conditioning is based upon a stimulus eliciting a response, the stimulus occurring before the response. Such conditioning procedures are of minor importance to sociologists since the behaviors involved are usually eye blinks, salivation, and galvanic skin responses. Much more important are operant behaviors, those behaviors emitted in the presence of given stimulus conditions and maintained by their consequences, that is, the changes they produce in the environment[3]. The stimulus follows the response. Examples of operant behavior include verbal behavior, sexual behavior, driving a car, writing an article, wearing clothing, or living in a house. The concept of operant behavior is important to sociologists because most social behavior is of an operant nature. Social interaction is maintained by the effect it has on other people. Homans has used the concept of operant behavior to discuss what he calls elementary forms of social behavior[4].

Stimuli, or environmental conditions, can be divided into several categories. Contingent stimuli are the environmental conditions which are produced by and are contingent upon a given response of the actor. Such stimuli can be reinforcing or aversive. A reinforcing stimulus strengthens the response, that is, the response rate increases when a given stimulus is produced by a given response. This process is known as reinforcement. An aversive stimulus weakens a response rate, that is, the response rate decreases when a given stimulus is produced by a given response. This process is known as punishment. Reinforcement can be positive or negative. Positive reinforcement refers to the process whereby the presentation of a stimulus increases the response rate; negative reinforcement refers to the process whereby the elimination of a stimulus increases the response rate. Likewise, punishment can be positive, wherein the presentation of a stimulus decreases the response rate, or negative, wherein the elimination of a stimulus decreases the response rate. These relationships can be diagrammed as follows:

	response up	response down
stimulus presented	S^r positive reinforcement	S^a positive punishment
stimulus eliminated	$S^{\bar{a}}$ negative reinforcement	$S^{\bar{r}}$ negative punishment

S^r refers to a reinforcing stimulus, S^a refers to an aversive stimulus, and a bar over the symbol refers to the elimination of the stimulus.

There are also controlling stimuli. Whereas the contingent stimuli occur after the response, the controlling stimuli are present when the response occurs, and they control the occurrence or nonoccurrence of the response. Stimuli in whose presence a response is reinforced or punished are called S^d (S dee), whereas those stimuli in whose presence a response is not reinforced or punished are called S^Δ (S delta). These are known as discriminative stimuli. A telephone is answered only when it rings; the ring is an S^d for answering the telephone. A child is punished only when the mother is present. The mother is an S^d for punishment.

Those stimuli which are in the environment but which are not differentially related to the consequences are known as constant stimuli (SS^c). Variables which make a stimulus reinforcing or punishing, such as satiation and deprivation, are labeled V (variables). The diagram thus looks like this[5]:

$$SS^c \quad S^{d\Delta} \to R \to S^{ra} \overset{V}{\underset{\downarrow}{\rceil}}$$

THEORY OF DIFFERENTIAL REINFORCEMENT

Criminal behavior is operant behavior; that is, it is maintained by the changes it produces on the environment. A criminal response can produce money, a car, a radio, sex gratification, or the removal of an enemy. Most crimes are property offenses, and there the reinforcing stimulus is the stolen item. Crimes against the person may involve negative reinforcement, that is the removal of an aversive stimulus. Murder and assault are behaviors of this type. Voyeurism, fetishism, exhibitionism, and homosexuality are behaviors that are maintained by their consequences on the environment, though the nature of the reinforcement and the conditioning which led to this association of sex gratification with such consequences is not well understood at this time. What is involved, however, is the association of sex behavior with a forbidden sex object, such as occurs in the case of fetishism or homosexuality. The homosexual selects a male rather than a female as the sex object because of his past conditioning history in the sexual area. Narcotics and alcohol are reinforcing stimuli because of the biochemical changes they produce in the body. In the case of narcotics addiction negative reinforcement is involved, that is, the removal of an aversive stimulus (withdrawal distress).

Coupled with reinforcement for criminal behavior, however, is punishment. Society through its legal system attaches aversive consequences to criminal behavior. A criminal act may lead to reinforcement, but it also may lead to punishment. The theory of differential reinforcement states that a criminal act occurs in an environment in which in the past the actor has been reinforced for behaving in this manner, and the aversive consequences attached to the behavior have been of such a nature that they do not control or prevent the response. Criminal behavior is under the control of reinforcing stimuli. An act of robbery produces money; it also may produce being shot at by the victim or the police, being arrested, being imprisoned, etc. However, if the aversive consequences of the act control the behavior, then the behavior does not occur, e.g., if a thief regards the consequences of his act as being shot or arrested, he will not steal in that particular situation.

The theory assumes that (1) the reinforcing quality of different stimuli differ for different actors depending on the past conditioning history of each; (2) some individuals have been reinforced for criminal behavior whereas other individuals have not been; (3) some individuals have been punished for criminal behavior whereas other individuals have not been; and (4) an individual will be intermittently reinforced and/or punished for criminal behavior, that is, he will not be reinforced or punished every time he commits a criminal act. However, intermittent reinforcement will maintain a response pattern, and a large part of our social behavior is maintained on an intermittent schedule of reinforcement. For example, if one man steals and another does not under similar circumstances, at least three variables can be noted immediately: (1) the reinforcing quality of the stolen item; (2) past stealing responses which have been reinforced, and (3) past stealing responses which have been punished. One of the criticisms often leveled at the theory of differential association is that it does not adequately account for the differences in behavior of those living in the same social environment: same family, same slum area, same ethnic group, and so forth. There are people living in high delinquency areas who are not delinquent; there are Negroes who are not delinquent; and there are young adult males who are not delinquent, though from a statistical point of view these social factors are important. This is a very selective process, the reason being that each individual has a different conditioning history even though he is in an environment similar to others.

CRIMINAL ASSOCIATIONS

Sutherland's theory states that other human beings act as reinforcers for criminal activities. Human beings often act as social agents for reinforcers such as food, sex gratification, employment, medical aid, housing, trips, entertainment, and the like. We associate with those from whom we receive reinforcement.

In the case of criminal activity, other people can reinforce the behavior in several ways. They can use verbal praise to strengthen criminal behavior, which is what is meant by a reputation in a criminal or delinquent gang. Delinquents talk a great deal about their exploits and conquests in order to be praised. Another person can also act as a confederate in the commission of a criminal act, or can be an accessory after the fact: hiding the criminal, "fencing" stolen goods, and so forth. People also apply aversive consequences to criminal behavior by verbally reprimanding, arresting, or shooting the criminal. These behaviors constitute what Sutherland calls "attitudes" favorable or unfavorable to the commission of a criminal act.

A research problem presented by the theory of differential association is the problem of what environmental consequences maintain criminal behavior. Is it the material gain, or is it the social approval and group membership? Sutherland's theory assumes that the important variable is social reinforcement, and his theory ignores the obvious fact that money, cars, and sex are in themselves powerful reinforcers in our society. For this reason whenever one attempts to test the theory of differential association one discovers cases of criminals without criminal associations, or noncriminals with criminal associations. Criminal behavior can be maintained by money or cars without social approval. A man without prior association with criminals may murder his wife after a quarrel or when he discovers she has a lover. This act cannot be explained by the theory of differential association; it can be explained by the theory of differential reinforcement, since the removal of an aversive stimulus is negative reinforcement. The husband's interaction with his wife is crucial in this act of murder, but this interaction is not of a criminal nature until after the husband has killed his wife.

Stealing is reinforcing in and by itself whether other people know about it and reinforce it socially or not. Sutherland limited the learning of criminal behavior to situations involving criminal attitudes and associations. A stimulus for a criminal response need not involve a criminal component. A person learns to respond to food in legitimate ways. As a baby he was fed, and gradually he learns a series of behaviors associated with the acquisition of food—buying food, cooking food, verbally requesting food, and so forth. Among the responses which may in time be associated with or conditioned to food might be a response called "stealing food." If a boy asks his mother for a cookie and she refuses his request, he learns he can raid the cookie jar when mother is not looking. Stealing a cookie is reinforced by the cookie, not by the mother or a delinquent gang. This child has had no contact with a delinquent pattern, and yet learning has taken place which later on can generalize to other situations.

A person rides in an automobile as a child. He learns to drive a car as an adolescent. If an automobile is available to him either because he can afford one or because his father owns one, then there is no need to steal automobiles. However, if access to automobiles is only by stealing, then he steals. A girl can get a fur coat by working for it, by having a rich parent, by marrying a rich man, or by exchanging sex favors for a fur coat. Criminal behavior is learned, though this does not imply as Sutherland did that the learning process itself involves criminal associations.

The theory of differential association limits the learning process to criminal attitudes; the theory discussed in this paper states that criminal behavior can be learned in situations not containing criminals or criminal attitudes. For this reason a person living in a criminal environment will often not be a criminal, while criminals are found in non-criminal environments.

Other individuals are probably as important, if not more important, in the behavioral process as discriminative stimuli rather than reinforcing stimuli; that is, the presence of a given person will signal that a given act will or will not be reinforced. It is a well established sociological fact that individuals behave differently in the presence of certain people than in the absence of these same people. A man behaves differently when his wife is in the room than when she is absent; a worker behaves differently in the presence of the boss, and so forth. The reason is obvious; certain behaviors are reinforced or punished in the presence of a given person, and not in his absence. An obvious example from the area of criminology is the fact that people often behave differently in the presence of a policeman than in his absence. Motorists try to figure out when the patrolman is around and when he is not. A father may send his son out to commit criminal acts, or a delinquent companion may serve as a stimulus for a delinquent act. Certain criminal acts are reinforced or punished in the presence or absence of a given person. Associates therefore help to maintain criminal behavior either as reinforcing stimuli or as discriminative stimuli.

SOCIAL VARIABLES AND CONDITIONING

Most official criminal and delinquent acts are committed by young adult males who are members of a minority group and who live in slum areas. One of the characteristics of a slum area is deprivation; the inhabitants are without the important social reinforcers in our economy. They are not reinforced for lawful behavior. A middle class person can secure food, clothing, and automobiles by noncriminal means.

Behavior theory takes into account the level of deprivation and satiation of the actor. A person deprived of food will respond to food in a manner in which a satiated person will not. A sexually deprived person will respond to stimuli which will not arouse a sex response in a sexually satiated person. In prison camps inmates eat rats and engage in homosexual acts which they do not do when they have access to beefsteak and females.

Young adults are more criminalistic than older adults for the reason that they lack the responses necessary to produce reinforcement. If they develop acceptable responses for the reinforcers they want, the criminal responses are extinguished. Also, if they persist in a pattern of criminal behavior they are likely to come to the attention of the police and a new series of contingencies comes to control the behavior, such as imprisonment.

The influence of television and comic books upon behavior is also better understood in terms of conditioning principles. Let us take, for example, one hundred wives watching a television show wherein a wife murders her husband. After viewing the program ninety-nine wives go back to their chores, the hundredth wife kills her husband. Ignoring for a moment the fact that we cannot really relate the behavior to a specific situation such as a television show (she might have killed her husband even if she did not see the show), we must further ask the question: "Why was it reinforcing for this woman to kill her husband, but not for the other ninety-nine?" We can assume that because of the nature of her relationship with her husband she wished to have him out of the way. She was responding as people do respond to aversive situations—she was removing the aversive stimulus.

It is sometimes assumed that if a child watches violence on television he will then behave in a violent manner. This argument assumes that the stimuli controlling the behavior are those presented on a television screen, whereas in fact the controlling stimuli are those in the child's own environment. Generalization of responses from a television program to those who observe the television program depends upon the extent to which the two environments are the same or similar, and upon the past conditioning of the observer. If we watch a television program in which Jewish children are placed in a gas chamber, this does not mean we are going out and place Jewish children in a gas chamber. We might, rather than imitating the Nazi, behave in such a manner as to prevent such acts from taking place in the future. The belief that a television stimulus will produce a given response in a viewer is based on the classical Pavlovian S——R paradigm; however, the behaviors involved are usually operant rather than classical responses, and as such they depend upon environmental contingencies for their existence, not upon the television set.

PUNISHMENT

As was stated earlier, punishment is defined as the withdrawal of a reinforcing stimulus or the presentation of an aversive stimulus. There are several contradictory notions concerning the effect of punishment on behavior.

Punishment will reduce a response rate but, unless it is severe, punishment will not eliminate a response rate. Once the punishment is discontinued, the rate of response will return to its normal pattern. Some authors have stated that punishment is not the opposite of reinforcement, since the withdrawal of punishment results in an increase in the response that was formerly punished. However, it should be remembered that the withdrawal of a positive reinforcer results in a decrease in a response that was formerly reinforced.

The problem lies in the fact that punishment is usually paired with a response that is strongly maintained by other reinforcing stimuli, whereas a reinforced response is not paired with other contingencies. There are two stimuli—not one—controlling a punished response: the reinforcing stimulus (food), and the aversive stimulus (shock). If we punish a food response, we can expect that the response will continue because of the strength of food as a reinforcer. The removal of food as a reinforcer will eliminate the response. Punishment will completely eliminate the response if food is not contingent on the response. Is the elimination of the food response due, however, to the removal of food (extinction), or is it due to punishment? Since we can accomplish the same results without punishment, we must conclude that the effective control is one based on extinction. We must, however, provide an alternative response pattern for obtaining food. Under these conditions punishment is an adequate control of behavior. Given two responses, one of which leads to food, the other to food and punishment, the organism will soon cease responding in the latter and respond only in the former situation[6].

Continuous punishment will not control behavior either, for satiation takes place the same as with a reinforcing stimulus. Food and money are not effective reinforcers except as they are placed on an intermittent schedule. Likewise, to control a delinquent by punishing him 24 hours a day is like trying to control him by feeding him ice-cream 24 hours a day.

Holz and Azrin have shown that punishment can become a discriminative stimulus if it is followed by reinforcement[7]. If a rat is shocked before the food mechanism operates, it will administer a shock to itself in order to get food. This experiment led to the so-called "masochistic rat." The statement is often made in psychiatric circles that masochistic people "like pain" or "must punish themselves" in order to get rid of guilt feelings. The literature is filled with case histories of men who committed crimes so that they could be punished. Such notions must be questioned in the face of experimental evidence. A person will not punish himself unless this punishment is paired with reinforcement. A child who is punished and then comforted or given candy will in future misbehave in order to get attention or sweets. Abrahamsen cites the example of a masochistic delinquent, a boy whose mother would punish him and then reward him with candy or ice-cream[8].

Mild punishment will be followed by a reduction in a response rate *if* it is a discriminative stimulus for non-reinforcement. Heavy punishment will be followed by an increase in a response rate *if* it is a discriminative stimulus for reinforcement.

These observations help to explain many of the contradictory statements about punishment and human behavior. *Under no condition, however, will punishment increase a response rate.* The Holz-Azrin experiment is often cited as evidence of the increase in response rate through punishment. Likewise, experimental work in the area of brain stimulation has led to observations of pleasure centers in the brain. A rat will shock itself at a high rate if an electrode is implanted in the proper area of the brain. This is used as another example of increasing the response rate by administering punishment. The problem here lies in the fact that the experimenter has classified shock as a painful stimulus. Rather the psychologist should talk about electrical stimulation to a given area of the brain as reinforcing, since it increases the rate of response. It is a well established fact that the stimulation of a nerve center can be pleasurable or reinforcing under some conditions but painful under others. A warm bath, for example, is reinforcing; but to be boiled alive is painful.

The Holz-Azrin experiment could be repeated wherein food was an S^d for shock—food would be presented and followed five seconds later by a shock. Under such conditions food would become a conditioned aversive stimulus, and the presentation of food would result in anxiety and conditioned suppression. Punishment is defined procedurally as a decrease in the response rate due to the presentation of an aversive stimulus contingent on the response. Yet punishment is followed by an increase in the response when punishment is an S^d for reinforcement. The increase in the response rate is due to reinforcement (food) and not to punishment; and, since reinforcement is defined in terms of an increase in the response rate, there is no contradiction in such statements.

The experimental evidence supports the classical school (Bentham-Beccaria) of criminology in its statement that it is the certainty of punishment—not the severity—that deters people from criminal acts. One of the basic principles learned by every student of criminology is that "punishment does not deter." It is pointed out that for hundreds of years criminals have been punished by execution; yet we have an increasing rate of crime. Such statements are in gross error concerning the influence of punishment on behavior.

The statistical evidence on capital punishment reveals the source of one difficulty. About one percent of those eligible to be executed are thus punished. The *uncertainty* of capital punishment is one major factor in the system. Another factor is the *time* element. A consequence must be applied immediately if it is to be effective; yet in Chessman's case the consequence was applied eleven years after the behavior. Such punishment does not recondition or rehabilitate. There is also present the fact that execution makes further rehabilitation impossible. The lesson to be learned from capital punishment is not that punishment does not deter, but that the improper and sloppy use of punishment does not deter or rehabilitate.

The immediate consequence of a crime—rape, murder, robbery, burglary—is the presentation of a reinforcing stimulus: money, sex gratification, or the removal of an enemy or hated individual. When one commits a criminal act, the behavior, like all behavior, is under the control of reinforcing stimuli. There are no aversive stimuli in the environment at that moment. If a robber is caught in the act and is immediately punished, then the effect of punishment on behavior is radically different.

These statements on punishment are not to be interpreted as supporting any wholesale drive to pass laws that inflict heavier penalties on criminals. Increasing the penalties for crimes has the negative effect of making the punishment less certain. Throughout the history of penology an increase in punitive measures has been accompanied by an increase in measures, legal and otherwise, by which punishment is avoided. Severity of punishment can be gained only by sacrificing certainty. The Holz-Azrin experiment definitely established the fact that mild punishment can control a response, whereas heavy punishment under different conditions will not control the response. Legislators think in terms of severity of punishment, which is an inappropriate and harmful way to use punishment.

The use of punishment as it is currently administered by the legal system does not eliminate criminal behavior, although undoubtedly it does reduce the crime rate; but it does shape other behaviors, known as *avoidance responses*. An organism will respond in such a way as to avoid an aversive consequence. This, of course, is negative reinforcement. Escape responses, which are like avoidance responses except that they terminate an aversive stimulus rather than avoid it, likewise increase in rate in the face of aversive stimuli.

The avoidance and escape responses available to the criminal are many: avoid detection, don't leave fingerprints, hire a good lawyer, bribe the police, plead guilty to a reduced charge, plead insanity, tell the probation officer the right kind of story, etc. Law enforcement procedures shape a great deal of avoidance and escape behavior, but this can be quite unrelated to the behavior the law is trying to prevent and control.

It must also be kept in mind that the effects of punishment upon different people differ according to what they have to lose as a result. As an example, a university professor who was accused of a misdemeanor (contributing to the delinquency of a minor) was dismissed from his position, lost status in his professional community, and was divorced by his wife. He was never convicted, and he never served a day for this minor offense, and yet the aversive consequences to this man were much greater than a five to ten year sentence would be to a felon who had already served three terms in a prison.

DELINQUENT SUBCULTURES

The theoretical work of Cohen, Cloward and Ohlin, Miller, Bloch and Niederhoffer, and Yablonsky could be reformulated in terms of reinforcement principles[9]. The work of Cloward and Ohlin comes closest to the theoretical scheme presented in this paper; in fact, some readers might feel that it is a new way of talking about means, ends, and opportunities. A goal or end is obviously a general term referring to the environmental contingencies which have been labeled herein reinforcers. When Cloward and Ohlin note that different behaviors emerge in different subcultural groups, they are saying that in certain environments a response is reinforced, whereas in other environments it is not. There is nothing in the Cloward and Ohlin treatment of delinquency that contradicts what has been said in this paper concerning criminal behavior as learned behavior. The difference is that this paper attempts to look with a microscope at individual responses in a given environment, whereas Cloward and Ohlin were looking at social organization rather than individual behavior.

However, if we wish to deal with delinquent behavior, we must deal with individual behavior. We now know a great deal about the environment from which delinquents come; we know very little about the variables in this environment controlling individual responses. A systematic application of learning principles to criminal behavior might be appropriate at this stage in the development of criminology since criminality involves both an environment and a response to an environment. Research in learning processes has provided us with some principles with which we can investigate in greater detail the interaction of the criminal with his environment.

SUMMARY

Criminal behavior is learned behavior. Sutherland's theory of differential association is basically correct; however, it needs to be revised in terms of recent advances in the psychology of learning. Operant behavior is behavior that is maintained by its consequences. Criminal behavior is maintained by its consequences, both material and social. Such social variables as age, sex, social class, ethnic membership, and residential area influence the manner in which criminal behavior is conditioned.

Punishment decreases a response rate only if it is used in a consistent manner, and is applied near the time of the occurrence of the forbidden act. As it is used to control criminal behavior, punishment is likely to create avoidance and escape behaviors rather than law abiding behaviors.

NOTES

[1] Sutherland and Cressey, *Principles of Criminology*, 74, 5th ed., 1955.

[2] Cressey, "Epidemiology and Individual Conduct," *Pacific Soc. Rev. Sociological Rev.*, Fall 1960, p. 47; "The Theory of Differential Association," *Social Problems*, Summer 1960, p. 2; Giaser, "Criminality Theories and Behavioral Images," *Am. J. Soc.*, March 1956, p. 433.

[3] Sidman, *Tactics of Scientific Research*, 1961; Nurnberger, Ferster, and Brady, *An Introduction to a Science of Human Behavior*, 1963; Bachrach, *Experimental Findings of Clinical Psychology, 1962;* Hill, *Learning*, 1963; Lawson, *Learning and Behavior*, 1960; Staats, Arthur and Carolyn, *Complex Human Behavior*, 1963; Wolpe, *The Conditioning Therapies*, 1964.

[4] Homans, *Social Behavior: Its Elementary Forms*, 1961.

[5] Goidiamond, "Perception," in Bachrach, *Experimental Foundations of Clinical Psychology*, 1962, p. 295.

[6] Azrin, "Punishment and Recovery during Fixed-Ratio Performance," *Journal of the Experimental Analysis of Behavior* 2 (1959): 301–305; Azrin and Holtz, "Punishment during Fixed-Interval Reinforcement," *Journal of the Experimental Analysis of Behavior* 4 (1961): 343–347.

[7] Holz and Azrin, "Discriminative Properties of Punishment, *Journal of the Experimental Analysis of Behavior* 4 (1961): 225–232; Holz and Azrin, "Inner Actions between the Discriminative and Aversive Properties of Punishment," *Journal of the Experimental Analysis of Behavior* 5 (1962): 229–234.

[8] Abrahamsen, *The Psychology of Crime*, 65, 1960.

[9] Cohen, *Delinquent Boys*, 1955; Bloch and Niederhoffer, *The Gang*, 1958; Kvaraceus and Miller, *Delinquent Behavior*, 1959; Cloward and Ohlin, *Delinquency and Opportunity*, 1960; Yablonsky, *The Violent Gang*, 1962.

II

PERSPECTIVES ON THE APPLICATION OF THEORY TO TREATMENT

INTRODUCTION

Theories from the behavioral sciences have formed the basis for correctional treatment ever since the classical school of criminology postulated the concept of free will two hundred years ago. Basic to the application of this concept was a pleasure-pain punishment model in which punishment was supposed to deter criminal behavior. Approximately one hundred years later, this concept of free will was challenged by advocates of biological determinism, and later by those who believed in social determinism.

In more recent times, with the advent of psychology and psychiatry, the emphasis in seeking the cause of deviant behavior shifted from biological and environmental factors to emotional forces within the individual offender. Crime and delinquency, once held to be a rational choice, an expression of free will, came to be explained as a symptom of some underlying emotional illness, the expression of which was beyond the individual's control. This transition from punishment to treatment gave rise to the medical model and culminated in the 1960s with what has been called the "therapeutic state."

In the first article, Paul E. Lehman places the development of this medical model in historical perspective. His research shows that the intent of penologists in advocating this model was not to equate crime with disease, but to provide a rational and more humane approach to handling criminals. The relationship of disease to criminality became superimposed on this model by Lombraso's biological determinism and later by psychological determinism.

Although Lehman terms this model an "archaic standard" for modern corrections, he does not call for its complete demise. Rather,

45

he criticizes those who cling to it as a panacea and refuse to recognize the potential offered in alternatives. What is needed, according to Lehman, is a differential approach, in which treatment can be selected from a variety of programs and strategies according to the needs of the offender. To accomplish this, however, Lehman states that correctional administrators and personnel must first define their goals. Differential treatment programs can then be designed to achieve them.

Susan Rose in her article does not treat the medical model so kindly. She contends that we cannot correct—that is, cure—anyone with the application of this concept because we do not understand what it is that we are attempting to cure. The results of relying on psychological determinism have meant failure for the correctional system and more harm than good for the offender. Her argument supports the search for alternative approaches which consider a broad range of causal factors.

Many of these criticisms of the medical model have been well heeded. Sociological and economic factors are playing an increasing role in the study of crime and delinquency. Fortunately, the reaction against the medical model has not caused the pendulum to swing back to the point where environmental determinism is replacing psychological determinism. Today, correctional casework takes its direction from a multidimensional frame of reference that includes elements from the medical model, but is not limited to them. In broadening the theoretical basis for casework, the term *treatment* has taken on a new meaning much wider in scope and application than implied in the concept of pure therapy.

In the third reading, Professor Charles E. Newman explores the concepts of treatment as they are applied in probation and parole supervision. His practical application offers an invaluable experience for the reader in relating theory to actual casework. Professor Newman describes treatment as a three-stage process of investigation, diagnosis, and treatment supervision; he emphasizes that this process begins with the first contact between offender and caseworker.

Newman also stresses the need to use an array of strategies and to implement them relative to the situation. One further ingredient of casework discussed by Professor Newman is the therapeutic relationship. To a large extent the climate formed in this relationship is the key to effective counseling.

In the concluding article, Dr. Jose Arcaya extends Newman's practical view of probation counseling. His "multiple reality" approach creates a composite role which accounts for the requirements of law, the feelings of the offender, and the role of the counselor. Dr. Arcaya offers the concept of a "dwelling stance" in which agent and client relate as equals in a therapeutic relationship to create a climate of mutual trust and constructive growth.

4

The Medical Model of Treatment
Historical Development of an Archaic Standard

PAUL E. LEHMAN

Chief, Excelsior House, NIMH Clinical Research Center,
Lexington, Ky.

Parole Officer, State of Indiana, 1961–63; Pre-Release Administrator,
USPHS Hospital, Fort Worth, Tex., 1964–67

MSSW, University of Louisville, 1964

The medical model of treatment in correction was first used as an analogy to promote more humane treatment of offenders. Later it gained prominence because crime was considered a symptom of an organic or mental disease, and its acceptance has continued partly because of the prestige of the medical profession. This standard of therapeutic treatment, with its emphasis on the one-to-one relationship, is unrealistic for the vast majority of offenders. Moreover, acceptance of an unattainable ideal has retarded the development of alternative experimental models by providing correctional administrators who are primarily interested in maintaining the status quo with rationalizations for failures of the existing system. Consequently, little real treatment is done in correction today. What is called "treatment" is usually some type of administrative processing. Until correctional goals are more carefully delineated and until new methods are tried and evaluated, administrators and correctional personnel are in a position to justify anything they do to offenders as "treatment." As long as this situation continues, little progress will be made.

Based on a talk given at the American Correctional Association conference, Cincinnati, October 11, 1970.

Reprinted, with permission of the National Council on Crime and Delinquency, from *Crime and Delinquency*, April 1972, pp. 204–212.

The term "medical model" is used rather broadly in this paper. It refers to a treatment approach that considers the commission of a crime primarily the result of an emotional disturbance in the individual offender. Remedial treatment, therefore, consists mainly of talk therapy designed to give the client insight into his underlying problems. The assumption is that once the offender has this insight he will be able to channel his antisocial impulses along socially constructive avenues —hence criminal behavior will cease. The medical model includes a range of therapies along a continuum from social casework to a strictly Freudian psychoanalytic approach. To be effective, it must be practiced by therapists who have special training in its use. Although the one-to-one relationship is the preferred method of application, certain types of small-group therapy can also be considered under the aegis of the medical model.

The medical model has changed over the years. Healy's case-study method is different from the dynamic, process-oriented techniques that were developed by Freud and his successors. Nevertheless, the concept that crime is a symptom of personal disease, defect, or maladjustment—i.e., an illness demanding individualized diagnosis and treatment —is common to all types of medical models.

These remarks are not intended to imply that the medical model has no place in a spectrum of correctional treatment rationales. Certainly for some offenders it is the preferred treatment approach: moreover, the medical model has greatly contributed to the development of a humane attitude toward the handling of prisoners. What I am reacting against is the medical model as the *standard* or the ideal treatment model in the correctional setting.

A HISTORICAL PERSPECTIVE

Adoption of the medical model as the standard for correctional treatment seems based on historical reasons rather than on the inherent value of the method. Correctional therapeutic treatment has traditionally followed the leadership of the mental health field.

Smith traces what he calls three mental health revolutions.[1] The first dates back to the nineteenth century, when insane persons were offered asylum from almshouses and jails. This approach stressed "moral treatment" and was an effort at a more humane approach to the mentally ill.

The second revolution was a result of Freudian insights and techniques. With its emphasis on one-to-one talk therapy, it proved impractical for the large numbers of inmates housed in institutions.

Smith maintains that, to be effective, the third mental health revolution must discard "the constraints of the doctor-patient medical model." He stresses the need for community treatment based on models other than the medical one.

The same general pattern described by Smith has been followed in correction. To the prison reformers in the latter part of the nineteenth century, crime was a moral defect of the offender. The term "treatment" was used at this time to describe the administrative handling of prisoners and did not refer to therapeutic intervention. The reformers of the period strongly believed that the representatives of society had a Christian obligation to treat their charges in a humane but firmly disciplined manner.

The Isolation System

It was generally agreed that hard work and fair treatment would undo the harm done by the previous penal policies of degrading punishment. However, most of the reformers also realized that staff attempts at reformation were hindered by the adverse effects of the inmates' evil influence on one another. Various experimental institutional models were tried in an effort to correct this situation. One model favorably publicized during the late 1880's was Richard Vaux's attempt to modify the old Pennsylvania system. Vaux referred to his program as "The Individual Treatment Method of Applying Punishment for Crime." In this system, established at Eastern State Penitentiary, convicts were physically isolated from one another; they were allowed to visit only with "good" people. Advocates of the system pointed out that segregation protected the inmate not only from the other convicts but from the "public gaze," thus preventing unfavorable publicity from hindering his chances of employment after discharge. An inherent part of this separate system was the concept of an indeterminate sentence, which was justified in terms of the medical analogy. An enthusiast of the separate system wrote in 1885:

> Instead of so many years for certain crimes, let it be the medicine of restraint for the prisoner until he is cured. Treat crime as a disease, the criminal as a patient. A physician of intelligence will prescribe the remedy until recovery, and cease administering when there is a cure.[2]

The question of what criteria should be used to decide when the isolated prisoner was reformed did not seem to bother Vaux and his followers. It appeared obvious to them that "experts" could accurately make such decisions.

The Congregate System

An alternative to physical separation of each individual inmate was treatment by a system of classification that provided for group segregation. Treatment in this sense did not concern itself with the individual's moral nature; instead, treatment was used to separate the "deserving" or "nonprofessional" criminals from the "real" or "professional" criminals. Generally speaking, deserving criminals were the young first offenders. Once these youngsters were confined away from the evil influence of older prisoners, the congregate system attempted to use group influences and living situations as tools of reformation. It also provided a graded system of marks by which an inmate could earn his release. The best use of the congregate system is illustrated by the work of Z. R. Brockway, superintendent of the Elmira Reformatory from 1876 to 1900. The 1885 report of an investigation of Elmira stated:

> It is the very purpose of the discipline of a reformatory to subject its inmates, as near as may be, to the conditions of actual life, *plus* some restraint. The values of rivalries, contentions, emulations, tests of progress in industry, morals, mental growth, and of resistance under temptation, can be realized under association. . . . Indeed, the legal and social theory upon which modified restraint and discipline are based is that they are patients under treatment, and not convicts under sentence.[3]

Both congregate and separatist systems reported good results by their methods. Brockway reported a recidivism rate of 20 per cent for his institution[4] while Vaux's success rate was reportedly about 75 per cent.[5]

The medical analogy used in describing both systems reflects the level of medical treatment that was being practiced at that time. The penal reformers of the period were not saying that crime was a disease; they were advocating a rational, humane approach to dealing with criminals. For lack of alternative models, they accepted the medical one because it best fitted the purpose they were espousing—i.e., Christian compassion and logical handling of the criminal to promote his reformation. They were not saying that the criminal was diseased but that he should be handled humanely, as an ill person would be.

The Beginning of Probation

As it was originally conceived, probation was not meant to be a therapeutic treatment process but rather a further example of humanitarian influences on penal administration. Adult probation was set up during the 1800's to help "nonprofessional criminals" who had committed offenses without evil intent. In 1880 the probation officer was delineated as follows:

> [He] should be a man of large experience in dealing with criminals, if possible; should possess good common sense, and be a superior judge of human nature, competent to discern between the really deserving

and the host of prisoners who will impose on him, if possible. He should have a large and warm heart, balanced by a good "level" head.[6]

Thus probation developed as a custody classification that could be used as an administrative alternative. The motivating force behind this innovation was the humanitarian desire to prevent future criminality by not exposing the "nonprofessional" criminals to the prison experience.

In 1891 the first act establishing a statewide use of probation officers was passed in Massachusetts. In referring to the operation of this legislation, Charlton J. Lewis, an active prison reformer, remarked:

The question for the court, upon the information of the probation officer, is simply whether it is safe for society that the prisoner go at large. It is not complicated by the irrelevant question whether the offense for which he is convicted bears one name or another—whether it is assault, robbery, arson, or murder.[7]

Thus the criterion for those "deserving" of various treatments was their potential risk to society; this risk was assessed not in terms of the criminal act but in terms of the violator's character. To comprehend the real character of the criminal, correction turned to a scientific, medical model for guidance. Under the influence of the works of Lombroso and the organically oriented psychiatrists, the idea gradually developed that criminals committed offenses because of some organic disease or congenital defect.

The Concept of Disease

There is a closer connection between crime and insanity than has been generally supposed. It will be increasingly recognized in the future. *Inherent* depravity is due to physical abnormality, or, in other words, to disease. . . . But, if inherent depravity is to be regarded as disease, then induced depravity is also probably the result of morbid physical condition; for bacilli of disease do not often settle in perfectly healthy tissue.[8]

The notion that crime is a symptom of disease was supported by a growing belief in professional circles that determinism had replaced individual free will. Soon it became fashionable to employ medical doctors as wardens of penal institutions.[9]

Measures advocated by the physician-wardens as therapy, however, were usually no different from those espoused by most progressive penal administrators—i.e., kind, firm treatment, and moral and vocational training. Nonmedical correctional administrators had difficulty accepting the concept that crime was a disease. They believed that the application of a medical model to a basically moral problem provided little guidance for changing their inmates into constructive citizens. As Thomas Mott Osborne, the warden of Sing Sing, remarked in 1916:

> The worst feature of the disease theory is that it cancels the responsibility of the criminal for his acts; and the moment you relieve a man of such personal responsibility, you are adrift upon a sea of intellectual doubt, with neither chart nor safe anchorage.[10]

In rejecting the medical model, Osborne saw treatment as education for "a better outlook upon life." He tried to give his prisoners educational experiences and to develop in them a feeling of self-worth by permitting them to participate in prison government. He wrote, "If you want the good results which come from bearing responsibility you must be prepared to grant the responsibility."[11]

Terms such as "undeserving" soon disappeared from use. Under the influence of scientific methodology, criminals were to be classified as either "congenital" or "occasional" offenders. Congenital criminals, it was generally believed, could not be changed and should be permanently removed from society. The occasional criminal, on the other hand, should be given remedial treatment. Harry Elmer Barnes, a strong advocate of the scientific approach to crime, put it this way:

> As the criminal, in nearly every case, is defective in one way or another, it is necessary to take positive remedial action with the aim either of eliminating his defects or rendering these defects no longer a danger to society. . . . A certain number of convicts will be revealed at once upon examination to be of a type that should never, under any circumstances, be again restored to a life of freedom, but should be permanently segregated or painlessly exterminated. Feeble-minded criminals, paretic criminals, and other types of low-grade degenerates or incurables would make up the bulk of this class.[12]

The Case Study Method

To better determine what should be done with which offenders, the American Institute of Criminal Law and Criminology established a committee in 1910 under the chairmanship of Dr. William Healy.[13] Healy and his associates were the first criminologists to use the case-study method to explore the causes of crime. Healy's position was that if enough facts were gathered on the individual offender, common sense would tell one what remedial measures needed to be applied. He used a multiple-factored approach, and the classification system he developed was later used to obtain material for his classic book, *The Individual Delinquent.*[14]

At the time Healy was conducting his research, the correctional personnel most concerned with diagnosing offenders were probation officers. Prison officials, with the exception of some persons like Osborne, were doing little to remedy the causes of crime. Reformers were still trying to introduce some kind of humanitarian changes into the institutions. Reading the literature of the period gives the impression that a primary focus of scientific criminology was to promote probation as the salvation of the penal system. Probation officers of the period were encouraged that scientific knowledge could give them the methodology they needed to be effective. The professional identification of probation workers was with the field of social work.[15]

Referring to the theoretical foundation established by Healy and others, Edwin J. Cooley (New York City's chief probation officer) wrote in 1918:

> One of the current developments in our Probation work is the realization that there is a definite methodology in making a comprehensive diagnosis of a delinquent.[16]

Imbued with the philosophy of social work and encouraged by the development of a "scientific methodology," Cooley had great hopes for the future of probation. Some years later he received a unique opportunity to put his ideas into operation. In 1925, Cardinal Hayes of New York funded a project described as an attempt "to demonstrate the full potentialities of probation functioning under favorable conditions, with adequate equipment, resources and personnel, which in all its history had never before been available."[17] The program focused on the individual offender with the specific objective of "working out an effective and comprehensive probation methodology which, when once definitely established and tested, was to be offered to the country at large."[18] The project, directed by Cooley, was staffed with college-educated probation officers who had social work experience.

As a consequence of this two-year experiment using highly trained staff, limited caseloads, carefully selected clients, and no real follow-up investigation, Cooley formulated a set of sixty proposed standards for treatment, evaluation, and probation practice. Most of these standards were officially adopted in New York and were later proposed as national standards.[19] The presentence report recommendations advocated by Cooley were basically those of Healy and, with certain modifications, are the ones currently prescribed.[20]

Cooley genuinely believed he had developed a truly scientific and effective method of treating offenders, but for all his work he may actually have retarded progressive efforts by providing correction with a rationalization for failure. After the completion of the New York experiment correction was able to explain recidivism rates simply as the failure to meet "professional standards" rather than admitting inadequate treatment methodology.

In accepting the medical model as the standard for correctional treatment, Cooley believed that the success of his probationers was based on the ability of his staff to diagnose and treat the underlying problems of the individual client. However, because the clients selected for probation were such good risks, the "cure rate" may have been based more on the quality of the probationers than on the therapeutic treatment they received. Moreover, the highly individualized treatment model could not be adequately transferred to the large penal institution.

Thus the diagnostic techniques based on the Healy type of psychiatric model became irrelevant as a treatment modality for the vast majority of offenders. The dilemma of the correctional administrator was expressed by Cabot in 1930:

> *Character diagnosis is essential and we lack it. But it is not treatment.* . . . Call in the psychologist and the psychiatrist! Study the patient's emotions, his thought-processes, his inhibitions, his reflexes and reactions. By all means, but what then? Psychiatry and psychology have given thus far few if any clues of proved usefulness in the treatment of crime.[21]

THE PRESENT

The problem became even more acute after 1930 as psychiatry and social work became more psychoanalytically oriented. The Freudian dynamic model further stressed the one-to-one relationship as the optimum choice of treatment and emphasized minute detail and lengthy diagnostic procedures. However, as psychiatry professed to become more scientific, it was also accused of having strong moral overtones.[22] Some have charged that with the passing of the concept of crime as a symptom of an organic disease, the medical or psychiatric model developed into an approach using permissive techniques of moral re-education. If this charge is true, then perhaps much of the medical model's appeal comes not from its efficacy but from its association with the prestige of the medical profession.

The question, of course, is not whether moral re-education should be a goal of correction; penologists have been advocating this for at least a hundred years. The question is whether the medical model should be the standard for accomplishing it in the correctional setting.

Correctional administrators have been slow to seek out and test alternatives to the medical model. One reason for their lack of aggressiveness in this area is that administrators obtain money for their operations by convincing legislatures that they are dealing with offenders in such a way that society is being protected. When the results show that the correctional apparatus is not doing its job effectively, administrators can blame insufficient resources. However, when the money is granted to implement programs that reduce caseloads, employ professional staff, and provide psychiatric consultation and if, even then, evaluation shows no increase in effectiveness, the administrator is caught in an embarrassing impasse: either he must admit that the medical model is inadequate (and then attempt the difficult task of experimenting with new models to find more effective aproaches) or he simply suppresses any research findings that endanger the agency's public image.[23] Of course, he can dodge the dilemma by avoiding program evaluation in the first place.

WHAT CAN BE DONE?

If correction is going to fulfill the tasks given it by society, new and alternative models will have to be developed. We can no longer simply advocate more of the same thing. In one sense, time is running out for making effective changes. In the past, society has granted much discretion to those working in criminal justice. However, because this discretion was often abused, the gradual tendency of the courts has been to limit the power of various governmental agencies. So far the police have been primarily affected; nevertheless, it is a reasonable assumption that in the future the courts will more and more demand that correctional administrators be able to justify the decisions they make in the name of "treatment."[24] The initiative for change should come from within the correctional field and not be imposed by the courts. We cannot continue to blame public apathy and recalcitrant clients for our failures.

The first thing we must do is say precisely and realistically what the goals of correction are. The medical model proposes the ideal of "complete" rehabilitation; as Cooley noted, "No matter how well the probationer appeared to be adjusted to his environment or his social contacts, no permanent rehabilitation could be said to have been effected until a thoroughgoing modification had taken place in his mental and emotional life, beliefs, attitudes, habits, and conduct."[25] A more attainable goal would be reduction of the offender's inclination to commit crime. Correctional workers must also acknowledge that not all their clients are deviant personalities. Many "normal" persons are caught up in the correctional cycle. The fact that an individual is processed into the correctional apparatus is no reason to believe that he is necessarily a psychopath or the victim of some type of character disorder.

If the goals of correction can be agreed upon, programs can be designed to achieve them. Evaluation information on the results of the programs can be fed back into the programs to insure that the outputs are in harmony with stated objectives. The key to successful correctional programing is determining which treatment rationales are effective for which types of offenders. Effective programs can be evolved only by imaginative experimentation and strict evaluation of results. Correctional theory must be accepted or rejected according to the practical consequences that result from its application.

One of the dominant trends in modern theoretical criminology is the development of classification systems on various taxonomic groups.[26] By exposing different theoretical systems to various treatment modalities, we can determine which policies are destructive or constructive to different kinds of persons. We need to develop a mosaic of treatment alternatives rather than rely on any one model.

When the medical model ceases to be viewed as the standard for correctional treatment, other resources become available to deal with correctional problems: If treatment no longer has to be done only by highly trained professionals, "sub-professionals" (including ex-offenders) become a source of potential manpower. If the casework model no longer applies exclusively, probation and parole caseloads do not have to be wedded to the fifty-unit standard; instead, we can experiment with intense counseling for some offenders and minimum or no supervision for others.

The following remarks made in 1911 are still true today:

> Tendencies in this country in the problems of the treatment of the criminal have been overwhelmingly administrative rather than analytical. . . . The extravagance of sole adhesion to [this] method is increasingly obvious. . . ."[27]

Correction must develop alternatives to the medical model—alternatives that are operationally and theoretically sound and that can be objectively evaluated.

NOTES

[1] M. Brewster Smith, "The Revolution in Mental Health Care—A 'Bold New Approach,' " *Trans-action,* April 1968, pp. 19–23.

[2] George W. Hall, "Prison Discipline," in *Proceedings of the National Conference of Charities and Corrections,* 1885, p. 302.

[3] Henry M. Hoyt, "The Evaluation of Prison," in *Proceedings,* 1885, pp. 291–92.

[4] Charles D. Warner, "The Elmira Reformatory," in *Proceedings,* 1885, p. 282.

[5] Hoyt, in *Proceedings,* 1885, p. 292.

[6] Warren F. Spalding, *Proceedings of the National Conference of Charities and Corrections,* 1880, p. 66.

[7] Charlton J. Lewis, "The Probation System," in *Proceedings of the National Conference of Charities and Corrections,* 1897, p. 45.

[8] Philip C. Garrett, "Necessity of Radical Prison Reform," in *Proceedings,* 1897, p. 29.

[9] E. E. Southard, "The Desirability of Medical Wardens for Prisons," in *Proceedings of the National Conference of Social Work,* 1917, pp. 591–92.

[10] Thomas Mott Osborne, *Society and Prisons* (New Haven: Yale University Press, 1916), p. 32.

[11] Ibid., p. 235.

[12] Harry Elmer Barnes, *The Repression of Crime* (New York: George H. Doran Company, 1926), p. 31.

[13] William Healy, "A System of Recording Concerning Criminals," *Journal of the American Institute of Criminal Law and Criminology,* July 1910, pp. 84–96.

[14] William Healy, *The Individual Delinquent* (Boston: Little, Brown, 1918).

[15] For one example, see R. O. Harris, "Probation in Its Relation to Social Welfare," *Journal of the American Institute of Criminal Law and Criminology,* January 1917, pp. 810–16.

[16] Edwin J. Cooley, "Current Tendencies in Adult Probation," in *Proceedings of the National Conference of Social Work,* 1918, p. 143.

[17] Edwin J. Cooley, *Probation and Delinquency* (New York: Catholic Charities of the Archdiocese of New York, 1927), p. ix.

[18] Ibid.

[19] Edwin J. Cooley, "Standards of Probation," *The Newer Justice and the Courts,* Proceedings, National Probation Association, 1927, pp. 48–59.

[20] For examples, see California Department of the Youth Authority, *Standards for the Performance of Probation Duties* (Sacramento, 1965); also, *The Presentence Investigative Report* (federal presentence report outline adopted by the Judicial Committee on the Administration of the Probation System, Feb. 11, 1965), Publication No. 103, Division of Probation, Administrative Office of the United States Courts.

[21] Richard Cabot in the foreword to Sheldon and Eleanor Glueck, *500 Criminal Careers* (New York: Alfred A. Knopf, 1930), p. x.

[22] Philip Rieff, *Freud: The Mind of the Moralist* (Garden City, N.Y.: Doubleday, Anchor, 1961).

[23] Daniel Glaser, "Correctional Research: An Elusive Paradise," *Journal of Research in Crime and Delinquency,* January 1965, pp. 1–11.

[24] For example, see Eugene N. Barkin, "Interpretation and Implementation of Civil Rights Legislation in Penal Institutions" *American Journal of Correction,* September-October 1966, pp. 36–37, 39.

[25] Cooley, *Probation and Delinquency,* p. 141.

[26] For example, see Albert Morris, "The Comprehensive Classification of Adult Offenders," *Journal of Criminal Law, Criminology and Police Science,* June 1965, pp. 197–202; P. McNaughton-Smith and L. T. Wilkins, "New Prediction and Classification Methods in Criminology," *Journal of Research in Crime and Delinquency,* January 1964, pp. 19–32; J. Douglas Grant and Marguerite Q. Grant, "A Group Dynamics Approach to the Treatment of Non-Conformists in the Navy," *Annals of the American Academy of Political and Social Science,* March 1959, pp. 126–35.

[27] O. F. Lewis, "A Report to the Committee on Law Breakers," in *Proceedings of the National Conference of Charities and Corrections,* 1911, p. 51.

5

The Fallacy of the Medical Model as Applied to Corrections

SUSAN ROSE
University of Oregon

In the quest to find new ways of resocializing those who make up our prison populations, criminologists have adopted proven models of therapy from other fields. The best known model, especially for its therapeutic success, comes from the field of medicine. Thus, the medical model is now widely used in corrections work. It is the author's contention that of all the fields employing this model, corrections work is least suited to it. An exploration of the underlying pre-requisites for the success of the medical model seems to explain why the abysmal failure in corrections as well as the reason for overwhelming success in medicine.

The medical model consists of a series of three steps: (1) *diagnosis* of a specific problem which manifests itself through symptoms (e.g. criminal activity); (2) *treatment* either aimed at the problem itself or the symptoms; producing (3) a *cure* or, at least, amelioration of the problem or symptoms. In other words, the medical model assures a "cure" if proper diagnosis is followed by equally proper treatment. The American physician, who certainly has the most familiarity with this model, also possesses the ultimate superior rank in the authoritarian structure. He is the sole source of knowledgeable information about medical ailments and remedies for ills. While men and women may have a choice of physicians, clinics, health centers, or hospitals, and even may prescribe for themselves, the fact remains that the omnipotent power over our lives is held by the physician. He can not only do forbidden things, explore dangerous, alluring and taboo regions of body and mind; he also knows how to save us from pain and suffering, how to keep us well, how to thwart death, and how to restore life. For twenty-five cen-

Reprinted, with permission of the California Probation, Parole and Correctional Association, from *Crime and Corrections, The Journal of the California Probation, Parole and Correctional Association,* Vol. 1, No. 1 (Spring 1973): 27–29.

turies, mankind has benefited from these practitioners of the art of Hygeia and the science of Asclepius.

Medicine, unlike the natural, physical and social sciences, has dealt with a relatively stable and confined phenomenon—the human body. With the advances in knowledge that have been made with such astounding rapidity, especially during this century, very few aspects have been left unexplored. Today's physician, by comparison, assuredly has more *complete* knowledge about his subject than do the host of social scientists together. The key is "complete". While the physician has a great deal of knowledge to which to refer; the corrections official, the psychiatrist, the psychologist, and the sociologist take an educated guess at best. Advances in the behavioral sciences have not had a chance to proceed at nearly the same rate as they have in medical science.

It follows, logically, that without a comparable fund of knowledge, usage of the medical model is like employing a whale net to catch guppies. The corrections field is fraught with unknowns. Perhaps the darkest area is why an individual sees criminal activity as a viable alternative to conformity and from society's viewpoint, how best to induce him to return to "acceptable" behavior. Our prisons and rehabilitation programs are shackled by old myths (medicine has a few to overcome as well!) and are confounded by Puritan ethics—punish the evil-doer! Since we do not understand what it is we are supposed to be curing, the methods of treatment cannot help but be bizarre, not to mention the harm done to the "patient" who is tossed from one bewildered authority to another. All that can be said truthfully about one who commits a criminal act is that he/she is a non-conformist and American society has always been inclined to mete out punitive treatment to its nonconformists in the absence of trying to understand them.

The erroneous use of medical research techniques has continued to lead investigators up one blind alley after another. According to René Dubos, the doctrine of specific etiology has unquestionably been a very constructive force in medical research, but it has yet to provide a complete account of the causation of disease. He suggests that better results may be produced by investigating indirect outcomes of a constellation of circumstances rather than attempting to locate the direct results of single determinant factors. Criminologists would probably do much better to concentrate on this phenomenologically oriented approach and stop pursuing fleeting antecedent causes of criminal behavior. For every cause proposed: poverty, lack of education, fetal malnutrition, XYY syndrome, broken homes, etc., etc.; there have been just as many exceptions noted.

The phenomenological approach requires a participant-observation methodology in which the investigator immerses himself in the world of his observees. When the observer can not only visualize the world through his respondents' eyes, but also can comprehend the impact of their environment, he will find his conclusions to be much more valid. This process is illustrated strikingly by G. Thomas Gitchoff *(Kids, Cops, and Kilos)*. Participant-observers were able to strongly identify themselves with their respondents and eventually could approach problems almost entirely from their subjects' point of view. This methodology also requires broadly based questions. For example, sociologists tell us that social unrest is preceded by a rejection of the boundaries of conformity placed on people by society. It is the nature of the human being to accept the given order as the only way of life; but if for some reason, the legitimacy of that order/authority is challenged and questioned, one discovers that societal restraints are no longer sufficient to produce conformity. Societal norms soon become de-legitimate and cease to be binding, hence criminal behavior loses its sanctions. Furthermore, suppose that non-criminal behavior is dependent on a critical amount of socialization; if so, perhaps inadequate socialization of an individual may make criminal activity an acceptable alternative for him. This hypothesis could account partially for the fact that not all children from broken homes engage in criminal activity. Perhaps an attempt to document these processes might yield more fruitful results, and even might lend itself to establishing new modes of dealing with offenders. The time is long past for a new approach in corrections, if only because old methods result in such consistent failures.

REFERENCES

Dubos, René. *Mirage of Health: Utopias, Progress, and Biological Change.* New York: Anchor Books, 1959.

Gitchoff, G. Thomas. *Kids, Cops, and Kilos.* San Diego: Malter-Westerfield Publishing Company, 1969.

6

Concepts of Treatment in Probation and Parole Supervision

CHARLES L. NEWMAN

The word "treatment" is probably one of the most overworked words in the correctional lexicon. Whatever its semantic meaning, treatment and the treatment approach have come to suggest several connotations: that "it" replaces an "old system" of dealing with offenders; that trained people can do "it" better than untrained ones; that "it" is more effective than other systems of dealing with offenders; that "it" considers the person, his needs, strengths and limitations, as they differ from other individuals around him. Increasingly within the correctional field, we have come to accept the idea that the treatment approach to the offender is better than any other method. Hopefully we can eventually demonstrate the greater effectiveness of this method over any other "nontreatment" oriented approach.

These are values to which we must subscribe even though the research to date does not substantially support our position. Part of the difficulty rests with the fact that the treatment approach requires of the field not only an ideological acceptance of the philosophy, but also the preparation and existence of a corps of suitably trained persons with the technical know-how, and the actual implementation of treatment practices. Even when so-called intensive treatment programs have been tried, it has frequently been with the use of personnel with limited professional training, in an atmosphere which is suspicious or even hostile to new approaches.

Within the correctional field we are probably further ahead in an acceptance of the philosophy involving treatment of the offender than we are with adequate staffing, but this would be hard to support in the face of punitive and coercive restriction which is so much a part of the entire correctional cycle: police, courts, probation, institutions, and parole.

Redirection and reeducation of persons who have demonstrated antisocial and illegal behavior are complex matters requiring both time

Reprinted, with permission from *Federal Probation*, Quarterly, March 1961, pp. 11–18.

and skill. Involved is the discovery of strengths within the individual offender which can be mobilized for constructive social behavior. Not infrequently, it will involve modifying the social situation in which he finds himself. But so long as we continue to assume, as we seem to do in so many jurisdictions, that probation, parole, and institutional treatment services can be provided by anyone with the proper political affiliation, one head, a good heart, and a meagre appetite for the luxuries of life, then it will be a long time off before we can truly implement the philosophy and goals of the correctional field.

Most correctional institutions make no claim to the provision of more than a custodial program for their inmates. But continuously, in both probation and parole, we claim to provide community treatment. Query: can we, or do we, under the circumstances?

We recognize that the basic purpose of probation and parole is the protection of the community. Any system which runs contrary to that precept cannot be acceptable to society. When an offender has been institutionalized, we are reasonably assured that, for a while at least, he will not be involved in further depredations against the community. But in our wisdom, we have learned to recognize that not all offenders need the physical control which an institution provides. This decision-making process must involve more than sentimentality, sympathy, charity, or a count of prior violations. Rather it demands a meaningful diagnosis and a prognosis that the individual does have sufficient internal strength to return to the community where essentially the same physical, social, and psychological forces are present as were at the time of commission of his criminal act, and to make an adequate adjustment in spite of those factors.

TREATMENT AN INTERRELATED THREE-STAGE PROCESS

In order to assist the individual to adjust to the community, the field correctional worker implements a three-stage treatment process: *investigation, diagnosis,* and *treatment supervision.* Contrary to the popular misconception that a given set of preliminaries is necessary before the treatment stage can be implemented, it should be clearly recognized that interaction (and consequently, treatment) occurs from the very first moment of contact. Obviously, if we are to work successfully with a person, we must be able to understand his inner-working.

In the *investigation* stage, we attempt to find out what is and was within him and outside him that made him the person with whom we are dealing. With skillful questioning, he will find himself looking at aspects of his life, so very necessary if he is to gain insight into the nature of his behavior. From this frame of reference it is not too difficult to see the investigation as a very vital part of the treatment process.

In our culture, we place a great deal of emphasis on putting labels on all sorts of things, including behavior. The words "neurotic," "psychopath," "psychotic," "behavior disorder," and many others are used with such ease that we sometimes think we know what they mean. In the diagnostic process, the goal is not to attach a label to the person. Rather, the *diagnosis* is the codification of all that has been learned about the individual, organized in such a way as to provide a means for the establishment of future treatment goals. It becomes immediately obvious that as we learn more about the individual through future contact, the diagnosis will be modified, and the treatment goals raised or lowered as the case may be.

The *treatment supervision* process, as it will be discussed here, entails the elaboration of knowledge about the individual through the process of communication, so that the individual will gain a more realistic appraisal of his own behavior, thereby enhancing his own ability to function more acceptably in the community. The provision of certain material services may also be involved in the treatment process.

INVESTIGATION FOR TREATMENT

In the finding-out process, the most important source to help the officer is the offender himself. He frequently is also a most difficult source. The offender may consider it to his interest and advantage to give a misleading picture. Here is the real test of the correctional officer's skill—the art of understanding and dealing with human nature. The extent to which a person reveals himself is in direct proportion to the degree of confidence (rapport) which the worker has succeeded in developing. Other sources of information lie outside the offender himself and require tact in approach and intelligence in selection. A problem which every worker faces is to obtain, within the limits of time, as many illuminating facts as possible without causing discrimination against the offender. The investigation should give a comprehensive picture of the offender's own world, his personality, his relationship to others, and his immediate environment as seen in relation to himself. We should know something about his likes and dislikes, his hopes and desires, his values and disappointments, his ambitions and plans (or lack of them), his assets and qualities as well as shortcomings. However, we should not let our own cultural biases and values seduce us into giving "feeling content" to the material which the probationer or parolee may not have. But truly knowing what are his feelings in regard to past and present experiences is central to dealing effectively with him in a treatment relationship.

Listing a series of isolated physical and social facts about a person provides only a bare skeletal diagram of that person. So frequently, for example, presentence, classification, or preparole reports will be limited to a cursory statement about the family composition, designating the names, ages, and occupations of family members. What do these facts mean? Without elaboration or interpretation, such facts are of limited value in arriving at a recommendation or in providing meaningful supervision. What we really need to find out is the type of relationship which has existed between the person and other significant people in his life: natural family, family by marriage, friends, neighbors, coworkers.

We have no hesitation about discouraging continued contact with previous associates. But what about family? Are these relationships always worth maintaining? With knowledge about those interrelationships, it may be most desirable to encourage the person to stay far away from his family as well as previous associates. Even though our culture strongly supports the notion of enduring marriage, we cannot assume, *a priori*, a positive family relationship exists solely because a man and woman are living together in marriage. Nor can we assume that a person has necessarily been damaged emotionally by the fact of growing up in a broken home. These are things we must find out.

Basically, the point is this: in the treatment relationship, the generalizations about human behavior (to which most of us subscribe) have applied value only to the degree that they fit the circumstances and the personality of the individual situation. We must know the individual first in order to understand him and to counsel with him.

An interview is a conversation with a purpose. In his role, the correctional worker is not interested in persons in the aggregate, but in the specific individual. Our goal, through the interview process, is to be able to know the offender's personality in action. We are interested in his immediate environment, the way he reacts to frustrations and opportunities. We want to know his attitudes toward others and himself. From that point, we can assist him to gain a better self-understanding thereby affecting his ability to function constructively in the community around him.

Whether the interview occurs during the presentence investigation or during the period of supervision, it is important to recognize that both the worker and the offender bring prior life experiences into the interview situation. If the worker has been able to develop insight and self-awareness about his own behavior, there is a likelihood that he will be more tolerant and effective with the persons with whom he is working. This is particularly necessary in the implementation of authority. The mature worker will recognize that it is the situation and not his own need for power, which calls for the use of authority.

TREATMENT BEGINS WITH THE FIRST CONTACT

While it can be true of every session, the first contact between the worker and the offender is of extreme importance. In all probability the person will be experiencing a certain amount of anxiety which, with skillful handling, can be mobilized from the very beginning to achieve the treatment goals. The person should be given the feeling that there is no need to hurry in exploring the many avenues which may develop in the initial interview. If the worker takes time to listen, the probability is that he will hear more than if he devotes the time to talking himself. At the beginning, the offender is making a number of observations about the officer, the office, and comparing his current impressions with his own preconceptions. At the same time, the worker should be making his own observations, such as the person's appearance, the way he enters the office, the way he conducts himself, how he sits down, how he talks, the tone of his speech, and other nonverbal communicative aspects. Whether we are capable of observing it or not, in many instances a *transference* occurs from the individual to the officer from the very beginning. The mature worker will recognize that fact, and interact accordingly.

The content of the first interview, as with all subsequent contacts, will vary with the individual. Part of the time is spent in gathering factual information. However, unless there is reason to believe that information already on file is erroneous, generally there is no need to repeat the operation. Being asked the same questions over and over again can easily give the impression that it does not matter too much what you say since no one pays any attention to the answers. Accurate recording (even though it takes time) is of vital necessity if we hope to do a respectable job of treatment. By recording basic information as well as progress contacts, we are in a better position to see the progress which has been made in the case and alter treatment goals accordingly. Without such information, a shift in caseload requires the new worker to start out from the beginning, which we would agree is a great waste of time and effort.

After the initial interview, the officer is faced with the monumental task of making a fast appraisal, on the basis of a single interview, of the person's ability to reside in the community with only limited external controls. One of the better means of appraisal comes from an understanding of the degree of discomfort which the individual feels in relation to his social or emotional problem. Further, the officer will have to determine what part others may have in the problem, and the extent to which they are affected.

The timing of subsequent interviews must, in large measure, be determined by a variety of factors, including the type and immediacy of the problem, the size of caseload, and the need of the person for support and control. Unfortunately, too much of probation and parole supervision is little more than routine monthly reporting. Admittedly, in some cases, this minimal type of control may be quite adequate. But generally speaking where problems of adjustment to the home and community exist, it is questionable whether any value is derived from infrequent contact. In too many probation and parole offices, moreover, a person is seen only after he has demonstrated some emergent problem situation. To insure the protection of the community, as well as to assist the person in adjustment, probation and parole supervision *must* provide preventive as well as remedial treatment services.

SURVEILLANCE VERSUS COUNSELING

Within the context of the need for sound correctional treatment programs, several elements emerge. First, we must recognize that the community continues to be concerned about the activities of the probationer and the parolee. Whether or not he is involved in further illegal activity, the law violater has demonstrated his capacity to disregard society's rules and regulations. By virtue of his prior behavior, the community is justifiably concerned.

Secondly, we must recognize that it is neither feasible nor desirable to maintain continuous surveillance of the offender's activities. At best, we can sample his behavior at various moments and *hope* that we are able to detect certain indicators which suggest that the person is *more* of a presumptive risk to himself and to the community. Greater protection than this to the commmunity through surveillance is not possible in a democracy. Moreover, surveillance, as opposed to treatment supervision, is essentially a police responsibility. It involves techniques for which the therapy-oriented and trained practitioner in corrections is unprepared to handle with maximum effectiveness. This does not obviate the need for surveillance, but rather places its implementation in the hands of the police, whose responsibility it is in the first place.

It becomes obvious, then, that the correctional worker (whether in the institution or field services) should be in a position to recognize, understand, and deal effectively with subtle as well as obvious shifts in the behavior and personality of the offender. Not infrequently, these shifts can be indicative of problems which the individual is experiencing and for which he is unable to find a solution. I do not mean to suggest that to find a person in a particularly irritable mood during a field visit is cause for revocation. On the other hand, such irritability, persistently detected, may be a clue which directs our attention to the movement of the person into behavior which ultimately may get him into difficulty.

RULES AND TREATMENT

Recalling our intention to protect the community through probation and parole services, we impose a number of controls upon the offender and his behavior. Not uncommonly, the person is instructed to abide by a series of rules and regulations which are universally applied to all offenders within the particular jurisdiction. Many times, the specific rule may not have any particular relationship to the offender and his prior conduct. The imposition of rules and conditions can have a therapeutic value. However, to do so, the rules must have a relationship to the prior behavior pattern of the individual upon whom they are imposed. Moreover, the officer must see these rules as a part of his treatment plan rather than external controls imposed by someone other than himself, and which, reluctantly, he must enforce.

Limit-setting involves specifying what behavior the officer, as the community's representative, will or will not accept from the person under supervision. First, however, the limits must be clear in the officer's own mind. Reluctance or vacillation in the enforcement of rules can easily lead to a situation where the officer will be manipulated by the person under supervision. If limits and rules are consistently applied, the spurious argument that one concession calls for another is easily overcome.

The point should be quite clear: if the boundary limitations or prohibitions are specified for an individual because it is known that he will endanger himself or others if he violates, then the officer has a clear course of action. Failure to be consistent adds only to confusion on the part of the person under supervision. If the violation of a rule does not result in the offender doing harm to himself or others, then the rule is not necessary in his case, and should not be invoked.

THE THERAPEUTIC RELATIONSHIP

One of the first major accomplishments of treatment comes about when the offender becomes aware both intellectually and emotionally that the officer represents not only authority with the power to enforce certain restraints and restrictions, but that he is also able to offer material, social, and psychological adjustmental aids.

Hardly a day passes that the correctional worker does not come upon a situation where a statement made has fallen somewhat short of the truth. Sometimes these statements may be the consequence of faulty recollection, or they may involve outright misrepresentation. The "natural" reaction is to feel irritated. From a treatment focus, however, one would have to ask the question: since the account seems unreasonable, what defenses are being used that prevent a more truthful representation? Then: what purpose do these defenses serve for the individual? Do they contribute to his sense of well-being, or do they provide him with the needed sense of discomfort? The next step in counseling emerges from this knowledge.

I do not mean to suggest that probation and parole officers should attempt to practice psychiatry, or otherwise involve themselves in depth analysis with their caseloads. In correctional work, we should be dealing primarily with conscious level material. Thus we do not get into dreams or use narcotherapy. But there is a wide range of difference between depth therapy and a "go forth and sin no more" approach. Few correctional workers have the skill or training to approach depth therapy with competence, and the moralistic approach does not work too well over the long run.

In the therapeutic, clinical management of the probationer and parolee, crime prevention is incorporated in the treatment process. As was pointed out earlier, probation and parole supervision must go beyond mere surveillance, for recognition of possible future antisocial behavior through an awareness of the individual's deteriorating personal and social relatonships are more effective for community protection than periodic barroom visitation.

The officer's awareness of the fact that the person is having a problem in adjustment is seriously handicapped when interviews are held across a counter in a crowded office, and limited to a 2- to 5-minute examination of the previous month's activity report. The "how-are-things going?" probe question is more suited when sufficient time, interest, and understanding are provided than when the response of "okay" or "so-so" is expected.

The correctional worker will lose one of his most important tools if he defines very carefully and structures very rigidly the interrelationship which he will allow between the offender and himself. If the probationer or parolee is not permitted to express anxiety, hostility, or other feelings toward the officer, employer, wife, or even the next-door neighbor, then the interview is forcing a response pattern which does not give an accurate picture of the person's feelings. Nor does it allow for the implementation of counseling techniques which interpret and assist in the resolution of the problem with the person. This is not to suggest that the probation or parole supervision interview should be devoted solely to ventilation. Rather, the officer must be in a position to recognize that, as a social therapist in an authoritative setting, certain types of interrelationships are desirable and necessary. The interaction must be geared to the dynamics of the offender's personality, and not to the exclusive satisfaction of the worker's own ego.

Beyond this, the officer must go into the field, into the family home, the neighborhood, and the job setting. No offender exists in a vacuum, and it is not improbable that adjustmental problems will be related to external as well as internal, intrapsychic factors. Discretion, of course, is both desirable and necessary because we do not want to jeopardize what acceptance the offender may have been able to reestablish for himself in the community. It is essential, however, that we constantly remember that the offender must do his adjusting in the community and not in the probation office exclusively. Adjustment is a great deal more than showing the necessary and expected deference to the wishes of the correctional officer.

A not-uncommon type found in probation or parole offices is one who appears to be unable to function effectively in the working world. Our middle-class morality suggests that work is desirable, and that "good" people want to work. Hence, failure and unemployment are often considered to be related to lack of motivation, laziness, or a configuration of morally-related values. Frequently, we find that these same individuals express a feeling of paralysis in what appears to them to be a hostile world. We can write off these complaints as characteristic of the convict culture, or we can seek more definitive answers for the individual case. In evaluating the situation, there are a number of questions which the officer can explore. When attempting to find out how long a problem has existed, the officer should also evaluate the degree of discomfort which the person feels about it. Are his feelings appropriate to the situation, and are his actions consonant with his stated feelings? Looking to the employment situation, for example, the officer can ask: Is what has been demanded of this person really compatible with his true potentialities? What has been the relationship between the offender and his employer, and to what extent do these external factors impinge upon the stability of the family relationship? Obviously, this is not the sort of information which can be obtained when the only knowledge about employment is taken from the monthly income report.

A person's previous employment record can be a very valuable diagnostic tool if it is evaluated in depth. And from that evaluation, certain treatment goals come to the fore. It is wise to look at the direction of change in position of employment, as well as the frequency. Did the person move from job to job with no appreciable improvement in position or salary? Has he been on the skids? Or, has the direction of change been in terms of upward mobility? Have external factors put demands upon him to move upward socially? If so, why? We can see then that a variety of reasons may account for vocational instability. It is vital that the officer does not try to implant his own moral values on the facts, but rather, that he derives their values from those who are directly affected by them.

In a reported situation, George A. was constantly in and out of work before he got into difficulty with the law. His references were poor, in that they showed him to be quick-tempered, with a "holier than thou" attitude. George had married in his second year of college, and with great struggle managed to graduate shortly before his wife bore them a second child. The wife appeared to be a very passive, yet demanding person. Her demands were always in terms of an improved living situation, which in her own eyes, at least, were realistic demands. George's change of jobs in part reflected her demands. But the job changes also reflected his inability to present himself in a desirable perspective so that he might get a much wanted promotion and increment in salary. Writing checks in nonexistent accounts finally led to his downfall.

Placed on probation, George was able to adjust quite readily in the counseling relationship. A job was found, and the position lasted for almost a year. Then, one day, George came in to report that he had just had an argument with the office manager of the firm where he was employed and that he had quit. The officer asked about the circumstances, but George was sullen and uncommunicative, somewhat daring the officer "to do something about it." Referring to his record, the officer then reviewed some of the glowing comments that George had made about the employer: how kind and considerate he had been, etc., etc. Yes, those things were true, but not that blankety-blank office manager. Then for the next 5 minutes George ventilated about the office manager, and covered most of the transgressions of man and nature. Finally, in a very tired voice, he told the officer that his wife was pregnant again, and that she was putting the pressure on him to get a better job. Had the worker responded with authority at the beginning, he would have lost what eventually developed into a situation where effective counseling could be accomplished.

Only as a person is able to gain insight into the nature of his behavior will he be able to make a satisfactory adjustment within himself. If the behavior seems unreasonable, then the counselor must seek to find out what defenses are preventing a more accurate perception of reality. Importantly, though, the officer must know how vital it is to the probationer's or parolee's sense of equilibrium that he maintain a self-defeating defense pattern. Creation of anxiety in the counseling situation is an important factor in precipitating change, but such a technique must be handled with a great deal of dexterity, and with the knowledge that it will not push the person into undesirable behavior, which may have been his pattern of reaction under earlier circumstances.

The correctional officer must be aware continuously of the concept that man's behavior and thinking are the outgrowths of his life's experiences. But man is not the blind product of social and physical forces around him. From the moment of birth, a relationship is established between the outside world and himself, and for which a reciprocal interrelationship evolves. Mother influences child and child affects mother-husband-other-child relationships. The whole confluence on the individual is extremely difficult to evaluate, particularly in the face of the large number of interactions we experience during the course of a lifetime.

THE NEED FOR SECURITY

Although human needs can be stated in an almost endless variety of ways, survival is a deep-rooted impulse of the organism. In order to survive it is necessary to be safe, and any threat to security causes a person to feel either anger or fear. Anxiety is the response to an internal feeling of threat. Whether that threat is directed from physical survival or from psychological and social concommitants, excessive anxiety interferes with physical and mental well-being. Further, when anxiety exists, a person strives to resolve it or defend himself against it. There are specific psychological mechanisms which he may employ as a defense against anxiety-producing situations, and the consequences may take either adjustive or socially disapproved forms.

THE NEED TO EXPRESS NEW FEELING

A person's feelings are mixed when he experiences a mutually incompatible combination of feelings. When feelings are mixed, anxiety arises, and the greater the anxiety, the more the feelings are mixed, and so on. Conflict is almost inevitable when feelings are mixed. Some of the kinds of behavior whose roots lie in conflict are: inconsistency, procrastination, hostility, unreasonableness, seclusiveness, inability to make up one's mind, rigidity. Chiding the person, or shaming him for these and related behaviors serves only to alienate the relationship, and does not get beyond the symptom of the disturbance. When the correctional therapist understands the motivating forces behind such behavior, he is then able to provide the needed help.

One way is to help the person bring out true feelings in the open for an airing, and to help him grasp the idea that double feelings are universal and that there is nothing wrong in having them. This is not to suggest that we condone destructive behavior either inner-directed or vented against the external world. But we do accept the person as an individual and help him to cope with the mixed feelings. In the matter of criminality, offenders probably experience every conceivable degree and every possible combination of positive and negative feelings: from joy of not being institutionalized (as on probation or parole) to bitter resignation and resentment at being tricked by fate.

The correctional worker can sometimes provide a desired treatment effect by listening and feeding back (nondirectively) what has been said with patience and acceptance. At other times, particularly with individuals whose response patterns reflect a primitive level of development, the officer may find it necessary to *teach* how to behave less disturbingly in confronting life situations. Some instances call for support; other situations call for the creation of anxiety to accomplish given treatment ends.

CONCLUSION

Treatment is a sophisticated process involving both time and skill. It is not something which starts after a given set of preliminaries, but rather, gets under way, desirably, with the very first contact. Obviously, there is no one method of treatment with all law-violators, or any other group of individuals who manifest unacceptable behavior. There are certain generic similarities to be found among all people, and the offender is no exception to this rule. But each personality is made up of a number of elements which are blended together in proportions and relationships which are unique to the individual. External changes can be accomplished through a change in the social environment of the individual, but without the vital internal changes in personality, we cannot expect more than a repetition of the previous unsuccessful and unsatisfying behavior. The objective, regardless of the approach, is to create in a person a self-acceptance which did not exist before.

7

The Multiple Realities Inherent in Probation Counseling

JOSE ARCAYA*

Psychologist, Allegheny County Adult Probation Department,
Pittsburgh, Pennsylvania

The probation officer, in dealing with his clients in the counseling relationship, confronts a problem inherent to all psychotherapeutic relations—the problem of multiple realities.[1] The term "multiple realities" refers to the array of different *experiential* (versus intellectual) meanings that the individuals participating in a common social relationship use to understand that relationship. This is to say, any human relationship always is made up of as many different perspectives of that situation as there are individual members involved in it. While these participants share some general, common expectations about the significance of their association, these are generally objective, legal, or formal understandings of the situation. They bear little, if any relevance to the subjective, attitudinal, or informal meanings held by the individuals involved. This difference in experiential interpretation, perspective, or assumption about the meaning of any given relationship is the phenomenon of multiple realities.

In probation work this issue of multiple realities is dramatically present. Here we find a situation where two individuals are joined by legal force in a counseling (and supposedly) trusting relationship. From the beginning, the probation officer is confronted with a problem which not only entails communicating meaningfully with an unknown individual (a meeting of two realities, difficult enough under voluntary conditions), but one which, if he is at all flexible, constrains him to pay heed to two different perspectives simultaneously: his obligations as a court-appointed supervisor of probationers, and the idosyncratic needs

*The author gratefully thanks Miss Mary Anne Murphy for her valuable suggestions in rendering clarity to some parts of this article.

Reprinted, with permission, from *Federal Probation Quarterly*, December 1973, pp. 58–63.

of the probationer as client in a counseling relationship. Inherent in the job of a probation officer is this tension of perspectives. It localizes itself between the officer and the court (how closely to abide by its formal rules of supervision), the officer and the client (how many breaks to give an offender), and between the officer and himself (what kind of officer to be).

It is from this general problem that we will examine the nature of probation work. To this end we will (1) try to describe some features prevalent in a typical, first-time counseling situation; (2) attempt to highlight the conflicts present there; (3) discuss the way these are often handled; and (4) suggest approaches which might mitigate these conflicts.

A DESCRIPTION OF A MEETING

When a probationer enters a probation office for the first time part of his awareness is occupied by a nagging feeling of apprehension. Viewed from the eyes of the probationer, the office represents a power that can, and does, limit his freedom. It is an institution to which he must submit involuntarily (as a "client," euphemistically put). In the background of this submission is an implicit assumption made by our legal system that a probationer is in need of supervision, rehabilitation, or guidance. Thus, even before the first contact is ever made between officer and client, the client is already led to believe that he is considered less than a responsible human being. It is not surprising, therefore, that the probationer encounters his supervising officer with a mixture of fear, wariness, and defiance. Generally, in the beginning of his introduction to the probation system, the probationer's attitude is to obey the formal rules of probation and maintain a respectful, if distant, relationship with whoever might be assigned to work with him. During this initial contact period the probationer's "sniff out" evaluates his officer, determining to what extent he may be trusted.

At the other pole of this meeting is the officer himself who has little say with regard to who is assigned to his caseload. He, too, meets a stranger for the first time. Like the probationer's experience, fear and apprehension accompany the initial meeting. The officer is fearful because he knows nothing of the individual's capacity to cooperate, follow the rules, or give a hard time. He is apprehensive because he knows that there might come a day when he will have to reprimand, admonish, or even incarcerate his new client. Maybe, from past experience, he feels he has failed to really help many of his probationers. Perhaps the memories of these failures haunt him now. Yet, in spite of these discouragements, he maintains an optimistic hope that the relationship will be worthwhile for the probationer. He desires the probationer's betterment through his experience on probation. With these feelings in mind, the officer chooses one of two broad counseling approaches toward his new ward.[2]

ROLES

First, he may choose to put out of his awareness the ambiguity of his position—that he is both a counselor of the individual and the representative of a legal institution. Instead of integrating the two responsibilities, he may dichotomize the functions and choose to act on one more than the other. In doing this he adopts what might be called a "nonthinking" stance, since he eliminates from his considerations the different ways in which he could be helpful. Instead he presents a constant role to each client, well-planned and rehearsed in advance of any actual encounter. This role has few creative or spontaneous elements, and even bores the officer himself. In this stance, two possibilities for behavior are open: To be an "authority figure" or a "nice guy."

The *authority-figure* role is inevitably presented by an officer hoping to cover his own fear of the interpersonal counseling experience. He conveys an image characterized by a determination to show the client "who's boss." He sees probation work to involve the legal surveillance of his cases. To this end, his major occupation centers around keeping paperwork in order, taking appropriate legal action when a clear violation of rules has occurred, and providing the person on probation with clear and strong reminders of the latter's probation responsibilities. Normally this officer "has all the answers" to any predicament. He is an "authority." Because he surrenders his ability to spontaneously react, to make decisions appropriate to the individual situation, he entrusts his thinking to the black and white answers contained in the probation rulebook.

The *nice-guy* officer is as inflexible and thoughtless as the authority figure. This individual chooses the other extreme of the spectrum by giving the probationer power over *him*. He has little consideration for the rights of society as a whole or, for that matter, the basic welfare of his client. He is an example of someone who believes that any rule broken is unimportant. By his silence, he subtly fosters and condones antisocial behavior on the latter's part. This officer is "bent" on being liked, proving that he is "humanistic," that he is, in short, a "nice guy." Like the authority figure, he fears the intimacy of an open counseling relationship because in it he might have to reveal anger, disagreement, or other negative feelings which he wants to deny. This "type" is perhaps the more difficult to describe of the two because its thoughtlessness leads to what is very socially desired—being liked. However, in this role the officer is out of touch with the full gamut of spontaneous emotions. He would rather repress an unkind or critical word needed by the client than to risk the loss of a potential friend.

AN ALTERNATIVE

The alternative stance is what is here termed a "dwelling" presence.[3] This attitude openly accepts the ambiguity of feelings and responsibilities attached to probation work and uses this ambiguity to bring the client an awareness of the officer's own humanity. Here the officer attempts to share with the person on probation the personal tensions he experiences in counseling within the legal system and discloses his difficulties in accomplishing this feat. The client is not made to feel that he confronts an unerring, larger-than-life, authority who has all the answers or a permissive, easily deceived fool. The officer has no interest in either having power over the probationer or having the probationer have power over him. Rather, in the dwelling stance the officer creates a relationship that encourages both to relate as equals. A respect for the inherent worth of both individuals is presumed in spite of the fact that one is a convicted criminal and the other a court-appointed supervisor. This stance acknowledges that there are no privileged positions in authentic human communication: The lasting benefits of a counseling relationship derive from the mutual trust and lack of power conflicts.

To accomplish this rapport the client and officer must develop a common ground of communication as a result of the experience with each other. This means building a *shared world* of meanings which occurs principally from a willingness to not only talk, but also listen. To truly listen implies to dwell in what the other says. It is not the absence of talk which characterizes listening, but the effort to interpret the other's words from his perspective. Communication proceeds only to the extent the speaker feels that someone is trying to understand him. In the most fundamental sense, listening communicates more than talking. The problem of multiple realities is no more than the challenge of really understanding what the other says.

CONFLICTS CONTAINED IN EVERYDAY LANGUAGE

If we were to overhear a typical client-officer conversation certain words and phrases, such as "cooperation," "honest," "responsibility," "helping yourself," might arise. These probably would be spoken by the officer in the hopes of conveying to the client the need for him to participate openly in their relationship.

Let us suppose the officer's newly designated probationer has had a long history of excessive drinking. He has been placed on probation after causing a near-fatal accident in which he himself was almost killed. The task which the officer sees before him now is how to keep the client from driving after drinking. In accomplishing this goal, the officer might urge the individual to go to an Alcoholics Anonymous chapter, see a psychiatrist or psychologist, maybe even live in a residential treatment center. In explaining his recommendation to the probationer, the officer might state that it was time that the offender "help himself," become "honest about his problems," and take "responsibility for his life." These words he would justify to himself by reasoning that he was helping to rid the public byways of a driving menace as well as helping the individual come to grips with his deep-seated emotional problems.

To the probationer, however, such talk smacks of personal rejection, lack of acceptance, or, simply, unconcerned advice. Perhaps such ethical-sounding terminology has been spoken to him by hypocritical authority figures (teachers, parents, government officials, employers) all his life. Now he lumps the words "responsibility," "honest," "self-help," and their ilk into a highly personal "language-to-make-me-do-something I-don't-want-to-do" category. From this perspective he answers that he has been helping himself, that he does not drink anymore, and that he is "as honest as anyone else" with his emotions. Yet even as he speaks, the tone in which he makes his reply reveals a mood of anger and defensiveness which is not evident explicitly from the spoken words themselves. Perhaps the officer perceives that the probationer's eyes narrow as he talks, that his hands clench into fists, that his body tightens—all tacit signs that the probationer understood something offensive in what he said. Maybe both will speak for awhile longer and then the client will leave. Later, the officer, in thinking back over the incident, will have a subtle intuition that they really did not communicate, that he did not "reach" the client. The client, on the other hand, will feel that he was reprimanded like a misbehaving child or objectified "like some kind of a nut."

What occurred here? Viewed from the perspective of their *lived* meanings, the words used by the officer were of a different reality than those employed by the probationer. A conflict occurred between the "languages" of the two individuals and their perceived realities of the situation. For the officer, reality demanded that he convince the client to cure his drinking problem, stay off the road, and, in an indirect way, become happier. For the probationer, on the other hand, reality informed him that the officer is "just like all the rest," someone who is "pushing me around," who, in some way, "rejects me." Perhaps, if the probationer had confronted an extreme case of the "authority figure," he would have been right. However, even if the officer had no value-judgments in mind and did not want to exhibit power over the individual, no communication occurred. Permit me to cite a nonprobation example.

Suppose that a husband and wife are continuously bickering to the point that each considers it best that they divorce. However, they do not want to be hasty in their decision so they appear before a marriage counselor to obtain his services before going through with the action. They say to the professional, each in turn, that the other spouse does not "love" him or her. The wife complains that she feels neglected by the husband, that he fails to show her affection or be around when she needs him. Moreover, she suspects that he is really interested in another woman because he seems to be away at his job more than he should be. The husband, on the other hand, fervently denies that he is unfaithful. He asserts that she does not love him because she does not respect his privacy and his solitude. The reason why he stays away at the office, he says, is because he gets engrossed in his work and forgets his other responsibilities. He claims that he does not want to deliberately neglect her.

At the core of their problem seems to be their different understandings of "love." From the wife's perspective love means attention, presence of her husband, and demonstrative affection. To the husband "love" translates as tolerance and respect for the other, as well as quiet and nondramatic affection. Both seem to have presuppositions about the meaning of "love" which are not only different but actually antagonistic. Basically, their problem reduces to the fact that each cannot see the context of the other's comprehension of that word and notion. They have smugly assumed, each in his own way, that the idea, "love," can only have one possible significance. They have lost sight of the fact that its meaning for them arises from their particular point of view.

The argument which we wish to make, in brief, is that no language in human dialogue is complete without an attempt to concretely ground the meaning of the words used. No fixed definitions of terms exist apart from the significances, explicitly or implicitly, given them by the people who are involved in the speaking relationship. Language, in order to communicate a meaningful reality, must be situated. One can only understand the words of the other when he has taken into account the other's entire speaking context. In turn, one's own words can be understood by the other only if the meanings to one's personal "language" are disclosed, in as complete a way as possible. Dialogue occurs in a rate proportional to the degree that the two individuals risk revealing and reacting, emotionally and intellectually, to the words of the other. Yet, simultaneous with reacting and revealing, it is necessary that one "actively" listen and "responsively" speak.

TOWARDS AN INTEGRATION OF REALITIES

In order for the probationer to feel that the counseling relationship is of benefit, it is necessary that he feel he is understood *as he understands himself.* This is important because no one trusts someone else if he feels that that other is not "with" him. Only when the client experiences the feeling of being understood will he, in turn, listen to what the officer has to say. He cannot be forced to listen. To lead the person on probation to voluntary listening, the officer must be responsive to his words. This means that he has to be a listener who respects the client sufficiently to let the latter's words *count*. This is to say that in a dwelling stance with the probationer, the officer tries to make sense of what his client has to say from the reality of the client's own "words." To meaningfully "be" with the other necessitates entering into his "world," trying, as much as possible, to leave one's own world apart. Let us examine two dimensions of responsiveness: listening and speaking.

Active listening[4] means that the officer actively attempts to put aside his preconceptions of what the client is saying. He tries, instead, to silently remain with the language which the probationer uses as much as possible, allowing him to describe what he means in his own words. The officer does not try to define the reality and experience of the client for him. He accords the individual enough respect to assume that he will relate his story better than the officer could. Nevertheless, it will occur that, as the officer listens with this end in mind, many uncertainties about what is actually said will arise. When this happens, the officer may ask the probationer to clarify what he means. This request, however, must be phrased also in the "language" of the client if the question is to be meaningful to him. Let us illustrate:

In our example of the "highway menace" some ambiguity arose between what the officer meant by "help" and the client's understanding of that word. Moreover, when the probationer stated that he *"was helping"* himself, he emphasized his difference with what appeared to be anger: The tone of his voice seemed harsher, his body tightened, his facial expression changed. The officer, in turn, overlooked the client's response and only later did he suspect that maybe he had not communicated effectively with him. However, if he had been sensitive at that moment to the body-language of the client, to the tone of his words, to the general interpersonal counseling "atmosphere," the officer might have been dismayed and angered at the reception which his well-meant suggestions received. He might have lashed out with a reprimand ("Why you dirty so-and-so I'm only trying to help and look at the way that you treat me!") or, on the other extreme, suppressed any mention of his feeling at all while silently dismissing his client as a "hothead" or as dangerous and disturbed ("some kind of a nut"). None of these actions, however, would have served the purpose of understanding the client's perspective.

Yet if he had been actively listening, trying to make sense of the client as he sees himself, the officer would neither have overlooked his own immediate feelings, reprimanded the client, nor dismissed him privately with demeaning labels ("hothead," "nut"). Instead, he would have attempted to set aside his own wounded pride in order to understand why the client responded as he did. An inquiry to the client about why he reacted as he did to the officer's suggestions would have been made in nonjudgmental, descriptive terms. Thus the officer might have stated: "You appeared disturbed just now. Your hands were clenched into fists, your body was tightened, and the tone of your voice grew harsher as you said 'I *am* helping myself.' You look like you were angry about something. Am I right? If not, then what was the matter, if anything?"

By grounding and contextualizing his question in this manner, the officer lets the probationer perceive himself as the officer perceives him, and permits him to realize the rationale which motivated the question in the first place. Contained in this inquiry are no hidden, evaluative terms ("Why were you being *defensive, hostile, irrational,* etc."). No motives, causes, explanations, or evaluations are ascribed with this concrete, descriptive language. Unlike its opposite, evaluative terminology, it permits a freedom of response to the client without having him feel as though he were admitting to a character flaw in the process. This language is open-ended, allowing the client to explain himself as he thinks he is—"Yes, I am angry at being pushed around," or "No, I'm not mad at you but I don't like myself for being in this fix," etc.

Through this and numerous other clarifications of the probationer's language and behavior, the officer slowly builds up an image of the style and perspective of the probationer. As a result of this type of inquiry, he actively listens to what the other says by having him serve as his own source of "reference." Meanings of words and body gestures are understood not through some independent "dictionary" definition but in terms of the inner "logic" of the client. Thus, the probationer is, for the listening officer, a self-defining being. Success in understanding someone as he understands himself comes only slowly and laboriously. In the above example it could be that the client is surprised or threatened that the officer was so close to his emotional world. Chances are that no breakthrough in communication would be accomplished through one inquiry. This does not matter. What is of greater importance is that the client see that the officer cares enough to consult with *him* about what *he* means without prejudging his experience. Of greater benefit than any discovered "facts" is the feeling conveyed to the probationer that someone is attempting to hear him. Listening requires patience.

Responsive talking has been reserved for the last topic of discussion because meaningful talk only follows as a consequence of meaningful listening. To talk, as understood from this stance, means really to *respond*. One talks as a consequence of having understood the client as he himself allows one to understand him. This means that the officer works together with the client through dialogue to contextualize and situate the latter's world. Any suggestions, recommendations, or, even, orders originate from the mutual dialogue. A set of probation goals is not the outgrowth of unverified and unshared prejudices of what *should* be best for the client. The client always serves as his own best advisor to action.[5]

While certainly this does not mean that the officer must capitulate his responsibilities to the courts and not abide by the guidelines of probation, it does mean that any rules enforced or any unpopular decisions made by him must, at the very least, be documented to the probationer in terms of the latter's concrete behavior. Hence in our example of the "highway menace" the recommendation that he seek professional help might be justified by citing the particular offenses which even the client admits to enacting ("yes, I was drunk while driving," "yes, I have drunk a little too much in the past and gotten into trouble," etc.). Even if the client remains unhappy about the officer's decision, solid ground work would have been established between the officer and client where the latter realizes that the officer effects decisions only from specific instances of behavior and shares his reasoning with the client. Again the client is consulted even if the final decision, after due consideration has been given, is not to his liking.

By way of conclusion, we must emphasize that all of the above suggestions (active listening, responsive talking, contextualization of language) are not intended to be understood as manipulative *techniques* to control the behavior of the probationer. These approaches to counseling cannot replace an original desire on the officer's part to be with and help the client. There is no substitute for simple human concern. Only if the officer respects the humanity of the other can our ideas have lasting benefits.

NOTES

[1] Schultz (1971) has spoken very cogently about this theme in a philosophical context.

[2] We draw these distinctions only in a general way. No individual officer completely fits either of the "pure" approaches which will now be described. These characterizations are solely intended to convey overall *tendencies* which, in many cases, are found to be typical in the normal probation counseling situation.

[3] Heidegger (1966) speaks of a similar idea when he contrasts "calculative thinking" (spurious, superficial understanding) with "meditative thinking" (dwelling with the ambiguity of thought without dichotomizing it).

[4] Thomas (1970) employs the same term in the context of parent-child communication problems.

[5] See Fischer (1969, 1970) for an elaborate discussion of the merits contained in using the client as a source of reference for formulating his own psychological recommendations.

REFERENCES

Fischer, C. T., "Rapport as Mutual Respect," *Personnel and Guidance Journal*, 48 (1969): 201–204.

"The Testee as Co-Evaluator," *Journal of Counseling Psychology*, 17 (1970): 70–76.

Gordon, Thomas, *Parent Effectiveness Training: The No-Lose Program for Raising Responsible Children*, Wyden Press, 1970.

Heidegger, Martin, *Discourse on Thinking*. New York: Harper Torchbooks, 1966.

Schutz, Alfred, "The Problem of Multiple Realities," *Collected Papers*, 1. The Hague: Martinus Nijoff, 1971, pp. 207–259.

III

CASEWORKER ATTITUDES AND COUNSELING STYLES

INTRODUCTION

Whether or not correctional casework is successful, perfunctory, or destructive depends to a large degree on how the caseworker perceives his own role in the counseling relationship. The dynamics of that relationship involve an interplay of many emotions, ideas, values, and needs on the part of both the worker and the client. All these reactions create a climate in which correctional change can occur, for better or for worse.

The basic question one must ask himself as he assumes a role in counseling is, Whose needs am I meeting; society's, the client's, or my own? The appropriate answer, obviously, is all three. However, the point of asking the question goes beyond the obvious answer. The real issue is the priorities assigned the needs. Stated more directly, At what cost will I, the caseworker, satisfy my own needs to help others? The counselor must also ask himself, What are the conditions under which change occurs and who is responsible for change?

This part attempts to deal with the issues raised by these questions. Regardless of his knowledge and understanding of human behavior, if the caseworker cannot clearly define his role as a counselor, and effectively deal with the agent-client relationship, his efforts will again be little more than a process of "muddling-through."

In the first article, Professors Jay Hall and Martha S. Williams say that the correctional worker is a manager of forces and an agent of change. In this role the agent must be sensitive to the forces for change and the climate in which change takes place. Two conceptual models are utilized in their analysis: Kurt Lewin's force-field theory, in which the conditions, motivations, and responsibility for change are examined; and the Johari Window, designed by Joe Luft and Harry Ingram, which serves as a model for diagraming communications between agent and client.

Psychologist Jack R. Gibb then gives a more specific analysis of the concept of help and the ingredients of a helping relationship. As he points out, "help is not always helpful." It can create a dependent individual, and a destructive climate in which effective change cannot occur. Against these destructive elements Dr. Gibb counterposes a model for a constructive relationship.

A more personalized characterization of the helping relationship is given next by Robert W. Resnick. He speaks to the relationship between professional therapists and their patients in a way particularly appropriate for those in corrections. The reader merely needs to insert "correctional caseworker" for "therapist," and Dr. Resnick's message will come through loud and clear. If "help" as he defines it can kill the humanness of the patient in therapy, it can brutalize the client in correctional counseling. In that event, not only is the offender's potential for personal growth thwarted, but his ability to contribute to society, rather than take from it, is seriously diminished.

In the fourth article, Probation Officer Claude T. Mangrum takes a different tack in discussing the helping relationship. Correctional casework is unique because the agent is an arm of the court, responsible to the law, and has the power and authority to force treatment on the client. If the client does not respond or cooperate appropriately, the agent can bring sanctions into play that can put the client in an untenable position.

Mangrum focuses on this aspect of the relationship, and emphasizes the element of coercion in counseling. His views suggest that the correctional worker is, above all, responsible to society, and corrective restraint and coercive direction may be necessary at times to meet this responsibility.

This dual nature of the correctional worker's role, enforcement and treatment, is extended in the article that follows by an author who chose to remain anonymous. A parole agent, he graduated from college with a master's degree in social work and faced the dilemma of enforcing the law while serving the needs of the offender. Excluding his digression on the courts in the conclusion of his article, Anonymous clearly describes the climate in which correctional counseling is conducted. The fact that he had difficulty resolving this dilemma is his problem, not that of the correctional system. However, it is a problem that all who enter the field of corrections must resolve.

In the concluding article, a supervising probation officer, John Stratton, shifts the focus back to the concept of "help" in the relationship between a probation officer and his client, and poses the question, Is the agent a helper of people or a con man? Within this context, Stratton introduces a third variable, the bureaucratic nature of the correctional agency. He follows with an exposé of the various cop-out techniques used by probation officers; instead of providing honest help, they create a relationship intended to keep their clients dependent and helpless.

8

The Correctional Worker as an Agent of Change[1]

JAY HALL AND MARTHA S. WILLIAMS
Southwest Center for Law and the Behavioral Sciences

As Warren Bennis and his colleagues have suggested, radical change is the one constant which seems to characterize this age.[2] The correctional worker is all too familiar with problems of change for he is confronted with the problem of trying to change the behavior patterns of those who have disobeyed the laws of the community. His is the task of sorting out planned change from accidental change so that only the more constructive aspects of the process may be realized and people returned to their society. Change in this instance may be the basic condition for the freedom without which life becomes increasingly difficult and unrewarding. And yet, from the standpoint of short-range needs, it is often more comfortable for individual offenders not to change. The reluctance of an individual to give up old ways of doing things is understandable when one considers the meanings change may have for those confronted with it.

Demands for change actually represent alterations in the lives of people and touch most of the elements and processes upon which they depend for day-to-day security. Weldon Moffitt,[3] in a conference on change, has suggested that change affects a whole range of beliefs, values, norms, and goals which individuals hold. It is little wonder that people often feel threatened when change is demanded of them in areas of such importance. They may comply; but by-products of apathy, suspicion, and resistance are frequently manifested as well.

The correctional worker, because of the nature of his task, must see to it that offenders make certain changes in their behavior so that they are no longer a threat to society. Certain kinds of antisocial behaviors must be altered without damaging the more positive traits

Reprinted, with permission of the authors and the publisher from *Readings in Correctional Change*, The Hogg Foundation For Mental Health, University of Texas, 1970, pp. 1–18.

which the individuals might possess. This places the correctional worker in the role of an *agent of change*.

Whether change occurs smoothly and is constructive or whether its occurrence is marked by resistance and hostility is determined to a great extent by the skills of the change agent. These skills, in turn, are determined to a large extent by the degree to which the change agent understands the dynamics of the change process. At best, change is complex and the failure to conceptualize it clearly can result in damage to the changee and frustration for the change agent.

A CONCEPTUAL MODEL OF CHANGE

The correctional worker is in need of some theoretical framework for analyzing the total process of change so that its effects might become more predictable and understandable. An approach with which many are already familiar is that suggested by Kurt Lewin,[4] a noted behavioral scientist. Lewin has theorized that any ongoing system may be thought of as a level of activity; for example, the current crime rate in a given locale usually reflects some level of relatively stabilized activity. Such a level is seen by Lewin as the resultant of a number of forces. There are forces which cause more of the activity and, therefore, tend to increase the level; and there are forces which oppose the activity and tend to decrease the level. These are called *driving* and *restraining* forces respectively. Within the framework of Lewin's model, driving and restraining forces are conceptualized as working in opposition to each other, much as credits and debits work against each other on the accountant's balance sheet. The level of activity, as a resultant of these opposing forces, is sensitive to changes in either the driving or restraining forces and fluctuates rather than remaining completely stationary.

In most situations, as the level of activity shifts in one direction, the strength of opposing forces increases. Thus, for example, an increase in crime may elicit increased demands for more restraining forces in the form of more effective law enforcement practices. Change, therefore, is thought of as an attempt to either raise or lower the level of ongoing activity and is seen as occurring within a field of forces, some of which facilitate and others of which oppose the modification. Within the correctional context, therefore, change would seem to involve a number of forces which correctional workers—if they could influence their strength—could utilize in effecting constructive change.

By way of example, a familiar problem which communities face might be considered. This is the problem of a high rate of juvenile delinquency in the area. A look at some of the driving and restraining forces which affect the amount of delinquency in a given locale can provide some insights into the change process and an understanding of Lewin's force field model as an analytical tool for creating change. The first question to be asked is "What are the forces leading to delinquency in the community and what are the forces opposing it?" One possible field of forces is shown on the following chart in schematic form.

As may be seen in the diagram, forces leading to juvenile crime in a community may stem from a variety of sources. The manner in which the driving and restraining forces are handled will dictate the success of the program for change. It may be predicted, for example, that should the driving forces be ignored and a program for change introduced, the strengths of those driving forces could increase, under tension, thus tending to block an effective shift in the level of activity. Similarly, as the driving forces increase in strength, a concomitant need for increased restraining forces is experienced, thus further increasing the tension in the total system. Some tension-wracked systems are characteristic of many social problems today. How then may the forces at work be managed to achieve smoother and more constructive programs for change?

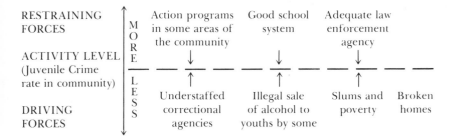

Succinctly, changes in the activity level of Lewin's model may be produced by either adding forces in the desired direction or by diminishing forces which serve as barriers. The two methods, however, have dissimilar consequences associated with them. As mentioned previously, the addition of forces may cause change to occur, but it is change accompanied by increased tension and, therefore, is less stable. On the other hand, a reduction in forces allows change to occur with a concomitant diminution of psychological tension; albeit more slowly. Thus, within the example used, a change toward less crime could perhaps be produced by placing a curfew on juveniles (*i.e.*, by increasing the restraining forces) or it could be achieved by reducing the poor slum conditions which breed crime (*i.e.*, by reducing some of the driving forces). Enough communities have tried increasing controls such as strict curfews, increasing the police force and so on to appreciate the forms increased tension can take when restraining forces are increased. Few communities, although there are increasingly more, have had first-hand experience with the by-products associated with attending to and reducing driving forces, however. The traditional approach to change has obscured the importance of driving forces and focused the attention on those functions which are primarily instrumental in increasing restraining forces.

The correctional worker, therefore, must reconsider his role if he is to function effectively as a change agent for his community. He is, within a change context, something more than a helper or controller. He is in addition to all of these a *manager of forces*. If he can identify most of the forces operating in the field within which change is contemplated, determine which of these forces is amenable to his influence, and devise ways of both reducing and increasing appropriate forces he may find that his task as a change agent will become more rewarding. Hopefully, the force field model presented here will aid the correctional worker from the standpoint of analyzing change; but in order to plan for the reconstitution of forces, he must know something of the forces themselves.

Essentially, the forces the correctional worker must learn to manage in effecting change in the offender are forces relevant to (1) the motivations for change, (2) the responsibilities for change, and (3) the conditions for change. It should be recognized at the outset that these are "people" forces rather than technical and represent, therefore, a domain traditionally of interest to the behavioral scientist. The skill with which the forces of change are managed, however, often reflects the assumptions people hold about motivation, responsibility, and the way these two interact to determine the conditions for accomplishing community goals. For this reason, such considerations cannot be too quickly dismissed or parceled out on the basis of a "theory-practice" criterion, but must be confronted by change agents head-on.

THE MOTIVATION FOR CHANGE

As Maslow has observed, man is a wanting animal.[5] By and large, therefore, the need for change by an individual will be felt when he recognizes that a current behavior is no longer adequate for satisfying his wants. The matter of such recognition is of importance to the change agent for ultimately the decision to change or not to change rests with the changee. Thus, the task confronting the agent of change is one of creating conditions under which this recognition is most likely to occur and then providing guidelines relative to the direction of change. This is no easy undertaking, for few people—regardless of their status in the community—enjoy having both life goals and pathways of attainment spelled out for them. Unless they can somehow come to share the perceived value of both the goals and the routes of attainment, individuals tend to resist attempts to change them. For the correctional worker, the issue of motivation constitutes one of the pivotal elements of change which can significantly affect the success or failure of his change-inducing strategies. For this reason, any plan for change must begin with an awareness and appreciation of the motivational components active in human behavior.

Kelman[6] has suggested three types of motivation which can underlie changes in both attitudes and behavior. The first of these—and, unfortunately, the most commonly encountered—is a motivation to avoid punishment and/or gain rewards which results in overt change. Kelman has attributed change based on this motivation to the process of *compliance,* which is designed to gain a specific *social effect.* A second motivation which might lead to change is the desire to establish and maintain a satisfying *personal relationship* by behaving in such a way as to please some admired person or group, regardless of the quality of the behavior required. Motivation of this type results in the process of *identification,* according to Kelman, and the specific content of influence attempts by the influencing person or group is less relevant to the changee than is the relationship. The third motivation for change occurs as a result of *internalization, i.e.,* acceptance by an individual of influence, and he changes because the content of the induced behavior is intrinsically rewarding and congruent with his value system. The motivation operative in internalization is due to the *credibility of the content* of the influencing message. Since the motivations for change may take such diverse forms and in view of the fact that the behavior manifested under each form may look quite similar on the surface, some further consideration of these elements of change from the standpoint of strategies, duration, and side-effects would seem to be in order.

Change via Compliance

Kelman indicates that each change process is characterized by a distinctive set of antecedent conditions in terms of the power of the influencing agent, prepotency of the changed behavior, and the relevance of the change issue. Under compliance, the power of the influencing agent must be higher than that of the changee *and* some means of surveillance must exist for the behavior of the changee to be maintained. Such a condition may be created by giving the change agent formal power in the situation. Kelman has demonstrated that conformity behavior which occurs under conditions of high change agent power remains ongoing only so long as there is surveillance by the influencing agent of the changee. Removal of surveillance, however, results in a decrease in conformity behavior and a return to more prepotent modes of behaving. Thus, change based on compliance represents an unstable form of induced behavior which relies on external controls and forces for its continued practice. Reduction of either surveillance or the change agent's power to mediate rewards and punishments may result in abandonment of the compliant behavior.

Change via Identification

As under compliance conditions, identification requires a fairly high amount of power on the part of the change agent; but in this instance, power accrues primarily from the salience of the relationship in the mind of the changee. The attractiveness of the change agent in terms of his personal charismatic qualities is the greatest determinant of his power over the changee and, consequently, of his effectiveness in inducing change. The motivation on the part of the changee to conform to the change agent's wishes stems from his desire to nurture and maintain his relationship with the change agent. Thus, surveillance is not necessary under these conditions for sustained change, but rather high change agent power is the *sine qua non*. Kelman has demonstrated that conforming behavior based on identification will continue when surveillance is withdrawn. Given a reduction of attractiveness of the change agent or the salience of the relationship, however, behavior becomes less conforming and the change agent less effective as an influential person in the life of the changee. Thus, again, change obtained under conditions of identification is unstable and relies on the continued ability of the change agent to function as a "significant person" in the changee's life. Such an ability is tenuous at best since the whole concept of attractiveness-unattractiveness is colored by implicit conditional value judgments on the part of the changee which are subject to change themselves at any time.

Change via Internalization

Unlike change based on compliance or identification, internalization-based change does not require either high power on the part of the change agent (either formal or social) or surveillance for its ability to produce prolonged conformity. Rather, internalization occurs as a result of the credibility of the content of the influence attempt. While high change agent power and surveillance may well facilitate change via internalization, Kelman has found that conformity behavior resulting from changee internalization remains ongoing even when power and surveillance have been reduced. This occurs because the change in behavior is based less on any external mediators than upon internal awareness and understanding. Thus, change based on internalization would seem to represent the only enduring and relatively stable form of induced conformity behavior.

The implications of these approaches to motivating changees to conform to one's influence attempts are primarily important in terms of the duration of change effects. Neither change via compliance nor change via identification can be characterized as enduring stable forms of induced behaviors. Internalization emerges as the only motivational source for such change. The task of the change agent, therefore, in contributing to the motivations for change of changees would seem to be one of creating the proper conditions for internalization to occur. Put another way, this says that the task of the agent of change is one of providing the conditions under which changees can see and appreciate the credibility of the content of the influence message. Such conditions may best be understood through a discussion of the responsibilities and conditions for change.

THE RESPONSIBILITY FOR CHANGE

Traditionally, change agents have viewed the responsibility for change as a one-sided affair. The norm of "fixing the responsibility" for an activity is well ingrained. Thus, change agents have come to "fix" the responsibility for change as their own. Too often this assumption of responsibility by but one party to the endeavor has been manifested in attempts to force change by emphasizing the authority relationships between change agents and changees. The well known "shape up or ship out" mandate has wider application than within the military organization which fostered it. The change agent—much as the squad leader—is frequently compelled to alter the performance of persons who may be seen as "bad risks" and "troublemakers." Failure to do so is perceived as increasing the probability that one's agency might be discredited or that one's own skills might be questioned. Thus, the assumption of the total responsibility for change by the change agents may well reflect their concern that they demonstrate the ability to adhere to implicit agency norms and, at the same time, function as effective agents of change.

The earlier discussion of the motivations for change, however, would seem to dampen the assumption that any single person can be totally responsible for a program of change which affects others if it is to be effective. If the needs of both change agents (as individuals, as well as agents of the organization) and changees are equally important determinants of the direction and success of attempted change, ultimately the responsibility for change needs to be shared as well. It should be stressed that the principle of shared responsibility is applicable to a greater or lesser degree to all phases of activity, but it is particularly important to those areas in which the internalization of new attitudes and behaviors on the part of changees is especially valued.

The all too common reactions of changees to proposed change, which were discussed earlier, may not be entirely reactions to change *per se,* but may well be an index of the degree to which individuals experience frustration and a loss of self-esteem under authority-obedience conditions of the type described. What is seen by the change agent as behavior completely in violation of the changee's obligation to perform effectively may be viewed by that changee as the only means available to him of demonstrating his feelings of alienation. Has the changee failed his obligation to perform effectively or has the change agent failed to manage effectively?

The question begins to evolve into one of not *who* is responsible, but rather one of *what* are the responsibilities which must be considered in undertaking programs of change. Since the decision to change or not to change rests finally with the changee—regardless of the number or strength of the changer's attempts to induce change—it seems apparent that the responsibility for effective change is inevitably shared. Thus, the responsibility of the change agent in a program of change becomes one of creating the proper conditions for shared responsibility, which in turn involves concern with other elements in the change process.

Goal-setting and Planning

Probably one of the most effective ways to clear up the issue of conflicting motives is to accurately identify the goals toward which behavior is to be geared. While this may constitute a difficult and time-consuming task, in the long run clearly defined goals provide the most adequate and realistic criteria for gauging the kinds of changes which must be made and the ways in which the various individuals involved in the program relate to the problem. Clear goals bring the issues of change more sharply into focus by narrowing the range of alternative methods which seem feasible for achieving change. Anxiety, frustration, and hostility all represent the effects that unclear goals may have on behavior.[7] When changees have the expectation that these are going to result from the introduction of change, it is little wonder that they sometimes feel less committed to the program than is necessary. Similarly, unclear standards—as a basis for establishing the criteria for evaluation of a changee's performance—compound the natural anxieties people feel when confronted with change in the first place. Therefore, in order to provide a clearer understanding of what is desired, as well as providing anxiety reducing insight into how the individual changee relates to the total program of change, the change agent has the responsibility of *identifying the goals and planning the steps* for a program of change.

Participation in the planning for change by those individuals who must do the changing is critical if permanent change is the goal. It has been suggested that the reason for this is that participation may not only increase goal clarity, but it may also establish the relevance of the goals of change for one's self and thereby elicit commitment.[8] Thus, a second responsibility the change agent might assume is that of *seeing that those who are directly affected by proposed change are involved in the planning of that change.*

Setting the Climate for Change

Goal-setting and planning for change coupled with involving those affected by change interact to form the third responsibility inherent in inducing change; *viz.,* the responsibility of setting the proper climate for change. Jack Gibb, in a discussion of interpersonal climates and their effects, has spelled out two types of interpersonal "atmospheres" which seem to have implications for achieving personal change. These are the *Defensive* and *Supporting* climates.[9]

The *Defensive* climate may be seen as a product of the change agent's own actions and behavior. Behaviors which are seen by many as part and parcel of the correctional worker's prerogatives may, in fact, contribute to defensiveness on the part of his clients. For example, Gibb has suggested that censoring, controlling, and punishing types of behavior are most instrumental in creating the *Defensive* climate. The effects of these behaviors—and consequently of the climate created —are increases in defensive protective responses on the part of the changees, decreases in individual growth and learning, perceptiveness, and empathy. The change agent may be deluded, however, because as Gibb points out the *Defensive* climate may also yield an increase in responding behavior; *i.e.,* as mentioned earlier, changees may yield to controls and censoring, and seek rewards or conform to avoid punishment. In effect, the change agent may succeed for the moment in "keeping the changee in line," but he does so at the expense of long-term commitment.

The *Supportive* climate also is a product of the change agent's behavior. In contrast to the *Defensive* climate, however, it is determined by an attitude of willingness to share in the planning for change. The change agent communicates his willingness to enter into a cooperative relationship for the purpose of exploring issues which confront and affect them both. Behaviors described as reflecting an attitude of shared problem solving, acceptance, empathy, and willingness to listen are instrumental in the creation of the *Supportive* climate. These, in turn, result in decreased defensiveness on one hand and increased growth, creativity, perceptiveness, acceptance, and empathy, on the other. In addition, increases in the incidence of individuals taking initiative may be observed under the *Supportive* climate. Change agents and changees alike are freed from the dread of negative judgments being levied against them and are thus enabled to focus their attention on the task-relevant problems at hand, rather than on ego-defensive aspects of the change situation.

Conclusions

In retrospect, it would seem that the real issue active in determining the responsibility for change is an issue of defining *what the respon-*

sibilities are, rather than who is responsible for change. The tradition of "determining accountability" has worked to obscure this facet of responsibility in programs of change. Assuming that some climates are more conducive to lasting and constructive change than others, it seems that the primary responsibility of the change agent is one of setting the climate under which change can effectively take place. This may best be done by recognizing and assuming the following responsibilities:

The goals of change must be identified and the steps in achieving these goals must be planned. The greater the clarity of goals in programs of change the more systematic and effective becomes the program of change.

Those who are directly affected by proposed change should be involved in the planning of those aspects of the program affecting them. In this way goal clarity is extended downward to those who must change their own attitudes and behavior, and issues of personal relevance and credibility of programs of change may be resolved constructively.

A supportive climate free of censure and threat must be created before constructive change can occur; and this climate is usually determined by the extent to which the change agent is willing to accept the two former responsibilities.

Assuming the effective discharge of these responsibilities, the change agent will find that substantial progress toward the creation of the conditions for change has already been made.

THE CONDITIONS FOR CHANGE

It has been suggested that participation in achieving change is characterized by several valuable by-products, not the least of which are recognition of the credibility of the program, commitment and acceptance, and earlier identification of barriers to change. The goal of participation is to communicate to the parties involved that they can truly become worthwhile members of the community; and the correctional worker must believe this if such a message is to be communicated. Thus, the attitudes and assumptions held by correctional workers about their relationships with clients are critical determinants of the conditions under which change will be introduced. This point was spelled out earlier in discussing the effects of *Defensive* as opposed to *Supportive* climates on client behavior. To extend the point further, it would seem that the behavior which is instrumental in creating either of these climates is a direct consequence of the attitudes and assumptions change agents have about the role of the changees in the community. These beliefs affect not only the kinds of expectations change agents will have and create in changees, but the basic strategies they will employ in working with them, as well.

Expectations and the Perception of Change

A condition which has commonly interfered with the successful intro-duction of programs of change has been that manifested by suspicion, distrust, and antagonism toward the change agent on the part of changees. Feelings such as these reflect a whole set of expectations that clients have about their roles and their relationship with the correc-tional officer. The expectation that "nobody gives a damn about us; we're just faces to them" is a significant factor in shaping the relation-ship. Another common expectation—that "he's pushing for himself; he wouldn't hesitate to cut your throat with the boys upstairs if it would do him some good"—can seriously distort the relationship between a cor-rectional officer and parolees or probationers. People come to expect certain things as being characteristic of their relationships with other people, and these expectations—be they valid or invalid—serve as indi-cants of the appropriate ways of responding to particular individuals or situations.[10]

Thus, relationships built around expectations of distrust and sus-picion can only lead to responses designed to disrupt, block, and frus-trate the correctional officer's attempts to induce change. Operating under the expectation that they are being manipulated and dealt with unfairly, clients quite naturally find themselves resisting efforts to change them. Regardless of the true state of affairs, their perception of proposed change is often that it is just another gimmick to control or punish them or some equally unworthy motive.

Correctional workers frequently dismiss the importance of client expectations and expressed feelings as being the products of "peculiar" personality traits. "Don't mind Joe; he's always been hard to get along with. He can't stand to be bossed;" or, "The guy's paranoid! You ask him about his job and he'll bite your head off for spying on him." To the extent such reactions are based on a person's expectations, how-ever, they are less a problem for a psychiatrist than they are a problem for the correctional worker. The expectations people hold and act upon, either positive or negative, are learned patterns of thinking. They come into being as a result of actual experience with target per-sons, by word-of-mouth from comrades, as well as being a result of the idiosyncratic needs so often blamed for them. In considering the condi-tions for change, this *learned* aspect of expectations is important for it raises some questions about the origins of the anxiety-ladened expecta-tions typically encountered by correctional workers. Have these foundations of suspicion and mistrust been learned also, or are they simply figments of the collective imagination of the offenders who experience them? The individual correctional worker must ultimately answer this question for himself; and he may be able to do so more adequately by answering a second more germane set of questions. These are "To what extent have I dealt openly and aboveboard with clients and to what extent have I been as ready to discuss *my* performance with them as I have been to discuss theirs?" It will be seen that the quality of the conditions of change will be determined by the extent to which norms of openness and give-and-take evaluations characterize the relationship.

Facades and the Process of Exposure

Correctional workers, too, have expectations and these affect the way in which they characteristically behave toward changees. One expectation which people in general, and some correctional workers in particular, seem to employ readily is the "I'd tell them, but they wouldn't cooperate" rationale. As Weschler, Massarik, and Tannenbaum[11] have pointed out with reference to the management situation the need to demonstrate personal control and an outward appearance of confidence and normalcy gives rise to a form of behavior called facade-building. Thus, managers learn to "play it close to the vest" in an attempt to keep ever tighter the controls over ongoing activity. Similarly, organizations frequently keep the lid on developments which affect the power structure or changes in procedures. Often neither organizations nor their managers feel comfortable if too many people know too much of what is going on. This has been a common pattern and one of the ingredients of the traditional climate of organization life.

This same kind of situation can arise in relationships between correctional workers and their clients. The correctional worker and parolee do not "level" with each other. Part of the problem is that one of the pair is often too insecure to risk tipping his hand to the other. The correctional worker may become isolated from the changee because of this. This isolation is a result of the barriers to communications which are erected during attempts by one to reinforce his facade. The other's reaction is to reciprocate, and thus each finds himself wondering what the other is doing and thinking. Another paradox of change exists here; for in feeling that the other person in the relationship will not understand or trust him—as presumably he would like—the correctional worker and his client do not give each other the chance to understand or trust. The support, acceptance, and respect which should underlie the relationship and its goals are never given an opportunity to manifest themselves. Therefore, the correctional worker and his client become caught up in a vicious circle. Stereotypes are perpetuated; relations become strained; and the conditions for change are further undermined by the existence of too many facades. People resent the withholding of information and manipulating of relationships which can occur when facades are used to divert attention from hidden agendas.

An alternative to facade-building is exposure and leveling. By this is meant simply a willingness to call a spade a spade; a willingness to explore the enriching potential which may be present; a willingness to put one's self on the line by comparing the perceptions one has with those held by others; and, finally, the courage to drop the constricting defenses of personal inhibitions and confront problems directly within the context in which they exist. By proceeding on the assumption that "we are partners and, therefore, have the same goals at heart," a wealth of resources can be released. These resources may well prove to be beneficial if given the opportunity to emerge. By adopting a norm of openness, the correctional worker may free others to be open as well; and, in so doing, he may find that the energy he has customarily invested in facade-building is now available for a more determined assault on the problems at hand.

In attempting to improve the conditions for change through the process of exposure of ideas and goals, the correctional worker must be prepared to shoulder a good deal of apprehension. Anxieties about the success of this approach—and the irrevocable consequences once his hand is tipped—are bound to beset the correctional worker. Resistance and the residue from old suspicions on the part of clients must be faced and resolved; for the adoption of openness and the use of exposure will in itself constitute a change which may be perceived by changees as just another facade. Since expectations are learned, however, they may also be unlearned and new expectations substituted in their place. It is on this phenomenon that the principle of openness through exposure is based. The correctional worker who chooses the option of openness will beget openness and the need for facades, both his and the client's, will tend to disappear. In so doing, the correctional worker will have vastly improved the conditions for change.

Blind Spots and the Process of Feedback

While the process of exposure may be used to create an atmosphere of openness and freedom of communications, and thereby eliminate facades, still other steps must be initiated by the correctional worker if he is to profit fully from these new conditions. Succinctly, the correctional worker must begin to reduce the size and number of his blind spots; i.e., he must accept the fact that there are facets of his relationship with clients of which he is unaware. If he is to effectively utilize the new resources which a program of openness makes available to him, he must also create the opportunity for his clients to apprise him of those aspects of the situation which they know but which he does not. For example, the correctional worker may not be aware of his effect on a client from the standpoint of interpersonal relations or job skills possessed by changes which are not being utilized. All information of this type, if known, could allow the correctional worker to perform his task more effectively. Implicitly, this means that such information may also pave the way for smoother, more constructive change.

The process by which blind spots may be eliminated is a natural concomitant of conditions of openness and exposure. It is the process of feedback. Feedback in its simplest form represents knowledge of results stemming from some action which has been taken. As such, it is one of the most critical mechanisms in the learning process yet discovered. Beginning with Thorndike[12] theorists and practitioners alike have recognized the importance of feedback for improving performance via learning. A number of studies of single individuals, groups and organizations have strongly suggested that knowledge of the results of a person's or group's performance by that person or group facilitates the improvement of performance.[13,14,15,16,17,18,19] The correctional worker-client relationship is no exception to the rule.

It would seem that if a correctional worker is to function more effectively and if a client is to adjust, they each must know the effects of their own behavior on the other; whether it is the result of a hostile remark or the introduction of new controls. If this is so, then the correctional worker and the client must create openings for feedback. Too often, however, people do not want feedback. This is one of the prime reasons why it is difficult to experiment with openness through exposure, for openness implies a free exchange of feedback on performance. No one is sacred and the protection of a facade is diminished. The correctional worker may feel that he stands "naked before his enemies."

The alternative to encouraging feedback is to accept one's blind spots and the prohibitions they place on effective behavior. The correctional worker must decide what he is willing to risk to achieve his goals and in serving the community. He must decide whether or not he can tolerate having less information about the effects of his own performance than is potentially available. By entering into a relationship characterized by a mutuality of feedback the correctional worker avails himself of any number of new pieces of information. This information, in turn, may lead to a reevaluation of his role or procedures and the best means for accomplishing goals. In effect, feedback is the mechanism which creates the awareness that previously adequate performance is no longer adequate and thereby lays the foundation for change. Motivationally, therefore, feedback may constitute the most valuable process available to the correctional worker if it is used correctly. A word of caution should be interjected, however, lest the correctional worker yield to an impulse to give feedback without accepting it and thereby defeat his purpose of motivating by contributing to a defensive climate.

Facades, Blind Spots, and the Johari Window

Since the concepts of facade and blind spot and the processes of exposure and feedback may be difficult to interrelate, it may be helpful to spend a few moments in looking at a conceptual model designed by Joe Luft and Harry Ingram for use in National Training Laboratories programs to illustrate these interrelationships. While the Johari Window, as it is called, was first conceived as an aid in sensitivity training for understanding one's self, it seems that its implications go beyond this and are generalizable to the typical correctional worker-client situation. The Johari Window presented in Figure 1 represents four types of information about on-going activity which affect the relationship between correctional workers and clients. These information-types may be broken down as follows:

  a. Knowledge the correctional worker has about the interpersonal situation, himself, and his feelings about the client.
  b. Knowledge of the situation, himself, and the client, which the correctional worker does not have, *i.e.*, the emergent and existent aspects of these things of which he is not aware.
  c. Information clients have about themselves, the correctional worker, and the interpersonal situation.
  d. Knowledge of the interpersonal situation, agency, and attributes of the correctional worker which the client does not have, *i.e.*, those emergent and existent facets which the client may come to know or may never know.

As indicated below, the relationships between these information-types are the same whether they exist for peers, correctional workers and parolees, managers, and subordinates, or for organizations and their employees. Similarly, the diagram below—while designed to reflect correctional worker behavior—can be "flipped" to reveal the behavior of the parolee, *e.g.*, the correctional worker's facade (Area III) is likely to be the parolee's blind spot, while the correctional worker's blind spot (Area II) may be due to parolee facades.

By referring to the schema, one can see that the various interrelationships between the information-types discussed earlier create quite different kinds of situations and, consequently, conditions for change. Four dissimilar areas are presented to represent the possible conditions for change which might exist at the time change is introduced. These areas may be thought of in the following manner:

Area I; *The Arena:* This area represents the thoughts, standards, and skills which the correctional worker is willing to present openly to others and which clients perceive. The Arena represents the area of public knowledge and free activity within which both operate in accomplishing goals.

	Known by Correctional Worker	Unknown by Correctional Worker
Known by Client	I. The Arena (Area of free and open activity)	II. The Blind Spot (Area of unrecognized realities)
Unknown by Client	III. The Facade (Area of the hidden agenda and defenses)	IV. The Unknown (Area of future-time, latent and/or unconscious aspects)

Figure 1.   Correctional Worker's Johari Window

Area II; *The Blind Spot:* The Blind Spot area represents these motivations, thoughts, and behaviors manifested by the correctional worker of which he is unaware. While other people—particularly clients—may perceive these behaviors and be affected by them, the correctional worker is neither aware of the operation nor is he sensitive to the effects they have on his client.

Area III; *The Facade:* This area represents those behaviors and motivations of which the correctional worker is aware and may potentially manifest when he deems it opportune or which he may hide and never present. Many of these thoughts and objectives are kept hidden by the correctional worker because he feels that they are either unacceptable to the client or inappropriate for his behavior. The clients, therefore, remain unaware of this area of behavior and thoughts.

Area IV; *The Unknown:* Area IV includes those aspects of the situation of which both the correctional worker and the client are unaware. Many facets of this area will become manifest in time, due to exploration or because of critical incidents. Unknown capacities of the client or correctional worker may become manifest if conditions permit, or developments associated with future events may occur. This is the "diagnostic" area and the area of concern in parole prediction.

The goal of correctional workers, in terms of achieving the conditions for change, should be to make Area I as large as possible. In view of the benefits of openness for allaying anxieties and suspicions and forestalling resistance in the induction of change, it would seem that The Arena, *i.e.*, the area of openness and free activity, should receive maximum attention from the correctional worker contemplating change. Within the Johari Window format, an enlargement of Area I necessitates a decrease in the size of Areas II, III, and IV. That is, the correctional worker's blind spot must be reduced in size and his use of the Facade must be held to a minimum or abandoned entirely. Similarly, as communications are improved by the reduction of Areas II and III, it may well be that elements of the Unknown Area become more predictable and less foreboding.

It is in the enlargement of The Arena by a reduction of the Blind Spot and Facade areas that the processes of exposure and feedback become important tools for the correctional worker. Since exposure is the antithesis of facade-building, the tendency of the correctional worker to reveal for inspection his thoughts, information and objectives results in an enlargement of Area I downward. That is, exposure decreases the number of hidden agendas, defenses, and ploys which the correctional worker knows he is using but which are not known to clients. As suggested previously, enlargement of Area I by this process resolves distrust and suspicion on the part of clients. By increasing the size of the area of free activity, the correctional worker can overcome his isolation from his clients and create conditions for the understanding necessary for gaining commitment to programs of change.

Reduction of the correctional worker's blind spot occurs because of the availability of information about the effects his behavior and strategies are having on others. Feedback is the process employed to both give and receive such information. The concurrent effect on Area I of reducing the blind spot via feedback is to enlarge it laterally. Thus, by creating the opportunity for getting feedback on ideas, feelings, attitudes, and the like, the correctional worker gains information about himself from those people most affected by these actions—the clients. By enlarging the Arena laterally, the correctional worker avails himself of many new resources both in planning and in forecasting the effects of various alternative programs of change. As Area I is enlarged, clients begin to feel that more and more they are in fact an integral part of the enterprise and that the responsibility for change is theirs as well as the correctional worker's. Thus, many of the barriers to successful change may be surmounted by the correctional worker's efforts to create a larger Arena as the basic condition for change.

Conclusions

The general climate of the work situation determines what conditions will be in existence at the time change is introduced. Thus, the correctional worker must be sensitive to the current conditions and what implications they have for a program of change in initiating his program. Should prevailing conditions not be perceived as supportive of change, by understanding the reasons for these conditions and the processes for creating a more facilitative atmosphere, the correctional worker can set the stage for a smoother period of transition. These basic concepts should be kept in mind in analyzing the existing situations:

> Clients relate themselves to the correctional worker and react to pressures on the basis of learned expectations regarding the meaning of the correctional worker's behaviors. Expectations of a negative character result in resistance to change.

> Correctional workers can help substitute positive expectations for negative ones by dealing openly with clients and by allowing mutual evaluations of performance. This results in an increase in the size of the area of free activity by abolishing the need for facades and by illuminating areas of insensitivity.

> The two processes of exposure of ideas and objectives and bilateral feedback are the most effective tools in the correctional worker's repertoire for achieving a free flow of communications, understanding, trust, and commitment among clients.

> An atmosphere of free activity reflects a situation characterized by a sharing of information between correctional workers and clients and this, in turn, constitutes the condition most conducive to the successful induction of lasting change.

SUMMARY

The task of achieving change does not emerge as a simple matter of identifying the area and type of change needed. Rather, it represents a difficult undertaking which must be well planned and based on an understanding of the forces of learning and interpersonal relations. The forces of the motivations for change must be identified and taken into account. The locus and types of responsibility for attaining change must be determined; and the conditions—both extant and potential —which aid or inhibit change must be considered. Implicitly, it has been suggested that in coming to understand change the correctional worker himself may need to change also; for he is, as the agent of change, a critical factor in the program of change.

    Thus, the correctional worker has been tossed a king-sized dilemma. It is his job to mesh together considerations of motivation, participation, norms, goals, interpersonal relations, and so on, into a theoretically sound proposal of change. It has been suggested that the correctional worker must be a manager of forces. In effect, it begins to sound as if the correctional worker is being asked to become a lay behavioral scientist, and to the extent that it is necessary for him to understand the behavior of clients and himself, this is true.

NOTES

[1] Prepared by the Southwest Center for training purposes.

[2] Warren G. Bennis, Kenneth D. Benne, and Robert Chin. *The Planning of Change* (New York: Holt, Rinehart, and Winston, 1962).

[3] Weldon Moffitt, "My Role in Working with Groups and Organizations in the Community," paper presented at the Community Leadership Training Laboratory, Bethel, Maine, 1962.

[4] Kurt Lewin, *Resolving Social Conflicts* (New York: Harper, 1948).

[5] A. H. Maslow. *Motivation and Personality* (New York: Harper & Brothers, 1954).

[6] H. C. Kelman, "Compliance, Identification, and Internalization: Three Processes of Attitude Change," *Journal of Conflict Resolution*, 2 (1958): 51–60.

[7] Bertram H. Raven and Jan Rietsema, "The Effect of Varied Clarity of Group Goal and Group Path on the Individual and His Relation to His Group," *Human Relations*, 10 (1957): 29–44.

[8] Coch and French, Ibid.

[9] J. R. Gibb, "Factors producing Defensive Behavior within Groups, IV," in *Annual Technical Report* (Office of Naval Research, November 15, 1957).

[10] J. Hall and V. O'Leary, "The Effects of One's Expectations on His Perception of Others" (Manuscript, National Parole Institutes, 1963).

[11] I. Weschler, F. Massarik, and R. Tannenbaum, "The Self in Process: A Sensitivity Training Emphasis," in *Issues in Training*, eds. I. Weschler and E. H. Schein (National Training Laboratories, 1962).

[12] E. L. Thorndike, *The Fundamentals of Learning* (New York: Teachers College, 1932).

[13] H. J. Leavitt and R. A. H. Mueller, "Some Effects of Feedback on Communication," *Human Relations*, 4 (1951).

[14] H. J. Leavitt, *Managerial Psychology*, (Chicago, Ill.: University of Chicago Press, 1958).

[15] Margaret Pryer and B. Bass, "Some Effects of Feedback on Behavior in Groups," *Sociometry*, 22 (1959): 56–63.

[16] M. B. Miles, "The Learning Process during Human Relations Training," in *Forces in Learning* (Washington, D. C.: National Training Laboratories, 1961).

[17] J. N. Mosel, "How to Feedback Performance Results to Trainees," in *Studies in Personnel and Industrial Psychology*, ed. E. A. Fleishman (Homewood, Ill.: The Dorsey Press, Inc., 1961).

[18] Jane S. Mouton and R. Blake, "University Training in Human Relations Skills," in *Forces in Learning* (Washington, D.C.: National Training Laboratories, 1961).

[19] R. Zajonc, "The Effect of Feedback and Probability of Group Success on Individual and Group Performance," *Human Relations*, 15, no. 2 (1962): 149–161.

9

Is Help Helpful?

JACK R. GIBB
Consulting Psychologist

People in the service professions often see themselves as primarily engaged in the job of helping others. Helping becomes both the personal style of life and a core activity that gives meaning and purpose to the life of the professional. The youth worker, the camp director, the counselor, the consultant, the therapist, the teacher, the lawyer—each is a helper.

Helping is a central social process. The den mother, the committee chairman, the parent, the personal friend, the board member, the dance sponsor—each is a helper.

Help, however, is not always helpful. The recipient of the proffered help may not see it as useful. The offering may not lead to greater satisfaction or to better performance. Even less often does the helping process meet a more rigorous criterion—lead to continued growth on the part of the participants.

To begin with, a person may have varied motivations for offering help. He may wish to improve performance of a subordinate, reduce his own guilt, obtain gratitude, make someone happy, or give meaning to his own life. He may wish to demonstrate his superior skill or knowledge, induce indebtedness, control others, establish dependency, punish others, or simply meet a job prescription. These conscious or partially conscious motivations are so intermingled in any act of help that it is impossible for either the helper or the recipient to sort them out.

Depending upon his own needs and upon the way he sees the motives of the helper, the recipient will have varied reactions. He may feel gratitude, resentment, or admiration. He may feel helpless and dependent, or jealous of the helper who has the strength or resources to be in the helper role. He may feel indebted, or pressured to conform to the perceived demands or beliefs of the helper.

Reprinted, with permission of the author and publisher from the *Y.M.C.A. Association Forum and Section Journal*, February 1964, pp. 25–27.

We have all noticed that in certain cases the recipient of the help becomes more helpless and dependent, less able to make his own decisions or initiate his own actions, less self-sufficient, more apathetic and passive, less willing to take risks, more concerned about propriety and conformity, and less creative and venturesome. We have also seen circumstances in which, following help, recipients become more creative, less dependent upon helpers, more willing to make risk decisions, more highly motivated to tackle tough problems, less concerned about conformity, and more effective at working independently or interdependently. Help may or may not lead to personal growth and organizational health.

Under certain conditions both the giver and the receiver grow and develop. In general people tend to grow when there is reciprocal dependence—*inter*-dependence, joint determination of goals, real communication in depth, and reciprocal trust. To the degree that these conditions are absent, people fail to grow.

From the standpoint of the organization, help must meet two criteria: the job or program must be done more effectively, and the individual members must grow and develop. These two criteria tend to merge. The program and the organization are effective only as the participants grow. The same conditions that lead to organizational health lead to personal growth. The following table presents a theory of the helping relationship. Seven parallel sets of orientations are presented. One set of conditions maximize help and a parallel set of conditions minimize help.

TABLE ONE

THE HELPING RELATIONSHIP

Orientations that help	*Orientations that hinder*
1. Reciprocal trust (confidence, warmth, acceptance)	1. Distrust (fear, punitiveness, defensiveness)
2. Cooperative learning (inquiry, exploration, quest)	2. Teaching (training, advice giving, indoctrinating)
3. Mutual growth (becoming, actualizing, fulfilling)	3. Evaluating (fixing, correcting, providing a remedy)
4. Reciprocal openness (spontaneity, candor, honesty)	4. Strategy (planning *for*, maneuvering, gamesmanship)
5. Shared problem solving (defining, producing alternatives, testing)	5. Modeling (demonstrating, information giving, guiding)
6. Autonomy (freedom, interdependence, equality)	6. Coaching (molding, steering, controlling)
7. Experimentation (play, innovation, provisional try)	7. Patterning (standard, static, fixed)

Reciprocal trust. People accept help from those they trust. When the relationship is one of acceptance and trust, offers of help are appreciated, listened to, seen as potentially helpful, and often acted upon. The receiver accepts help from one whose perceived motives are congenial to him. He tends to reject offers from people whose offering is seen as a guise for attempts to control, punish, correct, or gain power. "Help" is most helpful when given in an atmosphere in which people have *reciprocal* feelings of confidence, warmth, and acceptance. When one feels that his worth *as a person* is valued he is able to place himself in psychological readiness to receive aid.

Distrust. When people fear and distrust each other, even well-intended help is resisted, resented, or seen as unhelpful. Offers of help are sometimes given in service of motivations that are unacceptable to the receiver. That is, one offers help in order to place the other person in a dependent position, elicit expressions of gratitude, assert one's superiority, or punish him. In distrust the recipient's guard is up. He is likely to project his distrusts into the helper and to resist or resent the help.

One often gives help to camouflage or assuage his desire to change another person—change his character, habits, or misconceptions. The desire to change another person is essentially hostile. At a deep level, one who genuinely accepts another person does not wish to change him. A person who is accepted is allowed *to be,* become, determine his own goals and follow them at his own pace. The person who genuinely wishes to help offers the help that *the recipient wishes.* Genuine help is not foisted upon the receiver. Neither the punisher nor the child really believes that the punishment is given "for the good of the child."

Punishment or censure may be given with a conscious desire to help but usually is accompanied by a deep component of retaliation, or by a desire to hurt, control, or assert superiority. The giver often speaks of his act as "helpful" in order to rationalize to himself and to the receiver acts that are done for other motivations.

Cooperative learning. People are helpful to each other when they are engaged in a cooperative quest for learning. The learning atmosphere is one of joint inquiry and exploration. Needs for help and impulses to give help arise out of the demands of the common cooperative task. Help is thus reciprocal. The helper and helpee roles are interchangeable. Each participant has the *intent* to learn and feels he can learn from the partners and from the common task. The boss and the subordinate, the teacher and the student, the professional worker and the youth—all are most helpful when each member of the pair sees the relationship as a quest with potential learning for each. An effective project team is guided by the task and not by the teacher. It is motivated by the shared potential for learning.

Teaching. When one participant in a project sets out to teach, train, advise, persuade, or indoctrinate the other members or is *seen* as wanting to do so, the learning of each member is reduced. People cannot be taught. People must learn. People cannot be trained. They grow and develop. The most deeply helpful relationship is one of common inquiry and quest, a relationship between co-learners and co-managers in which each is equally dependent upon the other for significant help and in which each sees and accepts this relationship.

Mutual growth. The most permanent and significant help occurs in a relationship in which both members are continually growing, becoming, and seeking fulfillment. Each member participates in a mutual assessment of progress, accepts this reality of growth, and participates in a way that will maximize the growth of both participants. In a fundamental sense one can only help himself. The helper can only participate with another in an effort to create a climate in which growth can occur.

Evaluating. Growth is often hindered when one member of the helping team sets out to appraise or remedy the defects in the other member. Help is most effective when it is seen as a force moving toward growth rather than as an effort to remove gaps, remedy defects or bring another person up to a standard criterion. The limits of growth of any person are extremely difficult to foresee or to assess. The potential for growth is consistently underestimated by both participants in the helping relationship.

Reciprocal openness. One of the essential conditions for effective human learning is the opportunity for feedback or knowledge of progress. Feedback is essential in acquiring skills, knowledge, and attitudes. In the areas where professional help is most commonly sought or given, the essential progress in learning and growth is blocked most often by the failure to obtain adequate data on people's feelings and perceptions of each other. In order to do effedtive work one must know how others feel and how they see things. In the usual situations in which professional helpers find themselves, there are many pressures which camouflage or distort the relevant data necessary for efficient work and best learning. Many factors reduce the availability of the relevant data: differential status, differential perceived power, and fears that one can hurt or be hurt.

Strategy. When some part of the helping process is closed or unavailable to all participants, people are likely to become anxious, resentful, or resistant. Neither participant in the helping process can "use" the other for his own needs. The helping process is most effective when one plans *with* another, not *for* another. One is not helped when he is maneuvered into some action which he does not understand. Gamesmanship and gimmicks are antithetical to the helping process.

Shared problem solving. The productive helping relationship focuses upon the problem to be solved. Problem solving involves a joint determination of the problem, continual redefinition of the problem as successive insights are gained, joint focus upon possible alternative solutions, joint exploration of the data, and continual reality testing of the alternatives. The expertness and resources of each person are shared. The aspect of the behavior about which help is given is seen as a *shared problem*—not as a defect to be remedied or as something to be solved by the helper as consultant.

Modeling. A common image of the helping relationship is one where the helper offers a model for the advisee to follow. The expert gives a demonstration of how the recipient may solve his problems. The problem is defined by the expert. Diagnosis is made by the expert. The expert is challenged to offer additional alternatives to the solution of the problem and perhaps even to test the solutions. The process is uni-directional. The limitations of modeling are many. Dependency is increased. The pupil seldom gets better than the model. The worker tries to conform to the image of the supervisor. Growth is limited.

Autonomy. The ideal relationship for helping is an interdependent one in which each person sees the other as both helper and recipient in an exchange among equals. It is essential that each participant preserve his freedom and maintain his autonomous responsibility for guiding himself toward his own learnings, growth, and problem solving. The helper must work himself out of the helping job. The supervisor, youth worker, and counselor must become decreasingly necessary to the people being helped. Psychological weaning, however painful to both helper and recipient, must continue if help is to be truly helpful.

Coaching. The coach molds, steers, or controls the behavior of the recipient, much as a tennis coach or physical education director molds the behavior of the athlete or skill-directed recipient of help. This is another uni-directional process in which the coach is assumed to have special diagnostic and observational powers which he applies in a skilled way to the behavior of the recipient, who puts himself in the hands of the coach. The recipient of help is encouraged to maintain respectful dependency upon the coach, to not challenge his authority or expertness, to put implicit trust in his abilities and powers, and to receive from the coach motivational or inspirational guidance. Both coach and pupil suffer under this pattern. Each *may* gain in skill. Neither grows *as a person.*

Experimentation. Tentativeness and innovative experimentation are characteristic of the most productive helping relationship. There is a sense of play, excitement, and fun in the common exploratory quest for new solutions to continually changing problems. The helping process is viewed as a series of provisional trials. Each participant joins in the game and adds to the general excitement. Errors can be made —and are perhaps expected. Help is a search. Finding creative solutions to newly defined problems is a game—full of zest and intrinsic drives that keep the game going.

Patterning. Help is limited when the process is seen as an attempt on the part of one person to help another meet a prescribed standard, come up to a criterion, or reach a goal specified in advance. Helping is a creative synthesis of growth and a continual search for new forms.

"Help" is not always helpful—but *it can be.* Both the helper and the recipient can grow and learn when help is given in a relationship of trust, joint inquiry, openness, and interdependence. Growth-centered helping processes lead to healthy groups and effective organizations.

10

Chicken Soup Is Poison

ROBERT W. RESNICK, Ph.D.

Clinical Psychologist, Past President, Gestalt Therapy Institute of
Los Angeles

In order to make chicken soup, you have to kill a chicken. Although not particularly leading to self-actualization for the chicken, this sacrifices the bird to a greater cause—being helpful. Combined with onions, greens, carrots, water and seasoning, the resulting elixir is ready for its role as a helper. The giving of chicken soup is an attempt to "help" the other—to do for him, to make him feel better. The chubby, sponge-like matzo ball, not unlike the unconscious, lies 90% below the surface of the soup. By the time the unaware gourmet has had enough of this brew, the soup around the submerged matzo ball has cooled and, like a dead submarine, it spews forth its fatty oil slick. CAUTION: Chicken soup is likely to be as fatal to the recipient as it was to the contributing poultry. Now don't run around like a submarine with its head cut off—there is an antidote.

Many therapists see themselves as members of the "helping profession" engaged in the "helping relationship." Beware! Such people are dangerous. If successful, they kill the humanness in their patients by preventing their growth. This insidious process is somehow worse realizing such therapists typically want the reverse. They want their patients to grow, to live and to be, and they guarantee the antithesis with their "help." The distinction between true support and "help" is clear: *To do for the other what he is capable of doing for himself insures his not becoming aware that he can stand on his own two feet.* The difficulty is in judging whether or not the person is potentially capable of doing or being himself. This depends on your own convictions about human beings and possibly your own need to be "helpful." If you are convinced (sucked in) that the person is as helpless, as impotent and as incompetent as he plays, then you are "helpful."

Reprinted with permission of the author from *Voices: The Art and Science of Psychotherapy* Vol. 6, No. 2 (Fall 1970): 75–78.

Gestalt therapy has as a basic goal the substituting of self-supports for environmental supports. Perls talks about the therapeutic impasse—what the Russians call the "sick point." Typically people experience confusion, helplessness and nothingness at such a point. There usual attempts to manipulate their environment for support by playing deaf, dumb, by misunderstanding, by crying, by demanding, by playing crazy, by pleading, etc., are not working. If the therapist (or anyone else) walks into the manipulation by trying to be "helpful" he successfully keeps the other an infant. In order to achieve integration and to potentiate growth, the patient must "do his own dirty work." Perls, in a more poetic mood, states that the essence of Gestalt therapy is allowing (by frustrating) the patient to discover that he can "wipe his own ass." He illustrates this point by talking about the human embryo in utero. Here, the organism does nothing for himself. He is completely dependent on environmental supports. Sustenance, warmth and oxygen are all provided by the mother. At birth, the child enters his first impasse: He can breathe for himself or he can die. Throughout development the neonate becomes more and more able to crawl on his own four limbs. At birth he cannot stand by himself. Soon, if allowed, he stands autonomously. Carry a baby around all the time and he may never learn to walk. His muscles may atrophy and he may even lose the possibility of ever walking by himself. In western cultures mothers are "helpful" and their babies walk, on the average, amost a year later than children in some other cultures where the child is allowed to experiment, to make mistakes, to grow, to be. Children who get others to satisfy their needs with baby-talk never need to learn to speak. As long as they have someone helping them—taking responsibility for communicating their needs to the world—they never need speech. Without their "helpers" they are like a Robisperre without his Baby Snooks. Initially, they may scream and cry for others to support them. Eventually, they will learn to communicate directly themselves or die.

No one can be completely without some environmental supports nor is it easy for me to conceive of wanting to be in such a position. There is a great difference in getting from the environment that which I cannot do for myself and conning others into doing what I can do for myself. Most of us to varying degrees are under the illusion that "we can't." Typically I have found that "I can't" really means, "I won't." I won't take the risks involved. To want the environment to help, to comfort, to support, even when I can rely solely on my own self-supports entails taking the risk of asking for such help. I take the responsibility of asking for help rather than manipulating the other into offering what he believes I am incapable of generating for myself. Even the manipulation can be self-supporting if I am aware that *is* what I am doing. Such awareness allows me the choice and freedom to do this or do otherwise. I am then still me—not relinquishing my autonomy, my power, unless *I* want to do so.

People coming to therapy usually want something. Often they ask for "help" and what they want from therapy is a way to change the consequences of their behavior without changing their behavior themselves. They state that they eat spicy foods and get heartburn. "Can't you do something about my heartburn since I am sure I can't stop eating spicy foods? Stop the heartburn or at least help me find out 'why' my eating spicy foods gives me heartburn." (They are under the illusion that the only possible way for them to change *what* they are doing is to find out *why* they are doing it.) Their cop-outs vary. The unconscious, although diminishing in popularity, probably still gets the most blame. Parents are always popular as are wives, husbands, social systems, economic systems, world situations and the "soup-man" (or Superman, depending on how you see your therapist). As long as they attribute responsibility for *their* behavior to another person or concept *they* remain powerless. More exactly they are *giving* their power/ autonomy/humanness to the other person or concept. Their implicit therapeutic request is: Let's you and he (or it) fight. The therapist, if he is unaware, willing or both, is pitted against the free-floating unconscious or whatever via the patient's manipulation while the latter drools over the flow of chicken soup and is never sated. Slow down or, noodles forbid, stop the soup, and the patient tries that much harder to unclog his lifeline. When the help is not forthcoming and the patient has not yet discovered his own ability to give himself his own chicken soup, he then encounters his impasse. If the therapist successfully frustrates the patient's attempts to manipulate, the impasse is pregnant with growth. If the therapist is "helpful," he assures the patient's remaining impotent and up comes the oil slick from the murky depths of the soup. Even when a person breaks through his own shackles as often happens in encounter groups, sensitivity groups, nude groups, marathon groups and drug groups, he typically has great difficulty in integrating his behavior and experience into his everyday life. I am convinced that his freedom to be was given to him by the situation, the group, the leader, fatigue or drugs. Chicken soup comes in many flavors.*

The most popular way patients avoid standing on their own two feet is by looking for reasons. Simkin calls this the "why merry-go-round." (I'm sure you're all familiar with the tune.) The patient hops on the "why merry-go-round" and plays thirty-two bars of "why, why,

*With this statement I in no way wish to condemn encounter groups, etc. I feel they can play an extremely important role in potentiating human growth by allowing people to experience possibilities. This, however, is not enough. It is only a beginning. The work then is to find out how (not why) I prevent myself from enjoying my possibilities.

why does this happen to me?" After finding the reason, he hops off the merry-go-round only to find that nothing has changed. He crawls back on his outside horse looking for the brass-ringed "why"—spends more time, effort and money so that this time his new reason is elevated to the status of an insight. Stumbling off his horse, brass ring in hand, he finds nothing has changed. Some people have been on this carousel of "therapy" for five, ten or twenty years. Many of those who got off the merry-go-round have changed their tune. The first eight bars go something like: "So now I know all the reasons and I'm still miserable." Indeed, if you allow them, they'll delight in relating their insights interminably (Excedrin headache No. 2002). It's as if the purpose of therapy is to find out "why." I'm convinced the purpose of therapy is to change behavior, experience or both. Behavior is caused and knowing the whys has nothing to do with change.

The most popular way therapists help their patients to avoid standing on their own is to first deny that they have the blueprints and answers the patient is asking for. (Of course, the therapist doesn't believe this.) This done, the therapist "helps" the patient with the content of his problems (e.g., he manipulates the patient into discovering for himself what the therapist knew all the time). Even if I assume (and I do not) that the therapist is better equipped to make decisions than the patient himself, I am convinced that this leaves the patient no better off than when he started. If anything, he is a worse cripple. The lyrics of his problem change over the months and years but the melody lingers on and on and on. The process by which he stops himself from fuller functioning continues as long as he deals with the content of his problem to the exclusion of the process. Blaming his parents *for making him weak or insecure* is not his problem . . . *HIS BLAMING IS.* What he is doing is making his parents responsible for who he is *now*. *How* he is doing this is by playing "victim" and blaming them. *Why* he is doing this is irrelevant to changing and if pursued guarantees his staying stuck. Is it any wonder he remains "weak and insecure." Only when he becomes aware of *his* blaming his parent for who he is *now*, does he have a chance to grow. When he is in touch with *his* "response-ability"—his ability to respond—he enters a world of possibilities, choices and freedom. As long as he blames the other, he remains impotent.

The making of chicken soup is a fine, old art with many variations. However, one thing remains unchanged: In order to make chicken soup you have to kill the chicken.

11

The Function of
Coercive Casework in Corrections

CLAUDE T. MANGRUM

Director, Adult Division, San Bernardino County Probation
Department

One hears a great deal today about social permissiveness, individual freedom, right of free speech, and allowing everyone to "do his thing." These ideas have been made the topics of books, magazine articles, newspaper editorials, protest demonstrations, and political speeches; everyone seems to be getting into the act. On the one hand our courts are badgered for legal approval of more liberal expressions of individual freedom and on the other hand they are ridiculed for their lenient rulings which protect the criminal and tie the hands of law enforcement. There are alternating cries of anguish over the breakdown of law and order and of indignation over the development of a police state.

The writers, speakers, and demonstrators cite the rising crime rates, campus disorders, police brutality, the generation gap, youthful disrespect for authority, authoritative disregard for the individual, and a host of other themes to support their respective theses. They all imply, and often state, that it is a matter of unrealistic leniency or unconstitutional restriction—depending on which side the complainant finds himself—which is at the root of all our problems.

These are not tides of controversy which swirl outside the field of corrections. Indeed, some of our new recruits, especially those young people just out of college, may be particularly susceptible to being caught up in these controversies. They have been trained in times of less social restraint, exposed to the philosophy that every man should be free to "do his own thing," and, perhaps, influenced by the spirit of disrespect for law, order, and authority which infects our society today. Yet, they are coming into a field specifically assigned the responsibility of protecting society through the exercise of restraints, the enforcement of law and order, and the use of authority. It is little wonder that

Reprinted, with permission from, *Federal Probation*, Quarterly, March 1971, pp. 26–29.

some of the young enforcers of society's regulations may have conflicts of identification between society and the violators of society's laws.

In this setting, it seems important—indeed, imperative—to draw the attention of the newcomer and the veteran to these conflicts and to explore some ideas which may help to orient us to a resolution of them.

WHAT IS COERCIVE CASEWORK?

At the heart of the philosophy of correctional work is the twofold concept of social control and social treatment. They are not mutually exclusive or separate entities, but intertwined—the one impinging on the other, modifying and shaping, being modified and shaped in turn. Ideally, of course, we attain the goal of control through the means of treatment. However, this statement taken alone is easily misconstrued; therefore, it needs some explanation and analysis.

There is, in the minds of many practitioners of the "helping professions," an irreconcilable conflict between the use of casework techniques and the use of authority. This apparent dichotomy has been the topic of many debates and journal articles and need not be belabored here. The conflict remains unresolved and will probably continue so for a long time to come: We do not expect to resolve it here; only to try to approach it from a slightly different perspective.

The definitions of social casework are almost as numerous as are the numbers of persons defining it. However, they all generally are focused on the processes by which the individual is helped to more effectively function within his social environment. The emphasis is on the individual in the recognition that no matter how similar one's situation may appear to be to that of another, each problem, and each attempt and method to resolve it, has its own unique meaning to each individual. The method which works for one person may not work with another. One of the basic and most important tasks of the caseworker is to fit his treatment methods and techniques to the unique needs of his client.

To coerce is to restrain or constrain by force, especially by the use of legal authority. "Restrain" carries the idea of holding in check, controlling, curbing. "Constrain" gives the idea of forcing into, compelling, obliging to action.

By coercive casework, then, we mean the use of restraining and constraining legal authority in the processes of helping the offender to function in his social environment without resorting to illegal or antisocial behavior.

This is, ideally, the underlying philosophy of establishing and enforcing specific conditions of probation and parole because those conditions are to be used for guidance of the client's behavior. He is placed under restraints when instructed not to associate with certain kinds of people, not to leave the jurisdiction without permission, or not to possess a weapon. He is constrained when instructed to report regularly to the probation or parole officer, to maintain gainful employment, or to make restitution to the victim of his offense.

Perhaps a graphic example of this approach is the condition of probation which requires the probationer to participate in a program of psychotherapy. Despite some objections that such an order violates the basic need for client motivation for such therapy to be effective, most of us know of specific instances where the proper motivation has developed *after* the therapy program has begun.

There are many who hold that the foundation of effective casework is the belief that motivation to improve or to resolve problems must come from within, that casework is not effective unless it is desired and voluntarily requested by the client. Somehow, the client must engage himself in grappling with his own problems if they are to be resolved. They believe that every man has the right of choice and it is wrong to impose on him official values or solutions to problems from without.

We do not deny the innate dignity of man, nor his right to freedom to make choices. We do not deny the validity of the above-noted ideas, nor of the basic responsibility of the individual to deal with his own problems with his own resources; but, neither can we deny the necessity of the orderly functioning of society, nor of all citizens to behave so as not to disturb that orderly functioning. Neither can we deny the importance of client and worker alike recognizing that the exercise of the right of choice carries with it the necessity of accepting the consequences of that choice.

It is essential to recognize that underlying our highly developed society are orderly behavior and relationships, without which society could not exist. When individuals act so as to disrupt this order, some action must be taken to restore it. In the case of the criminal offender (and many others, for that matter) this action may be through coercion—for his own and society's welfare.

THE FUNCTION OF COERCIVE CASEWORK

While it is true that effective casework is not something done *to* or *for* the client, but *with* him, it is also true that sometimes it is a matter of some action which "gets his attention" or "holds him still" long enough for him to recognize that there *is* motivation from within; he may only need to make way for it to begin to function. Or, it may be necessary, through restraint and constraint, to structure action until the validity of it can be understood and accepted for itself as a way of life.

In this initial stage of the correctional treatment process, one need not necessarily be complicated in the design of his casework methods and techniques. He may need only to set, and enforce, some behavioral limits—to inform his client, "You can go this far, but no further"; to say, "No! You cannot do that."

If it is true that "nothing succeeds like success," it is also true that nothing fails like failure. In direct proportion to his lack of success, the individual is likely to feel ineffectual, then powerless, then useless, then helpless. At this point he also ceases to care; and that is when he is the most disruptive and dangerous.

The offender, often habitually unsuccessful in his attempts to adjust to the pressures and demands of society, needs to have successful experiences—even if they are at first coerced. A definite "shall and shall not" approach is often necessary until the client reaches the point where he can be comfortable with the restraints and constraints imposed on his conduct; until the motivation for lawful and acceptable behavior comes from within himself, from the knowledge of the benefit to be derived from avoiding the kind of disruptive behavior which subjects him to penalty and social rejection.

The aim of providing success experiences is to persuade the offender of the validity of society's ideals and to have him internalize them as his own. He must come to view his behavior in the light of its impingement on others and learn to regulate it accordingly. To reach this goal requires not only casework treatment but behavior control as well.

There is a common misconception that delinquent and criminal groups have "their own set of values," so will not accept and live by the values of the larger community. However, making the values of society meaningful and relevant to these groups can provide the motivation for them to modify their own value systems and to incorporate society's values into their own codes of conduct.

This will entail the application of realistic values that are relevant to present conditions, not merely harping on traditional concepts based on outmoded social codes. To sharp and inquiring youth, it will also require pertinent explanations of the "why" of these values.

It is imperative, in this regard, for society to propagate its value of the necessity to behave in accordance with law. Various subgroups, including the criminal and delinquent subcultures, actively propagate their value codes. It is no less acceptable for society to vigorously engage in such activity—despite current criticisms of such practice. The correctional worker needs occasionally to remind himself—and others, including his clients—that society also has rights and needs.

A POSITIVE APPROACH

We readily recognize the necessity of forcible restraint of those who represent a violent threat to society; and, for the protection of others, we put these persons behind bars. This is a negative action. There is a positive side to this same coin, however, especially in regard to those offenders who are not placed or continued behind bars, but are allowed to remain in the community on probation or parole.

This positive action—what we have termed coercive casework—is that restraint and constraint on the individual's behavior designed to help persuade him of both the short- and long-run validity of accepting society's values and regulating his conduct accordingly. The goal, of course, is to have him internalize these values, making coercion unnecessary. It is the same kind of discipline we enforce with our children as we try to instill within them acceptable standards of conduct. These standards are at first enforced through various restraints and constraints. As the child matures and restraint becomes self-discipline, the enforced standards become clear through understanding and habitual through regular observance.

It is behavior, illegal and antisocial, which brings the individual into the correctional system. It is both behavior and the attitudes leading to it which we must help to change. While the techniques for accomplishing this goal may be varied and require individual application according to need and circumstances as well as an explanation of "why," the underlying philosophy is as simple as "thou shalt not" and "thou shalt." This is not a new concept, certainly; but it is a basic and necessary one both in terms of individual benefit and the ongoing and orderly functioning of society.

12

The Community and Corrections: Hard Answers to an Old Problem

ANONYMOUS*

My supervisor was glad to see me come on board. An MSW with an acceptable Army record, I was surely the harbinger of a new day in corrections. V-J Day was still recent; it was reasonable to expect that more like me would soon apply for employment as parole officers. He was a humanist, a man with a mission to civilize corrections. Every day he contended with the remnants of the old guard in the Bureau of Parole, men who had seen the cons come and go and who hadn't needed a college degree to do their job. A famous penal reformer, now the agency director, had picked him for the assignment. Unfortunately, penal reform is a war to be waged on many fronts, and my supervisor was mostly left to his own devices. I was a new ally, perhaps a building block to better things.

After a week of orientation, I was introduced to my predecessor, who went over his casebook with me, case by case, about a hundred of them. Here was a young bastard who needed constant attention; the next guy was in jail on our hold, awaiting parole action; here was another who was coming along all right now that he had a steady job. My colleague thought he had been helping some of these parolees and expressed a mild regret at leaving them. Having briefed me as best he could, he handed over the leatherette binder and bought me a drink. The last ritual, I thought, before I passed from my brief novitiate to a professional career as a parole officer.

It wasn't.

My supervisor called me in for a final briefing. He began with some disarming reflections on the place of the professional social worker in a correctional agency during the transition from old ways to new. It was clear that I had nowhere to go but up, and rapidly. It was a heady hour. I wondered how long I would keep that casebook with all its fragments of information about all those sad young men.

Reprinted with permission from *The Prison Journal*, Autumn-Winter 1968, 17–22.

*Name withheld at request of author.

He had a check-list showing who had seen me during my orientation week and what I had seen. There were a couple of blank spaces at the bottom.

"You'll have to sign for these. I hope you won't have to use them."

A buzzer, neatly cased in leather, which could be flashed in the palm of your hand, just like a plainclothesman in the movies.

A pair of blue-steel hand-cuffs, with keys.

I signed. This was the *rite de passage*. I was now a parole officer.

So began my career as a caseworker in the authoritarian setting. Both buzzer and cuffs lay unseen but not unforgetten in my brief-case. I applied myself to interviews and dictation. I pursued parolees whom I couldn't find, and pursued jobs for those who dutifully flocked to my office as required. I put in fourteen-hour days without a murmur and agreed with my brother officers that we were all having the time of our lives.

Our social life consisted entirely of parole officers and their wives. We talked shop endlessly, and put our wives to sleep with our attempts to define roles and clarify functions. We tried to think of principles to guide the work of the day and the decisions which had to be made or recommended. How could authority and rapport be combined? How could we build the parolee's ego strength when there were so many decisions which were reserved to us or to the parole board? What were we supposed to do? What *should* we do?

We had no confidence in the agency's institutions. Their personnel were preoccupied with discipline and the maintenance of their dreary routines. We saw enough for ourselves and heard enough from our parolees to conclude that these institutions could never improve enough to provide more than sterile interludes from the streets for the offenders they confined. There were some hair-raising tales, but most of our parolees reminisced about their incarceration with a surprising lack of rancor. Their erstwhile custodians' want of common sense was related with relish. The benefits of counseling therapy or training were never mentioned.

Our consensus was that if anything could be done for offenders it would have to be done on the streets. We were clear on the logic if not the methods. Disentangling criminals from criminality had to be done in the community. The difficulties of the task were obvious to us, and we knew that it could not be done with caseloads of one hundred or more.

So if caseloads could be brought down to a reasonable size, probation and parole might be vastly improved. We seldom said so in so many words, but the implication was clear that lower caseloads would attract more dedicated and professional people like us to the field. The treatment of the criminal would reach a level of effectiveness which would limit incarceration to a correctional instrument of the last resort.

In spite of much sincere effort, it hasn't worked out that way. Why not?

I have lived with this question with mounting concern for a good many years. I conclude that the answer is to be found in the correctional dilemma which we have all faced so squarely in so many conferences. Learned academics, keynote speakers from the correctional establishment, and panel discussants from the firing lines have all defined the dilemma and proposed formulas for its resolution. On the one hand, custody; on the other, treatment, or at least a helping relationship. But perhaps custody could be used to help, perhaps authority was necessarily implicit in any treatment. As though it resolved the problem, the wise old-timers would tell us that we had to keep in touch with the parolee; we couldn't help him after he had absconded.

We could do better than that. We generalized that all offenders had problems with authority. The parole officer could offer an understanding, helping relationship by which this hostility to authority figures could be "worked through." Sometimes we listened to psychiatric consultants explain how we could do this highly professional kind of treatment.

It sounded plausible at the time, but there is little evidence that hostility is worked through in the way expected.

The obstacle is mistrust, which is fatal for a helping relationship. The hostility toward authority may indeed have deep psychodynamic roots, reaching back to classically oedipal situations, but the probation officer would have to be a virtuoso psychotherapist to intervene successfully from the official position he occupies.

The trouble is that he is a cop. He is a cop with a difference. He will seldom own up to this identity, but the buzzer and the cuffs are in his brief-case. It is true that he can help in limited but substantial ways. He can find a job for an out-of-work probationer. Sometimes he can pass the right word at the right time to a detective or a prosecutor which can get a guy out of a lot of trouble.

Most of the time he checks up, and some of the time he recommends revocation of parole. He cannot really be trusted. In the ambiguous world of the probationer or the parolee, he is a figure who may be manipulated, propitiated, evaded or deceived, but he must be dealt with. Few offenders need more ambiguity added to their burdens, but they get it, with assurances that the probation officer is there to help, even if it doesn't always seem that way.

The commitment to help is certainly sincere. Modern correctional administrators like to think that probation and parole are essentially social work. There is some queasiness about the designation. After all, most social workers are women, and work with law violaters is clearly for the virile and brave. Nevertheless, the officer's job is to help with the problems confronting the offender in the achievement of "reintegration," to use the term in favor with the Task Force on Corrections. The list of these problems is formidable: economic, social, psychological, marital, vocational, and legal, might cover the headings, but many offenders would have several concerns under each. The difficulty of these problems defines the offender's need for experienced help. It is easy to conclude that such help should come from a specialist; after all, this is an age in which all of us are increasingly dependent on specialists. It is easy, too, when medical practice has solved so many human problems of such great complexity, to assume that a highly trained specialist will be eventually able to diagnose and treat the offender's exceptional ills.

But the only problem which offenders have in common is the conviction of a crime. The rest of their problems are as various as those which face the rest of humanity. Nothing can be done about the status of the convicted offender, but the problems will be solved, if they are solved at all, only with the help of the best services in the community. He is not helped by the creation of professional services which are specialized for offenders only. At best his choice of services is restricted; at worst he gets the least competent services or none at all. So long as he is subjected to specialized services his label is accentuated. He is reminded, and so is the world around him, that he is in the community on sufferance. In return for the label, he gets such social services as the officer is able to give. Few officers have the training to counsel professionally or the time to do it even if trained. Aside from the constant search for employment for the jobless offender, it is difficult to identify social services which probation and parole officers generally attempt or perform.

But there are the reports, nearly always reports of the failures of their charges. It is difficult to see what this task requires which could not be performed by a literate police officer. So far as the surveillance and contact functions of correctional field service are concerned, there might be some reason to believe that the police could manage them better.

To sum up, probation and parole exist on the margins of law enforcement and social service. The practitioner can seldom perform either function well. There are exceptions. Anyone who has been in corrections as long as I have been observing it can remember gifted colleagues whose influence on all around them, including their clients, is pervasive and enduring. These are the memorable rarities. Most of their colleagues learn to prefer paper to people. The choice is understandable; judgments of professional worth are made on the quality of an officer's reports. The officer who passes the paper test will escape his clients entirely and will pass into the less ambiguous, more impressive and better paid tasks of management. To accommodate him, most affluent probation and parole systems will create multiple tiered hierarchies uniquely fitted to watch paper go up and down.

The officer who has not yet passed the paper test—and there are many who never do—is supervised, managed, and inspected with a concern which surely arises from an administrative awareness of his essential autonomy once his reports are written. Out there in the field he can do as he pleases. No one can watch him; no one can tell him what to say to his clients; no one can find out what he is doing until he has done it. It is a system in which the emphasis on helping people with hard problems can be easily lost. The record of a timely "no-call" is as essential to advance in the hierarchy as the completion of a successful series of casework interviews.

Probation and parole consist of unequal parts of police work, social work, and administrative routine. If this combination effectively reduced recidivism or achieved any other correctional objective, we might well wonder how such results could be obtained with such unlikely means. The high success rates claimed for probation bear no convincing relationship to any regularly administered process other than the careful selection of first offenders. For all that happens to such a probationer while he is supposedly under supervision, he might as well have been awarded a suspended sentence. Parole violation rates are much less impressive. Except that the "technical" violation rates can be controlled by cooperative decision-makers, there have been no studies which have successfully established a stable difference between a high caseload violation rate and the rate for a low caseload, with which increased services are possible and often performed.

The inference to be made from this state of affairs is that what might be reasonably expected is probably true: probation and parole service do not make a difference in the amount of crime committed by identified offenders. The influence on the novice offender exercised by the probation officer will be irrelevant to those who have been scared by the police and the courts into conformity, and insufficient to offset the crime-fostering influences confronting the more involved criminal. For the parolee it is highly probable that a combination of deterrence and opportunity are much more significant in achieving non-recidivism than the personal influence of an officer.

It follows that police work should be left to the cop and social work should be practiced in social agencies. The police can conduct surveillance without role conflict. The social worker can specialize on the real and definable problems of mental health, marriage counseling, vocational rehabilitation, and the other services which the community increasingly provides for the disadvantaged. The offender who is referred for such service can accept it without reference to a special correctional flavoring. The help he gets is offered and received on the same basis as any citizen needing assistance gets it.

What follows from the above is a proposal to dismantle probation and parole services. If we proceed as I think we should, some officers will find happy homes in police departments, and some MSW's will be welcomed into social agencies. There will still be some correctional services which will have to be conducted by specialists.

Civilized justice requires a rationally based structure for decisions.

Such a structure has yet to be designed. Its essential element is a flow of ordered and evaluated information. The pre-sentence investigation, for years the sign of a properly administered court, must be conducted by officers able to disentangle the meaning from feedback received on the consequences of decisions already made. Such officers will be social administrators capable of managing and using a complex information system. They must be fully cognizant of community resources and capable of making purposeful referrals of offenders needing services to agencies capable of providing them.

Both courts and parole boards will need these services. Officers able to provide them will be talented and highly trained civil servants. From the knowledge of the community which they will assemble, they will also become invaluable participants in community planning for services to all citizens, whether good, bad, or questionable. They will not waste their time going through the motions of surveillance, a task at which the police will always excel everybody else. Nor will they themselves attempt to provide second-rate services for people needing the best.

Advocates of the present order, if they have stayed with me so far, will be bursting with questions to demolish me. Let me anticipate some. What about the community which has no services to offer except those that the existing probation officer can himself provide? Although few communities are really so deprived, the evidence that the probation officer can make a difference in such a situation is hard to find. Let him make such referrals as he can—for employment, for medical services, for education—and let him advise the court as wisely and professionally as possible. Let him not waste time on attempting to do what cannot be done.

It might also be argued that with the evolution of probation and parole some complex legal and quasi legal structures have been erected. What will be the status of the offender who is now a probationer or a parolee? I would favor abandoning both terms as monuments to social experiments which have run their courses, from which we have learned much, but which are no longer relevant to an age in which the relationships between the citizen and his community have been radically altered. Let us settle for the suspension of a sentence subject to conditions to be enforced by the police.

Farewell then to the buzzer and the cuffs. Farewell to the leatherette casebook, too. Farewell to no-calls, to unread records, to the enduring dilemmas of probation and parole.

There is too much work to do to waste time and people on going through motions. The first task is to build an effective criminal court. It can be done if we can find people to put their minds to it. Hardly anything is so well worth doing in the administration of criminal justice, and hardly anything at all has been done about it.

13
Correctional Workers: Counseling Con Men?

JOHN STRATTON

Supervising Deputy Probation Officer, Los Angeles County Probation
Department

"Beware of any helpers. Helpers are con men who promise you something for nothing. They spoil you and keep you dependent and immature."[1]

This statement by Fritz Perls is one which requires examination and consideration by everyone in the so-called "helping" professions. Probation officers and parole agents are considered by society and themselves to be one group of social helpers. As a probation officer, observations over the years have led to the belief that some of the behaviors and techniques used in counseling by probation officers and parole agents fall into Perls' definition of a helper.

Employment criteria for either profession generally requires the possession of a bachelor's degree from an accredited college or its equivalent. As a result, the background can and does range from majors in home economics to accounting, without requiring any training in the fields of psychology and sociology. While some correctional workers do have extensive backgrounds in psychology or sociology, even these people seldom have any specific training or experience in counseling theory, techniques, or philosophy. But immediately upon employment, a large portion of their time is directly engaged in counseling aimed at rehabilitation. In a sense, this group along with other social agency workers become, by employment alone, the only unlicensed paid therapists in the country.

Ask any correctional worker why he decided on his profession and one of the most common responses will be "I wanted to help people." This discussion will be limited to the counseling role of the probation officer's and parole agent's function and will attempt to look at Perls' concept of helpers pointing out some of the ways members of these professions "con" those they supervise as well as "spoil" the people they

Reprinted, with permission, from *Federal Probation*, Quarterly, September 1973, pp. 14–17.

wish to help by keeping them dependent and immature. It will also offer some suggestions for becoming more effective in the therapeutic relationship.

THE HELPER AS A CON MAN

If asked to define a "con man," a common response would probably be: "Someone who gains your confidence and then proceeds to take something very important from you." "Deceitful," "dishonest," and "fraudulent" are words effectively used in describing a con man.

As a helper, what type of behavior would bring the worker into the con-man category? There is the matter of being dishonest in a relationship with the other person, which can occur in various ways. One of the most common ways is hiding behind the bureaucratic wall when the risk is more than the worker is willing to give.

The bureaucratic wall serves the same function as any other wall, it can be used to keep out those people whom you don't want to get close to. That agency wall also creates limits and defines areas of involvement through policies and procedures thereby giving the worker a means of avoiding responsibility for decisions he should make by hiding behind that wall and allowing him to "pass the buck" through the use of established rules and lines of command.

If he so chooses, the worker can interpret rules and regulations in such a way that he establishes a role for himself which leaves no leeway in establishing a meaningful relationship with the people under his supervision. In maintaining such a role, and never allowing the probationers to see him on a human level, the officer elicits the same nonauthentic role responses from the other person. The probationer interprets his role in response to the definition he receives of the worker's role, and if that consists of detached noninvolvement, with a better-than-you attitude, the probationer won't be willing to involve himself, and will let the officer talk at him—not with him. The interchange between these two people then becomes a communication between roles as determined by the worker and the rules, rather than two people communicating openly with each other.

A popularized method of politely "conning" the other person is by verbalizing interest or stating a desire to do something with them when in reality you are saying "No." In the bureaucratic structure, this is accomplished quite easily through use of the word "But" followed by a rule or role definition. Examples of this indirect "No" approach are such statements as:

"I'd really like to talk to your father *but* I only work until 5 p.m.." "I'd like to help you *but* my caseload is too large." "I really want to have you involved in a family treatment program *but* my supervisor won't let me." "Yes I'm very interested in discussing that with you *but* it will have to be at another time."

The specific words at times may be different, but the formula remains the same, with the probationer or parolee getting the message that the other person is not really concerned about him and is saying "No." If correctional workers wonder why those under their supervision are sometimes dishonest with them, it may be that they have learned some of their behavior from contacts with the bureaucratic structure.

If a correctional worker believes in what he is doing, is concerned for the welfare of the person he is working with, and has a solid foundation for what he wishes to accomplish, it then becomes possible with some risk, effort, and fortitude to be able to do something of value for the other person. However, in many social agencies with their defined policies and procedures, officers find it easier to do what has been done in the past, viewing the effort to do something new and innovative as being more than they are willing to invest of themselves or take the responsibility and time to do.

At times in the bureaucratic maze, it is worthwhile to consider the life style of the turtle. The turtle never moves forward until he sticks his neck out. The shell is a safe, warm, place and furnishes a turtle with the ability to retreat and hibernate for long periods of time. The correctional worker is also given the opportunity to retreat and hibernate in the bureaucratic shell, or he can take responsibility for what he does both with his probationers and the agency for which he works. The conning of the probationer is not done by the bureaucratic wall, nor by the rules, regulations, policies, or procedures—it is done by the correctional officer when he uses these as excuses or methods of avoiding the responsibility of telling the probationer what he as an individual is honestly willing or unwilling to do with the other person.

Another method of "conning" the other person is by attempting to impress him with the worker's pseudoassimilation of culture, image, clothes, and lingo. When the correctional worker's life style is different from the person he is supervising or investigating, an honest approach about different values and living patterns seems much more appropriate than attempting to be like the client as a method of establishing confidence and rapport. Such things as using street language, wearing clothing similar to the probationer's, identifying by hair styles, adopting handshakes and other mannerisms when these customers or fads are uncomfortable or foreign to the worker, make it equally uncomfortable for the other person, and begin the artificial relationship. These in themselves are dishonest representations of the probation officer or parole agent and what he really is. The gap between what a person really is and what he pretends to be is perceived readily, especially by people who have been conned and treated dishonestly in prior relationships—a rather common experience for probationers and parolees.

Another form of dishonesty is when the counseling process is used as a time to exchange social pleasantries rather than as a therapeutic encounter. When the worker uses only the socially acceptable words and behavior, those of the nature acceptable in interchanges with fellow workers or on a personal basis, the encounter is not a therapeutic one. The routine goes: "Hi, Mr. Jones, how are you? Everyting OK? Anything new? Great! See you in a month." This approach allows both parties involved to be very comfortable and feel superficially "nice" about each other but prohibits them from accomplishing anything toward the rehabilitative process, which, after all, is the purpose of this particular counseling relationship.

Oftentimes the safeness of a "nice" relationship stops the probation officer or parole agent from confronting the person under supervision and dealing with the responsibilities he has in determining what happens to him. It is much safer, in the socially appropriate context, to talk about what the situation was like in the past, and generalities about what is going to be different in the future. Really dealing with what is happening to the person, his feelings about his present situation, his responsibilities, attitudes, behavior, and what changes he must make, is risk involving. It takes real honesty on the part of the worker to be able to confront and deal with problems that create pain and emotional upheaval for the one he is providing service for.

In a true therapeutic encounter, there is the opportunity for having honest expression of thought and feelings, regardless of the discomforts to either person involved in the relationship, whether it be the officer or the person he supervises. While it is possible to keep the time devoted to counseling on a very pleasant nonthreatening level, it serves no purpose for the probationer and involves neither party of the relationship in the rehabilitative process. Being the "nice guy" may meet the worker's needs, but it also allows the other person an opportunity to avoid the reality of the situation and deprives him of the chances for change.

Counseling is a unique relationship between two people and by its very nature requires honest expression by both parties. If the probationer is willing to honestly express what his feelings are, then the worker should also be willing to reach into his own experiences and say, "I've felt something like that myself," allowing the other person to know him on a human level. The ability to say what is really felt by the probation officer or parole agent regardless of whether the other's feelings will be hurt or if he will become angry; this is the risk of relating honestly with another human being and allows the person the opportunity to honestly look at himself. By not letting the one being supervised know how his behavior, expressions, or appearance affect the worker, deprives him of an honest opinion of how he affects others, and the opportunity to be able to do something different if he chooses.

SPOILING CLIENTS, KEEPING THEM
DEPENDENT AND IMMATURE

A comfortable, easy way out for a probation officer is to do for the probationer what he is capable of doing for himself. This very act is one of the most degrading things one can do to another human being because it deprives him of the ability and initiative to perform the simplest acts for himself and creates a dependency that is unrealistic and unhealthy for both parties involved. Most people under supervision will readily accept the offer of "help" since one of the usual problems of clients is a believed inability to accept responsibility which coincides with the worker's need to do for others.

While this type of "help" can make the worker feel as if he is performing excellent services for the people he supervises, the only one he really helps is himself in polishing his own view of his role as a helper. The officer may receive the admiration of his fellow workers and oftentimes his supervisor feels good about the services he has performed. While there may be some uncertainty that the people receiving such help are always benefited, it seems much clearer that the people giving such help are profiting from their role.

In reality, the help given might be appropriate if this were a social situation. This relationship, however, is a therapeutic one where the thrust is to get the probationer to do the necessary things for himself, rather than doing them for him. The worker should discourage the use of crutches and unneeded supports, and at least attempt to establish a pattern of responsibility and initiative in the person being supervised.

One example is the case of a probation officer who tried to "help" a young probationer fulfill his "lifetime goal" of becoming an oceanographer. The probation officer spent hours in the library researching what requirements were necessary, and then proceeded to persuade various members of the community into donating the necessary expensive equipment for the underwater courses. The YMCA was willing to provide the lessons for the underwater qualifications and even transportation was arranged. The probation officer received a great deal of personal satisfaction in having arranged this marvelous opportunity for the young man. The probationer, however, didn't manage to get to one lesson. The experience gained from this situation was that some new insights were formulated regarding the role of helper by one probation officer.

If another approach had been used, one which placed the responsibility on the young man, a different result may have been reached. While he may not have followed through on meeting the requirements necessary to become an oceanographer, he at least would have been forced to evaluate whether this really was a lifetime goal, and one probation officer would not have wasted many hours and used up valuable resources in what turned out to be a futile gesture.

Letting the little things slip by, such as failure to keep appointments, make payments, or being consistently late, points out the dangers of spoiling the probationer. These little things, while not of considerable individual importance standing alone, generally form a habit pattern of irresponsibility extending into all areas of a person's life.

In asking what a person under supervision wants, that question should not be designed for the purpose of having the worker secure the wants for him. Asking what a probationer wants can be used in order to reinforce him to go out and secure those goals through efforts he expends himself. This relationship can produce support, not another creation of dependence which allows the person under supervision to fall back on the worker when everything doesn't work out quite right. It is often less taxing and more rewarding personally for the officer to secure a job for his probationer than to confront him to determine whether he really wants a job and if so provide him with methods and alternatives needed to acquire a job. If the worker locates the job, he has fulfilled his own needs but keeps the probationer dependent and immature by depriving him of the responsibility and self-satisfaction inherent in locating that job himself.

A different form of allowing individuals to escape responsibility occurs when a parent wants to be relieved of the discipline and care of his child. Rather than confronting the parent with the necessity for proper performance in his role as a parent, the officer offers to set limits, make rules, or even remove the child from the home. In the parent-child relationship when one party can dump responsibility, that relationship and its previous interactions are destroyed and chances for successful reintegration in the future are poor.

CONCLUSION

Throughout this article, examples have been given to demonstrate weaknesses in the counseling process with probationers and parolees. Creating a dependence by doing too much for another person, not forcing him to take responsibility in any area, and crawling behind that bureaucratic wall when the situation is risky, all deprive a probation officer or parole agent of his full effectiveness.

There is another way of approaching people who are on probation or parole, but it will create personal risk and takes basic honesty, caring and warmth. Being willing to break down some of the barriers which exist and open up to another person on a human level, that choice is an individual one and the pain and hurt that arise out of that caring is also a choice of an individual nature. The rewards are there, too, and much more fulfilling because of the risks and personal honesty involved in allowing a person to grow and become his own person.

The probation officer must be aware of, concerned about, and actively engaged in changing social conditions which contribute to the dehumanizing of individuals. He must be vitally concerned with social reform and with reform of the system for administration of criminal justice. But, in his concern for changing the system, he cannot afford to neglect his probationer. There is relatively little he can do as an individual to change the overall system; but he can determine that his treatment of the probationer will not be an extension of the brutality, callousness, unconcern, and delay which so frequently characterize the system prior to his getting the probationer for treatment.

—Claude T. Mangrum

NOTES

[1] Fritz S. Perls, *In and Out the Garbage Pail* (LaFayette, Calif.: Real People Press, 1969).

IV

INDIVIDUALIZED MODELS
FOR OFFENDER
CLASSIFICATION AND
TREATMENT

INTRODUCTION

The causes for criminal and delinquent behavior are as many and as varied as are the theories offered to explain them. A theory, however, is not intended to represent a definitive explanation, but rather to serve as a conceptual framework within which specific sets of variables can be isolated and their relationships identified.

Developing out of these theoretical macroconstructs is an increasing growth of new conceptual micromodels which include not only causal factors but also more precisely defined treatment methods and treatment goals. As a result, there is a significant increase in the variety of counseling strategies that recognize the differential nature of behavior. Also, each strategy addresses the worker's style and the agent-client relationship.

Strategies included in this part are applied in counseling the individual. In the first article, Ted Palmer describes the Interpersonal Maturity Level or I-Level classification and treatment method, based on the theoretical assumption that delinquents are not alike. Within this context, there is the further assumption that significant commonalities can be found in youths who are at similar stages of emotional maturity. In applying this model, individuals are classified into maturity levels based on their perceptions of themselves, of others, and of their environment. In addition, within each maturity level, subtypes are described according to behavioral responses.

The application of this typology has decided implications for treatment. Initially implemented by the California Youth Authority, followed by a number of California probation departments, I-Level is currently being used in correctional agencies across the United States and in Canada.

In the second article, Professor Don C. Gibbons criticizes the assumptions made by I-Level theory. His analysis, however, is not conclusive. Whether or not I-Level is valid, Professor Gibbons suggests that, since corrections is making increasing use of nonprofessionals, there is a need for a more simplistic treatment model rather than one as sophisticated as I-Level.

In the editor's opinion, the use of non-professionals does not represent a trend away from professionalization but, rather, it is a hiatus in professional development created by economic and social pressures. The progressive correctional administrators have been using this pause to redefine or, more accurately, to define the role of correctional casework and to evaluate their own direction. The trend beginning now is toward increased professionalization, including advanced education and training, that will culminate in rigorous procedures of certification and licensing. Whichever way the trend goes, the application of I-Level is not beyond the comprehension of paraprofessionals; its diagnostic concepts are simplistic. The application of I-Level can set the stage for effective treatment intervention, not only for counseling juveniles but for adults and families as well.

Next, in "The Dynamics of I-Level Interviewing," the editor takes a practical approach to classifying offenders into maturity levels and subtypes via the nondirective interview method. The typical interview environment is described, and the dynamics of the diagnostic process are detailed by focusing on the verbal and nonverbal communication involved in the interview.

The next two readings shift the focus away from classification typologies to FIRO (Fundamental Interpersonal Relationship Orientation), an individualized method of behavior analysis and treatment. In the first reading, which is an excerpt from his book, *The Interpersonal Underworld*, William C. Schutz postulates three interpersonal needs basic to all human relationships: Inclusion, Control, and Affection. He describes each need, how individuals develop their relationship orientation in each need area, and the implications that this development has for behavior.

Although FIRO is presented in this part, which deals with applying strategies to individual cases, it is equally appropriate for use with groups or in family counseling.

Following Schutz's conceptual discussion, the editor describes how to apply FIRO. In casework, the use of FIRO calls for administering two short projective questionnaires, FIRO-B and FIRO-F. By interpreting the results of these questionnaires, the counselor can develop a behavior-feeling profile which portrays his client's fundamental need orientation. The results are then used by the counselor to match his own style with the client's orientation, to identify dysfunctional behavior, and to develop an individualized treatment strategy appropriate to the needs of the client.

The application of FIRO-B in counseling is practically international in scope; the use of FIRO-F seems to be more limited. The apparent lack of training in interpreting F seems to account for this difference. Hopefully, this article demonstrates how to relate the two scales so that the counselor can develop a more comprehensive profile than that provided by B alone.

The focus shifts, in the next article by Richard D. Jones, to the concept of contract counseling. This approach, derived from a rational theory, assumes that man is fundamentally logical and, under the proper conditions, can develop his own problem-solving capabilities. Dr. Jones details eight steps to follow in contract counseling, and emphasizes the collaborative relationship between caseworker and offender.

The advantages of contract counseling are enumerated and attention is directed to the good results obtained when the offender assumes the responsibility for his own behavior. Although Jones does not dwell on the relationship of contract counseling to behavior modification, he does mention that the two concepts are compatible.

In the next article, Doctors Gaylor L. Thorne, Roland G. Tharp and Ralph J. Wetzel deal specifically with the application of behavior modification in counseling juvenile delinquents. The techniques of behavior modification are derived from operant learning theory; a conceptual model discussed, in theory, by Professor Jeffery in chapter 3, "Criminal Behavior and Learning Theory." Operant learning theory ignores the idea of root causes and concerns itself with changing overt behavior. The assumption is made that behavior is goal directed and is "governed by its consequences." The authors review the key concepts of learning theory, describe its application in counseling, and use case studies as examples.

Behavior modification relies on the use of reward and punishment to change behavior. However, these two forces for change are not always easily identified, primarily because they are being applied according to a definition made by the giver, not the receiver. A number of variables are involved in the composition of each, and caution is necessary in evaluating which is which, and for whom. What is punishment for one offender may be a reward for another.

In the concluding article of this section, J. Terry Saunders and N. Dickon Reppucci deal with this issue in a provocative way. Although their material comes from a closed environment, they share with the reader a number of keen insights on the dynamics of behavior change and the multitude of interfacing variables to consider when applying reward and punishment. Their method of punishment is not cruel or inhumane. When the behavior of an offender is truly dysfunctional, it is he who suffers most by allowing it to continue. What could be more humane than helping him change it, as long as he participates in selecting the behaviors that need changing?

14

The Youth Authority's Community Treatment Project

TED PALMER, Ph.D.

Principal Investigator, Community Treatment Project, California
Youth Authority, Sacramento

From 1961 to the present, the California Youth Authority (CYA) has
been conducting a large-scale, two-part experiment known as the
Community Treatment Project (CTP). Part 1 was completed in 1969.
Its basic goal was to find out if certain kinds of juvenile offenders could
be allowed to remain right in their home communities, if given rather
intensive supervision and treatment within a small-sized parole
caseload. Here, the main question was: Could CYA parole agents work
effectively with some of these individuals *without first locking them up for
several months* in a large-sized, State institution? The 1961–1969 phase
of the Youth Authority's experiment was carried out mainly in Sacramento and Stockton, with San Francisco being added in 1965. Within
each of these cities all areas or regions were included. We will now
describe part 1 of the experiment. After that, we shall turn to part 2
(1969–1974).

WHO PARTICIPATED?

Eight hundred and two boys and 212 girls participated in the
1961–1969 effort. All economic levels and racial backgrounds were included; and in this respect the CTP "sample" proved to be typical of
the Youth Authority's population within the State as a whole. Most of
the participants were between 13 and 19 years of age when first sent to
the CYA and placed into the experiment. Typically, these individuals
had been in trouble with the law on 5.8 occasions at the time they were
sent to the Youth Authority by the local juvenile court. Their "trou-
bles" had usually begun several years prior to the burglary, auto theft,
etc., which typically preceded their CYA commitment.

Reprinted, with permission from *Federal Probation*, Quarterly, March 1974, pp. 3–14.

Certain youths were not allowed to participate in the experiment. For example, it was necessary to exclude everyone who had been sent to the CYA for offenses such as armed robbery, assault with a deadly weapon, or forcible rape. (These nonparticipants were called "ineligibles"; participants were known as "eligibles.") Despite such restrictions, it was still possible to *include* a total of 65 percent of all boys and 83 percent of all girls who had been sent to the CYA for the first time, from the Sacramento, Stockton, and San Francisco Juvenile Courts. Along this line, it should be kept in mind that the presence of such things as the following did not, in themselves, prevent any youths from participating in the 1961–1969 experiment: Marked drug involvement, homosexuality, chronic or severe neurosis, occasional psychotic episodes, apparent suicidal tendencies.

THE PROGRAM

Part 1 of the CYA experiment was conducted in a careful, scientific manner: A "control" group was set up from the start. This made it possible to compare the performance of (1) youths who were placed directly into the intensive CTP program, without any prior institutionalization, against that of (2) "controls"—i.e., youths who were sent to an institution for several months prior to being returned to their home communities and then being given routine supervision within standard-sized parole caseloads which were operated by a different (non-CTP) group of parole agents.[1] Thus, all eligible youths were randomly assigned to either the *experimental (CTP)* or the *control (traditional)* program—both of which were operated entirely by the Youth Authority. Six hundred and eighty-six experimentals and 328 controls eventually became part of the 1961–1969 experiment, and all research costs were picked up by the National Institute of Mental Health (NIMH).

All CYA youths, or "wards," who were assigned to the *experimental* (CTP) part of the program were placed on a caseload which contained no more than 12 youths for each parole agent. Based upon (1) detailed initial interviews, (2) a careful review of written background material, and (3) a joint conference by responsible CTP staff, a "treatment plan" was developed for each experimental youth shortly after his assignment to the program. This plan tried to take into account each youth's major strengths, weaknesses, and interests, together with his overall "level of maturity," and various circumstances of his personal, family life, and social situation. Since the resulting plan could vary a great deal from one youth (or type of youth) to the next, the particular approach used in CTP was referred to as "differential treatment." This feature was separate and apart from that of *community-based treatment* per se.

The caseload of each CTP parole officer was limited to only certain "types" of youth or particular "levels of maturity." That is to say, it included only those youths who exhibited a particular *range* of personality characteristics, or who usually displayed certain distinguishing patterns of behavior. In order to make best use of the CTP parole agent's particular skills and interests, each such agent was selected to work primarily with only *certain types* of youth, or "personality patterns." In this sense, they were paired, or "matched," with all youths who were placed on their caseload; and as a result, they were not expected to be all things to *all kinds* of Youth Authority wards.

Certain principles, strategies, and techniques were followed in connection with all youths who were assigned to Community Treatment Project caseloads. Included were: (1) A determination on the parole agent's part to work with individual youths for a number of years if necessary; (2) careful placement planning (e.g., Exactly *where* is this youth going to live, and with *whom?*), especially during early phases of each ward's parole program; (3) parole agent contact on behalf of youths, with any of several community or volunteer agencies (e.g., probation, employment, school); (4) ready access to the parole agent, by the youths, if and when a need or emergency would arise on the youths' part; (5) flexible agent-youth contacts (office or streets; formal or informal), and on a daily basis if necessary; (6) extensive surveillance by the parole agent (e.g., during evenings or weekends) with respect to the youths' community activities, if and as needed.

The following were among the major program elements which could be made available, depending upon the youth's needs and life-situation at the time: (1) Individual and/or group-centered treatment; (2) group homes, individual foster homes, and other out-of-home placements; (3) an accredited school program which was located within the CTP "community center" building, and which included tutoring as well as arts and crafts; (4) recreational opportunities and socializing experiences (e.g., outings and cultural activities) both within and outside the community center.

The next section will contain the main results of the 1961–1969 effort. To help state these findings in a succinct yet meaningful way it will be necessary to: (1) Focus upon the Sacramento-Stockton area alone;[2] (2) talk about boys only—although, later on, the main results for girls will be mentioned as well; and (3) refer to three separate groups, or "types," of youth.

A few words must be said about the three groups of youth: *"Passive Conformist," "Power Oriented,"* and *"Neurotic."* These groups have long been recognized by perhaps the majority of practitioners and theorists. They are usually referred to by names which are similar to the ones which are used in this report. Each group is briefly reviewed in Section A of the Appendix. As to quantities, these groups accounted for *14 percent, 21 percent,* and *53 percent* of the 1961–1969 sample of boys, respectively. (Incidentally, the Passive Conformist group seems to account for a considerably larger proportion of the typical California *probation*—i.e., local city and county—population, when compared with that observed within the CYA.[3]) Thus, taken together, the three groups accounted for 7 of every 8—i.e., 88 percent—of the eligible boys.[4] The remaining 12 percent were made up of four rather rare groups of youth, and will be referred to later on.

For readers who are familiar with "I-level" theory,[5] it should be mentioned that many practitioners and theorists would refer to the Passive Conformists as "immature conformists" (Cfm's). Similarly, one may think of the Power Oriented group as being made up of "cultural conformists" (Cfc's) and "manipulators" (Mp's), whereas the Neurotic group would be comprised of individuals who are often referred to as "neurotic acting-out" (Na's) and "neurotic anxious" (Nx's).

MAIN RESULTS OF THE 1961–1969 EXPERIMENT

A.—First we will talk about the group which was by far the largest—*Neurotics*. These individuals appeared to perform much better within the intensive CTP program than within the traditional program (i.e., institution plus standard parole). For example, Criminal Identification and Investigation (CI&I) "rap sheets,"[6] which covered each ward's entire Youth Authority "career,"[7] showed that the controls were arrested 2.7 times more often than experimentals. (Offenses of minor severity were excluded.[8]) More specifically, the rates of arrest in connection with each month "at risk"—i.e., for *each month on parole, in the community*—were .080 for controls and .030 for experimentals. This amounted to a difference of about 1.4 arrests per youth, per CYA *career*. In practical terms, this would mean 1,400 fewer arrests per career, for every 1,000 "Neurotic" youths in the CTP program as compared with an equal number of these youths within the traditional program.

When offenses of minor severity were included, the arrest rates per month-at-risk were .101 for controls (C's) and .044 for experimentals (E's)—a difference of 130 percent in favor of the latter. Statistically speaking, neither of the C vs. E differences which have been mentioned could be explained on the basis of chance alone.

Additional information and findings are given in Section C of the Appendix. The present set of results, which of course apply to the Neurotic group alone, are probably of greater relevance today than they were during much of the 1961–1969 period. This is because the Neurotic group currently appears to make up an even larger proportion (perhaps 70–75 percent) of the Youth Authority's entire population of males, and of females as well. This increase seems to have been an indirect and rather complicated byproduct of the continually increasing average age of CYA first commitments and, of course, recommitments.

B.—*Power Oriented* youths who participated in the intensive CTP program performed substantially *worse* than those within the traditional program, particularly in connection with followup periods of relatively long duration. This was in spite of their better showing on a 24-month "recidivism index." See the Appendix, for details.

C.—On balance, *Passive Conformists* who participated in CTP performed somewhat better than those in the traditional program, at least while under Youth Authority jurisdiction. However, the subsample of experimentals who received a *favorable discharge* from the CYA performed somewhat worse than their controls in terms of convictions (but somewhat better in terms of arrests), when one looked at the 4-year period immediately following the termination of that jurisdiction. (See the Appendix.)

D.—*The Relatively Rare Types of Youth:* What about the four groups of youth who, when taken together, accounted for the remaining 12 percent of the sample? Basically, too few cases were present within each of these groups to allow for really firm or definite conclusions. Yet, it makes some sense to briefly state the findings which we do have, on at least a tentative or provisional basis, in contrast to reporting nothing at all about these individuals.

> In the case of one particular group, however, there happened to be a complete absence of cases within the Sacramento-Stockton, experimental sample; as a result, nothing can be said about them. In I-level terms, these youths are referred to as *"asocialized aggressives"* (Aa's). (I-level terminology will also be used in referring to the three remaining personality types: "Ap's, Se's, and Ci's" (see below)). Aa's, Ap's, Se's and Ci's accounted for *1 percent, 4 percent, 2 percent, and 5 percent* of the present sample of E + C boys, respectively.

(1) All things considered, the *"asocialized passive"* group (Ap's) seemed to perform somewhat better within the intensive CTP program than in the traditional Youth Authority program. (2) No substantial E vs. C differences were observed in relation to the *"situational emotional reaction"* group (Se's). Youths of this type appeared to perform consistently well, regardless of which particular program they were in. (3) The *"cultural identifier"* group (Ci's)[9] appeared to perform somewhat better in the traditional program than in CTP.

E.—*The Total Group of Boys (Viewed Collectively).* In this section, the results for *all* Sacramento-Stockton boys are reviewed. This includes the 12 percent which had earlier been set aside.

Based on CI&I rap sheets, the arrest rate was found to be .065 among controls and .040 among experimentals, for each month on parole. This 63 percent difference in favor of the intensive, CTP program cannot be explained in terms of "chance." (A similar nonchance difference was found when offenses of minor severity were included.) In practical terms, this would amount to at least 750 fewer arrests per CYA career, for every 1,000 experimentals as vs. 1,000 controls.

On 24-months-parole followup, experimental boys performed significantly better than control boys in terms of recidivism rate: 44 percent vs. 63 percent. (Recidivism is defined in Section C of the Appendix.) Other results are: Fifty percent of the controls, as vs. 69 percent of the experimentals, received a *favorable* discharge from the CYA within 60 months of their first release to the community. Twenty-three percent of the controls, as vs. 16 percent of the experimentals, received an *unfavorable* discharge within 60 months.

It seems clear from the above that boys who participated in the CTP program performed substantially better than those in the traditional program at least during the 2-to-4-year, typical duration of their Youth Authority jurisdiction.

What happened *after* some of these youths left the Youth Authority? If one looks at the subsample of individuals who received a *favorable* discharge from the CYA, control boys were found to have chalked up an average of 1.42 convictions within 48 months after they had left the CYA. The figure for experimentals was 1.67. (Focusing on arrests alone, the figures were 1.72 and 1.94—a difference of 13 percent. As before, nonsevere offenses were excluded.)[10]

It should be mentioned that this 18 percent difference, one which favored the traditional program, seemed to largely reflect the comparatively good performance which was chalked up by what amounted to a relatively large number of *Power Oriented* individuals among the "favorable-dischargee control-subsample," when compared with the performance of the relatively smaller number of control *Neurotics* who had also received a favorable discharge. (As seen in Section C of the Appendix, Neurotic *experimental* boys, taken by themselves, performed better than their controls, after having left the CYA on the basis of a favorable discharge. Very much the opposite was found in the case of Power Oriented experimentals.) In short, the Power Oriented individuals contributed enough "points" to have tipped the postdischarge balance in favor of the control group—i.e., when all youths were counted at the same time and when the performance of the Power Oriented youths was weighted according to the number of such individuals who were present in this subsample of favorable dischargees.

F.—*Girls.* The following relates to the total sample of girls: On balance, these individuals seemed to perform equally well in the traditional program and in CTP. We say "on balance" because control girls appeared to perform better when one focused on certain measures of effectiveness only, whereas results of an opposite nature were noted when still *other* measures were used. Even when these individuals were analyzed separately with regard to each of the three major personality groupings—Passive Conformist, Power Oriented and Neurotic—no really substantial, overall E vs. C differences were observed.

WHAT ABOUT COSTS?

What was the average cost of sending a youth through the traditional program, as compared with that of CTP? In addressing this question, the first thing we found was that costs for *both* programs rose a great deal from 1961 through 1969. This was mainly due to "normal" increases in salaries and wages, price-of-living, etc. Secondly, costs increased more within the *traditional* program than within CTP; moreover, this trend continued into the 1970s. (See below.)

> This "differential rise in costs" was largely related to the greater relative, and total, amount of time which the control youths were spending within the CYA's increasingly expensive-to-operate institutions, beginning in the middle and later 1960s. In other words, it was mainly a reflection of the amount of institutional time which was being accumulated by controls (particularly those whose parole had been revoked on one or more occasions[11]) as compared with that of experimentals. (Experimentals had been revoked and institutionalized less often than controls, on the average.)

The costs which appear below relate to all Sacramento-Stockton boys who had entered either CTP or the traditional program during 1961–1969, and who received either a favorable or an unfavorable discharge as of March 1, 1973. All reception center (NRCC), institution, camp, and parole costs were included. Separate analyses were made on these 162 C's and 192 E's, depending upon the year in which each individual had first entered the program (i.e., the experiment):

> For youths who entered during the experiment's early years, or *"early period,"* 1963 prices were used. For those entering during the *"middle period,"* 1966–67 prices were used. For youths who entered during the later years—the *"recent period"*—1971–72 prices were used.[12]

The average CYA career costs per ward were as follows:
Early period: C — $ 5,734:   E — $ 7,180
Middle period: C —   8,679;   E —   9,911
Recent period: C —   14,327;   E —   14,580
Thus, in earlier years the traditional program was noticeably less expensive than CTP. However, the C vs. E "cost-ratio" underwent a definite change as time went by. This was seen in relation to the early,

middle, and more recent cost-ratios, respectively: 0.80 to 1;[13] 0.88 to 1; and 0.98 to 1. As a result, the earlier advantage which was observed for the traditional program had largely faded away by the early 1970s. Stated directly, the actual C vs. E cost difference per youth amounted to *$1,446* during the early period, *$1,232* during the middle period, and *$253* during the more recent period. When one looks at the 1971–72 data in relation to the duration of the average youth's CYA career, the figure of $253 is found to involve a control/experimental difference of $66 per year, or 18 cents a day.

In light of price increases which have been experienced since the early 1970s, it is possible that the cost-balance has by now tipped in "favor" of the CTP program. Aside from this possibility, one which centers around the above figures alone, it should be pointed out that the 1971–72 "per ward costs" would be at least a few hundred dollars higher for the traditional program than for CTP if *capital outlay costs* were added to the picture. These costs, which were not included in the figures shown above, would relate to the construction of new institutions. They are estimated as being close to $10,000,000 for each "up-to-date," physically secure, 400-bed facility. Finally, the above figures do not take into account the fairly substantial, *non-CYA correctional costs* which were accounted for by unfavorable dischargees who had been sent directly to a State or Federal prison. In this connection, it will be recalled that a greater percentage of controls than experimentals had received a discharge of this type. (See also footnote 31.)

It appears, then, that current costs for the community program would in no event be substantially greater than those for the traditional program. To all indications they would, in fact, be a little less. This would be highlighted if one focused upon the "Neurotic" youths alone, regardless of whether any post-CYA "career costs" were brought into the picture.

THE PRESENT EXPERIMENT (1969–1974)

Despite the early promise shown by CTP with various groups of youth, it was quite clear by 1965 that there was much room for improvement with regard to still other groups. By 1967–1968, it was the consensus of CTP operations staff, and on-site researchers, that the difficulties and delinquent orientation of 25-to-35 percent of the eligible boys were hardly being influenced by the intensive CTP program. In fact, it had been found that at least one-third of these individuals were again involved in delinquency within a few weeks or months after having entered the program. Much the same was observed with similar types of individuals who had been assigned to the traditional program—i.e., with youths (control subjects) who had spent some 8 or 10 months in a regular CYA institution (or camp) prior to being paroled. These, then, were the type of experiences, findings and impressions which led to the present experiment—part 2 of the Youth Authority's Community Treatment Project.

"Part 2" has several objectives; however, its main thrust relates to the following question: Would many of the above-mentioned youths become less delinquently oriented if they began their CYA career within a certain kind of residential setting (described below), and *not within the community itself*? Thus the title of this 1969–1974 effort: "Settings for the Differential Treatment of Delinquents."[14]

To be sure, the idea of using a residential facility, on a fairly long-term basis if necessary, involved a definite departure from the philosophy which was behind the 1961–1969 effort. Under that philosophy, or set of hypotheses, the treatment-and-control of *all* eligible youths could just as well have begun within the community itself.[15] (Basically, only the research requirement that there be a control group prevented this from actually occurring.) Furthermore, during 1961–1969 the residential setting—in this case NRCC—was to be used (a) only *after* the youths' intensive community program had gotten under-way, and (b) on a short-term "temporary detention" basis alone, if at all.

The "Settings" experiment obtains its sample of youths from the greater Sacramento area. This consists entirely of males who (a) may be 13 to 21 years old at intake, and (b) are no longer restricted to being juvenile court commitments. The *key* "ineligibility criteria"—i.e., bases for exclusion—relate to the youths' commitment offense and offense history, as before. However the present set of offense-criteria allow for the inclusion, within the experiment, of a *broader range* of individuals than was possible in 1961–1969. (See below for details.)

PROCEDURES AND OPERATIONS (1969–1974)

The following question is asked by project staff in connection with each newly committed youth who—in accordance with the above criteria —seems likely to later be judged eligible by the Youth Authority Board:[16] "Within which type of setting would it probably be best to initiate the treatment-and-control of this individual"? The choice is between: (1) Initial assignment to an intensive, CTP-staffed-and-operated residential program—later to be followed by release to the intensive CTP community program (staffed-and-operated as in 1961–1969); (2) direct release to the intensive CTP community program (again as per the 1961–1969 pattern).

The project staffing team approaches the above question by first making a careful study of the individual's interests, limitations, immediate pressures and underlying motivations. The main object is to figure out what the most appropriate, yet practical, short-range and long-range goals might be. The resulting "close look" allows staff to next "check the youth out" in terms of written guidelines which are designed to further focus their attention on the question of *where* the given treatment-and-control plan might best be started. The guidelines relate to certain categories of youth who, as mentioned earlier, were found to be unusually difficult to "reach" during 1961–1969.

In these guidelines, a number of distinguishing characteristics are spelled out with regard to five groups of individuals. (According to the hypotheses of this experiment, youths who appear to "fit" any one or more of these descriptions "should" begin their CYA career within the above-mentioned residential setting.) More specifically, the guidelines contain short descriptions of (a) certain patterns of interacting with others, (b) outstanding personality characteristics, (c) underlying motivations, and/or (d) immediate pressures and life-circumstances.[17] The guidelines are outlined in Section D of the Appendix.

Individuals who are seen as needing an initial period of institutionalization are referred to as "Status 1"; those seen as *not* needing this type of initial setting are termed "Status 2." When the staffing team completes its evaluation of an individual and finalizes his "status," a random drawing is then made to determine whether his initial *placement* is to be within the CTP residential component (i.e., program) or else within its community-based component.[18] All CTP parole agents serve both parts of CTP. (Prior to the youth's actual placement into either one or the other of these CTP settings/components, the Youth Authority Board must declare him eligible for CTP per se. It makes this decision without having learned the outcome of the random drawing.)

This random assignment procedure results in the establishment of four separate youth-groups—two "residential" and two "community-based," with each of the two containing a subgroup of Status 1 and, in addition, Status 2 individuals. The research team later compares each one of these four youth-groups with each of the remaining three, in terms of community adjustment.[19] With certain planned exceptions, parole agents who participate in the experiment can have caseloads which contain individuals from all four youth-groups.

The parole agent who is assigned to work with a given youth, and who has therefore been part of the staffing team, remains assigned to that youth regardless of whether the latter's placement happens to be within the residential or the community section of CTP at any particular point in time. This helps promote continuity within and across settings, with respect to long-term treatment-and-control efforts.[20]

Before presenting the results to date, a few words should be added about the CTP residential unit. This unit ("Dorm 3") is located at NRCC and is a 5- or 10-minute drive from CTP's community center in Sacramento. Dorm 3 normally houses 23 to 25 youths at any one time—CTP youths (males) exclusively—although the number has ranged from 15 to 32. It is staffed by carefully selected "youth counselors" and "group supervisors," and is readily as well as continuously accessible to all remaining CTP personnel. Some parole agents have their office on the dorm. All dorm staff are individually, and officially, paired-up with one or two agents. This makes for better dorm-agent as well as dorm-dorm coordination of efforts with respect to implementing stated goals and strategies for residence-located youths who are on the caseload of the given agents.

Two additional points. (1) *Expanding CTP's Applicability.* Part of the 1969–1974 effort centers around the following question: Can the CTP approach[21] be applied to a *broader range and variety* of offenders than that which was available in connection with the 1961–1969 experiment? This question is dealt with at two levels: First, the "ineligibility criteria" which were used during 1961–1969 have been trimmed back in order to allow for the inclusion of many individuals who would otherwise be *excluded* on the basis of a) commitment offenses relating to armed robbery, forcible rape, etc., or b) offense histories of a particularly disturbed or aggressive-appearing nature.[22] However, the Board will declare these particular youths eligible for CTP only with the understanding that their program is to be initiated within Dorm 3. (For research purposes, all such individuals are therefore analyzed as a separate group. They are called "Category B" youths.[23]) Secondly, and aside from the matter of offenses, all first commitments to the CYA from the Sacramento County Superior Court have been made available for inclusion within CTP. This is the first time that adult court commitments have become part of the CTP studies. No restrictions are applied as to *where* these particular individuals may begin their program; etc. (2) *Terminology.* The following should facilitate the presentation of findings:

RR = Status 1 youths who were *appropriately placed:* These individuals were diagnosed as needing to begin their program within a residential setting. Their program *did* begin within a residential setting (i.e., Dorm 3).

RC = Status 1 youths who were *inappropriately placed:* Diagnosed as needing to begin in a residential setting; however, their program was initiated within a community setting, as in 1961–1969.

CR = Status 2 youths who were *inappropriately placed:* Diagnosed as being able to begin their program within a community setting; however, their program was initiated within a residential setting (i.e., Dorm 3).

CC = Status 2 youths who were *appropriately placed:* Diagnosed as being able to begin their program within a community setting. Their program *did* begin within a community setting, as in 1961–1969.

MAIN FINDINGS TO DATE (1969–1974 EXPERIMENT)[24]

Status 1 youths who were inappropriately placed are performing considerably worse than those who were appropriately placed: 94 percent of the RC's (inappropriately placed) as vs. 58 percent of the RR's (appropriately placed) have chalked up one or more offenses during their first year-and-a-half on parole.[25] The number of offenses per youth is 1.56 among RC's and 0.96 among RR's. For each month at risk the mean rate of offending is .140 among RC's as vs. .066 among RR's—in other words, one offense for every 7.1 months in the case of RC's, and one per 15.2 months among RR's.[26] This 112 percent difference in rate of offending cannot be explained in terms of "chance."[27]

These findings suggest that the delinquent behavior of the Youth Authority's more troubled, troublesome and/or resistive wards may be substantially reduced—provided that they are first worked with in a setting such as is represented by Dorm 3, as distinct from one which is community-based in the usual sense of the term. The scope, and the potential importance, of any such "reductions" should not be thought of as slight: Status 1 youths represent 46 percent of the total CTP sample.[28] It is likely that they comprise a sizable portion of the Youth Authority's total population, as well.[29]

What about the remaining 54 percent—i.e., the *Status 2* youths? (These youths, it will be recalled, are the less troubled, troublesome and/or resistive individuals.) On balance the present findings suggest that there is little if anything to be gained, with regard to parole performance, by initially placing Status 2 youths into a residential facility,[30] even of the type represented by Dorm 3: The average monthly rates of offending are .086 for CR's (inappropriately placed) and .068 for CC's (appropriately placed)—a difference of 26 percent. On the surface, these rates might suggest that an "inappropriate" (in this case, residential) placement would be slightly *detrimental* to the Status 2 youths, at least when compared with the more appropriate, alternate placement. However, this particular difference in rates of offending may be accounted for by "chance" alone. Together with results from three other measures of performance, the overall picture is one of few substantial and consistent CR vs. CC differences.

Inappropriately placed youths (RC's + CR's) are performing worse than appropriately placed youths (RR's + CC's): For each month spent within the community, the mean rate of offending is .107 among "inappropriates" (INP's) and .067 among "appropriates" (APR's). This amounts to one offense for every 9.3 months on parole in the case of

INP's, and one per 14.9 months among APR's. This 60 percent difference cannot be accounted for by "chance." Results from the remaining performance-indicators are consistent with this basic finding, although not as clear-cut.

The various findings which have been presented might seem to suggest the obvious: Delinquent behavior can probably be reduced in connection with community and residential programs *alike*, by means of careful diagnosis and subsequent placement of individuals into appropriate rather than inappropriate or less-than-optimal settings and programs. In short, it might be said that it matters *which* youths (or types of youth) are placed into *which* type of setting, and that careful selection may lead to higher rates of success for residential and community-based programs alike. Yet, it is recognized that such a viewpoint or conclusion would by no means be universally accepted as being "obvious," within corrections. For one thing, many people feel that nothing really has much effect on delinquent behavior; others believe that one single approach, and perhaps one particular setting, may well contain "the answer" for all but a tiny portion of the population. At any rate, the present findings will hopefully add new information to a long-standing placement issue which many practitioners do regard as being less than entirely obvious in the majority, if not large majority, of cases: Which youths would best be placed into which types of setting, or program?

Two final points in this connection. (1) The difference in rate of offending which is found *between* the Status 1 groups (RC's *vs.* RR's) is considerably larger than that found between the Status 2 groups (CR's *vs.* CC's). More specifically, Status 1 youths who were inappropriately placed are performing *considerably* worse than those who were appropriately placed; however, in the case of Status 2 youths *no substantial differences* are observed between individuals who were inappropriately placed and those who were appropriately placed. This raises the possibility that an initial placement within an inappropriate or less-than-optimal setting might make more of a difference to Status 1 youths than to those diagnosed as Status 2. It may be that the latter, presumably "stronger" individuals are in a better position to compensate for, or otherwise cope with and make the best of, an environment of this nature. (2) The significance, or possible differential significance, of the initial treatment-and-control setting is also suggested by the following: Appropriately placed youths (RR's *and* CC's) are performing about equally well on parole—i.e., regardless of status. However, *inappropriately* placed *Status 1* youths (RC's) are performing substantially worse than inappropriately placed *Status 2* youths (CR's). In other words, appropriate placement may perhaps help to offset or moderate certain pre-existing differences in level of coping ability, on the part of Status 1 vs. Status 2 youths. On the other hand, *inappropriate* or less-than-optimal placement may be more likely to accentuate or activate various differences which relate to their personal or interpersonal liabilities.

Thus far, the CTP approach does seem applicable to categories of offenders other than those which were studied in 1961–1969: Briefly, *Adult Court* commitments have presented few if any special operational problems, or, for that matter, diagnostic problems. Their treatment-and-control requirements differ only slightly from those of Juvenile Court commitments who fall within the 16-and-older age range. In addition, *Category B* youths have presented few unusual or serious operational and diagnostic problems. However, partly because of Board restrictions which are frequently placed upon these individuals with regard to day passes, furloughs or minimum length of residential stay, it has sometimes been difficult to develop treatment-and-control plans which closely resemble those observed in the case of many other residence-located youths. Operations staff nevertheless feel able to engage in productive interactions with most such youths. The parole performance of these individuals has yet to be evaluated in detail.

OVERVIEW AND CONCLUDING REMARKS

Within and outside of corrections, many concerned individuals are currently engaged in an ideological battle over whether to "keep almost all offenders on the streets," or else "lock up nearly all offenders, except for first-timers." This, of course, may be exaggerating the situation to a certain degree; yet at the same time, it may be accurate in its reflection of certain feelings which are often involved. Feelings aside, the facts which have emerged from California's 12-year experiment thus far suggest that both of the above positions may be too extreme, and that a more differentiated or flexible approach may be appropriate. (These considerations would at least apply to the type of individuals who have been studied thus far—youths who have had numerous contacts with the law.) A brief review may illustrate this point:

When an NIMH-funded research team combined several hundred Youth Authority males into a single study group (one which included the full range of CYA "personality types"), it found that (a) "experimentals" who participated in the intensive, 1961–1969 *community-based program (CTP)* had produced substantially less delinquent behavior than (b) "controls" who had participated in the traditional CYA program. (The experimentals and controls had been well-matched on such characteristics as age, IQ, socioeconomic status, race, etc.) However, the researchers also found that much of this difference in favor of the CTP—i.e., noninstitutional—program was accounted for by youths who were referred to as "Neurotics." During the 1960's, these individuals accounted for half of the CYA's population; they currently account for considerably more. By way of contrast, the *traditional CYA program* was found to have a greater influence than CTP in the case of individuals described as "Power Oriented." This particular group now comprises about one-tenth of the CYA population; it previously accounted for twice that amount.

Quite aside from these particular findings and developments, it was observed, prior to 1969, that roughly one-third of the *total* sample were responding somewhat indifferently, and often quite unfavorably, to the community-based and traditional programs alike. Included within this broad, "difficult-to-reach" category were some individuals from nearly all personality groupings. However, it was the difficult-to-reach Neurotics who accounted for the largest total number. (This was possible despite the relatively positive performance by the Neurotic group as a whole.) Since 1969, the distinguishing characteristics of difficult-to-reach "Neurotics" have been largely singled-out. In many cases (perhaps half) operations staff have helped them to engage in less by way of delinquent behavior while in the community. But before this could occur, it was necessary for these individuals to *begin* their Youth Authority program, (a) not within the community per se, (b) not inside a standard CYA institution, but rather (c) within a *medium-sized, CTP-staffed residential facility*—one which was operated in accordance with the 1961–1969 "differential treatment" philosophy. As to the difficult-to-reach "Power Oriented" youths, this same "residence-first" (CTP facility) approach seems to be resulting in relatively little overall improvement in terms of parole performance. Thus, the *traditional* program may still represent the Youth Authority's best alternative for the majority of these particular individuals—especially the sub-group known as "Cfc's." Finally, during 1961–1969 the "Passive Conformists" (now one-tenth of the population) performed somewhat, though not a great deal better in CTP than within the traditional CYA program. Nevertheless, their response to CTP's residential facility (1969–present) has been unfavorable. Thus, in this particular instance the 1961–1969 type of community-based approach would seem to be the treatment of choice.

CTP's originally stated ideal—that of changing delinquents into lifelong nondelinquents—is not being achieved in the large majority of cases. Obviously, the CTP program does not contain a "special potion" which, after having been taken, is capable of eliminating all traces of delinquency, and of fortifying the youths against every form of stress. Nevertheless, the "differential treatments" and "differential settings" which have been utilized in this program do seem capable of *reducing* the total volume of delinquent behavior on the part of many, but by no means all, eligible males. This holds true during the period of their CYA jurisdiction and, to a lesser extent, subsequent to the termination of that jurisdiction. In order to bring about this "reduction," it has very often seemed unnecessary to initially place these individuals within a residential setting (traditional or otherwise); in many other cases, it has seemed quite necessary. As suggested above, it is what goes on *within* the given setting that seems to count, and not just the setting itself. This, of course, may also vary from one type of youth to another. Nothing in our experience suggests that it is an easy matter to operate a program such as CTP. Implementation and maintenance of a community-based, intensive differential treatment-and-control program involves critical issues, and requires steadfast commitments, with respect to personnel selection, quality of supervision, administrative support, etc. In one form or another, issues of this nature will also be encountered outside the context of large-sized, State agencies such as the CYA. Although challenges of this type have been adequately met in certain instances, it might be well to recognize the fact that any thoroughgoing implementation of CTP—even of the 1961–1969 approach alone—is, at the present time, probably beyond the reach of most probation and parole departments within the USA on anything other than a limited scale. Even so, worthwhile modifications and adaptations of the California program do seem to be well within the realm of possibility; in several instances, they are already in existence.

Whatever the immediate future may hold for programs such as CTP, the research information which has been gathered since 1961 may continue to be of interest to practitioners, administrators and social scientists who still place value upon the concept of actively and directly intervening in the life of personally troubled, developmentally lacking and/or disturbing-aggressive youths and young adults. This should apply in relation to community-based and residential-centered programs alike.

Appendix

Section A

The three groups of youth which were first mentioned on page 4 may be briefly described as follows:

(1) *Passive Conformist:* This type of youth usually fears, and responds with strong compliance to, peers and adults who he thinks have the "upper hand" at the moment, or who seem more adequate and assertive than himself. He considers himself to be lacking in social "know-how," and usually expects to be rejected by others in spite of his efforts to please them.

(2) *Power Oriented:* This group is actually made up of two somewhat different kinds of individuals, who, nevertheless, share several important features with one another. The first likes to think of himself as delinquent and tough. He is often more than willing to "go along" with others, or with a gang, in order to earn a certain degree of status and acceptance, and to later maintain his "reputation." The second type, or "subtype," often attempts to undermine

or circumvent the efforts and directions of authority figures. Typically, he does not wish to conform to peers or adults; and not infrequently, he will attempt to assume a leading "power role" for himself.

Passive Conformist and Power Oriented youths are usually thought of as having reached a "middle maturity" level of interpersonal development. The group which is described next is said to have reached a "higher maturity" level. The "level of interpersonal maturity" concept is briefly explained in Section B of this Appendix.

(3) *Neurotic:* Here again, we find two separate personality types which share certain important characteristics with one another. The first type often attempts to deny—to himself and others—his conscious feelings of inadequacy, rejection, or self-condemnation. Not infrequently, he does this by verbally attacking *others* and/or by the use of boisterous distractions plus a variety of "games." The second type often shows various symptoms of emotional disturbance—e.g., chronic or intense depression, or psychosomatic complaints. His tensions and conscious fears usually result from conflicts produced by feelings of failure, inadequacy, or underlying guilt.

Section B

The following are brief definitions of the three main levels of interpersonal maturity which are observed within the CYA:

Maturity Level Two (1^2): An individual whose overall development has reached this level, but has not gone beyond it, views events and objects mainly as sources of short-term pleasure, or else frustration. He distinguishes among individuals largely in terms of their being either "givers" or "withholders," and seems to have few ideas of interpersonal refinement beyond this. He has a very low level of frustration-tolerance; moreover, he has a poor capacity for understanding many of the basic reasons for the behavior or attitudes of others, toward him.

Maturity Level Three (1^3): More than the 1^2, an individual at this level recognizes that certain aspects of his own behavior have a good deal to do with whether or not he will get what he wants from others. Such an individual interacts mainly in terms of oversimplified rules and formulas rather than from a set of relatively firm, and generally more complex, internalized standards or ideals. He understands few of the feelings and motives of individuals whose personalities are rather different than his own. More often than the 1^4 (see below), he assumes that peers and adults operate mostly on a rule-oriented or intimidation/manipulation basis.

Maturity Level Four (1^4): More than the 1^3, an individual at this level has internalized one or more "sets" of standards which he frequently uses as a basis for either accepting or rejecting the behavior and attitudes of himself as well as others. (These standards are not always mutually consistent, or consistently applied.) He recognizes interpersonal interactions in which individuals attempt to influence one another by means other than compliance, manipulation, promises of hedonistic or monetary reward, etc. He has a fair ability to understand underlying reasons for behavior, and displays some ability to respond, on a fairly long-term basis, to certain moderately complex expectations on the part of various peers and adults.

Section C

For the *Neurotic* group, the additional information and findings are as follows:

(1) Despite its known shortcomings, "rate of recidivism" has long been one of corrections' most widely used measures of parole *failure*. As used in this report, recidivism reflects the occurrence of any one or more of the following events: (a) Revocation of the youth's parole by the Youth Authority Board; (b) recommitment of the youth to the CYA, by either a Juvenile or an Adult Court; (c) unfavorable discharge of the youth by the Youth Authority Board, from the CYA itself. Any one of these events is usually the result of some type of police arrest and subsequent conviction. Events (a) and (b), above, are usually followed by a period of incarceration for several months, within one or another of the Youth Authority's large-sized institutions. (See below, regarding (c).) Thus, the higher the recidivism rate, the greater is the amount of "failure" in one sense of the term. Now then, on 24-months parole followup the recidivism rate was 66 percent for controls and 45 percent for experimentals.

(2) Within 60 months from the time of their first release to the community (literally, their date of initial parole), 40 percent of the C's as vs. 77 percent of the E's had been officially released by the Youth Authority Board from the CYA's jurisdiction—on the basis of a *favorable discharge*. Also, within a period of 60 months, 40 percent of the C's as vs. 17 percent of the E's were released on the basis of an unfavorable discharge. (It should be noted that depending upon an individual's behavior subsequent to one or more prior parole revocations which he may have received, the individual will still be able to eventually obtain *either* a favorable *or* an unfavorable discharge from the CYA.)[31]

(3) What happened *after* the CYA's jurisdiction had ended, in the case of Neurotic youths and young adults who had been given a *favorable discharge* (see (2), above)? At least this much is known: Many of these individuals did not entirely relinquish their delinquent tendencies—despite their experiences within the CYA. Be this as it may, those who had gone through the traditional CYA program seemed, on the average, to have remained somewhat *more* delinquent than those who had completed CTP: Within 48 months after having left the Youth Authority, controls chalked up an average of 1.88 convictions; the figure for experimentals was 1.58. (A somewhat larger C vs. E difference was obtained when one looked at *arrests*, and not simply convictions. As before, arrests of minor severity were not counted.) In practical terms, this would amount to a difference of about 300 convictions for every 1,000 experimental as well as control "favorable-dischargees," over a 4-year span of time. (The reader may note that this analysis of *post-CYA*, CI&I data has been completed on "arrests" and, also, on the "convictions" which related to those arrests. However, because the earlier-mentioned *parole (CYA-time)* CI&I data were first analyzed during 1973, only the "arrest" information has been looked at thus far, with regard to *parole* time. Judging from the "post-CYA" findings on arrests vs. convictions, the "parole time" results for these same two levels of analysis should be very similar to one another.) Using a 10-point scale, the penalties received for each conviction were somewhat more severe among controls than among experimentals—5.75 as vs. 4.25, on the average.

The following results relate to *Power Oriented* youths:

(1) CI&I rap sheets showed an arrest rate of .060 for controls and .071 for experimentals, with regard to each month spent within the community. This difference favored the traditional program by 18 percent. (Again, offenses of minor severity were excluded, although the picture hardly changed when they were included.) (2) On 24-months' parole followup, the recidivism rate was 66 percent for the controls and 40 percent for experimentals. (3) Despite the better showing by experimentals on the 24-month recidivism index, it was found that 53 percent of the controls as vs. 43 percent of the experimentals received a favorable discharge from the Youth Authority within *60* months of their first release to parole. Similarly, 15 percent of the C's as vs. 23 percent of the E's received an unfavorable discharge. (4) Within 48 months after being released from the CYA's jurisdiction, the Power Oriented, control *"favorable-dischargees"* had chalked up an average of 1.47 convictions; the figure for experimentals was 2.55. (The C vs. E difference was even larger when one focused upon arrests alone, rather than convictions alone.) This was a 73 percent difference in favor of Power Oriented youths who had successfully completed the Youth Authority's traditional program.

The following relates to *Passive Conformist* youths:

(1) CI&I rap sheets showed an arrest rate of .066 for controls and .037 for experimentals, for each month within the community. This difference favored the CTP program by 78 percent. (2) On 24-months' parole followup, the recidivism rate was 59 percent for controls and 51 percent for experimentals. (3) 54 percent of the C's as vs. 78 percent of the E's received a favorable discharge from the Youth Authority within 60 months of their first release to the community. Similarly, 14 percent of the C's as vs. 6 percent of the E's received an unfavorable discharge. (4) Within 48 months after termination of their CYA jurisdiction, the Passive Conformist, control "favorable-dischargees" had chalked up an average of 1.44 convictions; the figure for experimentals was 1.80. This was a 25 percent difference in favor of the traditional program.

Section D

Basic to the 1969–1974 experiment is the hypothesis that certain youths (five groups in all) would probably derive greater benefit from a course of treatment-and-control which would begin within a residential setting, in contrast to a community setting. Briefly, the groups are:

(1) Youths who are quite disturbed and openly disorganized relative to overall, everyday functioning, and who at times become highly agitated or even delusional when under the pressure of everyday life. (Mostly found among Nx's, Ap's and Aa's.)

(2) Youths who have an intensive drive to prevent other persons from exerting controls upon them, or from substantially influencing the direction of their lives. They are prepared to use virtually "everything" in their power —including runaway, physical resistance, etc.—to avoid the ongoing confrontation of concerned authority figures, and to avoid involvement in nonexploitive relationships with adults in general. (Mostly found among Mp's and Cfc's—the "Power Oriented" group.)

(3) Youths who are unable to recognize, or who vigorously attempt to deny, the existence and influence of the unusually destructive relationships and

loyalty-binds in which they are involved, at home and within the community. Were these youths released directly to the community setting, conditions such as these would undermine the youth/parole agent relationship at a time when this relationship would still be in its formative stage, and would operate so as to lead the youth into delinquent acting-out of a frequency or magnitude sufficient to result in an early parole revocation and removal from the community setting. (Mostly found among Na's and Nx's—the "Neurotic" group.)

(4) Youths who are nonneurotic and of a relatively high level of maturity, but who need to actually be shown that their freedom will definitely be withdrawn if they persist in their delinquent patterns. (Mostly found among Ci's.)

(5) Youths who—operating on the basis of underlying motivations of a self-defeating nature—have become increasingly committed to the use of drugs and/or a drug-using subculture, to the point of feeling little interest in coping with long-range social expectations or pressures, or in interacting with others in a nonexploitive manner. (Mostly found among Na's and Nx's.)

NOTES

[1] It should be mentioned that experimental and control youths both spent an average of 4 to 6 weeks at the Youth Authority's Northern Reception Center and Clinic (NRCC), immediately after having been committed to the Youth Authority. This period of "routine processing" consisted of necessary medical and dental work, standard diagnostic workups and related achievement testing, appearance before the Youth Authority Board, etc. Upon release from NRCC, youths were either sent to a CYA institution for a period which averaged several months or else they were returned directly to their home community, on parole status.

[2] In part, this is because the necessary, detailed analyses have not been completed relative to San Francisco youths. Nevertheless, relevant analyses which have been completed suggest that the overall results may be fairly comparable to those which appear in the present report, for the Sacramento-Stockton location alone.

Of the 1,014 eligibles, 72 percent of the boys and 58 percent of the girls were from the Sacramento-Stockton area.

[3] For example, an estimated 25 percent of the overall probation population—in contrast to the 14 percent which was observed during the CYA's 1961–1969 effort.

[4] They accounted for 94 percent of the eligible girls.

[5] See: Warren, M. Q. et al., "Interpersonal Maturity Level Classification: Juvenile. Diagnosis and Treatment of Low, Middle, and High Maturity Delinquents." (Sacramento: California Youth Authority, 1966), pp. 1–52, (mimeo.).

[6] These documents are compiled by the State of California, Department of Justice (D.J.). They are based on reports which are routinely, and directly, received by D.J. from police, probation, and sheriffs' departments throughout California. Among other things, the documents may include listings of antisocial activities which had not been mentioned in the (a) formal suspension reports, and (b) "special incident reports," of Youth Authority parole agents who participated in the 1961–1969 effort. (For a variety of reasons, omissions of this nature occurred significantly more often relative to the traditional program, as compared with the CTP program.)

[7] The figures which will next be given refer to all youths who received either a favorable or an unfavorable discharge from the CYA by the close of the 1961–1969 experiment, or shortly thereafter.

[8] Arrests of "minor severity" are those which relate to traffic (noninjuries/nonfelonies), runaway, incorrigible, etc.

[9] More recently referred to as higher maturity "delinquent identifiers" (Di's).

[10] As indicated in footnote 31, we have not completed the analysis of post-CYA offense behavior on the part of individuals who had received an *unfavorable* discharge.

[11] The periods of incarceration which resulted from these revocations are over and beyond the *initial* period of incarceration which was experienced by the controls, but not by the experimentals, shortly after their original commitment to the Youth Authority.

[12] In connection with the "recent period" the primary question was: What would the program costs look like on the basis of early 1970 prices—yet in relation to the performance of an actual sample of experimentals and controls who had entered the CYA during the later part of the 1961–1969 effort?

[13] Thus, 5, 734 divided by 7,180 yields a ratio of 0.80 to 1.

[14] As before, the research costs are picked up by NIMH.

[15] At any rate, there seemed to be little if any scientific evidence to suggest that it would be *inappropriate or impractical* to begin the treatment-and-control of eligible wards outside of a traditional institutional setting.

[16] As in 1961–1969, the Youth Authority Board gives the final, legal approval in regard to eligibility. (In the event that the youth is declared eligible, a "random drawing" will alone determine exactly *where* he is to begin his treatment-and-control. See the text.) Prior to the time that a ward is officially declared eligible, he would be referred to as a "pre-eligible."

[17] Since 1969, these descriptions have been found to be largely, though not entirely, mutually exclusive.

[18] As a result of the random drawing, it not infrequently happens that a Status 1 youth will have to begin his program within the community setting. By the same token, a Status 2 youth may have to begin within the residential facility. (These "less-than-optimal," initial placements serve an essential function in terms of the research design.) When this type of initial placement is called for, the Operations section of the staffing team prepares what is called a "modified treatment-and-control" plan. This differs in several respects from the "optimal . . . plan" which they had prepared just prior to the drawing. The main object of the modified plan is to (a) develop goals which are appropriate to the less-than-optimal setting in which the youth's program is to be initiated, yet which will remain relevant to the individual's needs, and (b) develop strategies which will allow for and at the same time encourage a maximum use of the resources which are available within the particular setting.

[19] The groups which are being compared thus serve as "controls" for one another.

[20] In many cases, individuals whose parole is revoked while they are in the community can be placed into, or returned to, the CTP residential facility. This allows them to remain part of the overall program.

[21] In the present case this includes the "differential treatment" feature in addition to the community-based aspect per se.

[22] That is, regardless of the possible lack of severity of the *commitment* offense itself.

[23] All other youths are referred to as "Category A."

[24] (a) These results relate to the first 106 eligible "Category A" males who were paroled as of December 15, 1972. (See footnote 23.) When "Category B" cases are included, the results hardly change. (b) Neurotic, Power Oriented, Passive Conformist, and "rare types" are combined into a single group—74 percent of which is comprised of the Neurotic category alone. (The findings which are reported—more specifically, the differences between comparison groups—are very largely accounted for by the latter individuals. They receive little if any support in relation to the remaining 26 percent of the sample, when the latter are viewed as a single, separate entity.) This population-distribution probably reflects a broader trend within the CYA as a whole. (c) The present results take into account offenses of all severity levels; however, they are virtually unchanged when those of minor severity are excluded. The latter account for 7 percent of the present, 120 offenses. (d) "Offense" is defined as any delinquent act which results in

any one or more of the following, official actions: Revocation of parole; court recommitment; adjudicated court referral to CTP; unfavorable transfer from CTP; suspension of parole. (During the coming year an analysis of CI&I rap sheets will be undertaken for the first time, relative to the 1969–1974 sample.)

[25] As before, "months on parole" is used synonymously with "months in the community" and "months at risk."

[26] By using a closely related yet possibly more refined statistical approach, an even larger difference was obtained between RC's and RR's with respect to the average (mean) monthly rate of offending. When the *median* rather than the *mean* was used in relation to this alternate approach, the monthly rate of offending was .180 for RC's and .060 for RR's.

[27] Nor can various background factors account for this difference. These factors include age, IQ, socioeconomic status, race, I-level, "subtype," and level of parole risk ("base expectancy").

[28] With "Category B" youths included, the figure is 49 percent.

[29] In 1968, research staff estimated that 39 percent of all eligible youths would receive a Status 1 diagnosis during the present experiment. Wards who were received by the CYA during the past few years appear to be more involved with delinquency than those received during the 1960's. For example, the present sample of eligible Category A subjects had accumulated an average of 7.1 delinquent contacts by the time of their commitment to the CYA. The figure for 1961–1969 eligibles was 5.8.

[30] This is generally consistent with the main results of the 1961–1969 experiment.

[31] Taking into account all "groups" of boys—i.e., all nine "subtypes"—50 percent of the experimentals and 50 percent of the controls who received an unfavorable discharge from the Youth Authority were sent to a State or Federal prison immediately upon receipt of their discharge. Their Court sentence commonly specified a maximum of several years' incarceration. Partly because of this, followup (i.e., post-CYA, postprison) analyses have not been completed for the unfavorable dischargee sample.

15

Differential Treatment of Delinquents and Interpersonal Maturity Levels Theory: A Critique

DON C. GIBBONS
Portland State University

The trend toward the use of diagnostic typologies in corrections is noted. The I-Levels (Interpersonal Maturity Levels) system employed in California is outlined in detail, including its applications to criminality. A number of questions are raised about the general validity of the theory, particularly as applied to offenders. In addition, several treatment projects are discussed in which this system has been utilized, with attention to limitations of these projects. In general, it is suggested that the results to date from the utilization of this framework in corrections are not encouraging. Finally, it is argued that correctional reform ought to be moving in a quite different direction from that of I-Levels.

In recent years, correctional agencies have been trying to increase the efficacy of treatment of criminal and delinquent behavior by the use of diagnostic models or offender types, along with differential treatment strategies based upon these types. This development has sometimes been termed the differential treatment model of correctional practice. Presumably, the diagnostic types used in rehabilitation would be drawn out of the criminological research literature, while the strategies of intervention linked to these types would be taken from the correctional treatment literature. The end result would be a situation broadly analogous to medical practice, in which forms of therapy would be linked to forms of disease and pathology. In the case of corrections, particular types of treatment would be specified for different patterns of criminality.

Reprinted with permission of the author, The University of Chicago Press, from *Social Service Review*, Vol. 44, No. 1 (March 1970): 22–23.

One instance of an appeal for the development of differential treatment can be found in the writings of the author (6, 10).[1] This view has also been voiced by an agency of the Department of Health, Education, and Welfare, which suggested four delinquent types: prosocial offenders, antisocial delinquents, pseudosocial manipulators, and asocial offenders (19). This perspective was also set forth by the President's Commission on Law Enforcement and Administration of Justice (20:20–22).

Although there has been a good deal of discussion of the notion of differential treatment, relatively little implementation of it has yet occurred, but two exceptional cases of differential treatment in application can be found in the San Mateo County Project in California (4, 13) and the Stonewall Jackson School Project in North Carolina (17), both of which involved the utilization of some of the programmatic recommendations in the author's book, *Changing the Lawbreaker* (6).

A good many obstacles lie in the path of rapid and general implementation of differential treatment notions. For one, correctional agencies are currently staffed by a hodge-podge of persons with widely varied social and educational backgrounds, so that it would be difficult to introduce into these agencies a system of diagnostic types and rehabilitation strategies upon which employees might agree.

Additionally, those who advocate the differential treatment approach are themselves in disagreement about which system of types and strategies ought to be utilized. The basic fact is that lawbreakers can be and have been classified in a variety of ways. There is not one offender typology; there are many. The existing evidence regarding characteristics of lawbreakers and causal influences in their backgrounds is incomplete, so that research data do not provide us with clear guidelines for adjudicating among competing classifications of delinquents or criminals. The result of all this disagreement is that psychologically oriented exponents of differential treatment go about arguing for typologies in which personality psychodynamics and pathology loom large, while those of a sociological persuasion contend that typologies which stress subcultural influences, social structural variables, and the like, ought to be utilized. Each group is able to point to some evidence to support its preferred diagnostic model. In short, diffusion of the differential treatment approach to correctional practice is impeded by lack of agreement about the system to be employed.

The application of a diagnostic system to correctional practice is currently under way in California in the form of Interpersonal Maturity Levels (I-Levels) theory, which is being employed by the California Youth Authority. In this instance, at least, action on differential treatment has gone well beyond the talking stage. The scheme involves a set of diagnostic types of delinquents, along with companion treatment strategies for these offenders. This differential treatment model is being used in the Community Treatment Project, the Preston Typology Study, the Northern Youth Center Research Project, and the Center for Training in Differential Treatment. An effort is being made to diffuse this approach through the California correctional system and into other state correctional programs. Thus, the I-Levels approach stands as a leading candidate to become the dominant one in differential treatment.

In view of the prominence being assumed by the I-Levels scheme, critical attention to it is called for, so that its strengths and weaknesses can be evaluated before we become totally committed to it as the basis for differential treatment. This paper is devoted to a critique of I-Levels theory. The article is designed to be critical in a positive sense, drawing attention to problems that need examination in the further development of the argument. Then, too, the critique is intended to identify a number of considerations which need to be kept in mind in evaluating rival diagnostic systems. The paper will examine in order (a) the structure of I-Levels theory and the question of its general validity or accuracy, along with applications of it as a theory of criminality; (b) current endeavors to use the theory in differential treatment in California; and (c) the possibilities for the diffusion of the system throughout American corrections programs.

I-LEVELS THEORY

Development of the Theory

The original statement of Interpersonal Maturity Levels theory was set forth by Sullivan, Grant, and Grant in 1957 (18). In brief, this was a socialization theory stressing that human development proceeds in a series of stages from neonatal dependence and nonhuman characteristics to adult maturity, interpersonal competence, and role-taking ability. At all stages there is a basic core structure of personality around which the actor's behavior revolves and which heavily influences his responses.

Not all persons go through the entire socialization process, so that some become held or fixated at one stage or another. The authors differentiate seven levels of interpersonal competence and contend that one must make the psychological integrations at a lower level before he can move on to a higher level of interpersonal maturity. The proponents of the theory set forth their ideas as follows:

> The normal pattern of emotional-social development follows a trend toward increasing involvement with people, objects, and social institutions. . . . The foundation for subsequent integrations is laid in preceding levels; the synthesis and integration of one set of stimuli or prob-

lems are essential to the perception of the next. . . . Each stage or level
is defined by a crucial interpersonal problem which must be solved
before further progress toward maturity can occur [18:373–75].

According to Sullivan, Grant, and Grant, the first level of interpersonal maturity involves the integration of separateness, by which they
mean that the person manages only to make self–nonself distinctions.
People are seen only as objects, hardly differentiated from other kinds
of objects. At the second level, the person is involved in the integration
of nonself differences, so that he now manages to deal with human
beings and objects differently, but his approach is an autistic one. Level
three involves the integration of rules, in which the actor perceives
rules and is oriented to them, but he views them as arbitrary, black-
and-white standards which are to be followed blindly. The fourth level
of maturity is one in which integration of conflict and response is a
major interpersonal problem to be solved. Here, the individual begins
to develop role-taking abilities in at least a rudimentary form, so that
his perceptions are more sensitive and his behavior is more mature
than at the preceding level. Level five involves the integration of continuity, in which the person develops awareness of stable action patterns in himself and others. The person at this level perceives continuity in the world of experience. The last two levels describe persons
who are quite well socialized, so that level six involves the integration of
self-consistency. Here the actor develops well-honed perceptions of the
differences between his core self and the social roles which he plays
from time to time. His behavior is more mature, he is more stable, and
his relations with others are more satisfactory than are those of persons
at lower levels. Finally, individuals at level seven are rarely if ever encountered in the real world, according to the authors. This level involves the integration of relativity, movement, and change (18:375–85).

Taking the Interpersonal Maturity Levels formulation first only as
a theory of socialization and personality development, it can be seen
that it is far from a novel theory. Indeed, as the authors themselves
acknowledge, it is in the tradition of symbolic interactional, Cooley-
Mead arguments about socialization. The theory seems plausible
enough in general terms, and there is little doubt that some kind of
cumulative process of interpersonal maturity development does occur.
The formal structure of the theoretical statement is relatively vague
and loose, but that is generally true of socialization arguments, so that
one cannot single this one out on that score. The major query which
might be raised about this formulation as a socialization theory is
whether the hypothesized elements or aspects of the various levels always go together as a package. Along the same line, one might ask
whether it is the case that individuals must necessarily proceed through
all the aspects of each level in order to attain a higher level of maturity.

Actually, no research has been conducted on the socialization theory, so that the authors simply assume that it is accurate and that it can be applied to delinquency. However, as will be apparent in a later section of this paper, there is some tangential evidence suggesting that the hypothesized elements of the various levels do not always occur together in real life.

Interpersonal Maturity, Criminality, and Delinquency

Interpersonal maturity theory is basically a personality development argument, but it has also been advanced as an explanation of criminality and delinquency. It constitutes a theory of criminal and delinquent behavior in that it has been argued that, somehow or another, persons at lower levels are often allocated to deviant roles, while, implicitly, those who are more mature are usually nondeviants. To quote the authors: "We do not believe that all who are described as immature along this scale will be delinquent, but we do predict that those who are immature are more likely to find themselves in difficulty and to be apprehended for delinquency than are others" (18:375).

In this original essay, the authors discussed the seven levels and also commented on the characteristics of adults who have remained at various of these stages, as well as of delinquents integrated at the various levels. In the case of adults, they contended that persons who are fixed at the first level are likely to be in the mental hospital, in hobo camps, or on skid road (9:429–32).[2] Those adults who are found at the second level are prone to see people as givers and to make unreasonable demands on them, so that presumably they are likely to be criminals in many cases. Adults at the third level are manipulative individuals who tend toward "con-man" kinds of adaptation (9:246–52),[3] while persons at the fourth level are likely to show a "tense, suspicious, bewildered, sometimes hostile, and always anxious personality, a person caught in a circular struggle with new and socially determined feelings of guilt" (18:382). Adults at the three higher levels of maturity are infrequently found in deviant conduct.

In the original essay on I-Levels, children at levels one through four were claimed to be frequently involved in delinquency, while youngsters at the fifth level were said to be infrequently implicated in misconduct, except perhaps in situationally determined lawbreaking. In more recent statements on I-Levels applied to delinquency, it is averred that most juvenile offenders fall into I-Levels two through four. In addition, recent elaborations of I-Levels notions have been made, in which subtypes within the several levels have been defined. Brief descriptions of the characteristics of delinquents at the several levels, along with the subtypes, are provided in the Appendix.

Some readers will no doubt notice the close resemblance of the I-Levels formulation on delinquency to the contentions of Harrison Gough concerning socialization deficiencies and criminality (12). Both of these are psychogenic arguments which maintain that delinquent roles and other deviant social positions are occupied by individuals who exhibit some degree of personality impairment, while nondeviant citizens are characterized by relatively healthy personalities. More than that, both argue that delinquency stems from interpersonal deficiencies; in other words, these are causal arguments. Both theories take an "other things being equal" stance, in which it is held that persons of low social maturity will usually be deviants, while individuals of high maturity will be conformists if various social contingencies do not intervene. But because of these contingencies, not all low-maturity individuals get into trouble, while some high-maturity persons may engage in deviance. Thus Gough asserts that "discrepancies are of course to be expected in individual instances between the sociological baseline and the psychological measurement if for no other reason than that the culture will occasionally make mistakes, in putting some men in prisons and others in positions of trust and responsibility" (12:23).

I-Levels and Delinquency: Validity of the Theory

As indicated above, no research test of the general theory of interpersonal maturity has been carried out in which efforts have been made to discover whether the various stages and internal elements occur as hypothesized. But if one assumes for the moment that the theory has been operationalized, investigated, and found to be correct, what then can be said about it as applied to delinquency?

The view of Sullivan, Grant, and Grant was that delinquents are usually at low levels of interpersonal maturity and that their lawbreaking is the product of immaturity, while nonoffenders are more mature, which accounts for their conformist behavior. But this is an untested assumption. No one has subjected the I-Levels formulation to research in order to discover whether delinquents truly are more immature than nondelinquents. While there is some plausibility to the argument, other lines of contention are also plausible possibilities. Among the possibilities are these: First, perhaps both delinquents and conformists are at higher levels of maturity than suggested by the theory, that is, both groups may be equally mature. Or perhaps both lawbreakers and nonoffenders are generally immature, with little variation in maturity between the two groups. In either of these cases, the theory would have to be rejected as an explanation of delinquency. Still another possibility is that there are some personality correlates of delinquency which differentiate offenders from nondelinquents, but they may be different from those set forth in I-Levels theory (8).[4] Empirical testing is the only way to choose among these possibilities. One cannot validate any single interpretation simply by fiat.

One issue which would quickly emerge were the theory of interpersonal maturity levels and delinquency subjected to research is that having to do with "hidden delinquents." There is an abundance of evidence that most youths who remain free from the label of "official delinquent" nonetheless do engage in lawbreaking conduct. What does the theory predict about these youths? The Sullivan, Grant, and Grant essay seemed to imply that these youngsters will be more mature than official delinquents. On this point, it can be argued that "hidden delinquents" remain undetected in considerable part because their acts of misconduct are relatively petty ones, and, indeed, the empirical evidence points to the relatively innocuous character of much hidden delinquency. Thus it may be claimed that relatively petty offenders are relatively mature interpersonally, differing in this regard from officially designated delinquents, and that their superior maturity serves to insulate them against serious lawbreaking. The point of this commentary is that the question of categories of delinquents to whom the formulation applies has not been satisfactorily addressed, so that there is an ambiguity which must be cleared up before any satisfactory test of the argument can be carried out.

Although no specific test of this theory applied to delinquency has been conducted, there is a collection of psychogenic research that does bear upon the argument and that can be utilized in arriving at a tentative estimate of its accuracy.[5] The thrust of most of this material is in the direction of suggesting that marked personality differences do not exist between delinquents and nondelinquents, notwithstanding all of the speculative claims to the contrary, claims advanced by social workers, psychologists, and psychiatrists. The work with the Minnesota Multiphasic Personality Inventory is a case in point. Offenders and nonoffenders did not turn out to vary markedly on the personality dimensions measured by that inventory (9:155). It is also possible to address more specific psychogenic claims in the I-Levels theory by examining other studies which have been conducted. Thus it is contended that, among Maturity-Level-four cases, neurotic delinquents are common, while it is implied that neurotics are less frequent among nondelinquents. Yet in one well-known and large-scale piece of research by the Gluecks, the nonoffenders in that study turned out to be more frequently neurotic than the lawbreakers, who were training-school wards and serious delinquents (11:240–43).

Along a somewhat related line, the I-Levels argument contends that relatively immature delinquents at level three are often manipulators. Here one might raise the question, similar to that for adults, as to whether manipulative individuals are actually more interpersonally sophisticated than this theory asserts. In much the same way, the empirical accuracy of the characterization of cultural conformist youths as at low levels of interpersonal maturity is open to question.

I-LEVELS THEORY IN APPLICATION

The Measurement of I-Levels

As noted earlier, the I-Levels framework has been applied in the Community Treatment Project, in which some wards who would normally be institutionalized are instead released directly on parole. It is also being employed in institutional treatment in the Northern Youth Center, while it was also used in the Preston Typology Study at the Preston School of Industry.

The California Youth Authority workers associated with these cases of I-Levels applications contend that nearly all Youth Authority wards do fall into one of the nine subtypes identified above. These researchers have managed to sort delinquents into these categories in the studies enumerated above. Thus, what is to be said about the criticisms advanced above? Perhaps delinquents truly are immature youths with marked interpersonal liabilities (although nondelinquents may also exhibit these liabilities). At any rate, this is the conclusion suggested in these several projects in which delinquent wards have been classified by I-Level.

The reader should be warned against quick acceptance of the conclusion that official delinquents are interpersonally immature. The diagnostic procedures used in the projects above are not highly objective ones about which one can have complete confidence. While it is probably necessary to utilize clinical, subjective techniques for assigning wards to diagnostic categories, at least in the early stages of differential treatment efforts, such procedures do introduce an element of doubt about the accuracy of diagnostic assignments.

In the Community Treatment Project, assignment of wards to types is based on semistructured interviews by two research workers. In the Preston Typology Study, an interview was conducted with each ward, combined with scores on a personality inventory and a sentence-completion test. The "judges" who made assignments of youths to I-Levels categories are not research skeptics, but instead are workers who are predisposed to the view that delinquents do fall into low levels of interpersonal maturity. Given these facts, one should not be surprised to find that wards were successfully sorted into maturity types. However, there is room to wonder if the same results would be obtained if diagnoses were attempted by skeptical observers not persuaded of the validity of I-Levels theory.

One indication of ambiguities in the I-Levels classification applied to delinquents comes from the Community Treatment Project. In one report on problems encountered in the San Francisco portion of this study, the investigators noted that a number of boys were found who did not seem to fit well within the diagnostic categories. Many of them seemed to exhibit characteristics cross-cutting several of the interpersonal maturity levels. The investigators also indicated that a good deal of difficulty was encountered in implementing the differential treatment program (16).[6]

Community Treatment Project

The Community Treatment Project was initiated in 1961 in several communities in California. In it, youths are diagnosed by I-Levels and the subtypes while at the Youth Authority reception center. Random assignment is then employed in order to allocate wards either to community treatment or to an institution. Those who are sent to training schools receive the regular institutional program, but the community treatment subjects receive differential treatment. The general outlines of the differential treatment tactics are indicated below:

> The essence of the treatment plan with I_2s is to place the youth in a supportive environment (usually foster home) and to attempt to meet some of his unmet dependency needs while helping him learn to perceive more accurately and respond more appropriately to the demands of society and its institutions. The treatment strategies for all I_3 subtypes involve an adult (the community agent) expressing concern for the youth by controlling his behavior. Group treatment is also used, taking advantage of the I_3's dependence on peers, in order to control behavior, change delinquent attitudes, and increase social perceptiveness. Treatment for the I_4 subtypes works toward reducing internal conflicts and increasing insight into personal and family dynamics which play a part in the acting-out behavior. These goals may be reached through family group therapy, individual psychotherapy, or group therapy. These treatment descriptions are much oversimplified since treatment goals and methods vary considerably among subtypes within maturity levels [2:3–4].

To date, results of the Community Treatment Project are available for that portion of it which took place in Sacramento and Stockton. The findings on parole-violation rates show that, for parolees from community treatment and regular institutional programs, those who had been exposed to parole for fifteen months had a violation rate of 30 percent in the case of community treatment wards and 51 percent in the instance of control-group cases. For parolees who had been exposed to parole for two years, the parole violation rates were 40 percent for the community project delinquents and 61 percent for the control-group cases (3:30). At first glance, these findings suggest that community treatment is an effective alternative to institutionalization, but, more importantly, they also suggest that the I-Levels pattern of differential treatment is pragmatically useful, contributing to increased correctional efficacy.

However, a cautionary recommendation is in order. Perhaps the I-Levels scheme is associated with marked improvements in correctional practice. Lerman has observed, however, that the community program parolees committed more offenses during the parole period than did the controls, so that over the fifteen-month period the community treatment parolees averaged 2.81 offenses, while the controls showed an average of 1.61 offenses. Lerman noted that the proportion of control-group offenders who had their paroles revoked for offenses of low or medium seriousness was higher than for the community treatment group, so that the total violation rate of the control-group offenders was higher. In Lerman's view, it is probable that, while community treatment agents saw more delinquencies on the part of project youths but took official action less frequently in their cases, the overall failure rates for boys in the two programs may well have been about the same (15:57–58). The Community Treatment Project results are misleading, for it appears that a kind of "halo" effect was involved, in which the experimental subjects were allowed more leeway in the form of misconduct in the parole period than were the control cases. The community program, and the I-Levels system involved in it, may not be markedly more productive of correctional success than other approaches.

One footnote from the community project is that this endeavor involved the matching of types of offenders, types of treatment, and types of correctional agents. The linking of offenders, tactics, and workers is also involved in other programs using the I-Levels framework, so that it ought to be noted that this model of differential treatment is an exceedingly complex one.

The Preston Typology Study (14)

The Preston Typology Study involved wards committed to the Preston School of Industry during 1966 and 1967. In this project, boys were classified according to I-Levels categories, and assigned to treatment or control groups. The experimental subjects were then placed into one of six living units, each of which was designed to provide a special program for a particular level of youth. Also, the project involved an attempt to realign staff assignments so that workers would be placed in therapy situations compatible with their therapeutic "styles." A rather elaborate program of differential treatment involving types of wards, strategies, and workers was tried out.

The Preston Study results were not very encouraging, although they must be treated somewhat gingerly. Parole performance data are available on treated and control youth for the first six months of the parole period. Over this quite short time period, the experimental cases had a parole failure rate of 21.9 percent, contrasted to the rate of 23.5 percent for the control subjects. These findings do not lend much support to the view that the I-Levels program will markedly improve the efficacy of delinquent treatment endeavors.

Other Projects

The Northern Youth Center project being conducted in Stockton involves the assignment of wards either to an I-Levels differential treatment program or to a behavior-modification program. This experiment is designed to continue until 1972.

The Center for Training in Differential Treatment, operating in Sacramento, is funded by a National Institute of Mental Health grant. Its purpose revolves around the training of workers from various California county and state correctional agencies in the application of the I-Levels approach. The center is the device through which the diffusion of this scheme is being attempted in California.

I-LEVELS AND CORRECTIONAL REFORM

The commentary to this point has identified a number of places in the I-Levels theory in which critical ambiguities are located. In addition, the version of this argument applied to delinquency was subjected to scrutiny in terms of the available evidence on juvenile misconduct. Some doubt was cast upon the validity of this perspective as a causal framework. Finally, it has been suggested that the results to date from the utilization of this framework in California corrections are not markedly encouraging. However, there is another basic issue to be raised about the I-Levels approach, even if this system of differential treatment were shown to be effective.

If one puts aside the doubts raised above and assumes that the I-Levels system turns out to be effective in rehabilitative ventures, what then? What are the prospects for reforming correctional practice by introducing I-Levels in widespread fashion into correctional systems?

The President's Commission on Law Enforcement and Administration of Justice has made some incisive comments on differential treatment, to which one might pay heed. It states:

> A failure to view data in sufficiently complex fashion and to classify subjects accordingly in a way relevant to management and treatment may defeat attempts to secure differential treatment. . . . And it may

be that classifications sufficiently subtle and complex to avoid the pitfalls of overgeneralization and to be of real help in management and treatment will ultimately prove too cumbersome to serve their original purposes [20:22].

The I-Levels framework certainly qualifies as a sophisticated, even elegant one. This program requires that a complex diagnostic process be carried out. The approach recommends a large number of strategies or tactics of therapeutic intervention. Finally, it calls for a body of well-trained agents to apply the tactics. Moreover, the correctional workers themselves are to be sorted into types and matched with particular collections of offenders.

It has already been noted that American correctional systems are now staffed with a hodge-podge of workers who share little in common. It is to be anticipated that any effort to draw all of these agents into an I-Levels program would encounter considerable resistance, given their diverse backgrounds.

Perhaps it could be argued that the I-Levels system could ultimately prevail in corrections if new employees were trained in it. Over time, these workers might predominate in correctional systems. However, such an argument presupposes that correctional training will continue to be the responsibility of a highly educated cadre of professional workers. In point of fact, some recent developments in corrections suggest that, in the future, increased reliance will be placed on subprofessional or paraprofessional employees and perhaps even upon offenders in the staffing of rehabilitative ventures. The time may rapidly be approaching when correctional agencies will find it impossible to continue employing treatment workers with five or more years of college preparation.

If these observations are accurate, the pressing need may be for the simplest and most parsimonious diagnostic scheme, not for rich and elaborate ones, such as I-Levels. Then, too, correctional reform may depend more upon experimentation and innovation within separate, specific agencies than upon the imposition of a standardized differential treatment model. There may be little hope that we can stem the flow of lawbreakers into the correctional machinery unless we can find ways to put plain people to work doing straightforward things to and with offenders. The real need may be for less elegance rather than for more of it.

APPENDIX: Some Characteristics of Delinquents at Maturity Levels 2, 3, and 4

Maturity Level 2 (I_2).   The individual whose interpersonal understanding and behavior are integrated at this level is primarily involved with demands that the world take care of him. He sees others primarily as "givers" or "withholders" and has no conception of interpersonal refinement beyond this. He has poor capacity to explain, understand, or predict the behavior or reactions of others. He is not interested in things outside himself except as a source of supply. He behaves impulsively, unaware of anything except the grossest effects of his behavior on others.

Subtypes: (1) *Asocial, Aggressive* responds with active demands and open hostility when frustrated. (2) *Asocial, Passive* responds with whining, complaining, and withdrawal when frustrated.

Maturity Level 3 (I_3). The individual who is functioning at this level, although somewhat more differentiated than the I_2, still has social-perceptual deficiencies which lead to an underestimation of the differences among others and between himself and others. More than the I_2, he does understand that his own behavior has something to do with whether or not he gets what he wants. He makes an effort to manipulate his environment to bring about "giving" rather than "denying" response. He does not operate from an internalized value system but rather seeks external structure in terms of rules and formulas for operation. His understanding of formulas is indiscriminate and oversimplified. He perceives the world and his part in it on a power dimension. Although he can learn to play a few stereotyped roles, he cannot understand many of the needs, feelings, and motives of another person who is different from himself. He is unmotivated to achieve in a long-range sense or to plan for the future. Many of these features contribute to his inability to accurately predict the response of others to him.

Subtypes: (3) *Immature Conformist* responds with immediate compliance to whoever seems to have the power at the moment. (4) *Cultural Conformist* responds with conformity to specific reference-group delinquent peers. (5) *Manipulator* operates by attempting to undermine the power of authority figures and/or to usurp the power role for himself.

Maturity Level 4 (I_4). An individual whose understanding and behavior are integrated at this level has internalized a set of standards by which he judges his and others' behavior. He can perceive a level of interpersonal interaction in which individuals have expectations of each other and can influence each other. He shows some ability to understand reasons for behavior, some ability to relate to people emotionally and on a long-term basis. He is concerned about status and respect, and is strongly influenced by people he admires.

Subtypes: (6) *Neurotic, Acting-out* responds to underlying guilt with attempts to "outrun" conscious anxiety and condemnation of self. (7) *Neurotic, Anxious* responds with symptoms of emotional disturbance to conflict produced by feelings of inadequacy and guilt. (8) *Situational Emotional Reaction* responds to immediate family or personal crisis by acting-out. (9) *Cultural Identifier* responds to identification with a deviant value system by living out his delinquent beliefs.

SOURCE: California Youth Authority, *The Community Treatment Project after Five Years* (Sacramento: California Department of the Youth Authority, 1968), pp. 3–4.

NOTES

[1] A general review of typological efforts in the area of delinquency can be found in Ferdinand (5).

[2] One might observe that this gratuitous assignment of skid-roaders and other vagrants to a category of being quite unsocialized fails to square with the facts concerning life patterns among skid-road residents (9:429–32).

[3] Again, much of the evidence on con-men portrays them as considerably more sophisticated in interpersonal terms than these authors grant (9:246–52).

[4] This is the view favored by the author. Thus we have argued elsewhere that automobile thief-joyriders may be responding to problems of masculine identity (8:301–8).

[5] Much of this research is reviewed in Gibbons (6, 7, 9).

[6] Another revealing study is Butler and Adams (1). In this investigation, girls in a training school were assigned to I-Levels by a staff member using interview and case-history information. About 20 percent of the girls were later re-assigned, on the argument that they had initially been misclassified. More critically, an attempt was made to identify these I-Levels through the use of an objective personality test. The behavioral types developed out of this interview, through Q-factor analysis, did not correlate with the clinically derived I-Levels assignments.

REFERENCES

1. Butler, Edgar W., and Adams, Stuart N. "Typologies of Delinquent Girls: Some Alternative Approaches." *Social Forces* 44 (March 1966): 401–7.

2. California. California Youth Authority. *The Community Treatment Project after Five Years.* Sacramento: California Department of the Youth Authority, 1968.

3. ———. *The Status of Current Research in the California Youth Authority.* Sacramento: California Department of the Youth Authority, 1968.

4. California. San Mateo County Probation Department. Adult Division. "The San Mateo County Typological Treatment Study." Preliminary research report. Redwood City, Calif., 1968.

5. Ferdinand, Theodore N. *Typologies of Delinquency.* New York: Random House, 1966.

6. Gibbons, Don C. *Changing the Lawbreaker.* Englewood Cliffs, N.J.: Prentice-Hall, 1965.

7. ———. *Delinquent Behavior.* Englewood Cliffs, N.J.: Prentice-Hall, 1970.

8. ———. "Problems of Causal Analysis in Criminology: A Case Illustration." *Journal of Research in Crime in Delinquency* 3 (January 1966): 301–8.

9. ———. *Society, Crime, and Criminal Careers.* Englewood Cliffs, N.J.: Prentice-Hall, 1968.

10. ———. "Some Notes on Treatment Theory in Corrections." *Social Service Review* 36 (September 1962): 295–305.

11. Glueck, Sheldon, and Glueck, Eleanor. *Unraveling Juvenile Delinquency.* Cambridge, Mass.: Harvard University Press, 1951.

12. Gough, Harrison. "Theory and Measurement of Socialization." *Journal of Consulting Psychology* 24 (February 1960): 23–30.

13. Hartjen, Clayton A., and Gibbons, Don C. "An Empirical Investigation of a Criminal Typology." *Sociology and Social Research* 54 (October 1969), 56–62.

14. Jesness, Carl, "Typology and Treatment." *California Youth Authority Quarterly* 19 (Summer 1966): 17–29.
15. Lerman, Paul. "Evaluative Studies of Institutions for Delinquents: Implications for Research and Social Policy." *Social Work* 13 (July 1968): 55–64.
16. Palmer, Theodore B.; Neto, Virginia; Johns, Dennis A.; Turner, James K.; and Pearson, John W. *Community Treatment Project, An Evaluation of Community Treatment for Delinquents: Seventh Progress Report, Part I, The Sacramento-Stockton and the San Francisco Experiments.* Sacramento: California Department of the Youth Authority, 1968.
17. Stonewall Jackson School. "An Empirical Evaluation of Don C. Gibbons' Typologies of Juvenile Delinquency and Robert K. Merton's Theory of Reference Groups." Concord, N.C., 1968.
18. Sullivan, Clyde; Grant, Marguerite Q.; and Grant, J. Douglas. "The Development of Interpersonal Maturity: Applications to Delinquency." *Psychiatry* 20 (November 1957): 373–85.
19. United States. Department of Health, Education, and Welfare. National Clearinghouse for Mental Health Information. *Typological Approaches and Delinquency Control: A Status Report.* Washington, D.C., 1967.
20. ————. President's Commission on Law Enforcement and Administration of Justice. *Task Force Report: Corrections.* Washington, D.C.: Government Printing Office, 1967.

16

The Dynamics of I-Level Interviewing

EDWARD E. PEOPLES

Assistant Professor, Administration of Justice Department, San Jose
State University

INTRODUCTION

I-Level, described in the two previous articles as a diagnostic model for
the classification and treatment of offenders, is derived from a theory
of personality which postulates seven stages of integration—maturity
levels—; stages that describe the psychological development of all individuals. It assumes that individuals are different one from another, but
that regardless of their differences, each passes through these stages on
the way to full maturity.

Each stage is characterized by the interpersonal problems that are
inherent in it and that must be resolved by the individual before he can
move on to the next stage. An individual's level of maturity can become
fixed at any given stage of development if he is unable to resolve those
interpersonal problems. Both treatment and treater must relate to the
individual at his specific level of development in order to effect behavior change.

It is the stage of development, then, that is being classified by
I-Level rather than the individual, an important distinction to keep in
mind. This paper focuses on the classification process itself, not the
assumptions or implications of I-Level theory. It is designed to serve as
a practical model for counselors and assumes the validity of the I-Level
construct and the reality of the dynamics involved.

This article was written especially for this book; it is assumed that the reader is familiar
with the characteristics of each maturity level and the subtypes within each level detailed
by Palmer and Gibbons in the two previous essays. For additional information on I-Level
theory see Warren, Marguerite Q., "The Case For Differential Treatment of Delinquents," *The Annals of the American Academy of Political and Social Science,* January 1969.
The author expresses his appreciation to Dr. Warren for reading his article and for her
suggestions during its preparation.

173

CLASSIFICATION BY INTERVIEW

The most successful and frequently used method of classifying the level of one's maturity is through the nondirective interview. The following steps are suggested as a guide in applying this method.

1. Arrange an appointment with the client in the agency office, the jail, or juvenile hall, which will allow for an uninterrupted period of approximately two hours. Ideally, the adjudication of the client has been completed and some minimum agent-client relationship developed. At least the two have met and talked and, hopefully, developed some level of mutual trust. This is ideal because it will create a more open climate during the interview, but it is not absolutely necessary. Successful interviews can be conducted with an offender who is awaiting sentence or disposition, and to whom the agent is a total stranger.

2. Before the interview begins, arrange the chairs so that the agent and client sit across the desk from each other, or so they sit opposite each other in the room. These positions are important only because the client will want to watch the agent's movements and facial expressions in the hope of gleening cues that will provide him some direction in responding to questions (direction that the agent must not provide).

3. The interview is recorded to allow for later classification by the agent, or preferably by a group of agents. No attempt is made during the interview to classify the client's maturity level because assumptions made early on may mitigate against the agent's efforts to make the interview comprehensive. Place the tape recorder (or video tape) in obvious view of the client and make it clear to him that everything will be recorded. Explain to him that the purpose of the interview is to allow the agent to get to know the client as a person and to provide the broad understanding that the agent feels is necessary to work effectively with the client under supervision.

4. Spend a few minutes in casual conversation so that both feel comfortable with each other. It is not necessary, however, that the client feel completely relaxed and open. Some degree of anxiety will always be present, but that does not matter. It does not even matter if the client tells lies throughout the entire interview. The essence of his responses will not be distorted in either event.

5. Turn on the recorder, adjust the volume, and begin the interview. It is essential that the style of the interviewer be nondirective. That is, the agent must phrase his questions in a manner that is absolutely value free and does not contain implied an-

swers or suggest expected responses. (Wrong: "Don't you agree that your father has been patient and fair with you?" Or, "Do you feel that your father has been patient and fair with you?" Or, "Don't you realize that what you did was wrong?" Or, "Do you realize that what you did was wrong?") In all of these examples the socially accepted answer is implied. The agent's values become obvious to the client, and it is obvious to him that the agent expects the good little boy to answer yes.

Questions must be open ended and neutral. (Right: "How do you feel you are treated by your father?" Or, "Tell me something about the way your father treats you." Followed by, "How do you feel about that?" And, "How do you feel about the offense?") It is equally essential that the agent does not reveal how he feels about the client's answers. No matter what the client says, the agent must not react verbally or behaviorally with any judgment cues. A smile, a frown, a laugh, a growl, a raised eyebrow, a pointed finger, folded arms, or a simple nod of the head can offer the client a hint about how his answer has been received. As soon as he figures out what pleases or displeases the agent, he can respond with *appropriate* answers rather than *his* answers.

This nondirective approach is a most difficult skill for the I-Level interviewer to develop. In the traditional dialogue between agent and client, the agent is often anxious to convince the client about the error of his ways, to explain to the client how he *should* act and feel, and to sway the client around to his way of thinking. The I-Level interview is concerned with how the client thinks, feels and acts—with *his* perceptions and *his* way of responding to those perceptions—not with the agent's perceptions. It is absolutely crucial to the accuracy of the classifying process that the agent does not impose his personality on the client.

The best way to develop this interviewing skill is by practice. Do it, and after each interview play back the tape, listen, and let other agents listen. The counselor new to the I-Level method will probably be surprised to hear how much direction he gives by cuing in the client on how he *should* answer. The nondirective skill usually improves with each interview; and once the counselor perfects it, he may be surprised to find that he is *listening* to the client, perhaps for the first time, rather than *talking* to him.

THE INTERVIEW STRUCTURE

Although the nature of the interview is nondirective, the scope is structured by the content covered. Questions in each area are designed to elicit responses which will reveal the client's interpersonal maturity level and his subtype within that level. The maturity level classification is derived from an analysis of the client's perceptions of himself, of others, of his relationships with others and the relationships between others, and of the forces within his environment. His subtype is determined by analyzing the way he responds behaviorally to those perceptions. The following steps are suggested for structuring the interview.

1. In advance of the interview, outline the appropriate content areas to be covered with each client. For example, (1) Offense—current situation and related background; (2) Expectation of probation (parole); (3) Family attitudes toward offense; (4) Perspective on father; (5) Perspective on mother; (6) Perspective on siblings; (7) Perspective on husband or wife; (8) Perspective on friends; (9) Perspective on significant others; (10) Perspective on self; (11) Perspective on work/school; (12) Ways of handling conflict; (13) Ways of expressing feelings; (14) Attitudes toward discipline, rules, laws; (15) Perspective on family life, marriage, the future. Under each area, list appropriate questions that can be asked in the nondirective style.

2. Guide the interview in a natural flow. The suggested areas need not be covered in any particular sequence, nor is it necessary to complete the questions related to one area before beginning the next. The interviewer should attempt to link each new question to the response made to the previous one and yet allow for maximum spontaneity.

    Guiding the interview in this manner requires the counselor to develop the "skill of structured naturalness" to the point where the structure does not impose itself. Sometimes the client offers one response, then free-associates and digresses into another area; this digression may be spontaneous or it may be an effort to avoid discussing the content area at issue. Either way, the counselor should make a natural shift to the new area, allow the client to share his perspectives there, then by contrived association guide the interview back to questions on the incomplete areas.

3. Move from the general to the specific; from the broadest possible scope down to specific issues. And even more important in discovering the client's perspectives, ask for clarification of specific terms and concepts. The articulate client may mask his actual perceptions by responding with pat phrases, glib jargon, or general value statements—"good personality," "a good person," "an honest person," and "treated fairly" or "treated badly." The inarticulate client may need time and effort to find the words to express his true level of understanding.

Questions must be designed to get under the concept statements to determine the depth of the client's perceptions. Too often the counselor will take it for granted that the client comprehends the abstractions implied in the words he uses. Sample questions used to qualify the client's terms might include the following: What is a good personality? What does personality mean to you? How do you tell whether someone has a good or a bad personality? What does honesty mean to you? How do you tell whether a person is honest or not? What do you think makes a person honest, or want to be honest? What does being fair mean? How does a person treat you when he treats you fairly/badly? Why do you suppose he does that?

These questions are not simplistic. The quality and depth of the client's responses to them reveal his level of perception and integration. The interviewer must probe the meaning behind every concept, descriptive term, or value statement offered by the client. Make no assumptions about his level of comprehension on any issue, check it out.

To structure an interview and to effectively qualify the client's level of perception, require skills that can readily be developed by the combination of practice, feedback (listening to the tape), self-evaluation, and practice. The following format serves as a useful practice-guide in developing content areas and related questions.[1]

I-LEVEL INTERVIEW STRUCTURE

Content Area	*Questions*
Expectation of Probation/Parole	1. What does being on probation/parole mean to you?
	2. What do you expect it to be like being under someone's supervision?
	3. What do you think the purpose of probation/parole is?
	4. In what ways will being on probation/parole affect your life?
	5. Why do you think the court placed you on probation (parole board put you on parole)?
	6. Do you see any ways in which you can benefit from probation/parole?
	7. How do you think probation/parole can help you accomplish those (benefits, goals, etc.)?
	8. Do you think you need help in those areas?
	9. Why do you suppose someone like me (any officer) would help you?
	10. Forget about me for a minute. What kind of a person do you think goes into probation/parole work?
	11. Why do you suppose that is (what motivates him, what does he get out of it)?
Attitude toward Offense and Offensive Background	1. Tell me something about why you're here. How did you happen to get involved in (nature of offense)?
	2. How did you feel about what you were doing at the time?

Content Area	*Questions*
	3. How do you feel about it now?
	4. (for the incorrigible) What does being beyond control mean to you?
	5. Why do you suppose they say you're beyond control?
	(For the incorrigible, focus in on his behavior, how he interprets it, how he thinks his parents interpret it, how he feels about that, how they usually respond to his behavior, how he feels and reacts to that, etc.)
	7. Do you think you'll get involved in something like that again?
(Here, you are examining his need for outer controls)	8. Why don't you want to?
	9. How do you think you'll go about staying out of trouble?
	10. Why do you want to stay out of trouble?
	11. What does it mean to you when you get caught?
	12. Have you ever been in trouble before?
(Is he a follower)	13. How did you happen to get involved then?
	14. Whose idea was it this time?
Perspective on Friends	1. What kind of guys are they?
	2. Are any of them what you would consider real friends?
	3. (if he names one) I've never met Joe, tell me something about him. What kind of a guy is he?
	4. How about Charlie—what kind of a guy is he?
	5. Do you see any ways that Joe and Charlie are different? (question for perceptions of differences in motives, attitudes, behaviors, etc.)
(Is his selection determined by behavioral characteristics or inner qualities)	6. How do you go about selecting your friends? *Or* What do you look for in a friend? *Or* When you meet a guy, how do you go about deciding whether or not he's going to be a friend?
Self-Perspective	1. Do you have any idea what your friends (guys at school/work) think of you?
	2. How do you feel about that?
	3. How about yourself—what kind of a guy are you? (clarify and qualify)
	4. How do you suppose you got to be the way you are?
	5. If you had to list all the things about yourself that you like/dislike, what would you put first?
	6. Is there anything about yourself that you would like to change? How would you go about changing that?
	7. If you could see into the future, what kind of a person do you think you'll be in 10 years, 15, 20?
(Ways of behaving)	8. What sorts of things make you angry (sad, happy, etc.)?
	9. How do you usually express yourself when you're angry (sad, happy, frightened, etc.)?

Content Area	Questions

Content Area   *Questions*

10. Do you remember a situation in which you really got angry (happy, sad, frightened, etc.)? How did you react then?

11. When you really get angry at someone you like, what do you do?

12. Can you think of someone you really like/love? How do you go about letting him/her know how you feel?

Perspective on Girl/
Boy Friend/Mate

(Does the client discuss internal qualities, or merely describe external behavior?)

1. (For singles) Do you have a boy/girl friend now? What kind of a person is he/she? If necessary, preface this by stating: I don't know whether I'll ever meet her/him, but let's assume that I will. What sort of a person will he/she be? Describe the kind of person I'll meet.

2. (For marrieds) You're married aren't you? Tell me about your wife/husband. What kind of a person is he/she?

3. (For both) What are the qualities you like best about her/him?

4. Does she/he have any qualities that irritate you? What do you usually do when she/he does that? If you could, what do you feel you'd really like to do?

5. Have you had any other girl/boy friends? Tell me about her/him. Do you see any way that she/he is like (present girl/boy friend)?

6. Do you see any way they are different?

7. (For juveniles) When you get older, do you think you'll get married? What sort of a person do you want to marry? Describe, if you can, what you feel would be the ideal married life.

Perspective on Family

1. Have your parents ever mentioned the kind of person they want you to marry?

2. How about your own parents. How would you describe their marriage? How do they get along?

3. Do you think they're happy? What makes them happy?

4. Who does the disciplining in the family? What does he/she do when you do something wrong? How do you feel about that? What would you rather he/she do? Why do you suppose he/she does that?

5. Do your parents treat you differently? What do you mean?

6. Do your parents treat you differently from your (siblings)? How? Why do you suppose that is?

7. How do your parents feel about you getting into trouble? For marrieds: How does your wife/husband/children feel?

8. Do they treat you differently now than they did before?

Content Area	*Questions*
	9. What do you think they expect of you? Why? How do you know that?
	10. In what ways are your parents different as people?
Perspective on Father	1. How about your father? What sort of a person is he? How do other people (mother, friends, etc.) feel about him?
	2. How do you feel about him, now, as a father? Have you always felt that way about him? Why do you think you feel differently about him now?
	3. What qualities do you like best in him? Least? How do you suppose he came to be that way?
	4. Do you see any ways that you are like him? Different from him? Why do you suppose that is?
	5. How do you think your father feels about you? How do you know he feels that way? How do you go about telling how he feels? Why do you think he feels the way he does? Has he always felt that way?
	6. How does he feel about (any other family members, his friends, his beliefs and values, etc.)?
Perspective on Mother	1. What about your mother? What sort of a person is she? (Repeat all appropriate questions from perspective on father, above.)
Perspective on School/Teachers	1. Where do you attend school? How do you feel about school? Why? Why do you suppose you have to attend school?
	2. What subjects do you like best? Least? Why? What is it about them that you like/dislike?
	3. Do you have a favorite teacher? What kind of a person is he/she? What do you like about him/her? Why? Why do you suppose he/she is like that?
	4. Is there a teacher that you don't like—who do you like least? Why?
	5. How are the two teachers different? How are they alike? How do you account for that?
	6. How do you get along with the kids at school? Do you hang around with a few guys regularly, or do you mix with most everyone?
Perspective on Work	1. Paraphrase the questions on school, above.
Perspective on World and Future	1. How about your leisure time—what do you enjoy doing? Any special interests, hobbies, etc.? What is it about them that you enjoy? Do you think that is something that everyone likes to do? Why/why not? What makes people like different things?
	2. What kinds of activities bore you? Why? Why do you suppose others find them interesting (enjoyable)?
	3. What kind of a neighborhood do you live in? Do

Content Area   *Questions*

you like it there? Why/why not? If you had your choice where would you like to live? How is that different from where you live now?

4. Do you have any desire to travel—to see the country (world)? Where would you like to go? What do you think it would be like? What kind of people would you expect to find there?

5. Can you think of some place that you never want to go? Why? What kind of a person would like living in that sort of a place?

6. Where do you think you might live when you grow up (get older/settle down)?

7. What do you think it will be like when you grow up/settle down and get a place of your own? Is that how you want it to be? Do you see any ways that you can bring that about?

8. What else do you think your future holds? If you had complete control, and could plan your life to turn out the way you want, what would it be like? Do you have any plans now that prepare for the future?

Closing

1. Well, we've talked about a lot of things during this past hour. Is there anything more that you want to say?

2. Do you have any questions that you want to ask of me?

3. How did you feel answering all those questions and talking as we did? If you were to rate your feelings on a scale from comfortable to uncomfortable, how would you describe those feelings?

At this point, turn off the recorder and bring the meeting to a close with casual conversation that seems appropriate. The client will probably begin to experience some anxiety over the purpose of the interview and will begin to wonder what is in store for him as a result. He will want some feedback and some reassurance. The counselor's closing comment might be, "I appreciate your coming in (or taking the time) for this interview. I believe that it will be helpful to both of us. I'm going to think about our conversation and I would like you to do the same, and we can talk about it more at our next meeting. Why don't we get together next week, say Wednesday at about this same time, and we can discuss what each of us thinks is necessary regarding your probation/parole? If anything comes up in the meantime, give me a call."

THE CLASSIFICATION PROCESS

While the interview is still fresh in the agent's memory, he should record his impressions and describe behavior of the client that seems related to his verbal responses. Ideally, classification is accomplished by a group of interviewers who evaluate each other's interviews. First, the individual, or group, listens to the recording. The procedure then calls for each individual to record his observations of the client's responses on a chart divided into the various levels. Response statements characteristic of each level and subtype are categorized under the appropriate heading. At the end, the counselors compare notes and discuss the points of their evaluation. When working alone, the counselor must be doubly sure that he is approaching the process with complete objectivity.

Individuals usually fall into maturity levels 2, 3 or 4, and occasionally, 5.[2] Rarely does one find a client whose responses fall completely within any one integration level. However, a significant theme or characteristic perception level will emerge.

An individual who is characteristically an I_2 will not discuss internal qualities in himself or others. He can describe the behavior he sees in rather basic terms, and is not able to explain cause-and-effect relationships or the motives behind that behavior. He will evaluate others on the basis of whether they take from him or deny him, or give to him and do for him. Behaviorally, the passive subtype will describe his reactions to others in terms of whining, childish pleading, or complaining. The aggressive subtype is more impulsive and acts out to meet his needs. He has few inner controls and his basic method of coping in the world is: fear → flight; wants → takes; angry → strikes out.

There is a low positive relationship between intelligence and maturity level; and the character Lenny in Steinbeck's *Of Mice and Men* comes to mind in describing the I_2. Actually, the I_2 individual does not necessarily have a low level of intelligence; rather, he is fixed at a low maturity level because of emotional deprivation. He is starved for love: heavy nurturing love, both emotionally and physically, although more than love is required in his treatment.

The individual whose integration level is characteristically at I_3 offers an interesting challenge to the interviewer. He expresses some basic understanding of cause and effect in relationships with others, and he sees himself as a generator of responses in others. However, he feels that everyone's motives are the same as his own; he can describe, but he cannot explain, the overt behavior of others and considers people in terms of whether or not they are useful to him. Often, his favorite term is *nice*, but he cannot describe any internal qualities about individuals that makes them nice. They are nice if they do things for him, if they give him a chance, if they don't hassle him, or if he can get along with them.

The first time a counselor interviews an I_3 he is frustrated by the inability of the client to deal with abstracts.

Question: "What kind of a person is your father? How would you
  describe him?"
Answer: "Oh, he's a nice guy."
Question: "What do you mean by nice guy?"
Answer: "Oh, he has a good personality."
Question: What do you mean by good personality?"
Answer: "Well, he . . . a . . . I . . . a . . . I get along real well with him."

There is just no way that he can describe abstract qualities such as nice,
good, bad, fair, honest, or fine. He either will stammer and stall and
say, "I don't know," or he will describe some overt behavior about the
person that he likes. When asked to describe himself, he is at a total
loss and cannot go beyond physical or behavioral characteristics.

The I₃ has a need to define the structure and rules of whatever
situation he faces, and to determine who is in charge so that he can
either conform or manipulate. This attitude is evident in the Cfm and
Mp particularly from their behavior during the interview. They attempt to qualify every question so that they can give the appropriate
answer. A pattern emerges by their initial response to every question,
"Do you mean . . . ?" Also, they are particularly frustrated by the nondirective interview and grope frantically for cues from the interviewer
on how to respond.

The immature conformist subtype wants to please the interviewer;
and if given the direction that his answers should take, he will parrot all
the *right* responses. The manipulator subtype wants to figure out where
the interviewer is coming from so that he can con him. The conformist
is a follower and will project the responsibility for his problems onto
some external source, usually his peers. The manipulator assigns responsibility to anyone, and both place the responsibility for staying out
of trouble on the agent, on the conditions of probation or parole, on
their parents, or on the fact that they will not associate with certain
peers. They are not inner directed. Values are not internalized, but are
described as expedients to be used to get what they want from the
environment.

The I₃ has no concept of self beyond his behavior and he cannot
describe differences between other individuals except in terms of physical or behavioral characteristics. One friend is different from another
because he smokes, has long hair, or dresses a certain way. Occasionally, when asked to describe what qualities he looks for in a friend, he
responds with a travelogue; he sets the stage and describes a scenario in
detail of meeting someone and how that person acts. He responds in
this same manner when describing almost any interpersonal relationship. The manipulator, especially, cannot articulate ideas, concepts, or
qualities; he can only describe scenes and behavior.

The immature conformist cooperates during the interview and seems to enjoy it; often the manipulator will too. This is usually not true of the cultural conformist. He will show little respect for the interviewer, and will express hostility toward everything and everyone outside of his reference group—his gang. For him, the gang provides structure, rules, and his own identity.

The individual who is characteristically an I_4 has a definite self-concept. In fact, he has a need to express his uniqueness and will articulate who he is and how he is different from others. Unlike the I_3, the I_4 goes beyond a mere description of how others behave and makes a value judgment about their behavior. He expresses certain internalized values by which he judges himself and others as good or bad. These values are not necessarily socially acceptable or acceptable to the agent, but they are his.

Since the I_4 can appreciate differences, he can describe himself and others in a relative ranking of status or prestige, or in relation to an idealized model. He can also articulate how people change over time, and can perceive some future to his own life. In fact, he wants to improve, he wants things to get better, and he wants to measure up to his own expectations and to people he admires.

An obvious distinction between an I_3 and an I_4, which emerges during the interview, is the manner in which each handles guilt. The I_3 expresses contrition and remorse if he thinks it will serve a useful purpose. The I_4 will hurt inside when he has violated his standard, and he will be able to articulate clearly why he hurts.

The I_4 neurotic anxious (NX) has internal conflicts that result in him being in a constant state of free-floating anxiety. This feeling of anxiety is apparent from the descriptions he gives of interpersonal relationship situations. He is intropunitive, and a pattern of "poor-me, bad-me" characterizes his descriptions of those relationships. Behaviorally, he controls the expression of his anxiety by blaming himself and hurting inside.

The neurotic acting-out (NA) subtype projects the blame for his behavior onto others (bad-mother, bad-father, bad-agent). The other two I_4 subtypes express far less anxiety than the NX, and the interview with them reflects fewer internal conflicts. The cultural identifier (CI) often appears cool, calm, and friendly, while the situational emotional reactor (Se) is forthright and responsive, and describes his offense within the context of a unique life situation. The NX and NA show obvious internal problems and the need for outside help. The Se has himself together fairly well; he may need some temporary guidance through his immediate situation, but otherwise will be conflict free and self-directed.

In differentiating between the I_4 and I_5, the interviewer must focus on the client's conceptual abilities. The I_4 narcotic offender, or the defender of a cause, may be very articulate and offer a number of mature-sounding ideas and arguments. He will have some understanding of what they mean, but for the most part he is merely spouting popular jargon to justify his situation. The interviewer must probe beneath the rhetoric.

The I₅ has a commitment to his way of life, and really believes that his cause is noble. In discussing his life and his interpersonal relationships, he can give a wide range of abstract complexities, variables, behaviors, and attitudes and make any number of connections among them. He feels comfortable living in a turbulent world, and can cope with his own feelings and needs.

SUMMARY

The dynamics of I-Level interviewing brings out authentic feelings; with skillful application, the integration level and behavioral subtype of an individual can be differentiated. The techniques require the interviewer to develop three skills: (1) the nondirective style of questioning; (2) the ability to structure the content areas and to guide the interview through a process of "structured naturalness"; and (3) the perceptive ability to recognize and categorize the responses of the client.

This paper is intended to provide a how-to model for using the I-Level method. Once the integration level of the client has been classified, counseling strategies that relate to the needs of the client may be developed. The purpose of I-Level is not to pigeonhole or label individuals, but to provide a basis for understanding and relating to them on their own terms.

NOTES

[1] This interview outline is offered only as an example of how an interview might be structured. The structuring of areas and phrasing of questions should always relate to the nature of the situation, age and verbal skills of the client, and the significant others in his life.

[2] For additional details on level characteristics, refer to the appendix in Palmer's article, Chapter 14.

17

The Postulate of Interpersonal Needs: Description

WILLIAM C. SCHUTZ

Postulate 1. *The Postulate of Interpersonal Needs.*

a. Every individual has three interpersonal needs: inclusion, control, and affection.

b. Inclusion, control, and affection constitute a sufficient set of areas of interpersonal behavior for the prediction and explanation of interpersonal phenomena.

Explanation: In studying interpersonal behavior it is important to isolate the relevant variables. "People need people" serves as a good starting point, but, if the frontiers of knowledge are to recede, the next question must be investigated: "*In what ways* do people need people?"

The literature is not lacking in contestants for the mantle of "basic interpersonal variables." French (35) in a recent report summarizes the factors found in the factor analysis of various personality tests; he was able to reduce the number of apparently unrelated factors to forty-nine! Clearly this number is unmanageable for use in future investigation.

If the strictly statistical techniques for reducing variables still leaves forty-nine, some other exploratory method must be employed or at least added. A developmental approach to isolating variables has several appealing features. It seems promising to attempt to trace the developing individual through his sequence of typical interpersonal dealings, as a method of identifying the most basic interpersonal areas from which others are derivable. A consideration of this developmental process (discussed in more detail below), and some formulations presented by certain investigators, notably Bion, led the author to the conclusion that three interpersonal areas seemed to cover most interpersonal behavior. Later analysis of certain relevant literature . . . lent weight to

Reprinted by permission of the author and the publisher from William C. Schutz, *The Interpersonal Underworld* (reprint edition) (Palo Alto, California: Science & Behavior Books, 1966), pp. 13–33.

the proposition that three areas would prove adequate for fruitful investigation.

As the description of these three areas, here called inclusion, control, and affection, progressed, the fable came to mind of the blind men who disagreed over the characteristics of an elephant because each was exploring a different sector. It seems that various investigators are describing different aspects of the elephant—the three need areas—but apparently they are describing the same elephant. Thus clinicians discuss unconscious forces, small-group investigators describe overt behavior, child psychologists report on early interpersonal relations, and sociologists are interested in roles and group structures. But there seems to be heartening convergence toward the same set of variables, even though the approaches differ. The problem, then, is to give a complete description of the "elephant" and point out which aspects are being described by each observer. This chapter attempts to provide a complete description of the three basic interpersonal areas as basic needs, by showing how they appear in personality structure, in overt behavior, and in pathological behavior. . . .

INTERPERSONAL NEED

The concept of interpersonal need, often called "social need," has been discussed by many authors (65), but because it forms the central part of this book it is important to describe in what sense the term will be used.

The term "interpersonal" refers to relations that occur between people as opposed to relations in which at least one participant is inanimate. It is assumed that, owing to the psychological presence of other people, interpersonal situations lead to behavior in an individual that differs from the behavior of the individual when he is not in the presence of other persons. An optimally useful definition of "interpersonal" is one such that all situations classified as interpersonal have important properties in common—properties that are in general different from those of noninterpersonal situations. With this criterion for a definition in mind, the following specifies the meaning of "interpersonal situation." (The term "interpersonal" shall be used as equivalent to the term "group.")

An *interpersonal situation* is one involving two or more persons, in which these individuals take account of each other for some purpose, or decision, D. It is described from a particular point of reference, usually either that of one of the participants or of an outside observer. It is also specified as existing during a stated time interval. Thus a complete statement of an interpersonal situation has the form:

"From the standpoint of O (or A, or B), A takes account of B for decision D during time interval t_1 to t_n."

"*A* takes account of *B* for decision *D*" means that when *A* considers what alternative to select for decision *D* one criterion for his choice is his expectation of *B*'s response to his choice. This expectation does not require that *A* make a different decision because of the influence of *B*; it simply means that his criteria for making the decision are supplemented.

For example, if a man who is sitting on a bus trying to decide whether or not to give up his seat to an elderly lady considers the reaction of the attractive young woman across the aisle, he is taking account of the young woman whether or not he gives up his seat. From *his* point of view the relation is interpersonal, since he takes account of her. From the standpoint of the young woman the situation may not be interpersonal at all, since she may not even be aware of his presence. Further, *A* may take account of *B* for one decision, for example, giving up a bus seat, as in the previous example, but not for another, for example, deciding which cobbler to patronize a week later. In addition, the degree to which *A* takes account of *B* varies with time. Our bus rider may be taking account of the lady during the bus ride (i.e., t_1 to t_n) but not at all when watching television that evening (i.e., after t_n).

The type of investigation will determine which point of reference for defining the term "interpersonal" will be most useful. Sometimes it is useful to consider an interpersonal situation from the standpoint of an individual, as when we speak of an interpersonal need. Sometimes it is more advantageous to consider a situation interpersonal only if the "taking account of" relation is reciprocal, that is, perceived by both members of a dyadic (two-person) relation. . . . Sometimes the point of view of observers will decide whether a situation is interpersonal, regardless of the reports of the individuals involved in the relation. For conceptual clarity the important requirement in describing an interpersonal relation is that the point of reference be specified.

The phrase "face-to-face" used frequently by other writers when defining "interpersonal" or "group" has been omitted from the present definition. As shall be elaborated below, the property of physical presence is an important variable within the scope of interpersonal behavior, closely related to the area of inclusion. Further, it is often useful to consider situations as interpersonal in which behavior is determined by *expectations* of the behavior of others, even if the others are not physically present. It therefore seems more useful to leave the term "interpersonal" free of the face-to-face condition and consider as a separate problem the effect of that condition on behavior.

The other term in the phrase under discussion is "need." A "need" is defined in terms of a situation or condition of an individual the nonrealization of which leads to undesirable consequences. An interpersonal need is one that may be satisfied only through the attainment of a satisfactory relation with other people. The satisfaction of a need is a necessary condition for the avoidance of the undesirable consequences of illness and death. A discrepancy between the satisfaction of an interpersonal need and the present state of an organism engenders a feeling in the organism that shall be called *anxiety*.

There is a close parallel between biological needs and interpersonal needs, in the following respects:

1. A biological need is a requirement to establish and maintain a satisfactory relation between the organism and its *physical* environment. An interpersonal need is a requirement to establish a satisfactory relation between the individual and his *human* environment. A biological need is not satisfied by providing unlimited gratification. An organism may take in too much water and drown, as well as too little water and die of thirst. The need is satisfied by establishing an equilibrium between the amount of water inside and outside the organism. The same is true for the "commodities" exchanged between people. An individual's needs may be unfulfilled either by having, for example, too much control over his human environment and hence too much responsibility, or too little control, hence not enough security. He must establish a satisfactory relation with his human environment with respect to control.

2. Nonfulfillment of a biological need leads to physical illness and sometimes death. Nonfulfillment of an interpersonal need leads to mental (or interpersonal) illness and sometimes death. Unsatisfactory personal relations lead directly to difficulties associated with emotional illness. Death, either through suicide or resulting from the more general loss of motivation for life, results when interpersonal dissatisfaction is prolonged.

3. The organism has characteristic modes, which are temporarily successful, of adapting to lack of complete satisfaction of biological needs. The organism also has characteristic ways, which are temporarily successful, of adapting to nonsatisfaction of interpersonal needs. For the interpersonal situation the terms "conscious" and "unconscious" needs are sometimes used to describe the phenomena at issue.

The distinction between a conscious and an unconscious need finds a parallel in a biological condition such as drug addiction. In drug addiction the immediate (conscious) need is to satisfy the immediate craving and to adjust the body chemistry so that the pain is reduced. The more basic (unconscious) need is to adjust the body chemistry back to the state where the drug is no longer required. The pain or anxiety felt when the organism is in a situation which does not allow for the satisfaction of these two needs is different in each case. In the first there is the immediate deprivation, analogous to an interpersonal situation in which an individual's characteristic psychological adjustment mechanisms (for example, defenses) cannot operate. To illustrate, if denial were the defense used by an individual in the affection area and he were placed in a situation in which close personal relations were called for, he would feel an *immediate anxiety* caused by the discrepancy between the demands of the situation and his most comfortable behavior pattern. The more *basic anxiety* or interpersonal imbalance stemming from the general inadequacy of the defense to ward off the need for affection is analogous to the physical discomfort caused by the discrepancy between the chemical balance produced by the drug addiction and the normal chemical balance.

This analogy assumes a particular interpersonal relation that optimally satisfies interpersonal needs, parallel to an optimal chemical balance. This assumption is made, although it is difficult to test. Perhaps it parallels the condition in which the psychoanalyst attempts to place his patient. The analyst has a conception of an optimal psychological condition for a given individual toward which the person strives. This condition goes deeper than the reinforcement of the patient's defense mechanisms, which protect him from undesirable impulses. The optimal state is one in which defenses are only minimally required. It is this psychological state that is analogous to the concept of an optimal interpersonal relation.

These parallels between the interpersonal and biological needs will be specified more precisely in the following discussion. Other aspects of this problem could be mentioned at this point, such as the phylogenetic continuity of interpersonal needs, their universality cross-culturally, and possible physiological correlates. However, this would take the discussion too far afield. The main point is that in many important ways interpersonal needs have properties closely parallel to those of biological needs.

INCLUSION, CONTROL, AND AFFECTION

Now comes the problem of describing the elephant, that is, providing a complete description of interpersonal variables sufficient to provide a framework for integration and future investigation in the field.

To construct such a schema it is necessary to determine the most relevant parameters for describing important aspects of the interpersonal variables. These parameters may then be used as the classification variables for generating a matrix to encompass the interpersonal behavior of interest. This process is called "substructing" by Lazarsfeld and Barton (55), and "facet analysis" by Guttman (45). It has the virtue of providing all possible combinations of parameter values so that omissions or duplications are easily recognized.

The parameters chosen should delineate salient differences worthy of preservation in personality description. Differences on these parameters represent important behavior differences which are helpful, even necessary, when behavioral characteristics are related to external factors, for example, childhood experiences, productivity, compatibility, leadership. The matrix generated by the parameters represents the *types of available data*. The methods of obtaining the data (such as introspection, questionnaire, observation, projective test) are independent of the matrix. Any method of data collection is permissible for any type of data. The parameters:

1. *Observability*—the degree to which an action of an individual is observable by others. This parameter is dichotomized into *action* and *feeling*. An action is usually more observable to outsiders, a feeling usually more observable to the self.
2. *Directionality*—the direction of the interaction with respect to originator and target. This parameter is trichotomized into a) self toward other, b) other toward self, and c) self toward self. The last category is interpersonal in the sense that it represents interaction between the self and others who have been interiorized early in life.
3. *Status of Acion*—whether the behavior is in the inclusion, control, or affection area.
4. *State of Relation*—whether the relation is desired, ideal, anxious or pathological.

Table 1 summarizes the terms and concepts discussed. . . . This table, in a sense, is the "elephant" (see p. 192).

The Three Interpersonal Needs

The interpersonal need for inclusion is defined behaviorally as the need to establish and maintain a satisfactory relation with people with respect to interaction and association. "Satisfactory relation" includes (1) a psychologically comfortable relation with people somewhere on a dimension ranging from originating or initiating interaction with all people to not initiating interaction with anyone; (2) a psychologically comfortable relation with people with respect to eliciting behavior from them somewhere on a dimension ranging from always initiating interaction with the self to never initiating interaction with the self.

On the level of feelings the need for inclusion is defined as the need to establish and maintain a feeling of mutual interest with other people. This feeling includes (1) being able to take an interest in other people to a satisfactory degree and (2) having other people interested in the self to a satisfactory degree.

With regard to the self-concept, the need for inclusion is the need to feel that the self is significant and worth while.

TABLE 2-1. Matrix of Relevant Interpersonal Data—"The Elephant"

		INCLUSION			CONTROL			AFFECTION		
		Self to Other (Actions)	Other to Self (Reactions)	Self to Self	Self to Other (Actions)	Other to Self (Reactions)	Self to Self	Self to Other (Actions)	Other to Self (Reactions)	Self to Self
DESIRED INTERPERSONAL RELATIONS (NEEDS)	Act	Satisfactory relation re interaction and inclusion behavior 1			Satisfactory relation re power and control behavior 19			Satisfactory relation re love and affection behavior 37		
	Feel	Satisfactory relation re feelings of mutual interest 2			Satisfactory relation re feelings of mutual respect 20			Satisfactory relation re feelings of mutual affection 38		
IDEAL INTERPERSONAL RELATIONS	Act	Social 3	People include me 4		Democrat 21	People respect me 22		Personal 39	People are friendly to me 40	
	Feel	I am interested in people 5	People are interested in me 6	Feeling that I am significant 15	I respect people 23	People respect me 24	Feeling that I am responsible 33	I like people 41	People like me 42	Feeling that I am lovable 51
ANXIOUS INTERPERSONAL RELATIONS (ANXIETIES)	Too much activity — Act	Over-social 7	Social-compliant 8		Autocrat 25	Rebel 26		Over-personal 43	Personal-compliant 44	
	Too much activity — Feel	I am not *really* interested in people 9	People aren't *really* interested in me 10	I am insignificant (I don't know who I am; I am nobody) 16	I don't trust people 27	People don't trust me 28	I am incompetent (I am stupid, irresponsible) 34	I don't *really* like people 45	People don't *really* like me 46	I am unlovable (I am no good, rotten bastard) 52
	Too little activity — Act	Under-social 11	Counter-social 12		Abdicrat 29	Submissive 30		Under-personal 47	Counter-personal 48	
	Too little activity — Feel	I am not interested in people 13	People are not interested in me 14		I don't *really* respect people 31	People don't *really* respect me 32		I don't like people 49	People don't like me 50	
PATHOLOGICAL INTERPERSONAL RELATIONS	Too Much	Psychotic 17			Obsessive-compulsive 35			Neurotic 53		
	Too Little	(Schizophrenia) 18			Psychopath 36			Neurotic 54		

The interpersonal need for control is defined behaviorally as the need to establish and maintain a satisfactory relation with people with respect to control and power. "Satisfactory relation" includes (1) a psychologically comfortable relation with people somewhere on a dimension ranging from controlling all the behavior of other people to not controlling any behavior of others and (2) a psychologically comfortable relation with people with respect to eliciting behavior from them somewhere on a dimension ranging from always being controlled by them to never being controlled by them.

With regard to feelings, the need for control is defined as the need to establish and maintain a feeling of mutual respect for the competence and responsibleness of others. This feeling includes (1) being able to respect others to a satisfactory degree and (2) having others respect the self to a satisfactory degree.

The need for control, defined at the level of perceiving the self, is the need to feel that one is a competent, responsible person.

The interpersonal need for affection is defined behaviorally as the need to establish and maintain a satisfactory relation with others with respect to love and affection. Affection always refers to a two-person (dyadic) relation. "Satisfactory relation" includes (1) a psychologically comfortable relation with others somewhere on a dimension ranging from initiating close, personal relations with everyone to originating close, personal relations with no one; (2) a psychologically comfortable relation with people with respect to eliciting behavior from them on a dimension ranging from always originating close, personal relations toward the self, to never originating close, personal relations toward the self.

At the feeling level the need for affection is defined as the need to establish and maintain a feeling of mutual affection with others. This feeling includes (1) being able to love other people to a satisfactory degree and (2) having others love the self to a satisfactory degree.

The need for affection, defined at the level of the self-concept, is the need to feel that the self is lovable.

This type of formulation stresses the interpersonal nature of these needs. They require that the organism establish a kind of equilibrium, in three different areas, between the self and other people. In order to be anxiety-free, a person must find a comfortable behavioral relation with others with regard to the exchange of interaction, power, and love. The need is not wholly satisfied by having others respond toward the self in a particular way; nor is it wholly satisfied by acting toward others in a particular fashion. A satisfactory balance must be established and maintained.

Inclusion, Control, and Affection Behavior

Thus far these key terms have been discussed only from the standpoint of their status as interpersonal needs. Since the value of the theory is dependent to a large extent on the cogency and clarity of these terms, it is important to describe them as fully as possible. . . .

Inclusion behavior is defined as behavior directed toward the satisfaction of the interpersonal need for inclusion.

Control behavior is defined as behavior directed toward the satisfaction of the interpersonal need for control.

Affection behavior is defined as behavior directed toward the satisfaction of the interpersonal need for affection.

In general, *inclusion behavior* refers to association between people. Some terms that connote a relation that is primarily positive inclusion are "associate," "interact," "mingle," "communicate," "belong," "companion," "comrade," "attend to," "member," "togetherness," "join," "extravert." Some terms that connote lack of, or negative, inclusion, are "exclusion," "isolate," "outsider," "outcast," "lonely," "detached," "withdrawn," "abandoned," "ignored."

The need to be included manifests itself as wanting to be attended to, to attract attention and interest. The classroom hellion who throws erasers is often objecting mostly to the lack of attention paid him. Even if he is given negative affection he is partially satisfied, because at least someone is paying attention to him.

In groups, people often make themselves prominent by talking a great deal. Frequently they are not interested in power or dominance but simply prominence. The "joker" is an example of a prominence seeker, very much as is the blond actress with the lavender convertible.

In the extreme, what is called "fame" is primarily inclusion. Acquisition of fame does not imply acquisition of power or influence: witness Marilyn Monroe's attempt to swing votes to Adlai Stevenson. Nor does fame imply affection: Al Capone could hardly be considered a widely loved figure. But fame does imply prominence, and signifies interest on the part of others.

From another standpoint, behavior related to belonging and "togetherness" is primarily inclusion. To desire to belong to a fraternal organization by no means necessarily indicates a liking for the members or even a desire for power. It is often sought for its "prestige value," for increase of "status." These terms are also primarily inclusion conceptions, because their primary implication is that people pay attention to the person, know who he is, and can distinguish him from others.

This last point leads to an essential aspect of inclusion, that of identity. An integral part of being recognized and paid attention to is that the individual be identifiable from other people. He must be known as a specific individual; he must have a particular identity. If he is not thus known, he cannot truly be attended to or have interest paid to him. The extreme of this identification is that he be understood. To be understood implies that someone is interested enough in him to find out his particular characteristics. Again, this interest need not mean that others have affection for him, or that they respect him. For example, the interested person may be a confidence man who is exploring his background to find a point of vulnerability.

At the outset of interpersonal relations a common issue is that of commitment, the decision to become involved in a given relation or activity. Usually, in the initial testing of the relation, individuals try to identify themselves to one another to find out which facet of themselves others will be interested in. Frequently a member is silent for a while because he is not sure that people are interested in him. These behaviors, too, are primarily in the inclusion area.

This, then, is the flavor of inclusion. It has to do with interacting with people, with attention, acknowledgement, being known, prominence, recognition, prestige, status, and fame; with identity, individuality, understanding, interest, commitment, and participation. It is unlike affection in that it does not involve strong emotional attachments to individual persons. It is unlike control in that the preoccupation is with prominence, not dominance.

Control behavior refers to the decision-making process between people. Some terms connoting a relation that is primarily positive control are "power," "authority," "dominance," "influence," "control," "ruler," "superior officer," "leader." Some terms that connote primarily a lack of, or negative, control are "rebellion," "resistance," "follower," "anarchy," "submissive," "henpecked," "milquetoast."

The need for control manifests itself as the desire for power, authority, and control over others and therefore over one's future. At the other end is the need to be controlled, to have responsibility taken away. Manifestations of the power drive are very clear. A more subtle form is exemplified by the current magazine advertising campaign featuring the "influential." This is a person who controls others through the power he has to influence their behavior.

The acquisition of money or political power is a direct method of obtaining control over other persons. This type of control often involves coercion rather than more subtle methods of influence like persuasion and example. In group behavior, the struggles to achieve high office or to make suggestions that are adopted are manifestations of control behavior. In an argument in a group we may distinguish the inclusion seeker from the control seeker in this way: the one seeking inclusion or prominence wants very much to be one of the participants in the argument, while the control seeker wants to be the winner or, if not the winner, on the same side as the winner. The prominence seeker would prefer to be the losing participant; the dominance seeker would prefer to be a winning nonparticipant. Both these roles are separate from the affectional desires of the members.

Control behavior takes many subtle forms, especially among more intellectual and polite people. For example, in many discussion groups where blackboards are involved, the power struggle becomes displaced onto the chalk. Walking to the blackboard and taking the chalk from the one holding it, and retaining possession, becomes a mark of competitive success. Often a meeting is marked by a procession of men taking the chalk, writing something, and being supplanted by another man for a further message. In this way propriety is maintained, and still the power struggle may proceed.

In many gatherings, control behavior is exhibited through the group task. Intellectual superiority, for one thing, often leads to control over others so that strong motivation to achieve is often largely control behavior. Such superiority also demonstrates the real capacity of the individual to be relied on for responsible jobs, a central aspect of control. Further, to do one's job properly, or to rebel against the established authority structure by not doing it, is a splendid outlet for control feelings. Doing a poor job is a way of rebelling against the structure and showing that no one will control you, whereas acquiescence earns rewards from those in charge which satisfies the need to be respected for one's accomplishments.

Control is also manifested in behavior toward others controlling the self. Expressions of independence and rebellion exemplify lack of willingness to be controlled, while compliance, submission, and taking orders indicate various degrees of accepting the control of others. There is no necessary relation between an individual's behavior toward controlling others, and his behavior toward being controlled. The domineering sergeant may accept orders from the lieutenant with pleasure and gratefulness, while the neighborhood bully may also rebel against his parents; two persons who control others differ in the degree to which they allow others to control them.

Thus the flavor of control is transmitted by behavior involving influence, leadership, power, coercion, authority, accomplishment, intellectual superiority, high achievement, and independence, as well as dependency (for decision making), rebellion, resistance, and submission. It differs from inclusion behavior in that it does not require prominence. The concept of the "power behind the throne" is an excellent example of a role that would fill a high control need and a low need for inclusion. The "joker" exemplifies the opposite. Control behavior differs from affection behavior in that it has to do with power relations rather than emotional closeness. The frequent difficulties between those who want to "get down to business" and those who want to get to "know one another" illustrate a situation in which control behavior is more important for some and affection behavior for others.

In general, *affection behavior* refers to close personal emotional feelings between *two* people. Affection is a dyadic relation; it can occur only between pairs of people at any one time, whereas both inclusion and control relations may occur either in dyads or between one person and a group of persons. Some terms that connote an affection relation that is primarily positive are "love," "like," "emotionally close," "positive feelings," "personal," "friendship," "sweetheart." Some terms that connote primarily lack of, or negative, affection are "hate," "dislike," "cool," "emotionally distant."

The need for affection leads to behavior related to becoming emotionally close. An affection relation must be dyadic because it involves strong differentiation between people. Affectional relations can be toward parental figures, peers, or children figures. They are exemplified in friendship relations, dating, and marriage.

To become emotionally close to someone involves, in addition to an emotional attachment, an element of confiding innermost anxieties, wishes, and feelings. A strong positive affectional tie usually is accompanied by a unique relation regarding the degree of sharing of these feelings.

In groups, affection behavior is characterized by overtures of friendship and differentiation between members. One common method for avoiding a close tie with any one member is to be equally friendly to all members. Thus "popularity" may not involve affection at all; it may often be inclusion behavior, whereas "going steady" is usually primarily affection.

A difference between affection behavior, inclusion behavior, and control behavior is illustrated by the different feelings a man has in being turned down by a fraternity, failed in a course by a professor, and rejected by his girl. The fraternity excludes him and tells him, in effect, that they as a group don't have sufficient interest in him. The professor fails him and says, in effect, that he finds him incompetent in his field. His girl rejects him, and tells him, in effect, that she doesn't find him lovable.

Thus the flavor of affection is embodied in situations of love, emotional closeness, personal confidences, intimacy. Negative affection is characterized by hate, hostility, and emotional rejection.

In order to sharpen further the contrast between these three types of behavior, several differences may be mentioned.

With respect to an interpersonal relation, inclusion is concerned primarily with the formation of the relation, whereas control and affection are concerned with relations already formed. Basically, inclusion is always concerned with whether or not a relation exists. Within existent relations, control is the area concerned with who gives orders and makes decisions for whom, whereas affection is concerned with how emotionally close or distant the relation becomes. Thus, generally speaking, inclusion is concerned with the problem of *in or out*, control is concerned with *top or bottom*, and affection with *close or far*.

A further differentiation occurs with regard to the number of people involved in the relation. Affection is *always* a one-to-one relation, inclusion is *usually* a one-to-many relation, and control may be either a one-one or a one-many relation. An affectional tie is necessarily between two persons, and involves varying degrees of intimacy, warmth, and emotional involvement which cannot be felt toward a unit greater than one person. Inclusion, on the other hand, typically concerns the behavior and feelings of one person toward a group of people. Problems of belonging and membership, so central to the inclusion area, usually refer to a relatively undifferentiated group with which an individual seeks association. His feelings of wanting to belong to the group are qualitatively different from his personal feelings of warmth toward an individual person. Control may refer to a power struggle between two individuals for control over each other, or it may refer to the struggle for domination over a group, as in political power. There is no particular number of interactional participants implied in the control area.

Control differs from the other two areas with respect to the differentiation between the persons involved in the control situation. For inclusion and affection there is a tendency for participants to act similarly in both the behavior they express and the behavior they want from others; for example, a close, personal individual usually likes others to be close and personal also. This similarity is not so marked in the control area. The person who likes to control may or may not want others to control him. This difference in differentiation among need areas is, however, only a matter of degree. There are many who like to include but do not want to be included, or who are not personal but want others to be that way toward them. But these types are not as frequent as the corresponding types in the control area.

TYPES OF INTERPERSONAL BEHAVIOR

For each area of interpersonal behavior three types of behavior will be described: (1) deficient—indicating that the individual is not trying directly to satisfy the need, (2) excessive—indicating that the individual is constantly trying to satisfy the need, (3) ideal—indicating satisfaction of the need, and (4) pathological.

In delineating these types it is assumed that anxiety engendered by early experiences leads to behavior of the first, second, and fourth types, while a successful working through of an interpersonal relation leads to an individual who can function without anxiety in the area. . . . For simplicity of presentation the extremes will be presented without qualifications. Actually, of course, the behavior of any given individual could be best described as some combination of behavior incorporating elements of all three types at different times, for instance, the oversocial, undersocial, and social.

Inclusion Types

The Undersocial. The interpersonal behavior of the undersocial person tends to be introverted and withdrawn. Characteristically, he avoids associating with others and doesn't like or accept invitations to join others. Consciously he wants to maintain this distance between himself and others, and insists that he doesn't want to get enmeshed with people and lose his privacy. But unconsciously he definitely wants others to pay attention to him. His biggest fears are that people will ignore him, generally have no interest in him, and would just as soon leave him behind.

Unconsciously he feels that no one ever will pay attention to him. His attitude may be summarized by, "No one is interested in me, so I'm not going to risk being ignored. I'll stay away from people and get along by myself." There is a strong drive toward self-sufficiency as a technique for existence without others. Since social abandonment is tantamount to death, he must compensate by directing his energies toward self-preservation; he therefore creates a world of his own in which his existence is more secure. Behind this withdrawal lie anxiety and hostility, and often a slight air of superiority and the private feeling that others don't understand him.

The direct expression of this withdrawal is nonassociation and interaction with people, lack of involvement and commitment. The more subtle form is exemplified by the person who for one reason or another is always late to meetings, or seems to have an inordinate number of conflicting engagements necessitating absence from people, or the type of person who precedes each visit with, "I'm sorry, but I can't stay very long."

His deepest anxiety, that referring to the self concept, is that he is worthless. He thinks that if no one ever considered him important enough to receive attention, he must be of no value whatever.

Closely allied with this feeling is the lack of motivation to live. Association with people is a necessary condition for a desire to live. This factor may be of much greater importance in everyday interaction than is usually thought. The degree to which an individual is committed to living probably determines to a large extent his general level of enthusiasms, perserverance, involvement, and the like. Perhaps this lack of concern for life is the ultimate in regression: if life holds too few rewards, the prelife condition is preferable. It is likely that this basic fear of abandonment or isolation is the most potent of all interpersonal fears. The simple fear that people are not interested in the self is extremely widespread, but in scientific analyses it, too often, is included as a special type of affectional need. It is extremely useful, however, to make clear the distinction between inclusion and affection.

The Oversocial.   The oversocial person tends toward extraversion in his later interpersonal behavior. Characteristically, he seeks people incessantly and wants them to seek him out. He is also afraid they will ignore him. His interpersonal dynamics are the same as those of the withdrawn person, but his overt behavior is the opposite.

His unconscious attitude is summarized by, "Although no one is interested in me, I'll make people pay attention to me in any way I can." His inclination is always to seek companionship. He is the type who "can't stand being alone." All of his activities will be designed to be done "together." An interesting illustration of this attitude occurs in the recent motion picture, "The Great Man." José Ferrer, as a newspaper man, is interviewing a woman about her reasons for attending the funeral of a television celebrity.

> "Because our club all came together," she replies.
> "But," Ferrer persists, "why did you come *here?*"
> "I came here because the rest came here."
> "Were you fond of the dead man?"
> "Not especially," she replies, "but we always do things together."

This scene (the dialogue is from memory) nicely illustrates the importance of being together presumably as an end in itself. The interpersonal behavior of the oversocial type of person will then be designed to focus attention on himself, to make people notice him, to be prominent, to be listened to. There are many techniques for doing this. The direct method is to be an intensive, exhibitionistic participator. By simply forcing himself on the group he forces the group to focus attention on him. The more subtle technique is to try to acquire status through such devices as name dropping, or by asking startling questions. He may also try to acquire power (control) or try to be well liked (affection), but for the primary purpose of gaining attention. Power or friendship, although both may be important (depending on his orientation in the other two interpersonal areas), is not the primary goal.

The Social.   To the individual for whom the resolution of inclusion relations was successful in childhood, interaction with people presents no problem. He is comfortable with people and comfortable being alone. He can be a high or low participator in a group, or can equally well take a moderate role, without anxiety. He is capable of strong commitment and involvement to certain groups and also can withhold commitment if he feels it is appropriate.

Unconsciously, he feels that he is a worth while, significant person and that life is worth living. He is fully capable of being genuinely interested in others and feels that they will include him in their activities and that they are interested in him.

He also has an "identity" and an "individuality." Childhood feelings of abandonment lead to the absence of an identity; the person feels he is nobody. He has no stable figures with whom to identify. Childhood feelings of enmeshment lead to confusion of identity. When a child is nothing but parts of other people and has not had sufficient opportunity to evaluate the characteristics he observes in himself, he has difficulty knowing who he is. The social person has resolved these difficulties. He has integrated aspects of a large number of individuals into a new configuration which he can identify as himself.

Inclusion Pathology.   Failure to be included means anxiety over having contact with people. Unsuccessful resolution of inclusion relations leads to feelings of exclusion, of alienation from people, of being different and unacceptable, and usually the necessity of creating a phantasy world in which the nonincluded person is accepted. Inclusion, because it is posited to be the first area of interpersonal relations to be dealt with by the infant, has strong narcissistic elements and other close similarities to the description by psychoanalysts of the interpersonal characteristics in the oral stage. Hence a pathological difficulty in the inclusion area leads to the most regressed kind of behavior, that concerned with belonging to people, being a significant individual. This syndrome is very much like the functional *psychoses*. In Ruth Munroe's description of the Freudian explanation of psychoses (66) these points are made clear:

> The essential feature of Freud's explanation of psychotic conditions may be stated as the greater depth of regression. The adult never lapses back to infancy all of a piece of course. . . . Freud felt, however, that the truly psychotic manifestations belong to the pre-oedipal period—indeed to the stage of narcissism before the ego has properly developed. The mechanisms of psychoses are the archaic mechanisms of the infant before secure object relations have been established. (p. 288)

The last line of this quotation is especially pertinent to demonstrating the close relations between the Freudian discussion of the psychosis and the area of inclusion. The phrase, "before secure object [interpersonal] relations have been established," certainly bears a close resemblance to the preceding discussion of the problems of becoming included in the social group.

It appears, then, that difficulty in establishing a satisfactory relation with other persons, with regard to inclusion or contact, when difficulty reaches a pathological state, leads to psychosis, especially schizophrenia. This statement does not mean that all conditions now called psychosis are caused by difficulties in the inclusion area, nor does it necessarily mean that all inclusion problems will, if pathological, become psychoses; nor does it even imply that there are "pure" inclusion problems uncontaminated with other areas. It implies only that there is a close relation between disturbance in the inclusion area and psychosis.

Psychosis, especially schizophrenia, appears to be related more to the undersocial pattern than the oversocial. The lack of identity and inability to be alone, if carried to the extreme, would correspond to the pathological extreme of the oversocial.

Control Types

The Abdicrat. The abdicrat is a person who tends toward submission and abdication of power and responsibility in his interpersonal behavior. Characteristically, he gravitates toward the subordinate position where he will not have to take responsibility for making decisions, and where someone else takes charge. Consciously, he wants people to relieve him of his obligations. He does not control others even when he should; for example, he would not take charge even during a fire in a children's schoolhouse in which he is the only adult; and he never makes a decision that he can refer to someone else. He fears that others will not help him when he requires it, and that he will be given more responsibility than he can handle. This kind of person is usually a follower, or at most a loyal lieutenant, but rarely the person who takes the responsibility for making the *final* decision. Unconsciously, too, he has the feeling that he is incapable of responsible adult behavior and that others know it. He never was told what to do and therefore never learned. His most comfortable response is to avoid situations in which he will feel helpless. He feels that he is an incompetent and irresponsible, perhaps stupid, person who does not deserve respect for his abilities.

Behind this feeling are anxiety, hostility, and lack of trust toward those who might withhold assistance. The hostility is usually expressed as passive resistance. Hesitancy to "go along" is a usual technique of resistance, since actual overt rebellion is too threatening.

The Autocrat. The autocrat is a person whose interpersonal behavior often tends toward the dominating. Characteristically, he tries to dominate people and strongly desires a power hierarchy with himself at the top. He is the power seeker, the competor. He is afraid people will not be influenced or controlled by him—that they will, in fact, dominate him.

Commonly, this need to control people is displaced into other areas. Intellectual or athletic superiority allows for considerable control, as does the more direct method of attaining political power. The underlying dynamics are the same as for the abdicrat. Basically the person feels he is not responsible or capable of discharging obligation and that this fact is known to others. He attempts to use every opportunity to disprove this feeling to others and to himself. His unconscious attitude may be summarized as, "No one thinks I can make decisions for myself, but I'll show them. I'm going to make all the decisions for everyone, always." Behind this feeling is a strong distrust that others may make decisions for him and the feeling that they don't trust him. This latter becomes a very sensitive area.

The Democrat.   For the individual who has successfully resolved his relations with others in the control area in childhood, power and control present no problem. He feels comfortable giving or not giving orders, and taking or not taking orders, as is appropriate to the situation. Unconsciously, he feels that he is a capable, responsible person and therefore that he does not need to shrink from responsibility or to try constantly to prove how competent he really is. Unlike the abdicrat and autocrat, he is not preoccupied with fears of his own helplessness, stupidity, and incompetence. He feels that other people respect his competence and will be realistic with respect to trusting him with decision making.

Control Pathology.   The individual who does not accept control of any kind develops pathologically into a psychopathic personality. He has not been adequately trained to learn the rules of behavior established for respecting the rights and privileges of others. Ruth Munroe (66) says,

> The major Freudian explanation for this condition is that there has been a serious failure of superego development. The parental image has not been adequately internalized in the form of conscience but remains the policeman at the corner—an external force. Truly, the behavior of the psychopath is childish without the limited experience of the child. When the resources of adulthood are used without the inner controls of adulthood the resultant behavior is very likely to be deplorable. Object relations generally are poor of necessity since good early object relations would have led to more adequate superego development. (p. 292)

Affection Types

The Underpersonal.   The underpersonal type tends to avoid close personal ties with others. He characteristically maintains his dyadic relations on a superficial, distant level and is most comfortable when others do the same to him. Consciously, he wishes to maintain this emotional distance, and frequently expresses a desire not to get "emotionally involved"; unconsciously he seeks a satisfactory affectional relation. His fear is that no one loves him. In a group situation he is afraid he won't be liked. He has great difficulty genuinely liking people. He distrusts their feeling toward him.

His attitude could be summarized by the "formula," "I find the affection area very painful since I have been rejected; therefore I shall avoid close personal relations in the future." The direct technique for maintaining emotional distance is to reject and avoid people to prevent emotional closeness or involvement actively, even to the point of being antagonistic. The subtle technique is to appear superficially friendly to *everyone*. This behavior acts as a safeguard against having to get close to, or become personal with, any *one* person. ("Close" and "personal" refer to emotional closeness and willingness to confide one's most private concerns and feelings. It involves the expression of positive affection and tender feelings.) Here the dyadic relation is a threatening one. To keep everyone at the same distance obviates the requirement for treating any one person with greater warmth and affection.

The deepest anxiety, that regarding the self, is that he is unlovable. He feels that people won't like him because, in fact, he doesn't "deserve" it. If people got to know him well, he believes, they would discover the traits that make him so unlovable. As opposed to the inclusion anxiety that the self is of no value, worthless, and empty, and the control anxiety that the self is stupid and irresponsible, the affection anxiety is that the self is nasty and bad.

The Overpersonal.   The overpersonal type attempts to become extremely close to others. He definitely wants others to treat him in a very close, personal way. His response may be summarized by the formula, "My first experiences with affection were painful, but perhaps if I try again they will turn out to be better." He will be striving in his interpersonal relations primarily to be liked. Being liked is extremely important to him in his attempt to relieve his anxiety about being always rejected and unlovable. Again, there are two behavioral techniques, the direct and the subtle. The direct technique is an overt attempt to gain approval, be extremely personal, intimate, and confiding. The subtle technique is more manipulative, to devour friends and subtly punish any attempts by them to establish other friendships, to be possessive.

The underlying dynamics are the same as those for the underpersonal. Both the overpersonal and the underpersonal responses are extreme, both are motivated by a strong need for affection, both are accompanied by strong anxiety about ever being loved, and basically about being unlovable, and both have considerable hostility behind them stemming from the anticipation of rejection.

The Personal. For the individual who successfully resolved his affectional relations with others in childhood, close emotional relations with one other person present no problem. He is comfortable in such a personal relation, and he can also relate comfortably in a situation requiring emotional distance. It is important for him to be liked, but if he isn't liked he can accept the fact that the dislike is the result of the relation between himself and one other person—in other words, the dislike does not mean that he is an unlovable person. Unconsciously, he feels that he is a lovable person who is lovable even to people who know him well. He is capable of giving genuine affection.

Affection Pathology. Neuroses are commonly attributed to difficulties in the area of affection. Ruth Munroe (66) says,

> The early bloom of sexuality, which cannot possibly come to fruition, is called the phallic stage to differentiate it from true genitality leading to mature mating and reproduction. At this period attitudes are formed which are crucial for later heterosexual fulfillment and good relations with people generally. For this reason it is the stage most fraught with potentialities for neurotic distortion. (p. 199)

Combining early experience and present behavior with the pathological classification will provide a more complete picture of the process of personality development and disintegration.

Summary

To summarize, difficulties with initiating interaction range from being uncomfortable when not associating with people ("can't stand to be alone"—the *oversocial*) to not feeling comfortable initiating interaction ("can't stand being with people"—the *undersocial*). Difficulties with controlling others range from not feeling comfortable controlling the behavior of anyone ("can't tell anyone what to do"—the *abdicrat*) to not feeling comfortable when unable to control everyone ("always have to be in charge"—the *autocrat*). Difficulties with originating close, personal relations range from being uncomfortable when unable to establish a sufficiently close, personal relation ("can't get close enough"—the *overpersonal*) to being uncomfortable when getting too close and personal with someone ("don't like to get emotionally involved with people"—the *underpersonal*).

This description could be stated in psychoanalytic terms with little if any difference in meaning. In the struggle between the id and the superego to determine the individual's behavior the excessive response in each area represents the triumph of the id. The restrained response results from the triumph of the superego. The ideal response represents the successful resolution of the id impulses, the demands of the superego, and external reality; it therefore corresponds to the triumph of the ego.

In each of the nonideal (extreme) types described there are anxiety, hostility, and ambivalence. (One outcome of this analysis is to suggest that each of these widely used terms could be divided profitably into three types.) Anxiety arises from a person's (a) anticipation of a nonsatisfying event (for instance, being ignored, dominated, rejected) and (b) fear of exposure, both to self and others, of what kind of person he "really" is—his inadequate self concept. The anxiety indicates that these behavior patterns are inflexible, since anxiety usually leads to rigid behavior. The threat involved in changing behavior is too great to allow for much flexibility. Hostility also follows from anxiety; so the hostility, too, may arise in three ways.

Finally, ambivalence is also present in the nonideal behaviors, since the behavior pattern being utilized is necessarily unsatisfactory. In many instances an overpersonal individual, for example, will occasionally become underpersonal, and vice versa. Complete reversals are to be expected more than slight modifications, especially for the extreme behavior patterns. The characterization of a person's behavior can describe only his most usual behavior, not his invariable behavior.

REFERENCES

(35) French, T. *Summary of Factor Analysis Studies of Personality.* Princeton, N.J.: Educational Testing Service, 1956.
(45) Guttman, L. "The Basis for Scalogram Analysis," in S. A. Stouffer et al., *Measurements and Predictions.* Princeton, N.J.: Princeton University Press, 1950, 60–90.
(55) Lazarsfeld, P., and A. Barton. "Qualitative Measurement in the Social Sciences," in D. Lerner and H. Lasswell, *The Policy Sciences.* Stanford, Ca.: Stanford University Press, 1951.
(65) Miller, N. E., and J. Dollard. *Social Learning and Imitation.* New Haven, Conn.: Yale University Press, 1941.
(66) Munroe, Ruth. *Schools of Psychoanalytic Thought.* New York: Dryden, 1956.

18

The Application of FIRO in Correctional Counseling

EDWARD E. PEOPLES

This article is based on six years of applied research by the author, using FIRO with probationers, parolees and prison inmates, both juvenile and adult, as well as with probation, parole, and institutional officers. The author also provides training on the application of FIRO in correctional counseling, and in personnel selection and management.

Correctional caseworkers are not professional therapists. They are not educated, trained, or licensed to "treat" their clients as psychologists or psychiatrists are to treat their patients. Nevertheless, they are responsible for providing counseling to a significant number of juvenile and adult offenders for the purpose of changing a wide variety of dysfunctional behaviors. And, frequently, the nature and scope of this counseling requires them to possess the understanding, insight, and therapy skills that, although not professional in name, are professional in fact. In addition, the results of their efforts often have implications more far reaching than those of the so-called professionals. They can, and often do, have a resounding impact on our social environment.

Considering this heavy task, it is easy to understand why dedicated caseworkers take every opportunity to learn new counseling methods. One such method (perhaps "tool" is a better term) finding wide acceptance in probation and parole counseling is called FIRO. This construct was developed by Dr. William C. Schutz from his research on a theory of interpersonal behavior begun in the 1950s.[1] Over the years Schutz also developed a series of projective questionnaires used to test, validate, and actually apply his theory in various relationship situations.[2]

During the late 1960s two of these questionnaires, FIRO-B and FIRO-F,[3] have been used successfully in casework as an aid in matching a correctional treatment approach with the specific needs of the client. They have been used also as a management tool for matching the counseling style of the caseworker with the response style of the client so that an entire caseload is placed under the supervision of an agent whose needs are compatible with the client's.

Although FIRO is being used by an increasing number of probation officers and parole agents, very little has been written in the correctional literature about its application. The purpose of this article, then, is to describe what the FIRO questionnaires are, what they measure, how to interpret the results, and how to apply these results in casework.[4]

FIRO-B

The initials FIRO-B stand for Fundamental Interpersonal Relationship Orientation—Behavior. It is a 54-item projective questionnaire designed to measure the expressed and wanted dimensions of three behavior needs: Inclusion (I), Control (C), and Affection (A). Based on his research, Schutz postulated that these three needs are basic to all human interaction.[5] Inclusion he defines as the need to establish and maintain a comfortable relationship with other people—in general, in social, or in group situations. This need, for any one individual, may be measured on a continuum from a compelling need to be with people to a compelling need to be away from people.

Control he defines as the need to establish and maintain a relationship with others relative to power, authority, and dominance or, at the other end of the continuum, dependence and submissiveness. It also reflects one's internal comfort with leadership, responsibility, and decision making. Affection is the need to establish and maintain a comfortable dyadic relationship based on friendship, personal warmth, openness, and intimacy.

The expressed and wanted dimensions of each need area are measured nine times; and the intensity of each dimension—the degree to which each is characteristic of one's behavior orientation—is scored from 0 to 9. The resultant score for each dimension is recorded in the appropriate position in a box on the front of the questionnaire (Fig. 1).

Figure 1

Generalized FIRO Profile

	I	C	A
e	0 | 9	0 | 9	0 | 9
w	0 | 9	0 | 9	0 | 9

Expressed (*e*) scores indicate one's overt behavior in each area—one's need-level and level of comfort in originating a particular behavior with others. Wanted (*w*) scores indicate the intensity of one's need to receive a particular behavior from others.

The individual, in answering the questionnaire, responds to 54 statements about his behavior by selecting a number from 1 to 6 which indicates the degree to which each statement is, or is not, characteristic of his behavior. The nine statements that measure each of the six behavior categories are mixed throughout the questionnaire; and the cut-off point for determining whether one's response (number selection) to each question is to be considered in arriving at a score for that need does not follow any obvious sequence or pattern. This makes the questionnaire difficult to manipulate. Since there are no right or wrong answers, only different responses, there is no reason to attempt manipulation.

The questionnaire takes approximately 15 minutes to complete; its construction and phrasing are relatively nonthreatening. Nevertheless, it should be administered in a relationship climate that is also nonthreatening. To score the questionnaire, merely lay a key beside the response numbers selected and follow fairly simple directions.

Scores fall into three general categories: low, average, and high. Low scores range from 0 to 2, average from 3 to 6, and high from 7 to 9. However, the closer a score is to either end of the scale, the more that person's behavior is characteristically low or high. Both low and high scores indicate a compulsive quality about the behavior need; a quality that will be an overriding concern in one's interpersonal relationship orientation (Fig. 2).

Figure 2

Low-High Characteristic

Low	Average	High
0-1-2	3-4-5-6	7-8-9

compelling ←——————————————————→ compelling

FIRO-F

The FIRO-F (Fundamental Interpersonal Relationship Orientation —Feelings) is also a 54-item projective questionnaire designed to measure the expressed and wanted dimensions of the feelings associated with Inclusion, Control and Affection. It is administered and scored in the same manner as FIRO-B; however, the scores have a somewhat different meaning. Inclusion is related to the concept of significance, Control to the concept of competence, and Affection to lovability.[6]

Expressed Inclusion scores measure the degree to which one *feels* that other people in general are significant and important—the extent to which the very existence of other people makes a difference to him. Wanted Inclusion scores measure the degree to which one has a need for, and is concerned about, having others *feel* that he is significant and important—that his being in this world counts for something.[7]

Expressed Control scores measure the degree to which one *feels* that others are competent, reliable, dependable, and capable—the extent to which one is comfortable trusting and relying on others. Wanted Control scores measure the degree to which one has a need for, and is concerned about, having others rely on him, and *feels* that he is dependable, competent, and capable.[8]

Expressed Affection scores measure the degree to which one *feels* that other individuals are likable, lovable, and basically good once he gets to know them. Wanted Affection scores measure the degree to which one has a need for, and a concern about, having others *feel* that he is likable, lovable and basically good as a person.[9]

THE FIRO PROCESSES

One additional ingredient of FIRO needs examining before an interpretation of the score can begin. Whenever people come together, for whatever reason and in whatever environment or situation, they pass through three processes: the Inclusion process, the Control process, and the Affection process. Individuals can be observed going through these processes when they move into a new neighborhood, begin a new job, enter into the agent-client relationship, or come together in any relationship situation. It is particularly noticeable in group counseling.

The Inclusion Process

When first entering the group situation, each individual feels out the climate, sizes up the other individuals, and evaluates the activities that the group will be involved in. Each then interacts on a social basis in an effort to achieve his required comfort level relative to the others. To the extent that each individual achieves his position of comfort, he is ready to include others and be included by them according to the intensity of his behavior needs for Inclusion. As a part of this, he is also ready to seek from, and give to, the others the amount of prominence and recognition that his needs require (see need score projections).

The speed and ease with which an individual will go through this process can be determined by his Inclusion scores on FIRO-B. Some complete this process quickly and are prepared to enter into a reciprocal relationship with the others. Some include themselves cautiously, but perhaps not completely; and some individuals do not include themselves at all. One of the most frustrating dilemmas is to counsel a client who does not even want to include himself in his own treatment.

The Control Process

As each individual completes the Inclusion process, he moves on to establish the relationship position that he needs with others relative to dominance or submission. Those with strong needs to control emerge as the informal leaders and attempt to direct the group's activities. If more than one leader emerges, they frequently encounter each other in playing "king of the mountain" while the followers wait for the play to end. Until the leadership is resolved in some manner, the activities of the group cannot effectively begin. In group counseling, the caseworker can observe that some individuals will look *to* him for leadership, some will participate *with* him in the leadership, and others will challenge him *for* the leadership. This behavioral phenomenon is most obvious in the "guided group interaction" form of group counseling.

The Affection Process

After each individual has established his position on Inclusion and Control with the others, he can move on to develop meaningful relationships with the others. Intimate and open behavior can begin between individuals, and they can get underway with the activities for which they are meeting.

At this point an observer can say, "Yes, the group really came together," or "No, it didn't." To the extent that a group does not "come together," it usually means that the relationships between some of the individuals are still fixated at the Inclusion or Control process. A variety of possibilities exist—some individuals have decided not to include themselves, or have been frozen out by others; perhaps the competition for dominance of the group has not been resolved; perhaps no leadership has been provided at all.

INTERPRETING FIRO

Some individuals behave as they feel, while others behave differently from the way they feel. In either case, behavior is goal directed. Behavior orientation on FIRO-B is directed toward need satisfaction and fulfillment, and away from anxiety-producing relationship situations.

Figure 3 represents the so-called ideal FIRO profile—the individual whose expressed and wanted needs are average and well-balanced, and whose behavior is in tune with his feelings:

Figure 3

Ideal FIRO Profile

FIRO-B

	I	C	A
e	5	5	5
w	5	5	5

FIRO-F

	I	C	A
	5	5	5
	5	5	5

Seldom does one find this ideal profile; remember that a profile deviating from it in any area is neither bad nor good, only different. Nevertheless, the 5/5 combination represents a useful point of departure for interpreting one's orientation in each need area.

As a rule of thumb, begin the interpretation by examining the FIRO-F scores. Note first which wanted needs stand out. Next, note the relative difference between the intensity of wanted and expressed needs in each area. With time and experience, the counselor will come across every conceivable arrangement of scores; it is beyond the scope of this article to cover them all. However, the following representative "F" profiles should serve as a guide (Fig. 4).

Figure 4

Representative Feeling (F) Profiles

Flat Affect

	I	C	A
e	0-2	0-2	0-2
w	0-2	0-2	0-2

Candide

	I	C	A
e	7-9	7-9	7-9
w	7-9	7-9	7-9

The Taker

	I	C	A
e	lo	lo	lo
w	hi	hi	hi

The Giver

	I	C	A
e	hi	hi	hi
w	lo	lo	lo

The Reciprocator

	I	C	A
e	med	med	med
w	med	med	med

To the degree that one extends to others the same level of feelings and the same regard in each area that he wants from them, he will stimulate a response that will meet his own feeling needs.

After an assessment has been made of the client's feeling orientation, examine his behavior profile, and relate the expressed scores of one questionnaire to the wanted scores of the other. Regardless of the profile represented by each, one should be a mirror image of the other to represent a harmonious relationship between feeling and behavior.

Take, for example, the individual whose primary feeling need is to have others feel he is a likeable person, and yet he is very selective about individuals with whom he will reciprocate this same feeling (0/6 in FIRO-F Affection). One of the easiest ways for him to meet this need is to behave in a friendly way toward others (6/0 in FIRO-B Affection). Another way would be for him to mix with people generally and express gregarious social behavior (6/0 in FIRO-B Inclusion). By behaving toward others in either of these ways, he can present the "nice guy" image that he wants others to hold of him.

The same relationship can be made in the Control area between the need a person has for others to *feel* he is competent and reliable and his exercise of authority and responsible behavior (0/6 in FIRO-F Control and 6/0 in FIRO-B Control).

In the examples above, the behavior of the individual is motivated solely to meet his feeling needs. He is not concerned that others reciprocate Inclusion or Affection behavior, but only that his overt behavior create a favorable image with others. In fact, his real involvement *with* others in a reciprocal behavioral relationship is quite limited. The 0 in these wanted behavior areas, however, does not mean that he cannot, or will not, become involved. It does mean that the scope of his wanted involvement will be limited far more than is suggested by his behavior. In the FIRO-B Inclusion area this pattern characterizes the person who is socially skilled but highly selective about people with whom he really cares to spend time. In the FIRO-B Affection area, this pattern characterizes one who is skilled in handling dyadic encounters but is highly selective about the persons he will allow to move close to him and behave intimately with him.[10]

Generally speaking, a wanted feeling need can be met by an expressed behavior need, either directly as in the mirror image relationship or indirectly in a cross-relationship. Frequently, however, individuals express a certain level of behavior in one need area in order to stimulate reciprocal behavior from others, as well as, or instead of, feelings. To the degree that an individual has a wanted need to be included by others, he may express Inclusion behavior. And to the degree that a person wants intimacy, or friendly behavior from others, he may well express it to others.

When the expressed and the wanted FIRO-B scores are balanced in Inclusion or Affection, their range on the 0-9 scale reflects a level of need-intensity in either area. Thus, a 0/0 score indicates a compelling need to *avoid* either social interaction (I), or intimate relationships (A), whereas a 9/9 score indicates a compelling need *for* social interaction or intimacy.[11] In both instances, the distinction to be made is between the quantity needed rather than the quality of the relationship. The 9/9 in

Affection , for example, suggests instant intimacy with many individuals, whereas the 0/0 suggests that real intimacy is slowly developed, and with very very few other individuals. However, the quality of these intimacies can be equally meaningful. Scores in between reflect the level of intensity inferred by their relative position on the 0/0→9/9 scale.

BEHAVIOR CONFLICT: INTERNAL

Behavioral conflict for an individual can stem from two sources, one internal and one external. Internally, an individual can experience conflict if his wanted FIRO-B score in Inclusion or Affection exceeds his expressed score. If this occurs in either area, it indicates an unmet need; and his hurt inside because of this can be determined by the relative degree that w exceeds e.

To the degree that this difference occurs in the Inclusion area, the individual will seem cautious, inhibited, shy, or awkward in social situations. He wants to be accepted and included by others, but he lacks the social skills or confidence required, and is uncomfortable while experiencing the Inclusion Process. In the Affection area, this e/w score difference is characteristic of an individual who experiences discomfort-originating behavior in dyadic relationships, and who will seem shy, inhibited, awkward, or cautious.

Individuals whose scores indicate the presence of this internal conflict are quick to feel either socially rejected (I) or discounted as a person (A). Dealing openly with these feelings in group counseling can be an effective method of exposing and resolving the "poor-me" posture that is often taken by these individuals. This intropunitive coping mechanism can be very dysfunctional for the client, and frequently it is nurtured and rewarded by the unaware counselor rather than corrected.

Other coping mechanisms are often manifested in the behavior of clients, and they are also projected in the FIRO-B scores. One functional behavior for an individual who needs intimate behavior from others but is uncomfortable originating it (lo/hi in Affection), is to develop his social skill behavior (hi/lo in Inclusion). With this profile, he can mix with many on an impersonal basis in order to maximize his opportunities to select individuals with whom it is safe to relate on an intimate basis (Fig. 5).

Another equally effective coping mechanism is shown in Figure 6. This profile represents an individual who will exercise assertive behavior and control others and his environment in such a manner that people will include him and behave in a friendly way toward him. He has a need to exercise Control; however, he will modify the expression of it so as to assure himself that others respond appropriately to his wanted needs in the other areas. This person can be contrasted with the individual whose profile shows hi/lo in FIRO-B Control as his only need. The former can be characterized as a smother-mother, while the latter is an absolute autocrat.[12]

Figure 5

Profile: The Selection Process for Intimacy

FIRO-B

	I	C	A
e	hi		lo
w	lo		hi

Figure 6

Profile: The Smother-Mother

	I	C	A
e	lo	hi	lo
w	hi	lo	hi

Behavior coping mechanisms, then, are utilized by individuals to meet wanted feeling or behavior needs that would otherwise go unmet and create internal conflict. Such mechanisms can also be used to avoid conflict-producing relationships; see, for example, the individual whose only projected high need is to exercise control (Fig. 7). This individual also has a compelling need to avoid social or intimate relationships with others, and will control his own position in the environment in order to protect himself.

Figure 7

Profile: The Autocratic

	I	C	A
e	lo	hi	lo
w	lo	lo	lo

BEHAVIOR CONFLICT: EXTERNAL

A second source of conflict that can be determined from FIRO-B is the reciprocity of need behavior between individuals. For example, the Affection scores of a husband and wife may indicate a source of incompatibility (conflict) if the wanted need of one is not reciprocated by the expressed need of the other.[13] In a relationship in which the husband's Affection scores are 2/6 and the wife's scores 6/8, an obvious degree of incompatibility is projected. The husband in this case will be content because his wanted need is being met by the expressed behavior of his wife; her need for Affection behavior, however, is not being reciprocated by him, and she will have to seek such satisfaction outside of their relationship. Children can serve as a source of satisfaction for her.

Control behavior is often another area of conflict between individuals, and this conflict can be an important factor for consideration in the agent-client relationship. The following mini-caseload will serve as an example (Fig. 8).[14]

Figure 8

Mini-Caseload

Parole Officer	Client A	Client B	Client C	Client D	Client E
C	C	C	C	C	C
e 5	e 9	e 5	e 2	e 3	e 1
w 4	w 0	w 5	w 8	w 6	w 1

The parole officer is a moderately assertive individual whose supervision style is participatory.[15] He is most comfortable working *with* his clients, and would be an ideal type for group counseling based on guided-group interaction. Client B is compatible with the officer, and would also relate effectively in group counseling.

Client A is an autocrat. He does not want the officer, or anyone else, exercising authority over him. He will resist direct guidance in one-to-one counseling, and will challenge the officer, and everyone else, for leadership in group counseling.

Client C is a dependent individual who looks to his environment for control. He will lean on the officer or the group for all decisions over his life, and he will expect others to be responsible for him. He will readily submit to Client A, and will feel more comfortable in that subordinate position than in any other available to him from the group described. He quite possibly has been institutionalized over a long period of time.

Client D is only moderately dependent and will *tend* to be other-directed. His primary need is for reassurance and occasional guidance rather than direct control. He is amenable to counseling that provides direction from environmental support to self-support, that encourages his move to independence rather than perpetuating any semblance of self-doubt or dependence. The parole officer in this case may well provide that type of supervision as long as he is supportive and reassuring, not dominating.

Client D may be overwhelmed in group counseling by the assertive posture of Client A, and give in to A's Control. However, if he does, he will resent his own weakness, but will project the blame and resentment onto A for being so domineering and onto the officer for not protecting him from A's authority.

Client E does not want to participate in any type of counseling relationship, group or individual. He wants to be completely inner directed, and will resist any attempt by others to control him. Also, he has a need not to impose his will on others in any form unless the situation will have a direct and significant effect on his life. In that case, he has the need to exert complete authority on his own terms. In one-to-one counseling his position will be, "Don't bug me." In group counseling his position will be, "Don't lay your trip on me, and I won't lay mine on you. Your problems are yours, and mine are mine. I can't decide anything for you, and you can't decide anything for me." This attitude will be especially strong if he has little confidence in the ability of others, as indicated by his expressed Control score in FIRO-F (0/?).

Incompatibility in the expressed and wanted Inclusion scores of individuals can also be a source of much conflict. Consider the husband who is a homebody (3/0) with a wife who needs people (8/8). He will be content with very limited social interaction, while she will have to participate in a number of social activities outside their relationship. Of course, the reverse situation can be a source of conflict equally as serious in a marriage.

Inclusion scores are also important to consider in forming a group for counseling, particularly during the early stages of the interaction. In the following example (Fig. 9), a group of offenders are meeting together in the first of a series of sessions:

Figure 9

Mini-Group

Parole Officer	Client A	Client B	Client C	Client D	Client E
I	I	I	I	I	I
e 4	e 5	e 9	e 9	e 6	e 0
w 3	w 5	s 9	w 0	w 0	w 0

The parole officer's scores indicate that he is moderately comfortable in group or social relationships. He will interact on the basis of give-and-take, and has no need to move toward, nor away from, people.[16]

Client A's Inclusion profile is similar, and represents a similar, though slightly more dynamic, orientation. Both individuals will work through the Inclusion process with relative ease, and will be prepared to establish a reciprocal and nonthreatening relationship with the group.

Client B's profile suggests instant Inclusion. He will immediately open up with social interaction at an intense level. Two process problems may present themselves in B's behavior. First, he will begin with a level of interaction that may initially overwhelm the others, especially clients E and F, and perhaps even the officer. Second, he will sustain that intensity throughout the meeting to a point where the others may become emotionally drained.

Clients C and D will be comfortable originating social behavior, and will *seem* to be including themselves in the process. Actually, they will play the gregarious role while they screen each individual, and the nature of the session, and decide if they really want to get involved, and with whom. They may or may not return next time the group meets.

If C and D do remain in the group, they will compete for prominence and recognition from the others. The officer may observe that A, B, C and D are really coming together as a group and sharing in a productive dialogue. This may be true of A, and perhaps B although he needs to relate, whereas A can take it or leave it. C and D are each delivering their own monologues *to* the others, rather than participating *with* the others in dialogue.

While this process is occuring, Client E will move away from B who seems to be engulfing him, and he may even move his chair back away from the table, or group circle. If he includes himself at all, he will do so very slowly, and at his own pace. Probably, he will completely ignore B, and will turn C off. In a group of this type, with so many incompatible behaviors, the chances are slight that he will get involved at all, even in his own treatment. He will return in body if he is ordered to, but not in spirit.

COUNSELING WITH FIRO

The use of FIRO in counseling serves many purposes. It is easy to administer, score, and interpret; it is economical, in terms of time and money. The counselor can complete a profile on himself and his clients, and can then adjust his own supervision style to relate effectively with each client and meet each specific need. Or the correctional supervisor can utilize it to match the various caseloads with the style most comfortable for each officer.

FIRO lends itself to use in group counseling in two ways. First, groups can be formed on the basis of the relative need compatibility desired. Second, and regardless of the group's compatibility, the profile of each individual can be used to facilitate the counseling process. The following steps suggest how this can be most effectively accomplished.

1. Select eight offenders from a caseload who have some commitment to their own correction and personal growth, and who volunteer to participate in group counseling.
2. Administer the FIRO-B and FIRO-F to each one in the group setting at the first meeting. Introduce it in a nonthreatening manner, explaining honestly the purpose it will serve, and that the results will be shared openly with the group for their benefit, but not with anyone else. To aid in creating a climate of openness and trust, the counselor should be willing to participate by sharing his own profile with the group.
3. Score the questionnaires then and there with the group. Have name cards prepared for each member, but instead of filling their names in, write their FIRO score in so that each one will have his behavior-feeling profile on the table in front of him.
4. Explain what behavior and feeling needs are measured and what the scores mean in general.
5. At the second meeting, be sure that everyone has his score profile displayed. Also, be sure that the Inclusion process has been worked out as much as possible. This process becomes more complete and more open with each session as the cohesiveness of the group develops.
6. Summarize the interpretations of the scores, in general, and clarify any misunderstandings. Proceed to each individual and interpret his projected orientation, leaving sufficient opportunity for responses from him, or others in the group.
7. Discuss the group profile openly and point out areas of conflict and compatibility, and make a comparative analysis of the needs of the members, as well as your own.
8. During each subsequent session, apply the counseling approach (guided-group, TA, etc.) that would be used without the aid of FIRO. Use the FIRO scores from time to time as a tangible reference point to make observations about the group or individual behaviors.

By following these eight steps, FIRO can make a significant contribution to group counseling. It will be a little scary and anxiety producing at first. Individuals will make joking remarks about their scores and attempt some humorous observations about the others. However, as the threat of self-disclosure is relieved and they realize that they are all in it together, they will relax and begin to use the scores to facilitate the group process and to deal with the behaviors of each other.

It is not uncommon to observe the 0/0 in FIRO-B Affection saying to the 9/9, "Hey, cool it a little. You're coming on too strong and I can't handle that. Don't you see my 0/0?" He would not say this before because he could not bring himself to articulate his feelings. Now he can point to a tangible external object and say, in effect, "It's not me saying something about you. It's these numbers out here on the table that are overwhelmed by your numbers."

It is also not uncommon for members of the group to refer to someone's score in order to handle his assertive, submissive, withdrawn or self-conscience behavior, or cool feelings. Example: "Hey, your heavy 9 is coming out (9/0 in Control behavior); reel it in a little"; "Come on Jack, help us decide on this issue (to a 0/9 in Control behavior); your opinion is as valid as ours, and we're not here to carry your bottom 9"; "Hey, 0/0 (in Inclusion behavior), pull your chair back up to the table"; "Come on, Charlie, we want you, we love you (to a 0/9 in Inclusion or Affection behavior), you're among friends here, but you gotta spread your bottom 9 around a little"; or "I understand why you think people see you as a cold fish (to a 0/? in Affection feeling), you don't express much warmth to others."

Although individuals in most groups will use the FIRO scores in this manner, they will also use them to deal more openly and honestly with their own motives, behaviors, and feelings. For many, it will provide a vehicle by which they can learn to own their own feelings. In a similar way, they will learn to appreciate the right of the others to be different; to have different needs and different motives. Tolerance for others, then, and an appreciation for self, are two meaningful by-products of FIRO in group counseling.

CONCLUSION

FIRO has limitations, like anything else under the sun. It measures only three behavior needs, and the three associated feeling needs, but that is all it is intended for.[17] It does not measure absolutes, only characteristic orientations, and these orientations will change over time and with experiences. But then people change, and no one wants to be pigeonholed as a thing, fixed forever in some position.

FIRO is not *the* tool to use. It does not provide *the* answer. However, it is *a* tool, and it does provide many answers. When considered from this view, FIRO can be one of the most effective single methods of counseling.

NOTES

[1] William C. Schutz, *The Interpersonal Underworld*, reprint ed. (Palo Alto, Ca.: Science and Behavior Books 1966).

[2] William C. Schutz, *The FIRO Scales Manual* (Palo Alto, Ca.: Consulting Psychologists Press, 1967).

[3] Questionnaires and additional interpretive material may be purchased at a reasonable price from Consulting Psychologists Press, 577 College Avenue, Palo Alto, California.

[4] As indicated, this article deals with the applied aspect of FIRO, not the theoretical foundation upon which it is based. A thorough reading of Schutz's *The Interpersonal Underworld* is suggested before using the questionnaires.

[5] Schutz, *Interpersonal Underworld*, pp. 13–33.

[6] Schutz, *FIRO Manual*, p. 8.

[7] Ibid.

[8] Ibid.

[9] Ibid.

[10] See Leo B. Ryan, *Clinical Interpretations of FIRO-B* (Palo Alto, Ca.: Consulting Psychologists Press, Inc., 1970).

[11] Ibid.

[12] Ibid.

[13] See Schutz, *The Interpersonal Underworld*, pp. 192–4, for a more detailed discussion of compatability.

[14] See Ryan, *Clinical Interpretations of FIRO-B*, for an additional discussion of control behavior. Much of the description given above is based on his research.

[15] This score was used for the parole officer because it represents the average profile, in control, of parole agents tested by this writer.

[16] This score represents the average Inclusion profile of parole agents tested thus far in research by this writer.

[17] Some counselors rely on FIRO-B alone in their casework. There is a disadvantage in this, for using FIRO-B without FIRO-F is like cruising on a ship through an ice flow. One sees only the top of the bergs.

19

The Use of Contract Counseling in Corrections

RICHARD D. JONES

Contract counseling can be seen as a recent behavioral development which can be utilized by a variety of correctional personnel. The author provides a guideline of the fundamental features of contract counseling and examples of contract counseling in actual practice.

Contract counseling is the second in a series of articles designed to introduce various intervention techniques which can be utilized by the correctional worker in helping the offender.

The primary purpose of the correctional system is to help an offender to do things differently from the way he did them before, since it's obvious that the way he did them before didn't work out well for him. In helping the offender we try to establish and maintain high levels of communication and understanding so that we can do something about the real problems involved. There are several stages that we go through in developing appropriate courses of action. The first step toward a solution is to agree on the existence of a problem or area of concern. The second step is to define the problem area as accurately as possible. Once this is accomplished the correctional worker then begins to formulate specific means to help. Next all the advantages and disadvantages of the action are considered. Finally the correctional worker must help the offender to develop a program that will give the offender the best chance of succeeding in his course of action.

There is no one course of action for all offenders. Just as the offenders bring a variety of problems to the correctional worker, so the correctional worker must bring a variety of intervention strategies to the helping process. In essence the correctional workers must establish and maintain a facilitative relationship and must have a large variety of intervention strategies. When the correctional worker uses a variety of

Reprinted, with permission of the author and publisher, from *Georgia Journal of Corrections*, Vol 2, No. 2 (August 1973): 40–41.

action courses with an offender he must remember that these intervention strategies will affect each other and that all must begin in relatively small steps.

CONTRACT COUNSELING

Contract counseling is a recent behavioral development. The underlying concept of contracting is old although its development in counseling is recent. The basic concepts of contract counseling are easily adaptable to the correctional system and can be used by a variety of correctional personnel.

While there are numerous variations, the fundamental features of contract counseling include:

1. The correctional worker and offender establishing and maintaining a high level of communication and understanding that builds trust between them.
2. The correctional worker and offender agreeing on the existence of a problem and defining this area as completely as possible.
3. The correctional worker and offender deciding on the behaviors that are needed in order to correct the problem. This may involve the offender agreeing to perform certain behaviors singularly and this may involve both the offender and correctional worker agreeing to perform certain behaviors.
4. The correctional worker and offender agreeing on the method or methods of evaluating how well the contract has been fulfilled and what the reward will be.
5. The correctional worker and offender deciding upon the terminal dates for the completion of segments of the contract or the contract as a whole.
6. The correctional worker and offender writing out the terms of the contract and both of them signing it. It may prove beneficial to have the terms typed and the signatures witnessed by a notary, warden, or someone important to the offender. When this is done it is necessary to complete two contracts, one for the correctional worker and one for the offender.
7. The correctional worker and offender proceeding to fulfill the terms of the contract. The correctional worker acting as a resource person while providing encouragement and support to the offender.
8. The correctional worker and offender determining if the contract has been fulfilled. If not, the offender may be granted additional time, the contract may be renegotiated or he may simply fail to receive the reward he contracted for.

When the interaction process between the correctional worker and the offender is such that some plan of action can be formulated, the correctional worker must decide whether or not contract counseling would be appropriate. Contracting will not work with all offenders. The correctional worker's decision concerning the use of contract counseling should be based on the nature of the problem and the needs and characteristics of the offender. In general, relatively simple behavioral problems involving a lack either of self-discipline, judgment, or motivation, lend themselves best to a contractual system. The contract system is also applicable in dealing with offenders in training or in a program of behavior modification. The discovery that present attitudes and behaviors are not successful in achieving his goals lead to the offender's desire to contract with a counselor, administrator, guard or teacher for the kinds of behavior or action that will facilitate his adjustment. In group counseling, a contract between the correctional worker and the group and/or among the group members may be functional. This often helps to mold the member to meet group norms and expectations.

Establishment of a contractual agreement necessitates a discussion of the system between worker and the offender. The correctional worker should not force acceptance of the system on the offender but should clearly indicate that (1) the contract will consist of a plan of action worked out together, (2) this plan will require certain kinds of different behavior, (3) the correctional worker will give support and assistance in checking on progress, and (4) the responsibility for the success or failure of the contract lies with the offender. The offender must then decide to accept or reject this approach to his problem.

Upon acceptance of the contractual approach, the offender should select the most satisfactory course of action. The contract thus becomes a list of desired behaviors consistent with the selected course of action. Initially, it may not be possible to develop the entire program. The contract can, however, be amended as new factors emerge or as previously designed courses of action are proven to be unworkable.

Through contract counseling the offender is encouraged to define his problems, work out the process that will lead to successful solutions, and take action on the plan. The correctional worker's role is to help the offender evaluate his progress, assist him in formulating new plans, contribute technical information, and provide encouragement and support to the offender.

CONTRACT COUNSELING IN ACTION

A description of some actual situations in which contract counseling was successfully employed will serve as an illustration. These situations occurred in Georgia and Alabama and were reported to the author by the correctional workers.

Bob, an inmate living in a dorm unit, was always receiving disciplinary slips for not having his area clean when the guard checked it. The situation seemed to be getting worse until Bob, the guard, and the counselor talked about the problem. Together they contracted to make up a checklist for Bob to follow each day. They went over his past slips and found the reasons for receiving them was usually related to not taking care of five basic items. They were (1) not putting away his personal things from the top of the stand next to his bed, (2) not hanging up his clothes in the locker, (3) not having his bed made, (4) not having his shoes under his bunk, and (5) not having his books stacked up. They contracted that if he were to follow the checklist each day and check off the items as he did them he would not receive any slips and would therefore not have any of his free time taken away as had happened in the past. This checklist gave Bob a structured system to follow that soon corrected the situation. Today Bob is still using the checklist and his area is now one of the best in the dorm.

Jim, a probationer, was having domestic problems and his wife had threatened several times to have him arrested. Jim and his P.O. discussed the problem and defined it as the wife being angry because Jim would not give her any money from his paycheck. Together, Jim, his wife and the P.O. sat down and worked out a contract that consisted of a planned budget where Jim would give a certain amount of money to his wife each week. From this, the wife was to buy food and pay all monthly bills. If he would do this the wife agreed not to have him arrested. The P.O. agreed to come by the house each payday for the first month, then once per month and then once every other month to help Jim and his wife stick to their contract and budget. So far this plan is working and Jim and his wife seem to have one less thing to argue about.

Mach, a guard, had a work detail that was not inclined to complete the jobs they were given. This caused Mach to ride the men and resulted in their working even slower, usually not finishing their daily work assignments. Mach talked this over with the social worker and psychologist and together they decided to try the contract system with the men. Mach then discussed this matter with the warden and received his permission to try it. The next day Mach called the men together and explained that when they finished their work assignment they could then go in and have any part of the day that was left as free time. The men agreed and instead of Mach having to ride them, all the men seemed well motivated to *finish* the job. The result is that the men now usually finish their daily work assignments about an hour earlier.

ADVANTAGES OF THE CONTRACT SYSTEM

The contractual system is similar in some aspects to the concepts of various counseling processes. It provides structural reinforcement and can be used by noncounselors in the correctional system. There are several other advantages:

1. The contractual system is based on trust between the correctional worker and the offender.
2. The contractual system helps the offender to assume responsibility for his own behavior.
3. The contractual system provides a written record of the commitments made by the offender and establishes the course of action that will lead to success.
4. The contractual system provides a quasi-legal document that often acts as a motivational device for the offender.
5. The contractual system introduces time limits which tend to act as a motivational force.
6. The contractual system is broken into various sections or subgoals, with evaluation taking place at various times. This provides the offender with intermittent reinforcement and gives him a feeling of progress.
7. The contractual system tends to insure that the offender will receive evaluations of his progress from the correctional worker at regular intervals.

CONCLUSION

The purpose of this article has been to demonstrate how the contract system may be used to provide an innovative approach not only to counseling but also to other aspects of the correctional system. Besides providing a logical, self-directed approach to problem solving, the contract system allows the offender to assume responsibility for his own behavior. While contract counseling is certainly not a panacea for every problem the correctional worker faces, it can prove to be a valuable addition to his repertoire of intervention strategies.

20

Behavior Modification Techniques: New Tools for Probation Officers

GAYLORD L. THORNE, ROLAND G. THARP, AND RALPH J. WETZEL

Dr. Thorne is director of the Behavioral Research Project of the Southern Arizona Mental Health Center. Dr. Tharp is director of the Psychology Department at the Center and co-investigator for the Behavioral Research Project. Dr. Wetzel is associate professor at the University of Arizona and consultant for the project.

Probation work with juvenile delinquents, as the authors have viewed it, has not been very rewarding to the probation officers and not very helpful to the youngsters. Far too many youngsters fail probation by committing further offenses and, unfortunately, a significant percentage move on to adult crime. Probation officers frequently point to their large caseloads and lack of professional training as causes for low success rates. The former certainly warrants concern, whereas the latter is probably overemphasized. The position of this article[1] is that juvenile probation officers could be considerably more effective than they are presently even with large caseloads and no graduate training.

Such a position is based on the burgeoning evidence that has become available recently in the field of mental health. Great changes are underway. The importance of the following is diminishing in modern treatment approaches: Talking therapies as a major curative method; the medical disease model; primary reliance on highly trained therapists; institutions operating as quasi-psychiatric centers; and the emphasis on "psychiatric" causation (particularly psychoanalytic) for antisocial behavior. The abandonment or severe curtailment of these traditional approaches has led to some badly needed changes.

The application of *behavior modification* techniques is certainly one of the most exciting and refreshing of the new treatment innovations. The techniques follow from operant learning theory—a theory that is elegantly simple, easily taught, dramatically effective, and useful in an almost unlimited number of settings (Grossberg, 1964; Schwitzgebel,

Reprinted, with permission, from *Federal Probation*, Quarterly, June 1967, pp. 21–26.

1964; Ullmann and Krasner, 1965; Wolpe, et al., 1964). The juvenile probation officer is in a key position to take advantage of these new techniques. This was recently pointed out by Judge Ronald B. Jamieson (1965) in his recommendation of the use of conditioning principles in probation work.

> Judges can keep learning theory and conditioning principles in mind in drafting conditions of probation. They can require the probationer to do things (1) which will tend to break habits and associations which led him into crime and (2) which will tend to create new habits and associations which will tend to lead him into constructive, non-criminal activity (p. 7).[2]

BEHAVIOR MODIFICATION TECHNIQUES

What are behavior modification techniques? Briefly, they represent the systematic application of a reinforcement learning theory largely developed by B. F. Skinner and his associates. The basic premise is: *Behavior is governed by its consequences.* Only observable behavior is dealt with; fantasies, dreams, the unconscious, ego, etc., are not considered legitimate data. The goal of modifying behavior is accomplished by altering consequences. One technique of such an approach involves the determination of these consequences (or more technically *reinforcers)* and applying them when a desired behavior is approximated.

A child's reinforcers can be determined by carefully observing his behavior. Each child has an idiosyncratic list of reinforcers which one can rank from most to least important. Aside from candy for young children, and money for all others, it is seldom that reinforcers can be accurately specified without observation and inquiry. In working with predelinquent children, the authors determine a "reinforcement hierarchy" by inquiring directly from the child and from his parents as to what motivates him—the people, things, or events which he seeks.

There are two general types of reinforcement schedules used to modify behavior. The first is a "positive schedule of reinforcement," and is characterized by such reinforcers as praise, attention, privileges, money, food, TV, use of the car, etc. Changes in behavior promoted by such a schedule tend to be relatively rapid and durable. The second is an "aversive schedule of reinforcement," and is characterized by such reinforcers as threats, physical punishment, confinement, withdrawal of rewards and privileges, ridicule, ostracism, etc. Psychologists have shown that behavior changes promoted on the latter kind of schedule tend to be relatively limited and temporary.

In actual practice the type of schedule used to modify behavior is usually mixed, i.e., both positive and aversive. The key to modifying behavior lies with that which is given the major emphasis. Many delinquent and predelinquent children are being raised primarily on an aversive schedule and, unfortunately, the steps usually taken by public agencies to correct such behavior are also very likely to be aversive—e.g., being expelled from school, incarcerated, etc. The challenge, from a behavior modification viewpoint, is how to get the youngster onto a more balanced schedule of reinforcement.

THE CONCEPTS OF SHAPING AND CONTINGENCY

Two more concepts are needed to round out the general description of operant principles before dealing with specific procedures to change behavior. The first is *shaping,* a term used to describe steps or approximations to a desired goal. When a behavior is selected as a goal, then all responses that approximate this goal are reinforced and all other responses are not reinforced. For example, when an otherwise very capable youngster is getting all failing grades in school one should not immediately ask for A's on his work. Instead, he should be shaped toward A's by rewarding D's and all behaviors approximating those needed for academic success (attending, opening book, completing some of the assignments). Once D's are attained the reward criterion can be gradually increased to C's, then B's, and finally A's. The same process would be used for antisocial behaviors. To illustrate, a boy who habitually fights could be rewarded for going a full day without a fight, then 2 days, then 5 days, until it was felt that he had learned new nonaggressive ways of relating to peers.

The second is the concept of *contingency* and it is absolutely essential in understanding operant principles. Contingency means that the consequences of an event are made dependent upon whether the event occurs. For example, telling a child he may have an ice cream cone only if he behaves means that ice cream is contingent upon good behavior; or, if parole depends upon acceptable prison behavior, then acting-out prevents parole. It is a very simple and straightforward concept that we deal with in a variety of ways during our daily lives. However, failure to understand the importance of rewarding or punishing *on contingency* is commonplace and can utterly destroy learning.

ALTERNATIVES TO TRADITIONAL THERAPY

The possible use of probation officers as agents to implement behavior modification would be highly consistent with some current outlooks on treating problem children. The traditional use of highly trained psychotherapists has not been particularly successful with children. The creation of an artificial relationship between a youngster and a caseworker, psychologist or other individual, takes considerable time and skill, yet its effectiveness can be questioned. However, the use of natural relationships (e.g., parents, friends, relatives, teachers) for bringing about changes in a youngster can be efficient and powerful. Parents have the primary responsibility for their children, and if they even display a modicum of cooperation there is a potential for bringing about behavior changes of a meaningful and durable nature.

The agents used on the Behavioral Research Project of the Southern Arizona Mental Health Center to teach new child management techniques to parents and teachers are all subprofessionals—bachelor's degrees or less. They were trained and are supervised by the authors. The training techniques could easily be taught to probation officers to improve their effectiveness.

The typical probation officer's effectiveness with youngsters could be improved with operant techniques because of the ways they usually fulfill their present roles. When a probation officer enters a child's life, his "treatment" plan is traditionally built around points of law, the prestige of the judge, threats of incarceration, the punishments and restrictions he can create in the home and community, lectures on bad behavior and society's right of revenge, lists of "Do Not" rules to follow, and the use of his presence in the home or school to prevent certain misbehaviors. Psychologists would describe this as an aversive schedule of reinforcement—only unpleasant or punishing consequences are used. They would also predict that such a reinforcement schedule will only produce circumscribed learning (Bandura, 1962; Skinner, 1953). The latter is further complicated by the fact that additional contacts with the child's parents rarely occur (while he behaves), so the changes in their behavior are not reinforced by the probation officer and thus not maintained. This represents a considerable waste of effort in a large percentage of cases, i.e., one instance of threat from the juvenile court motivates only a small number of parents to change their ways.

The error of focusing one's attention on misbehavior is certainly not unique to probation officers. It is a commonplace occurrence in schools and homes. School teachers particularly tend toward this, seldom realizing that the use of attention in this manner actually *stimulates* and *maintains* misbehavior in a large number of youngsters. It is, of course, only logical that probation officers must focus their initial attention on misbehavior since they have almost no other occasion for being in contact with a child. However, this does not justify the continuation of such a focus.

Probation officers should make use of their aversive controls, which can temporarily reduce misbehavior, and then build a treatment or rehabilitation plan around positive controls that would teach new socially acceptable behaviors. The whole purpose of behavior modification techniques is to introduce reinforcement contingencies that will encourage the emergence of nondeviant behaviors. The latter can rarely be done without teaching parents new child management techniques; juvenile probation officers are usually very remiss about doing this.

Some Case Examples

Perhaps several cases from the Behavioral Research Project will illustrate some of the alternatives available in working with the teachers and families of misbehaving children. All of this work was carried out by subprofessional staff, so in every case a juvenile probation officer (trained in operant techniques, of course) could have done the same.

Case 1. Claire is a bright, moderately attractive 16-year-old who was referred to the project for truancy, poor grades, and incorrigibility at home. The parents were divorced 6 years ago and the mother now supports the two of them as a maid. The father is out of state, as is Claire's older married sister.

When the referral came from a local high school, it stated that Claire was going to be expelled for truancy. The staff persuaded them to hold up expulsion for several days, which they were willing to do.

The mother was eager for help, although she lacked the physical or emotional resources to assist very much. Claire had been staying home from school for days and was now threatening to run away. Her mother had withdrawn all money, the use of the telephone, and dating privileges. These were all very powerful reinforcers to Claire but, unfortunately, her mother had not provided any clear way for Claire to earn them back.

Obviously, the most pressing problem was Claire's truancy and it was imperative that an intervention plan be prepared immediately to prevent suspension from school. Also, Claire's attending school would be very reinforcing to mother who was, at this time, somewhat dubious that a "noncounseling" approach would be successful. By winning her confidence it would be possible to begin shaping her to regard Claire in a more positive perspective, which would be necessary before a more amicable relationship could be worked out between them.

An intervention plan was agreed upon by mother, Claire, and a staff member. Telephone privileges and weekend dates were contingent on attending school all day. The school attendance officer would dispense a note to Claire at the end of each day if she had attended all of her classes. On presenting the note to mother, Claire earned telephone usage (receiving and calling out) for that day. If she received four out of five notes during the week she earned one weekend date night, and five out of five notes earned two weekend date nights. Phone usage on the weekend was not included in this plan.

Much to mother's astonishment Claire accepted the plan. Mother herself felt the plan "childish" and was apprehensive about Claire complying with it. Staff emphasized the necessity and benefit of praising Claire whenever she brought a note home. This would be difficult for mother, who was inconsistent, ineffectual, and emotional in all her relations with Claire. However, she was given support through several brief phone calls every week.

Despite frequent family upsets Claire attended school regularly from the first day of intervention. The plan was altered (in technical terms the schedule was "thinned") after a month so that Claire would receive only two notes a week. A note on Wednesdays would mean she attended all her classes on Monday, Tuesday, and Wednesday. This was backed up by the privilege of one weekend night out. A second note on Friday meant full attendance on Thursday and Friday, which was backed up by a second weekend night out. The telephone privileges were taken off contingency. About 7 weeks later the notes were stopped entirely.

The results were quite impressive. During the first 46 days of school (baseline period) Claire missed 30 days of school (65.2 percent absent). While working with the project for less than 3 months she was illegally absent twice (6.6 percent). She was *never* illegally absent again following termination, which covers the entire second semester of school. Grades were beyond redemption during the first semester mainly because of absences, thus causing her to fail two subjects. This dropped to one failure during the second semester.

According to her counselor at school, Claire continued to experience a poor relationship with her mother but did begin expressing positive attitudes and interests in her classes. Thus, the project was successful in preventing this girl from being expelled from school and probably running away. This was accomplished with a very modest expenditure of staff time.

Case 2. Mark is a 7th grade boy referred by the local juvenile court for (1) incorrigibility—refusing to do chores, disobedient, defiant; (2) destructiveness—toys and family property were often impulsively destroyed; (3) stealing—both at school and at home; and (4) poor peer relations—he has few friends and frequently fights with his siblings. He lives with his natural parents and two younger sisters.

The case is particularly interesting because of the great difficulty the staff had in gaining parental cooperation. The mother and father seemed to be people who derived little from experience. The father handled all discipline problems with a combination of extended lectures and punishment. His whippings were commonly followed by some destructive act by Mark, but the father still would not reduce his corporal punishment. The mother was also prone to lecture Mark, as well as being quite vague and inconsistent in her expectations of him. The destructive acts around home were serious enough to require immediate attention. Money, praise (especially from father), and a new bicycle were found to be highly reinforcing to Mark. His allowance had been placed entirely contingent on report card grades at school, which meant long periods of nonreinforcement. The parents were persuaded to reinstate the allowance contingent on daily nondestructive behavior at home. If he did destroy or damage something, he would lose money for that day, plus having to pay for repairs. In addition, Mark could earn points each day for the successful completion of chores at home, points that would accumulate toward the purchase of a bicycle in about 6 months. Regular assignments were encouraged from school so that Mark could be rewarded for studying at least 30 minutes after school. When father would arrive home from work he praised Mark for studying. Should he study each day of the week father would "bonus" him with an extra allowance or special weekend outings together. Father was to ignore Mark on any day that he did not study. The parents kept daily records on these behaviors. The records were collected every other week.

At the end of 7 weeks Mark had not committed a single destructive act, there had been no reports of stealing, he rarely missed completing a day of his chores, and he was studying at least one-half hour 6 nights a week. The parents were pleased but informed the project that Mark did not need to be praised and rewarded for appropriate acts—this was just "bribery." It was so alien to the nature of these parents to use rewards to shape behavior that they were seriously considering dropping the plan despite its considerable success. Fortunately, report cards came out at this time and Mark showed improvement in both academic and behavior grades. Therefore, it was possible to persuade them to continue.

A disaster did occur several weeks later, though. Mark broke his eyeglasses. This prevented any studying for a week, but worse still it precipitated an infuriated reaction in his father because of the expense. Mark was castigated and the bicycle point-chart was indefinitely suspended.

Some 6 weeks passed before any consistent plan of action was reinstated. School work, intermittently reinforced with father's praise, was maintained at its prior high level. Two minor acts of destructiveness occurred at home (he broke some bathroom tile and a toy) and he exhibited some defiant behaviors toward his mother. Completion of chores began dropping again, and probably was most responsible for the parents again accepting the suggestion to make a chart for the chores and reward completion of them. The "back-up" (reward) would be interaction with father plus his praise. Earning money and the bicycle were still not allowed by the parents.

About five weeks were spent in keeping a daily chart on Mark's completion of chores. He would place a star on the chart and then the parents would praise him. The frequency of chore completion soon rose to 100 percent and this so pleased the father he decided to reinstate the bicycle point-chart. Completion of chores and obedient behaviors would then earn points, and when an arbitrary total was accumulated he would get a new bicycle. Mark got the new bicycle in 34 days. In this period he had 170 individual behaviors that could earn points, and he was reinforced on 168 of them.

The parents are fully persuaded as to the importance of making rewards contingent, and the efficacy of shaping behavior with positive reinforcement. No daily charts are now kept on Mark. A 6-week followup shows no return to previous misbehaviors. Originally, he had earned two D's and an F in eight subjects on the midterm report card. His final report card had no mark below a C.

Case 3. Blaine is a 14-year-old boy whose limited ability (IQ in low 80's) had contributed to a number of adjustment problems at home and at school. His father referred him to the project because he had been setting fires in and around his home, and frequently messing up the home. The school complained of his antagonism toward peers and general incorrigibility. The father had tried occasional spankings, lectures, and restriction of TV (the most effective). The school had tried paddling, scolding, restriction of playground privileges, plus the principal inviting him to the gym to put on the boxing gloves!

The mother had died 2 years previously in an airplane crash. Blaine and his 12-year-old brother were cared for during the day by a neighbor, while the father worked as a policeman. The neighbor lady was capable of setting limits on Blaine, but was not a source of much reinforcement. The father was quite reinforcing and capable of using his reinforcers on contingency.

The most urgent matter of business was to stop the playing with matches. Several minor fires had been started by Blaine, and his father realistically feared a serious one. A daily chart was kept by the father and the babysitter. A star was put up each day that Blaine refrained from playing with matches. This was backed up daily by praise from his father and access to evening TV. A week of success also gained him 25 cents. If on any day he was caught playing with matches, he did not get his star, he lost his TV privileges, and his quarter on the weekend. A second chart was simultaneously begun for the completion of chores (the details are unimportant here). No intervention was begun at school.

In the 2 weeks prior to intervention, Blaine had been caught playing with matches four times. Blaine continued on the chart system for nearly 6 months. He had 161 opportunities for reinforcement (no playing with matches) and he missed only one of them. Equally interesting, though, were the side effects that occurred after he was put on a positive schedule of reinforcement. Both Blaine and his brother began doing their chores regularly, thus receiving attention, praise, and money. The school reported a steady improvement in Blaine's attitude and behavior. No misbehavior incident was reported on him at school from the time following intervention. Recent followup showed no changes—the school was full of praise for his behavior and playing with matches had not recurred.

Case 4. The final case is particularly instructive because it demonstrates some of the strengths and limitations of behavior modification techniques. Loren is a 16-year-old boy who lives with his stepfather, mother, and two younger brothers. He was referred for (1) assaultive behavior—threatening to shoot his stepfather and trying to fist fight with both parents; (2) defiance of nearly all parental requests (coming home early at night, completing his household chores, mowing the lawn, not taking the car without permission); and (3) habitual truancy. Police had been called for several of these incidents, and referral was made from the local juvenile court.

Assessment of the family revealed that Loren was on an entirely aversive reinforcement schedule. He was denied allowance, restricted to the house, restricted from the car, continually threatened with the police, and verbally abused. None of these was effective. Money, use of the car, and nights-out were considered positively reinforcing, but the parents were so angry with Loren they provided no clear way for him to earn these. An interview with Loren confirmed the latter.

Loren's parents were where many are at the point of referral —desperate. They had been meeting each infraction with punishment until a point of no return was reached. The thought of rewarding Loren for approximations of "good" behavior had not occurred to them and the suggestion was met with great skepticism. However, since they had exhausted their own repertoire of controls, the project staff member was able to persuade them to at least give his suggestions a try.

Two points in the family assessment were quite important. First, Loren apparently had never been given a clear idea of his parents' expectations. For example, instructions such as, "Be in at a decent hour," made for much uncertainty. Second, it became obvious that his stepfather wanted the boy out of the home and was trying to accomplish this through unrealistic and vacillating demands.

The intervention plan consisted of a carefully devised schedule —more nearly a contract—which would allow Loren to earn money for completion of chores and being obedient (e.g., on a weekend night he must be in by midnight). Failures brought not only a loss of money but also carried a fine in the form of 15-minute blocks of restricted time from use of the family car. For the first time he knew exactly how to earn money and time away from home, and exactly what the consequences would be for not conforming. The parents were not to hedge on the contingencies, and biweekly phone calls from our staff plus a posted copy of the "contract" were used to prevent this.

Rapid changes subsequently occurred in Loren's behavior. In the first 35 days, he was rewarded an average of 81 percent of the time in each of four areas of responsibility (range 75 to 89 percent). Prior to intervention he met these obligations rarely (0 to 10 percent).

At this point a second contract was drawn up because Loren's stepfather was continuing to nag him despite tremendous improvement and because Loren's car insurance had expired and his stepfather refused to renew it. The new contract was negotiated in the presence of both parents, Loren, and a project staff member. It allowed for points to be earned for chores and responsibilities which could be applied to the car insurance premium (stepfather agreed finally to this). Loren could earn a maximum of 50 points a week, and needed 250 for the premium. The first week he earned 22 points and then the full 50 on each week thereafter.

Loren began driving the car again, but only by meeting specific contingencies agreed to by his parents, himself, and staff. In addition, he re-entered high school, achieved satisfactorily, was not truant, and had applied for an after-school job. The case was maintained at this level of success for 24 days, requiring only one phone call to the parents and two brief home visits. Loren's stepfather and mother expressed satisfaction over the changes and felt that he was doing so well that the "contract" should be abandoned. Our staff member vigorously tried to discourage this, feeling that such a drastic change was premature. However, the parents persevered and abruptly ceased abiding by the agreements and contingencies.

Events following the parents' return to pre-intervention conditions illustrate an unfortunate collapse of environmental controls. Loren was truant for the succeeding 7 school days, and was arrested 11 days later for burglary. His parents refused to visit him during his 2 days at a detention home. In addition, they told the probation officer that Loren was "hopelessly" bad despite all the good things they had done for him. The court placed Loren on probation and reluctantly allowed him to return to his home. The project had recommended foster placement but none was available. His adjustment remains exceedingly tenuous at home, but the parents have refused further help.

Loren's case demonstrates the validity of behavior modification techniques—behavior can be changed by altering environmental consequences, while simultaneously exhibiting its limitations, and uncooperative parents can defeat productive change. Probation officers adopting operant techniques will thus have to accept a shortcoming common to all known forms of helping children, namely, bad parents yield bad results.

BEHAVIOR MODIFICATION AND JUVENILE PROBATION OFFICERS

What are the possible applications probation officers could make from these cases? The amount of time spent in devising intervention plans such as those used on the Behavioral Research Project of the Southern Arizona Mental Health Center probably would not burden court staff (all of these were arranged in 3 or less interviews). Once the intervention plan is underway staff contacts (by phone when possible) decrease steadily to three or four a month. Most importantly, though, the behavior modification techniques frequently *work* and the probation officer can begin experiencing positive changes in behavior rather than just suppression of misbehavior.

The authors see juvenile probation officers as having the potential for becoming experts in behavior modification. They could continue to approach their delinquent charges as representatives of the courts, and as such they would still be dispensers of aversive control. The real change, though, would be that aversive methods would no longer be their only source of control. They could also be skilled in teaching parents how to put powerful positive rewards on contingency. The combination, in the hands of a trained person, is most effective. Psychologists are increasingly available to teach operant theory and its application, and thereafter can be available on a consultative basis to juvenile courts and field offices. The time has never been more right for the people in probation work to reach out for new techniques.

NOTES

[1] This article is based on data gathered from the Behavioral Research Project which is supported by the Office of Juvenile Delinquency and Youth Development, Welfare Administration, Department of Health, Education, and Welfare.

[2] Ronald B. Jamieson, "Can Conditioning Principles Be Applied to Probation?" *Trial Judges' Journal*, 4 No. 1 (1965).

REFERENCES

A. Bandura, "Punishment Revisited," *Journal of Consulting Psychology*, 26 (1962): 298–301.

J. M. Grossberg, "Behavior Therapy: A Review," *Psychological Bulletin*, 1964.

R. B. Jamieson, "Can Conditioning Principles Be Applied to Probation?" *Trial Judges' Journal*, 4, no. 1 (1965).

F. S. Keller, *Learning: Reinforcement Theory.* New York: Random House, Inc., 1954.

R. Schwitzgebel, *Street Corner Research.* Cambridge: Harvard University Press, 1964.

B. F. Skinner, *Science and Human Behavior.* New York: Macmillan Co., 1953.

L. Ullmann and L. Krasner, eds. *Case Studies in Behavior Modification.* New York: Holt, Rinehart and Winston, 1965.

J. Wolpe, A. Salter, and L. J. Reyna, *The Conditioning Therapies: The Challenge in Psychotherapy.* New York: Holt, Rinehart and Winston, 1964.

21

Reward and Punishment: Some Guidelines for Their Effective Application in Correctional Programs for Youthful Offenders

J. TERRY SAUNDERS

B.A. (Psychology), 1968, Harvard University

N. DICKON REPPUCCI

Assistant Professor, Psychology Department, Yale University
Lecturer, Department of Social Relations, Harvard University, 1968;
Director of Graduate Training in Clinical Psychology, Yale University,
1969-70

Ph.D. (Clinical Psychology), 1968, Harvard University

This paper is intended to provide some guidelines for developing programs to rehabilitate, or change the behavior of, youthful offenders. The first section analyzes the principles of reward, punishment, and group pressure, stressing their combined use. The second section discusses the need for rigor and reviews certain factors that play a key role in the effectiveness of reward and punishment. Among these are environmental and developmental trends, consistency and immediacy of reward and punishment, and the continued use of rewards and punishments with high generalization potential.

A program to rehabilitate youthful offenders in a correctional institution may take several forms. Selection of an appropriate program must consider overall long-term goals, a theoretical pattern to guide the application of specific measures, staff size, inmate population, physical plant location, and available funds.

The following is an attempt to establish some general principles, basic to the science of behavior, that will serve as guidelines for the

Reprinted with permission of the National Council on Crime and Delinquency, from *Crime and Delinquency*, July 1972, pp. 284–290.

formulation of a program to rehabilitate young persons—a program to change their behavior.

THE PRINCIPLE OF REWARD

Behavior can be changed through the systematic use of rewards. A reward given to a person immediately following a certain behavior will tend to increase the frequency of that behavior. Likewise, an absence of reward following any particular behavior will tend to decrease the frequency of that behavior. For example, a baby is sitting on the floor surrounded by several of his toys; his father is reading in a nearby chair. On impulse the baby picks up a rattle and shakes it. Seeing this, his father is amused and laughs. The child sees his father laugh and shakes the rattle again. Once more the father laughs. Soon the child shakes the rattle repeatedly, each time watching his father laugh. As the novelty wears off, the father stops laughing and returns to his reading. Watching his father closely, the baby shakes the rattle a few more times; then, seeing that his father isn't laughing, he stops shaking the rattle, puts it down, and looks for another toy.

Let us analyze this example in terms of behavior and reward. To a child whose father is at work all day, his father's laugh is something special and pleasant—a reward. In the above example, the child found he could obtain this pleasant reward by shaking the rattle. The behavior was shaking the rattle; the reward was the father's laugh. When the reward followed the behavior, the particular behavior increased; that is, the child ignored his other toys and played only with the rattle. When the father tired of this play, the child learned that he could no longer obtain the reward by shaking the rattle and returned to other toys. When the reward did not follow the behavior, the behavior decreased and finally stopped.

THE PRINCIPLE OF PUNISHMENT

Behavior can also be changed through the systematic use of punishment. When a person is punished immediately following an enjoyable behavior, he will tend to perform that behavior less frequently. If the punishment is removed, the behavior will usually return to its previous rate of occurrence. Let us resume our example at the point where we left off.

The baby is looking for another toy. He picks up a few toys and gives them a cursory examination, but he is becoming bored. He looks around the room and spies a pretty vase on a nearby table. It is shiny, very colorful, and within reach. As the child moves toward the vase, the father looks up from his book to check on the baby. Seeing the baby's intended target, he says, "No!" The child hesitates, then continues to move forward. The father repeats his command with emphasis. Now the child stops and sits still. Shortly thereafter the father leaves the room. As he leaves, the child looks up, crawls to the table, and reaches for the vase, with fairly predictable results.

Let us look at the example in terms of behavior and punishment. The father did not want his child to play with the vase. When the child made a move to do so, the father used the punishment of saying *no*. (Saying *no* to someone is usually considered a mild reaction, but it is a form of punishment to a child who wants his father's approval.) Hearing his father say *no* for the second time, the child stopped the behavior. In other words, when the punishment immediately followed the behavior, the behavior ceased. Note, however, that soon after the father left the room, the child went for the vase again. The punishment was taken away, and as a result the behavior recurred.

THE PRINCIPLE OF GROUP PRESSURE

A third way to change behavior is the systematic use of group pressure. The basic assumption underlying the principle of group pressure is that persons who are often together as a group have considerable influence over one another's behavior and, through social pressure, can change one another's behavior. Let us take a real-life example from a correctional institution for boys.

> In a 60-man dormitory, the inmates brought their soiled towels to a central location where, after being counted, clean ones were issued. This had been a carefully monitored routine procedure. The correctional community staff in this dormitory decided to increase the prisoners' responsibility, beginning with a different procedure in distributing towels. One morning, it was explained in the large group that towels would be given out on Monday, Wednesday, and Friday of each week, by simply being placed on a conveniently located table, one towel for each inmate.
>
> The program started on the following day when 60 towels were placed on the designated table. The inmates scrambled for them. Some took more than one. Staff made no move to control the situation. The individuals who did not get towels were angry and attempted to manipulate the staff to get towels. Staff refused, explaining that 60 towels had been placed on the table, enough for all. The responsibility for towel distribution belonged with the inmates. Some inmates threatened that "something drastic" might result if staff didn't handle the problem.
>
> When their demands were not met, some inmates showered and came to the staff nude, dripping wet, and explained that they had no towels. The staff explained that they understood this situation, but did not supply towels. The inmates were bitter and again threatened that some inmate might be beaten up or "piped" that evening if the staff did not act. The threats were ignored. Thus frustrated, the wet in-

mates asked the staff what they should do and how they could dry off. Staff said they would have to work the problem out for themselves. The inmates then returned to the shower and used their underwear for towels.

The next morning, in the community-group meeting, the inmates let loose a barrage of hostility. They questioned whether the staff was really interested in helping them. They complained that the State of California was too cheap to provide enough towels. They made wild comments and menacing gestures in an effort to manipulate staff. When it became apparent to them that the staff would not be stampeded or manipulated, the atmosphere changed. One inmate suggested a solution. Those without towels could report to the gym and state that they were going to work out. The coach would then provide them with towels. Instead of working out, the inmates could return to the dormitory with these towels. The supervisor asked, "Isn't this a delinquent solution to the problem? Is it not in fact somewhat like the kind of behavior which had gotten you into the institution in the first place?" At this time the inmate blushed, others laughed.

Finally, one inmate pointed out that the group could assume the responsibility for seeing that everyone got a towel. But the group was not yet ready to accept this answer to their situation. This problem continued to be talked about in groups for six weeks. Some staff members became bored and wanted to change the subject. Actually, they were becoming more anxious and frustrated, and wanted to talk about more comfortable subjects. The supervisor maintained that this subject should be talked about until the community could handle this responsibility. By insisting that the inmates assume responsibility for proper distribution of the 60 towels, the staff was able to assist the inmates in accepting the responsibility of seeing to it that each inmate took only one towel, and that there was a towel for each. In this manner the inmates, rather than the staff, were responsible.[1]

This example illustrates the principle of group pressure. By insisting that the whole group assume responsibility for the towel supply, the staff mobilized inmate social pressure to constrain individual activity that was not in the interest of the entire group.

RELATIONSHIP OF THE PRINCIPLES

Now, using the examples presented above, we can discuss the relationship between the principle of group pressure and the principles of reward and punishment.

Staff-Inmate Interaction

By encouraging the inmates to assume responsibility for equitable towel distribution, the staff rewarded their responsible behavior. When the inmates wished to talk constructively about the towel problem, the staff, though anxious at times, discussed the problem. At the same time, try-ing to decrease irresponsibility among the inmates, the staff ignored their irresponsible behavior. When the inmates confronted them nude and dripping wet, their appearance and threats were ignored.

The outcome was analogous to what happened in the example given under the principle of reward: The father increased the inci-dence of rattle shaking and decreased the incidence of playing with other toys by rewarding the former and ignoring the latter. Similarly, in the group pressure example, the staff was able to increase the inci-dence of responsible behavior and decrease the incidence of irrespon-sible behavior by rewarding the former and ignoring the latter.

Staff-Staff Interaction

As anyone with experience in a correctional setting might predict, the inmates attempted to change the staff's behavior in the towel incident through the use of staff-directed punishment. Menacing gestures, threats of violence and "pipings," and the previously mentioned meet-ing where inmates confronted the staff nude and wet were all intended to break down the staff's unanimous demand that the inmate group assume responsibility for towels. The staff succeeded in setting up a new towel distribution system only through *mutually* rewarding support and an agreement to see the incident through as a group with one opinion. The importance of this intrastaff support and consolidation of opinion cannot be overemphasized. If the supervisor had not insisted that the entire staff continue to discuss the issue when some members became anxious, the inmates would have sensed disunity. Visible dis-agreement among the staff would have served as rewarding feedback for the inmate group, a sign that their punitive attitude toward the staff was successful. If they had detected staff disunity, the inmates would have increased staff-directed punitive behavior.

Inmate-Inmate Interaction

Several inmates did not get towels; their main concern was how to get them. At first they tried to use pressure against the staff, but it soon became evident that the staff would not hand out extra towels. Then the inmates turned to themselves to solve the problem. They began to punish one another for behaviors which would not solve their problem; for example, an inmate suggested that they get towels from the coach under the pretense of working out, but he was laughed at. In the example under the principle of punishment, the father was able to pre-vent the baby from playing with the vase by saying *no*—a mild punish-ment. Similarly, in the group pressure example, the inmates discour-aged damaging behavior among themselves by using another form of mild punishment—laughing at someone.

EFFECTIVENESS OF REWARD AND PUNISHMENT

Much of what has been said up to this point could be classified as "common sense." If someone is "good," he should be rewarded; if someone is "bad," he should be punished or ignored. Rules can be made to apply to groups, and people within the groups may enforce them. Parents, school teachers, and correctional staff in general are already aware of these principles. If these principles are powerful instruments for changing behavior, why has their everyday application often been ineffective in changing the behavior of young offenders?

The question of effectiveness has long occupied the minds of behavioral scientists. As with any emerging science, answers are scarce and theories plentiful. In the behavior sciences rigor has long been recognized as a key factor in the effectiveness of reward and punishment. To make outcome effective, one must define reward and punishment rigorously and then apply them rigorously. At the program-planning stage, consideration must be given, first, to factors that may affect the nature of reward and punishment and, second, to factors that relate to the application of reward and punishment. Each of these topics will be discussed separately.

The Nature of Reward and Punishment

There is no simple way to define reward and punishment rigorously. A punishment for one individual may act as a reward for another. For our purposes a reward is any stimulus whose presentation increases the probability that the behavior it follows will be performed again, while punishment is any stimulus whose presentation decreases the probability that the behavior it follows will be performed again. There are at least two sets of circumstances that affect the nature of reward and punishment.

Environmental conditions make up the first of these sets of circumstances. An individual's environment helps to determine what will be rewarding or punishing to him. For example, consider reprimanding. Most people think of a reprimand as a form of punishment, and most youngsters react to it as punishment. If you reprimand most youngsters for a particular behavior, the frequency of that behavior will decrease. However, there are individuals who seem to react to reprimands as if they were rewarding; that is, if you reprimand them for a particular behavior, the frequency of that behavior will increase. Why the discrepancy? Environment may be one reason for these reactions.

The environment of most young people is such that they receive more attention from their parents and other adults when they behave well. However, the environment of some "problem" children is such that they receive the greatest amount of attention from parents and authorities when they behave poorly. In a correctional setting, there are many youngsters who are accustomed to receiving parental attention and peer approval only when they have violated parental rules or the law. Correctional staff who ignore a "problem" child's satisfactory behavior and reprimand his unsatisfactory behavior may find his unsatisfactory behavior increasing. He is rewarded when staff reprimand him because this is the only attention he receives from them. In addition, he probably receives praise from his fellow inmates for being "cool" and giving staff a hard time. In this situation one solution would be to increase the amount of attention he receives for satisfactory behavior from both staff and peers, even if it seems artificial, and reduce or eliminate attention for his unsatisfactory behavior. This solution would take environmental influences on reward and punishment into account.

A second set of circumstances affecting reward and punishment is made up of *developmental differences.* An individual's development or maturity dictates the nature of the rewards and punishments he receives. Our society says that the same rewards and punishments do not apply to both children and adults. When his work is outstanding, an adult receives a promotion or a pay raise; a child, on the other hand, receives candy or a prize for good behavior. Likewise, punishments for an adult are typically a loss of status or a lesser job; short of physical punishment, children are scolded, told they are bad, or sent to bed without any supper.

The point is obvious but nevertheless extremely important. The developmental differences reflected in rewards and punishments tell a person how old you think he is. If you reward and punish him as you would an adult, you are telling him that you think he is an adult; if you reward and punish him as a child, you are telling him that in your opinion he is a child.

Well-meaning correctional planners often use rewards and punishments that are not appropriate for the age group in their institution. For example many institutions in our society punish individuals by restricting their freedom. Confinement to quarters is much like making a child stay in his room. A more appropriate punishment for a young adult might be the loss of a job he values in the institution, substituting more menial, less interesting tasks. Rewards must also be commensurate with age. Increased privileges and higher status jobs are appropriate for a young adult, while "prizes" and special outings have their greatest effect on children's behavior.

Effective Application of Reward and Punishment

Many factors, some of them situation-specific, contribute to the overall effectiveness of reward and punishment when applied to changing behavior. We will discuss three of the most important.

The first is *consistency*. If a person's behavior is to change in the desired direction, he must be rewarded and punished in a consistent manner. In other words, a person will not behave the way you want him to if you sometimes reward him for a certain behavior and at other times punish him for the same behavior, or if he is rewarded for a certain behavior by one person and punished for it by another.

It is difficult to maintain consistency in large correctional institutions. The counseling staff may initiate programs for certain youngsters without informing the custodial staff. With three shifts per day and only custodial staff present in the evening and at night, the youngsters involved may receive markedly different treatment as their day progresses. They may be rewarded for particular behaviors by counselors and other staff during the day and ignored or punished for the same behaviors by custodial staff in the evening. Inconsistent application of rewards and punishments will never increase desired behavior, except by accident. In order to maintain consistency in behavior change programs, correctional institutions *must* keep *all* personnel informed on inmate behavior as well as on goals and objectives.

The second factor is *immediacy* of reward or punishment. Especially in the early phases of any behavior modification program, the reward or punishment should immediately follow the behavior that earned it. The rationale for this is simple. People tend to associate a reward or punishment with what they are doing at the moment. If you want a person to associate a reward with something he has just done, then he should be rewarded at that time—not later. The same is true for punishment. If the situation does not allow this immediacy, the next best thing to do is tell the person that he will be rewarded or punished later, and then keep your word. Verbal approval is easy to give and with some youngsters, quite effective; for many, however, something concrete is more likely to be effective, such as tokens that can be cashed in for appropriate rewards.

Like consistency, immediacy of reward and punishment is difficult to attain in large correctional settings; in many, it is a virtually impossible task.

The third factor is *continuation* of rewards and punishments over an extended time period; i.e., seeing to it that behavior will be similarly rewarded or punished in the future. Since it may take an individual a long time to learn a new behavior, those people who punish or reward him now may not be the ones who will punish or reward him later. Decision-makers should design rewards and punishments that will be commensurate with those the individual will face in the future. This is especially true in a correctional setting, where the goal should be to effect behavioral change that will be maintained when the inmate is returned to the home community. A schedule of rewards—e.g., a progressive system of job placements that begins in a correctional setting and continues upon release into the community—makes any transition to the community smoother. Moreover, it may reduce recidivism by providing inmates with skills that are appropriate for the society outside the institution.

NOTES

[1] N. Fenton, E. G. Rimer, and H. A. Wilmer, *The Correctional Community* (Berkeley: University of California Press, 1967), pp. 73–74.

V

GROUP AND PROCESS MODELS FOR COUNSELING

INTRODUCTION

These readings are distinguished by their focus on process and on the dynamics of group counseling, rather than on individualized classification and treatment models. Because there is always a process involved in any change or in any counseling relationship, this distinction is arbitrary to some extent. Nevertheless, the essence of the following strategies *is* the process rather than the application of more tangible, or more mechanical, methods. The strategies are further distinguished by their emphasis on the client's responsibility for directing his own change, and by their concern with encouraging personal enrichment and growth for the client, with law-abiding behavior as a by-product.

In the first article, Herbert Vogt shows how a group of probationers become involved in their own, and in each other's, treatment. His method fits the style known as *guided group interaction*. The counselor merely guides the group process in a manner that will bring out the humanness of individuals in the group, and creates a climate in which the resources of each individual are utilized by the group to foster growth and constructive change.

Olive T. Irwin's article develops an alternative to the more traditional client-reports-to-agent approach. Her intent is to provide specific principles and techniques that guide the counselor in applying group therapy to juvenile probationers. The ingredients of her approach are consistency and absolute honesty from the counselor, and responsibility from the client. In her view, the client is responsible for his own life and for any changes that he or she wants. The purpose of group counseling, then, is to process the attitudes and behaviors of individuals in the group in a climate of honest reality so that they will assume that responsibility and participate in directing their own lives.

The third and fourth articles are excerpts from the book *Conjoint Family Therapy* by Virginia Satir, one of the nation's leading authorities on family counseling. Family therapy is not just another name for counseling families, however; it is a specific model for counseling, with specific assumptions about the nature and treatment of deviant behavior. As designed by Mrs. Satir, family therapy holds that the disturbed behavior of an individual is a symptom of pain within a dysfunctional family; that the individual is acting out, not because he is sick, but because the total family is dysfunctional. In applying family therapy, the counselor needs to treat the family as a unit or as a system of interdependent parts, each impacting upon the other.

Mrs. Satir first identifies the elements of family therapy and defines the terms used in this counseling model. The key element is the marital relationship. If the husband and wife, as parts of the system, are not in harmony, the entire family unit will become dysfunctional; and the child most affected by this dysfunctionalism will be identified as the disturbed one—the patient. Then, in "Concepts of Therapy," Mrs. Satir discusses how this dysfunctionalism is manifested by the family as a unit and by the individual members and describes what the counselor actually does in family therapy. At the core is the family's pattern of communications—it is dishonest but safe; it is also self-perpetuating and prevents growth. Counseling is directed toward creating an open family system in which members can be honest with each other without their feelings of self-esteem being threatened.

The concept of communication patterns is next examined from the perspective of Transactional Analysis (TA) by Richard C. Nicholson. TA is a counseling strategy widely used in county, state, and federal corrections, and by an increasing number of noncorrectional agencies and individuals. For those who accept its principles, TA is more than a model for analyzing communications and behavior patterns, it is a way of life. Nicholson reviews these principles and then applies them to counseling with a group of probationers. He clearly expresses TA's goal, as helping "a person to become responsible for his future; to feel OK." TA is also successful in providing a person with a vehicle for self-fulfillment and personal growth.

One of the most significant contributions to the literature on TA is *Born to Win* by Muriel James and Dorothy Jongeward. In a unique and provocative style, they blend TA with Gestalt therapy and offer a comprehensive rational-emotional model ideally suited to correctional casework. The sixth reading in this part, which is the first chapter of their book, describes the principles of each method and provides the framework of understanding necessary for their combined application.

Gestalt therapy is used often in counseling without TA, or any other blended approach. Whether the agent decides to combine it, or to apply it alone, is his choice. In either event, the next three readings serve as a basis for planning the appropriate strategy. In the first article of this group, Elaine Kepner and Lois Brien describe Gestalt therapy and how it explains personality development and behavior.

In the next article, Joen Fagan details how the counselor applies Gestalt therapy, and what is required of the therapist in establishing an effective counseling relationship. Then, Dr. Eric H. Marcus describes the specific application of Gestalt therapy to correctional counseling. As he says, the goal of Gestalt therapy is to move the client from a position of dependence to one of independence, from environmental support to self-support. No matter which strategy a caseworker uses, he has to deal with the issue of dependence vs. independence, both for himself and for his clients. Dr. Marcus gives useful suggestions for overcoming this problem.

From these three articles the reader may draw the conclusion that Gestalt therapy is used frequently in counseling the individual, and he may wonder why it was included in this part. Because Gestalt is the most process-oriented strategy, it is valuable in group sessions. When used in one-to-one counseling, the client experiences the process internally; it is for him a tremendous emotional self-processing. When used in group counseling, not only does each individual experience this internal emotional process as he "works out" on his own problem but, as each in turn "works out," the others experience the process vicariously, often in as moving and as rewarding a way as if it were their own.

In the reading that follows, Richard L. Rachin reviews the principles of Reality therapy and proposes a method for their application to correctional change. In Rachin's view, the mental health/mental illness approach to counseling is not only unsuccessful in changing behavior, it is also counterproductive in that it isolates and stigmatizes the law violator. Reality therapy does not attempt to *cure* because it rejects the notion that people are *sick*. Instead, it focuses on two basic psychological factors—on the need to feel lovable and significant, and on the client's position along the dimension of responsible-irresponsible behavior. After a thorough critique of Reality therapy versus conventional therapy, Rachin details a 14-step procedure to follow when applying Reality therapy to casework.

The concluding article is a critique of Reality therapy from the somewhat different and practical perspective of Robert J. Wicks. Although directed toward applying Reality therapy to institutionalized offenders, this excerpt from Professor Wicks' book *Correctional Psychology*, is presented so that it is equally appropriate for counseling offenders in the community. Wicks emphasizes three steps in the effective application of Reality therapy: (1) develop an honest personal relationship between agent and client; (2) create a climate of understanding based upon the realities of the offender's situation; and (3) provide learning experiences that allow the client to deal appropriately with his environment within the framework of reality.

22

An Invitation to Group Counseling

HERBERT VOGT

Supervising Probation Officer, United States District Court,
Washington, D.C.

About 10 years ago the probation office of the United States District Court for the District of Columbia began using group methods as an adjunct to its supervision techniques. Since that time a number of probation officers have conducted special types of groups. I have been especially interested in the long-term, ongoing, open-ended group for which 8 to 12 probationers are selected on the basis of their interests, problems, and needs. For the past 3 years, however, I have conducted orientation groups which include persons recently placed on probation and parole. We meet one evening a week for 4 weeks, for 75 to 90 minutes. The primary emphasis is on (1) specific goals the members wish to pursue, (2) evaluating the problem areas and treatment needs, (3) eliminating some of the distorted attitudes and feelings that our probationers and parolees have about probation officers, (4) interpreting the functions and role of the probation officer, and (5) determining whether the problem areas are related in any way to the offenses and what the probationers and parolees, together with the probation officer, might be able to do to resolve these problems and needs.

In the first meeting the group members tend to display some resistance and misgivings; they question the feasibility of men and women getting together to talk over problems. I find that a simple, honest, to-the-point presentation of the significance and meaning of group interaction and the constructive influence of human beings on one another conveys especially well the message I try to get across. The basic concepts of persons using their own resources to help each other needs to be reiterated and reemphasized at each of the four meetings.

The purpose of this article is to present an approach to the group which has been found to be especially helpful in capturing and holding their interest and attention, in getting them to listen and to become involved in looking squarely and objectively at where they have been,

Reprinted with permission from *Federal Probation* Quarterly, September 1971, pp. 30–32.

where they are at this time, what options are available to them, and what they might wish to do about their particular situation.

THE SUBSTANCE OF WHAT IS SAID

If you were to be a participant in one of these orientation sessions you would hear throughout each of the four meetings something along the lines of the following remarks and, in general, the sequence in which they are presented. In substance they give what I try to get across to the group participants. The remarks are not read. And at each of the four meetings they are interspersed with questions and answers and dialogue. The general remarks follow:

"Group counseling is one of the new ways in which probation officers are trying to give a helping hand. In the group, the officer tries to help people to help each other succeed on probation and parole as rapidly and as completely as possible. In several cities across the country probation officers are now meeting regularly with groups of persons under their supervision. Their experience has been that group members have been helped to get a firmer grip on their lives and move on to better things. This office wants to offer you the same kind of help.

"Making a successful community adjustment is no overnight matter. It takes time to work out the problems that come up. The counselor does not expect a person to progress all at once. He believes that if a person comes to the group and takes part in the discussions, he will begin to get some returns for his effort to learn about himself.

"Because most people's jobs prevent them from coming during the weekday, your group meeting will be held on the same weekday evening in each week or possibly during the day on Saturday. The meetings will last about an hour and a half because this is usually the best length of time to have a meaningful 'rap' session.

"As a probation officer, the group counselor wants to do his job well. His job is to help as many of his people as he can be free of trouble for good, and be successfully on their way. He believes that if a person is given a chance to solve the problems of everyday living, the chances are good that he will comply with the conditions of his supervision. The counseling group is a part of the probation officer's job. He will, therefore, consider a person's attendance at his group meetings a part of his efforts to succeed on probation or parole."

WHAT WILL I GET OUT OF GROUP COUNSELING?

"In a counseling group several people get together and talk about what is on their minds in trying to make it and to improve themselves. There is nothing mysterious or unusual about getting together as we do. In some respects, it is like a kind of free discussion between good friends who want to take the time to hear each other out and get each other's opinions.

"It has been our experience that when people can be encouraged to talk freely about themselves, about their problems, and their plans for the future, they can come closer to being the kind of person they have always wanted to be.

"Of course, this kind of open give-and-take will take a while to develop. At first, it is like any new experience. The people are strangers to each other or, at best, have only a nodding acquaintance. But it has one strong advantage that usually helps people solve their problems together. They all have one important interest in common that they may not share, as persons, with any other groups they are in; each wants to make his way toward being a completely free member of society, with no strings attached.

"This kind of group has another advantage that may not be easy to see at first. But after a while, it can get to mean a lot to the person in a group. The person who has to live up to conditions that someone else sets up sometimes worries about matters or has things on his mind that most other people can't understand. Sometimes he has trouble finding someone who will hear him out and will not back away from him. The person on probation or parole too often may feel cut off from help. On the other hand, people who have been in groups of this kind have reported that one of the things they valued most was the support and understanding interest the group gave them. 'If I couldn't have talked it over with the group,' one person said, 'I don't know where I could have turned.'

"There are no lessons in the group, no lectures, and no homework. Your group leader, a probation officer, acts as guide and moderator in the discussions. He will sometimes offer the benefit of his training and experience, but he will not shove anything down anyone's throat. Mostly, he would rather have group members come out with their own ideas. He realizes that he does not have any final answers. What he tries to do is help a person think through his own answers.

"There is probably no problem you can think of that at least one other person in the group has not had to face. Every person approaches problems in his own way. If you listen, you sometimes get new and sound ideas from the experiences, solutions, and suggestions of others who have been in exactly the same boat. Sometimes, the most valuable opportunity a person has is to sit down and figure it out by himself. Many of us, no matter who we are, know how tangled up a problem can get at times. Sometimes we want to get ourselves untangled. Other times we are pulled this way and that by different ideas about how to set things straight. We may have conflicting feelings that make us want to do first one thing and then another. At times we are not sure why some things bother us or why we want to do other things that really don't seem like such a good idea. Occasionally, we even wonder how we got ourselves into such a difficult spot in the first place.

"There is no shame in being bewildered or confused. Everyone of us who is trying to be his own boss gets his lines crossed at times. But it does take time to unravel all the knots. All of us have suffered the consequences of plunging ahead without thinking of what we were doing. The counseling group is set up for just exactly this kind of experience. In it, a person can sit still and take stock of himself, if he is so minded. He can learn what has happened to him, where he is in his life course right now, and where he is going.

"Since the group leader is also a probation officer, he is a representative of law and order. Group members, to some extent, are responsible to him, but far more to themselves for their conduct in the community. Now, this may not, at first, seem to be of any use at all. In fact, it may look like one good reason *not* to speak out in the group. Often, people who have power, legal or otherwise—police, courts, employers, teachers, or parents—have been the ones from whom a probationer has kept farthest away.

"The group leader's attitude toward a probationer getting into unlawful activity or breaking the rules of probation would have to be the same whether he heard about it in the group or privately. He is a probation officer and he, too, has his rules to follow. On the other hand, he is not running the group to check up on anybody. He could do that much more easily and quickly than by holding group meetings.

"He has learned that the people with whom he deals are much more to him than law violators. In his daily contact with them, he knows that they have many problems and that a lot of their other problems have had some bearing on their law violations. He figures that if he works to solve the other problems with them, the chances of helping them toward success are much better. This is why, in the group, you will discover that he wants you to take the time to get things off your chest. You will most likely have to check out the sincerity of his interest in your own way. But you will find that he, in his own way, will care about what is happening to you. One important result will be that some group members will find it a lot easier to act natural in front of a person with authority than they ever have before. Group members sometimes find new and even pleasant ways of working along with people as a result of their give and take with the counselor."

WHERE THE PROBATIONER OR PAROLEE NOW STANDS

"A person on probation or parole is young. Most are between 18 and 35. He is almost always moving away from one type of life and trying to move into another. The meaning of the word 'probation' has to do with a person proving himself. 'Parole' originally meant 'word of honor.' His teenage years are usually not too far behind him. The period of youth in our country is likely to be a mixed-up time for most of us; for some it is a wild period—a time of finding and doing our thing.

"For some probationers and parolees, their period of youth was time off from the business of maturing and making something of one's self. Some ended up pulling time in institutions, not too long ago, because they took too much time out from making time in their lives. For others, a close call in court reminds them that they took a wrong turn somewhere and it is now time to get their affairs back on the right track. Every person who comes into this office knows that he is up to bat.

"All around him, he may find that he has to catch up. Some people his own age may be further along because things went alright for them. In the meantime, they may have learned about a job, established more security for themselves, and gotten more training. Some of his old associates may be pulling him back to activities that he is trying to shake off. He may be finding it difficult to fall into step with new people. His personal and family life may be showing the effects of having been out of it either actually or in his interests. Many things may be unsettled, and he wants to take hold and set a true course for himself. Whether he thinks about it or not, he probably can use all the guidance and authority he can get."

This, then, is what I try to get across at each of our four group counseling sessions, not necessarily in the language or in the sequence presented nor at the same session. Parts may be reiterated and reemphasized at each of the meetings. And at each meeting I remind our participants that the constructive influence of human beings upon one another—a resource that has been with us since the creation of man —can be and is a potential for change.

In the past we have tended to rely primarily on an individual, probationer-to-officer type of interaction supplemented by casework services of the environmental manipulative kind. It is suggested that the time has come for us to examine other approaches, particularly those derived from the study of social psychology, group dynamics, human relations, and their practical application in group psychotherapy. Research studies indicate that in many instances (with alcoholics, for instance) a group approach is more successful than an individual technique in effecting an improvement in behavior and perception of societal norms.

—ALEXANDER B. SMITH, LOUIS BERLIN,
AND ALEXANDER BASSIN (1960)

23

Group Therapy with Juvenile Probationers

OLIVE T. IRWIN

Clinical Instructor, School of Social Work, Syracuse University

---

It was 4:15 on a weekday afternoon and the probation department waiting room was filled with boys and girls. Some had been there quite a while, waiting to see their probation officer. One or two leafed listlessly through a magazine, not really seeing the pictures or articles. Others, friends who came in together, talked desultorily. Most of them just sat, their faces expressionless, their eyes automatically following, without recognition, the movement of those who were called into inner offices and then somewhat later left.

A boy entered and told the receptionist he was to see Mr. Jenkins.

"Mr. Jenkins is out for the rest of the day. Come back next week."

The boy turned and left without a sound, as though he were used to not finding the probation officer in.

"Man, I been here an hour and I'd sure like to get back outside," a teenager murmured to his friend, as he restlessly picked up another magazine and flipped its pages. "I'd sure like to cut out."

"You better relax, man. I got told last week I'd get sent to the judge if I missed any more times. My P.O. said I better be on time, too, if I wanted to ever get off probation. Said I had to 'show responsibility.' "

His voice rose in elaborate sarcasm: "I'd like to know what that 'on time' means—I always wait about an hour. Every Tuesday. Sometimes he ain't ever here. Than *I* hafta go to the judge. Man, I could send *him* to the judge."

The two boys burst into suppressed frustrated giggles, which stopped suddenly as they caught the receptionist's disapproving eye. There was a momentary responsive stir among the waiting group, and then apathy returned to the faces and postures.

This theme with variations is repeated daily in juvenile probation offices. Probation officers are working conscientiously at their jobs, try-

Reprinted with permission from *Federal Probation* Quarterly, September 1967, pp. 57–63.

ing to be a model of acceptable behavior, trying to induce some willing imitation into the youths whose behavior they have accepted the awesome responsibility to change. Yet it is apparent that they have indifferent success. The oblique glances of their probationers are not admiring, cooperation is minimal, too often distrust and cynicism are only reinforced. What is wrong?

USE OF GROUP THERAPY IN TREATMENT

In this paper I shall discuss some principles and techniques of group therapy which were developed in a search for some way to lessen these basic relationship problems between probation officer and probationer which prevent therapeutic change. The ideas were tested and developed in a juvenile probation department with groups formed from probationers. Their customary experiences with probation were examined from a new viewpoint: What does the probation officer's behavior really communicate and what are the probationers really telling their officers? The experience in group treatment which evolved, it was agreed, might well be the treatment of choice in this setting.[1]

These principles are not unique in applicability to groups, but should be basic in treatment of adolescents. It is not the intention of this article to add to the numerous expositions of the advantages of the group method with adolescents.[2] Discussion will be limited to an explanation of some principles and techniques designed to guide the interested practitioner into a consistent approach to group treatment which can be modified to fit each person's unique abilities as leader.

DEFINITION OF TERMS

Everyone who wishes to discuss "therapy" or "counseling" must give his own definition of the terms, since meaning is far from standardized. In this paper I join the group which differentiates therapy from counseling primarily in its being conducted by professionals (psychologists, psychiatrists, or social workers). I further differentiate the processes I am describing from psychoanalytic psychotherapy in the emphasis on use of conscious material and the relative minimizing of insight development.[3] It is directed toward attitudinal and behavioral changes from which eventually may come some of the personality change which psychoanalytic group therapy seeks more directly.

SELECTION OF GROUP MEMBERS

The question of criteria for selection of members is generally considered to be important. Can all adolescents on probation be included in this kind of group, or is there enough difference among them to make careful diagnosis essential?

In literature on treatment of delinquents, there is fairly general agreement that most delinquents manifest varying combinations of traits warranting mixed diagnosis. Wasserman notes the common acceptance that the delinquent is reacting to innumerable forces, psychic and environmental. "Their differential impact determines whether he is labeled a social, a neurotic, or a psychopathic delinquent."[4] Symptoms are usually found to be similar, regardless of diagnosis, but in casework there has been insistence that differential diagnosis is the sine qua non for treatment.[5] Yet treatment techniques as described do not appear clearly differentiated. There is general agreement that in all treatment of delinquents firm limits must be set, the therapist must be incorruptible, he must play multiple roles—parent surrogate, teacher, advisor, and counselor. Reality must be kept evident, but with consistent warmth. And so on. The fine diagnostic distinctions become blurred in discussions of treatment, possibly because of the fact that no set of techniques has ever met widespread success.

Dr. William Glasser departs radically from the traditional position. He postulates that all people who are living ineffectively, including neurotic, psychotic, and delinquent, have a common problem—they are irresponsible. He proposes a kind of treatment (individual and group) with similarities in technique and intent to that outlined in this article, which can be applied regardless of diagnosis:

> Using Reality Therapy there is no essential difference in the treatment of various psychiatric problems . . . the treatment of psychotic veterans is almost exactly the same as the treatment of delinquent, adolescent girls. The particular manifestation of irresponsibility (the diagnosis) has little relationship to the treatment.[6]

Practitioners must face the reality that much practical therapy has to be done and is being done without attention to complex diagnosis or fine points of differential treatment supposedly based on it.

There is another factor in probation settings which makes diagnostic skill less important: the prior screening out through investigation and other judicial disposition of neurotics, psychotics, and psychopaths.

It is my contention that most children on probation are suitable for such groups as could be formed from a probation caseload. I would exclude only the occasional probationer who is so advanced in psychopathy that there is no likelihood of his becoming involved with other members, or who is so pervasively angry that he will do nothing but disrupt, or whose mentality is so defective that he cannot associate as an equal.[7] Beyond this, I would say simply that the group is intended to help members experience a new way of viewing their lives through each other; therefore an assortment of personality types, ages, offenses, and life styles—varied without restriction save the common sense or intuition of the leader—provides the best material to reflect life's problems to them.

SOME BASIC PRINCIPLES

The basic guiding principle of this therapeutic process is that the staff member—usually a probation officer, and hereafter designated simply as "the leader"—must be scrupulously honest with the group. If this sounds elementary, I can only suggest that there is in much of our counseling techniques (as in society at large) a depth of dishonesty so pervasive that it slips unobserved into our relationships with clients, no matter what the setting.

In correctional settings we are particularly susceptible to this attitude because we are more distinctly the agents of the community than social workers whose clients come voluntarily. We cannot always truthfully say, "Trust me and I will help you." We may find ourselves institutionalizing a delinquent, sending him to a place we know can offer no help, solely for the protection of the community. Yet how many times do we urge our clients to confide in us, because we are "only trying to help" them? It takes a high degree of self-awareness and self-control for a probation officer to face such situations honestly in the face of his inability to really help; yet dishonesty will only be more damaging, even when it is intended to save the child from the unpleasantness of the facts. In a treatment group any dishonesty, no matter how trivial, is detected immediately, sometimes before the leader is aware of it himself. It is used against him, he loses stature in the eyes of the group, and it may be some time before he retrieves his status with the members.[8]

A common expression of dishonesty is the refusal to admit knowledge of a probationer's untrustworthiness. Many probation officers, somehow feeling that a frank admission of lack of trust is unprofessional or discouraging to the probationer, hide behind evasions and vague reassurances of hope or faith. On one occasion, early in a group's experience, the leader was directly confronted by the outraged accusation of a girl: "You don't trust us!" He replied, in essence, "Of course I don't. Have you done anything to make me trust you? Do you trust everyone before you know that you can? Do you trust me before I prove to you that it is safe? Anybody who does that is heading for trouble."

Such a response does several things at once. It provides a basic reassurance that the leader can be frank; that he is ready to deal with negative emotions openly; that he will not become defensive when directly attacked, that he can see the world with a dispassionate realism; that he will not attempt to moralize. Such a response is likely to anger but intrigue the group members, and may relieve them of some anxiety. At the same time that it startles the group with its unexpectedness, it forces them to reshuffle their defense reactions and do some thinking. Most important, it begins to define the leader as someone quite different from the authority figures they have known and learned to distrust, someone who will make no attempt to mislead them, who will, on the contrary, always insist on making clear every move he intends to make in relation to them. Unfortunately, this kind of communication (and demonstration) is all too rare. The more common practice is to keep negative attitudes and intentions hidden, possibly from fear of angry retailation or flight, possibly from the leader's own need to give happiness and win approval. The authorities (parents, community, even social workers) with whom these children have dealt all their lives have probably misled them from much the same misguided motives. If the leader acts like them, he will get the same response—deserved disbelief and contempt.

Another expression of dishonesty is the insistence on observance of various middle-class virtues which adults—including probation officers—many of them successful and honored in the community, ignore every day. An example is punctuality: Punctuality in a probationer is somehow evidence of maturity, even if it leads repeatedly to cooling the heels in the waiting room, and besides, it will help probationers get ahead in the world. Or the repeated warning that continued misbehavior will only lead to more trouble. Young people can only react to this with cynicism. It is at worst a bad untruth in the face of everyday observances to the contrary; at best it is a long-accustomed moralistic lecture which arouses irritation and contempt in adolescents.

A better approach is: "If you continue to steal, you may get away with it, as lots of people do. But you have to take the chance that you will be locked up. Maybe it is worth that chance to you—nobody else can decide for you. If you really like living that way—taking those chances—it's up to you." Finding no opposition, no moralizing, no attempt to persuade or force, the adolescent is much more likely to readjust his values.

Achieving honesty requires a long, hard apprenticeship of self-examination. Often we are so well defended by our own needs to reach certain goals (e.g., the probationer's improved behavior), and by the ubiquity of accepted social dishonesties that we cannot detect our own blind spots. Periodic consultation with another staff member is helpful in gaining another point of view. As the leader repeatedly demonstrates his honest acceptance of responsibility, then only can he begin to help group members face their responsibilities. Acceptance of responsibility by group members is the ultimate goal.

THE BASIS OF RESPONSIBLE BEHAVIOR

In order to help these young people move toward acceptance of responsibility, it first must be understood that frustration and helpless rage are at the base of their problems. They maneuver in a hostile and ineffective way, all the while disclaiming responsibility, and so defeat themselves and compound their problems. Their own accounts of their lives depict a series of encounters in which they see themselves as innocent victims of rejection, discrimination, hostile fate or at least unfortunate accident. It is unthinkable to them that more often than not they contribute to their defeat. What makes the situation even more difficult is that their perceptions are not entirely distorted.

Corrective experiences are not easy to provide. These children are not in a condition to form a close relationship which might support another person. They cannot respond to generous gifts of services and supplies, which only increase the dependency and debt which they already have reason to fear or hate. Their anger at this combines with their experiences of failure in their encounters with the adult world, to immobilize them with fear of trying new encounters. Most adolescent probationers, despite their tough front and denial of interest in conformity, want desperately to belong. Their need for successful experiences in dealing with the world is deep; yet their fear of failure perpetuates their helplessness and anger.

While they take advantage of help, even demand it or do without what they want, they do not respect the giver or themselves for this collaboration in keeping them inexperienced and lacking in social confidence and skill. Learning to risk themselves in action, facing possible defeat and trying again is one of the most important and rewarding processes that occurs in the group. The leader must never in a misguided attempt to be approved of or simply to get things going do a favor which the probationer could do himself. It is hard to believe the importance to the youth of his own social accomplishment until one sees how it can change him.

Sally, a 15-year-old with deep feelings of inadequacy, asked the leader one day to go to the court office in an adjoining building for her and find out how much restitution she still owed. "It would be easy for *you*—you know them and they won't get mad at you. And besides, you're around there a lot." When the leader flatly refused, the entire group became angry, supporting Sally.

"We thought you probation officers were supposed to help people. You won't even do us an easy little favor."

The leader's bland refusal, as a matter of principle, explained but not excused, surprised and troubled them. They attempted to coerce her into the pattern they knew by appealing to all the traditional concepts of the good, accepting, helpful social worker. This failing, they implied selfishness, laziness, downright hostility on her part. The intensity of their attack indicated its importance to them beyond the immediate request. Most of the subsequent hour was spent discussing the implications.

The next week Sally and another of the girls arrived together, obviously pleased. They had gone to the office and braved the sour-faced clerk, and had gotten their information. The experience was a double success: The two girls learned directly that it is possible to deal successfully with a public official and the rest shared vicariously in the education. Episodes like this, through repetition, accelerate the members' progress. Sally was unable to say she was happier because she did it herself, but her attitude spoke plainly for her and the group was impressed. If, on the other hand, the encounter had been unpleasant and a failure, the group could offer support while the failure was examined and courage was developed to try again. The speed of integration into behavior of such experiences cannot be duplicated in individual counseling with most adolescents. Nor is it likely to occur in a group, if the leader is fostering resistance in them by being dishonest himself or is perpetuating dependency by being "helpful" when the help is not needed.

The individual by such experiences is widening his perception of choices open to him and is learning to manage his life with more awareness of the realities involved. It may be objected that these adolescents have already taken over too much of the management of their lives and this is what has gotten them into trouble. It is not the *fact* of self-management, but the choices made which are destructive. Young people in conflict with the adult community need to learn how to choose more wisely among alternative courses of action. Often, if they could only realize it, their goals are not really so divergent from adults' as they think. For example, one boy is confused about the reasons for trying to achieve in school. He has the idea that it is to "please" the teacher, whom he hates, so he refuses to get the lessons and does succeed in infuriating the teacher, which pleases him. Unfortunately he also fails, which doesn't really please him because of the trouble it causes him though he has to pretend he doesn't mind. Another boy, also hating the teacher, recognizes that failure would be harder on him than angering the teacher would be worth, and chooses more effectively to study and pass.

Group discussion of just such problems is the means of helping the first boy to the more effective choice. Adolescents are not to be excused from the realities of social living; they must be helped to realize that their behavior has an impact on the community which will respond to them in somewhat predictable ways. If they fail in school, they must accept the discomfort and limitations which follow. If they are caught burglarizing, they will go to court and may be locked up. If they act as though they were crazy, they may be sent to a mental hospital. But we are encouraging irresponsibility if we let them pretend that they don't have a choice. They can choose conformity to society's acceptable standards and have a measure of noninterference; or they can chose rebellion and take the chance of their partial freedom being taken away.

Exhorting and haranguing them, painting a dismal picture of the reform school, appealing to their reason or emotions, threatening or cajoling—these measures, all too often resorted to in probation, have no place whatever in the treatment group. They only reinforce the probationers' opinion of the leader as a phony and convince them that their resistance to adults is justified.

Improvement in communication is an essential concomitant of the process of accepting responsibility. When children come into probation, effective satisfying interaction with the adult world has long since been lost, if indeed it ever existed. They have abandoned any hope of an interested hearing from adults which might result in action favorable to them, and often the adults in their world feel equally frustrated. Alienation is deep. Effective interaction has been replaced by self-perpetuating defensive manipulation on both sides.

Until the child can have confidence that he can express himself fully, that he will be heard, and that he has a chance of some of his reasonable wants being supplied, he cannot rejoin the community. He does not know how to make himself heard and respected. He does not know that he can learn more effective ways of making adults listen and hear him clearly and respond with some of the supplies he needs. He needs to be retaught, step by step, with patience and repetition, that a different kind of question will receive a different answer. He has to be taught first to see that his communications provoke adverse responses, and then to see what other communications would achieve. This is done, not by lecture or advice, but by slow, repeated group experience with different kinds of communications and direct observations of their results. Focus of discussion is brought gradually from outside events to the interactions of the group itself where behavior being unlearned and relearned is dramatized. Then as he begins to practice his new techniques and finds them successful, he is finding his way back to acceptance by the community.

TECHNIQUES OF LEADERSHIP

Specific techniques in application of the above concepts vary with the individual and so are almost impossible to communicate in any but the most general terms. Each person must rely on his thorough understanding of the principles and his conviction that they are valid for him to guide him into his own methods of application. However, a few which appear to be readily transferable among workers will be described.

At the beginning, a "contract," or set of basic procedural rules, must be established and understood by all participants. Terms of attendance, responsibility for discussion topics, limits on acting out (if any)—minimal ground rules—are clarified by the leader. Since attendance is at first seen as threatening, I recommend ordering attendance for a specific period, possibly 2 months, with an option to change to individual interviews only at the end. In my experience no probationer has chosen to leave the group after giving it this trial. It can be made clear that members are responsible for the quality of discussion and for maintaining its level of interest. It is the leader's responsibility to keep them aware that they cannot abdicate without effects on themselves. He tells them and reminds them when necessary that the group will have value to them only if they try to give it value. Then the process itself begins to demonstrate that this is so.

Whatever the spoken content of the meetings, the leader's interventions must be of a quality that will get the group's instant attention. This is very important. He cannot challenge successfully or promote thought if he talks frequently. If the group becomes accustomed to his contributions, interest will soon be lost because they know what he is going to say and they will not listen. What he says must startle and puzzle them (even irritate them) into thinking themselves. Only infrequently can he indulge himself in an elaborated comment, and then it must be at a time when the group needs it enough that their attention will be caught and a strong reaction will result. The group learns to want his comments and to wait for them as they become aware that what he says somehow helps them to reshuffle their perceptions. His stance thus has seductive elements in it: They are captivated in spite of themselves by the glimpses he offers of a more satisfying life, or at least of a different way of viewing it.

Most social workers, especially those who never tape, have no idea how much their own repetitious, often sententious, contributions dominate their interviews. Adolescents are especially critical of such behavior. They are lulled, then irritated, then alienated by it. The leader must place high value on what he says or the group will not. Every sentence should be showing them that they can count on him to be different from all the adults they have ever known and be convincing them that they want to try to get him to say more. But in this they must not succeed. How each leader puts this principle into practice depends entirely on the kind of person he is and the depth of his understanding of the principles involved. His honesty, his consistency, his difference from others are his chief tools.

There are many gambits the leader uses to encourage the process. To mention a few: He picks up obscure clues or messages and confronts the group with them; for example, seating arrangements or the group's avoidance of a certain subject. He relates various aspects of the members' behavior to each other; for example, the formation of certain subgroups, or isolation of a member. He keeps the group stirred up, wondering, sometimes bewildered. Conflict is brought into the open, even promoted. All this is done by the leader's matter-of-fact observations about what he sees and hears.

He avoids expressions of warmth or praise. Praise of one will provoke demands for it from all the others, and to meet this request he can be quickly trapped into insincerities which will be spotted. He is as open about his own frailties as about those of the others. If his statements are proved to be inaccurate, he accepts correction. If he acts out of anger at times, he points this out and leads in the analysis of the act, but never attempts to justify it. His general attitude might be described as one of dispassionate interest.

SOURCES OF THE THERAPEUTIC RELATIONSHIP

All this may seem to some to be a cold and disinterested approach to young people in trouble. It is not. It is an attitude which the young people can respond to with a slow development of realistic trust. It may well be its consistency and its honesty which make it effective. These young people know too well the dependency which results from protection or repression disguised as warmth, services, and material gifts; they know it carries a big price: passivity, dependency, a false appearance of affection, agreement to live as the parents dictate. And the same is true to a lesser extent in all their dealings with adults. Their rebelliousness is an attempt to keep their identity, and if the group leader reflects to any degree the coercive (and dishonest) adult world they already know they can only resist him, too.

It is for this reason that he must be different, without any expectations for himself. If he offers the rewards of praise, or shows disappointment or displeasure, he will be using the same subtle coercion to prevent growth into autonomy. Praise is seductive; they will succumb (or have to resist) if it is offered. Either way, their anger and helplessness are intensified. It cannot help them at this stage. Instead, they want and need autonomy of actions within safe limits, and the only effective limit is the knowledge of undesirable consequences to themselves. More than love, they want the truth about the world, so they may know how to act responsibly.

When they learn that in the group they can discover some of the truth that has been denied them about their relationship to the world, there is evident relief. Their relationship to it shifts. An understanding, an unspoken, often unconscious, agreement develops in which they feel safe to risk themselves, to face their own limitations, to accept inevitable disappointment and pain. Although in the group they are provoked into conflict and confronted with their inadequacies, they are doing it themselves and the leader meets their struggles with impartial honesty. He has not set his own goals for them, he does not threaten to engulf them, he is not using them for his private ends; but more important, they cannot use him. He cannot be corrupted. There is unparalleled safety in this situation, but there is also challenge which must be met in some fashion.

A natural process seems to evolve. At first the group is watchful, suspicious, as members try to figure out what the leader is up to. Over and over, they try their old gambits but find themselves up against a situation and a person they cannot define according to old rules. Anger is expressed, attacks may be made on the leader, only to have them rebound in a startling, confusing, yet somehow intriguing way. The process begins to capitivate their interest in spite of themselves. A group feeling becomes strong. They stop complaining about how badly the world treats them and begin to regard their behavior with a new sense of responsibility. Soon they begin examining their self-concepts and gaining a sense of worth. Meanwhile, they begin to bring in reports of successful contacts with people and of decrease in problems. True warmth has developed, based on self-confidence and respect for the independence of themselves and others. They are taking hold of their lives in a new way.

NOTES

[1] I wish to acknowledge with gratitude the unstinting time and interest of Dr. Bertram Rothschild, Ph.D., former assistant director of the Onondaga County Mental Health Clinic, Syracuse, N.Y., under whose guidance these ideas were put into practice.

[2] For general discussion, see Joyce Gale Klein, "Social Group Treatment: Some Selected Dynamics," in *Social Work With Groups* (New York: National Association of Social Workers, 1961), pp. 35–47; also the several articles on group methods in *Crime and Delinquency*, 11, no. 4 (October 1965).

[3] For discussion of the various definitions, see: Rosemary C. Sarri and Robert D. Vinter, "Group Treatment Strategies in Juvenile Correctional Programs," *Crime and Delinquency*, 11, no. 4: 326–340; and Abraham S. Luchins, *Group Therapy: A Guide* (New York: Random House, 1964), pp. 11–16.

[4] Sidney Wasserman, "Casework Treatment of the Neurotic Delinquent Adolescent and the Compulsive Mother," *Social Casework*, 43 (November 1962): 487.

[5] There are many expressions of these concepts. See, for example, Bertram M. Beck, "What Can We Do About Juvenile Delinquency?," *Child Welfare*, 33 (1954): 3–7; Martin Falsberg, "Setting Limits With the Juvenile Delinquent," *Social Casework*, 38 (1957): 138–42; Hyman Grossbard, "Ego Deficiency in Delinquents," *Social Casework*, 43 (April 1962): 171–78; and Wasserman, *Social Casework*, 43: 487. Each of these articles cites, in turn, several other sources.

[6] William Glasser, M.D., *Reality Therapy: A New Approach to Psychiatry* (New York: Harper & Row, 1965), pp. 48–49.

[7] See for more detail my article, "Group Reporting in Juvenile Probation," *Crime and Delinquency*, 11, no. 4: 341–48.

[8] For an excellent discussion of some of our favorite professional lies, see Seymour L. Halleck, "The Impact of Professional Dishonesty on Behavior of Disturbed Adolescents," in *Social Work*, 8, no. 2 (April 1963): 48–56. In my opinion, this article should be studied by all social workers.

24

Why Family Therapy?

VIRGINIA SATIR

1. Family therapists deal with family pain.
   a. When one person in a family (the patient) has pain which shows up in symptoms, all family members are feeling this pain in some way.
   b. Many therapists have found it useful to call the member who carries the symptom the "Identified Patient," or "I.P.," rather than to join the family in calling him "the sick one," or "the different one," or "the one who is to blame."
   c. This is because the therapist sees the Identified Patient's symptoms as serving a family function as well as an individual function.
2. Numerous studies have shown that the family behaves as if it were a unit. In 1954 Jackson introduced the term "family homeostasis" to refer to this behavior (142).
   a. According to the concept of family homeostasis, the family acts so as to achieve a balance in relationships.
   b. Members help to maintain this balance overtly and covertly.
   c. The family's repetitious, circular, predictable communication patterns reveal this balance.
   d. When the family homeostasis is precarious, members exert much effort to maintain it.
3. The marital relationship influences the character of family homeostasis.
   a. The marital relationship is the axis around which all other family relationships are formed. The mates are the "architects" of the family.
   b. A pained marital relationship tends to produce dysfunctional parenting.
4. The Identified Patient is the family member who is most obviously affected by the pained marital relationship and most subjected to dysfunctional parenting.

Reprinted by permission of the author and the publisher from Virginia Satir, *Conjoint Family Therapy*, pages 1–7. Rev. Ed. Palo Alto, California: Science and Behavior Books, 1967.

    a. His symptoms are an "SOS" about his parents' pain and the resulting family imbalance.

    b. His symptoms are a message that he is distorting his own growth as a result of trying to alleviate and absorb his parents' pain.

5. Many treatment approaches are called "family therapy" but differ from the definition which will be presented here, since they are oriented primarily to family members as individuals rather than to the family as a unit as well. For example:

    a. Each family member may have his own therapist.

    b. Or family members may share the same therapist, but the therapist sees each member separately.

    c. Or the patient may have a therapist who occasionally sees other family members "for the sake of" the patient.

6. A growing body of clinical observation has pointed to the conclusion that family therapy must be oriented to the family as a whole. This conviction was initially supported by observations showing how family members respond to the individual treatment of a family member labeled as "schizophrenic." But further studies showed that families with a delinquent member respond in similar ways to the individual treatment of this member. In both cases it was found that:

    a. Other family members interfered with, tried to become part of, or sabotaged the individual treatment of the "sick" member, as though the family had a stake in his sickness.

    b. The hospitalized or incarcerated patient often got worse or regressed after a visit from family members, as though family interaction had a direct bearing on his symptoms.

    c. Other family members got worse as the patient got better, as though sickness in one of the family members were essential to the family's way of operating.

7. These observations led many individually-oriented psychiatrists and researchers to re-evaluate and question certain assumptions (109, 110, 114, 140, 142, 146, 162).

    a. They noted that when the patient was seen as the victim of his family, it was easy to overidentify with and overprotect him, overlooking the fact that:

      — Patients are equally adept at victimizing other family members in return.

      — Patients help to perpetuate their role as the sick, different, or blamed one.

    b. They noted how heavily transference was relied on in order to produce change.

      — Yet perhaps much of the patient's so-called transference was really an appropriate reaction to the therapist's behavior in the unreal, noninteractive, therapeutic situation.

— In addition, there was a greater chance that the therapeutic situation would perpetuate pathology, instead of presenting a new state of affairs which would introduce doubts about the old perceptions

— If some of the patient's behavior did represent transference (that is, his characteristic way of relating to his mother and father), why shouldn't the therapist help the patient deal with the family more directly, by seeing both the patient and his family together?

c. They noted that the therapist tended to be more interested in the patient's fantasy life than in his real life. But even if they were interested in the patient's real life, as long as they saw just the patient in therapy, they had to rely on his version of that life or try and guess what was going on in it.

d. They noted that in trying to change one family member's way of operating they were, in effect, trying to change the whole family's way of operating.

— This put the burden of family change-agent on the patient all by himself rather than on all family members.

— The patient was already the family member who was trying to change the family's way of operating, so when he was urged to increase his efforts, he only received a more intense criticism from the family. This also led him to feel even more burdened and less able.

8. Aside from all these observations, once therapists started to see the whole family together, other aspects of family life which produced symptoms were revealed, aspects which had been largely overlooked. Other investigators of family interaction were making similar discoveries. As Warren Brodey sees it, the mates act differently with the normal sibling than they do with the symptomatic sibling:

> . . . the parents in the presence of the "normal" sibling are able to relate with a freedom, flexibility, and breadth of awareness that one finds hard to believe, considering the limitations that exist in the relationship between the parents when involved with the symptomatic sibling. The pathological ways of relating seem to be focused within the relationship with the symptomatic member. One wonders how this has come about.[1]

9. But those psychiatrists who became increasingly devoted to family therapy were not the first to recognize the interpersonal nature of mental illness. Sullivan and Fromm-Reichmann, along with many other psychiatrists, psychologists, and social workers, were pioneers in this area of discovery. The Child Guidance movement was

another important development which helped break the tradition of singling out just one family member for treatment (159).

  a. Child Guidance therapists included both mother and child in treatment, even though they still tended to see mother and child in separate treatment sessions.

  b. They also increasingly recognized the importance of including the father in therapy, though they found him hard to reach, and generally failed to engage him in the therapy process.

— Therapists reported that the father felt parenting was his wife's job more than his; if the child acted disturbed, his wife was the one who should be seen.

— The Child Guidance therapists, being mother-child oriented anyway, tended to agree with the father's reasoning, so they could not easily convince him that his role in the family was important to the health of his child.

— Child Guidance Clinics remained primarily focused on "mothering," even though they increasingly recognized the importance of "fathering." And whether or not they included the father in their thinking, they continued to focus on the husband and wife as parents of the child rather than as mates to each other. Yet it has been repeatedly noted how critically the marital relationship affects parenting. Murray Bowen writes, for example:

The striking observation was that when the parents were emotionally close, more invested in each other than either was in the patient, the patient improved. When either parent became more emotionally invested in the patient than in the other parent, the patient immediately and automatically regressed. When the parents were emotionally close, they could do no wrong in their "management" of the patient. The patient responded well to firmness, permissiveness, punishment, "talking it out," or any other management approach. When the parents were "emotionally divorced," any and all "management approaches" were equally unsuccessful.[2]

10. Family therapists have found it easier to interest the husband in family therapy than in individual therapy. This is because the family therapist is himself convinced that both architects of the family must be present.

  a. Once the therapist convinces the husband that he is essential to the therapy process, and that no one else can speak for him or take his place in therapy or in family life, he readily enters in.

  b. The wife (in her role as mother) may initiate family therapy, but once therapy is under way, the husband becomes as involved as she does.

    c. Family therapy seems to make sense to the whole family. Husband and wife say: "Now, at last, we are together and can get to the bottom of this."

11. Right from the first contact, family therapists operate from certain assumptions about why a family member has sought therapeutic help.

    a. Usually the first contact is made because someone outside the family has labeled Johnny as disturbed. This first contact will probably be made by an anxious wife (we will call her Mary Jones), acting in her role as mother of a disturbed child, Johnny. The child is disturbed, so she, the mother, must be to blame.

    b. But Johnny was probably exhibiting disturbed behavior long before he became labeled disturbed by someone outside the family.

    c. Until the outsider (often a teacher) labeled Johnny as disturbed, members of the Jones family probably acted as though they did not notice Johnny's behavior; his behavior was appropriate because it served a family function.

    d. Usually some event has occurred which has precipitated symptoms in Johnny, symptoms which make the fact that he is disturbed obvious to outsiders. These events are:

      — Changes from outside the nuclear family: war, depression, etc.

      — Changes in the two families of origin: sickness of a grandmother, financial distress of a grandfather, etc.

      — Someone enters or leaves the nuclear family: grandmother comes to live with the family, the family takes on a boarder, the family adds to its membership with the birth of another child, a daughter gets married.

      — Biological changes: a child reaches adolescence, mother reaches menopause, father is hospitalized.

      — Major social changes: a child leaves home to attend school, the family moves to a new neighborhood, father gets a job promotion, son goes to college.

    e. These events can precipitate symptoms because they require the mates to integrate the changes. This requirement puts an extra strain on the marital relationship because it calls for a redefinition of family relationships and thus affects family balance.

    f. The family homeostasis can be functional (or "fitting") for members at some periods of family life and not at other periods, so events affect members differently at different times.

    g. But if one member is affected by an event, all are to some degree.

12. After the first contact with Mary Jones, the therapist may speculate about the relationship between Mary and her husband, whom we will call Joe. If it is correct to assume that a dysfunctional marital relationship is the main contributor to symptoms in a child, the relationship between the mates will be the therapist's first concern.
    a. What kind of people are Mary and Joe? What kind of families did they come from?
       — Once they were two separate people who came from different family environments.
       — Now they are the architects of a new family of their own.
    b. Why, out of all the people in the world, did they choose each other as mates?
       — How they chose each other gives clues to why they may now be disappointed with each other.
       — How they express their disappointment with each other gives clues to why Johnny needs to have symptoms in order to hold the Jones family together.

NOTES

[1] W. M. Brodey, "Some Family Operations of Schizophrenia: A Study of Five Hospitalized Families each with a Schizophrenic Member," *Arch. gen. Psychiat.*, 1 (1959): 379–402, p. 391.

[2] Murray Bowen, "A Family Concept of Schizophrenia," in *The Etiology of Schizophrenia*, Don D. Jackson, ed. (New York: Basic Books, 1960), p. 370.

25

Concepts of Therapy

VIRGINIA SATIR

In this chapter, I should like to restate in a more general way some of the ideas about psychic health and illness which we have discussed previously, in order to show their relevance to the interactional approach of family therapy. I also want to present my own picture of what a family therapist is and does, since he becomes, to an important degree, a model for his patients' subsequent behavior.

1. I am not trying to present a "philosophy of therapy." These ideas appear to me as working tools, helpful in organizing my own way of handling therapy, or as a conceptual core around which therapeutic growth may be structured, rather than as a system of thought possessing value in and for itself.

   Finally, let me say that this discussion of theory is admittedly schematic, not filled in. I intend to follow this volume with a later one in which I will be illustrating my basis of operations more fully with examples from actual family situations.

2. The most important concept in therapy, because it is a touchstone for all the rest, is that of maturation.

   a. This is the state in which a given human being is fully in charge of himself.

   b. A mature person is one who, having attained his majority, is able to make choices and decisions based on accurate perceptions about himself, others, and the context in which he finds himself; who acknowledges these choices and decisions as being his; and who accepts responsibility for their outcomes.

3. The patterns of behaving that characterize a mature person we call functional because they enable him to deal in a relatively competent and precise way with the world in which he lives. Such a person will:

   a. manifest himself clearly to others.

   b. be in touch with signals from his internal self, thus letting himself know openly what he thinks and feels.

Reprinted by permission of the author and the publisher from Virginia Satir, *Conjoint Family Therapy*, pages 91–105. Rev. Ed. Palo Alto, California: Science and Behavior Books, 1967.

   c. be able to see and hear what is outside himself as differentiated from himself and as different from anything else.

   d. behave toward another person as someone separate from himself and unique.

   e. treat the presence of different-ness as an opportunity to learn and explore rather than as a threat or a signal for conflict.

   f. deal with persons and situations in their context, in terms of "how it is" rather than how he wishes it were or expects it to be.

   g. accept responsibility for what he feels, thinks, hears and sees, rather than denying it or attributing it to others.

   h. have techniques for openly negotiating the giving, receiving and checking of meaning between himself and others.[1]

4. We call an individual dysfunctional when he has not learned to communicate properly. Since he does not manifest a means of perceiving and interpreting himself accurately, or interpreting accurately messages from the outside, the assumptions on which he bases his actions will be faulty and his efforts to adapt to reality will be confused and inappropriate.

   a. As we have seen, the individual's communication problems are rooted in the complex area of family behavior in which he lived as a child. The adults in the family provide the blueprint by which the child grows from infancy to maturity.

   b. If the male and female who were his survival figures did not manage jointly, if their messages to each other and the child were unclear and contradictory, he himself will learn to communicate in an unclear and contradictory way.

5. A dysfunctional person will manifest himself incongruently, that is, he will deliver conflicting messages, via different levels of communication and using different signals.

   a. As an example, let us take the behavior of the parents of a disturbed child during their first interview with the therapist. When the therapist asks what seems to be the trouble, they practically deny that there is any.

     M: Well, I don't know. I think financial problems more than anything . . . outside of that, we're a very close family.

     F: We do everything together. I mean, we hate to leave the kids. When we go someplace, we take the kids with us. As far as doing things together as a family, we always try to do that at least once a week, say on Sundays, Sunday afternoon, why we always try to get the kids together and take them out for a ride to the park or something like that.

   b. In words, they imply that there is no reason why they should be in a therapist's office. But their actual presence there, and the agreement they have already made to enter therapy, amount to an admission of the contrary. And the father presents a further contradiction when he reduces his claim that the family does "everything" together to a statement about the rides they take on Sunday afternoons.

6. In addition, a dysfunctional individual will be unable to adapt his interpretations to the present context.

   a. He will tend to see the "here and now" through labels which have been indelibly fixed in his mind during the early part of his life when all messages had survival significance. Each subsequent use of the label will strengthen its reality.

   b. Therefore, it is conceivable that he will impose on the present that which fits the past, or that which he expects from the future, thus negating the opportunity to gain a perspective on the past or realistically shape the future.

     — For example, a school-age girl was brought into therapy because she was acting strangely and talking in riddles. When the mother was asked, "When did you notice that your child was not developing as she should?" she replied, "Well, she was a seven-month baby, and she was in an incubator for six weeks." The child's present and past difficulties were thus connected in a very illogical fashion.[2]

     — Later she said that after she brought the baby home from the hospital, "She wouldn't give me any reaction, just as though she couldn't hear. And I'd take her around and hold her next to me, and she wouldn't pay any attention, and I know it upset me, and I asked the doctor and he said it was nothing, she was just being stubborn—that's one thing that sort of stuck in my mind with her."

     — By using the word "stubborn" for the baby's indifference, the mother has given the baby a label that does not suit the context of babyhood. It implies that the child can be held accountable for willfully refusing to return the mother's love. Later on, the mother applies the same explanation to the child's strange behavior.

     — By using the label "stubborn," and by implying in her first statement that the child's difficulties have a physical cause, the mother is able to absolve herself of blame; in fact, she has a double coverage. It is hard for such a mother to see her child's present problems objectively because she has already imposed her own interpretation on them.

7. Finally, a dysfunctional individual will not be able to perform the most important function of good communication: "checking out" his perceptions to see whether they tally with the situation as it really is or with the intended meaning of another. When two people are neither of them able to check out their meanings with each other, the result may resemble a comedy of errors—with a tragic

ending. Here is one possible misunderstanding between a husband and a wife:

Report: W: "He always yells." H: "I don't yell."

Explanation: W: "I don't do things to suit him." H: "I don't do things to suit her."

Interpretation: W: "He doesn't care about me." H: "She doesn't care about me."

Conclusion: W: "I will leave him." H: "I will leave her."

Manifestation: Wife uses invectives, voice is loud and shrill, eyes blaze, muscles stand out on base of neck, mouth is open, nostrils are distended, uses excessive movements. Husband says nothing, keeps eyes lowered, mouth tight, body constricted.

Outcome: Wife visits divorce lawyer. Husband files a countersuit.

8. Difficulty in communicating is closely linked to an individual's self-concept, that is, his self-image and self-esteem.
   a. His parents may not only have given him inadequate models for methods of communication, but the content of their messages to him may have been devaluating. . . .
   b. In order to form his self-image, the child has a demanding task. He must integrate messages from both parents (separately and together) telling him what to do with aspects of living like dependency, authority, sexuality and coding or labeling (cognition).
   c. If the parents' own attitudes are uncertain, or if they disagree with each other, the messages the child takes will be equally confused. The child will try to integrate what cannot be integrated, on the basis of inconsistent and insufficient data. Failing, he will end up with an incomplete picture of himself and low self-esteem.
   d. In addition, the child's parents may depreciate his self-esteem more directly. He looks to them to validate his steps in growth; if these are not acknowledged at the time they occur, or if they are acknowledged with concomitant messages of disgust, disapproval, embarrassment, indifference or pain, the child's self-esteem will naturally suffer.
9. Low self-esteem leads to dysfunctional communication:
   a. When there is a conflict of interests. Any relationship presupposes a commitment to a joint outcome, an agreement that each partner will give up a little of his own interests in order to reach a wider benefit for both.
      — This outcome is the best objective reality that can be arrived

at in terms of what is possible, what is feasible, what fits the best all the way around.

— The process used for reaching this outcome depends on the self-concepts of the persons engaged in it. If their self-esteem is low, so that any sacrifice of self seems intolerable, it is likely that the process will be based on some form of deciding "who is right," "who will win," "who is most loved," "who will get mad." I call this the "war syndrome."

— If a person operates by means of this war syndrome, it is inevitable that his ability to seek objective information and arrive at objective conclusions as to what fits will be greatly impaired.

   b. Dysfunction in communication will also follow when the individual is unable to handle different-ness.

— As we have seen, . . . an individual who has not achieved an independent selfhood will often take any evidence of different-ness in someone he is close to as an insult or a sign of being unloved.

— This is because he is intensely dependent on the other person to increase his feelings of worth and to validate his self-image. Any reminder that the other is, after all, a separate being, capable of faithlessness and desertion, fills him with fear and distrust.

— Some couples express their objections to each other's different-ness freely and loudly . . . but others, less secure in this area, prefer to pretend that different-ness does not exist.

— With such couples, communication becomes covert. . . . Any message which might call attention to the self as a private agent, with likes and dislikes, desires and displeasures of its own, is suppressed or changed. Wishes and decisions are presented as if they emanated from anywhere but inside the speaker himself; statements are disguised as symbolic utterances; messages are left incomplete or even not expressed at all, with the sender relying on mental telepathy to get them across. . . . For example, a couple who overtly behaved as if they had absolutely no problems responded in therapy to the "How did you meet?" question as follows:

H: "Well, we were raised in the same neighborhood."

W: "Not exactly the same neighborhood" (laughs).

This slight modification on the wife's part presaged many revelations of serious division between them.

10. Thus far we have been talking about dysfunctional behavior rather than the symptom that calls attention to it. What is the connection between them?

a. Dysfunctional behavior is, as we have seen related to feelings of low self-esteem. It is, in fact, a defense against the perception of them. Defenses, in turn, are ways which enable the person with low self-esteem to function without a symptom. To the person himself and to the outward world, there may appear to be nothing wrong.

b. But if he is threatened by some event of survival significance, some happening which says to him, "You do not count; you are not lovable; you are nothing," the defense may prove unequal to the task of shielding him, and a symptom will take its place.

c. Usually it is only then that the individual and his community will notice that he is "ill" and that he will admit a need for help.

11. How, then, do we define therapy?

a. If illness is seen to derive from inadequate methods of communication (by which we mean all interactional behavior), it follows that therapy will be seen as an attempt to improve these methods. As will be seen in the chapters on therapy, the emphasis will be on correcting discrepancies in communication and teaching ways to achieve more fitting joint outcomes.

b. This approach to therapy depends on three primary beliefs about human nature:

— First, that every individual is geared to survival, growth, and getting close to others and that all behavior expresses these aims, no matter how distorted it may look. Even an extremely disturbed person will be fundamentally on the side of the therapist.

— Second, that what society calls sick, crazy, stupid, or bad behavior is really an attempt on the part of the afflicted person to signal the presence of trouble and call for help. In that sense, it may not be so sick, crazy, stupid, or bad after all.

— Third, that human beings are limited only by the extent of their knowledge, their ways of understanding themselves and their ability to "check out" with others. Thought and feeling are inextricably bound together; the individual need not be a prisoner of his feelings but can use the cognitive component of his feeling to free himself. This is the basis for assuming that a human being can learn what he doesn't know and can change ways of commenting and understanding that don't fit.

12. This brings us to a discussion of the role of the therapist. How will he act? What picture will he have of himself?

a. Perhaps the best way that he can see himself is as a resource person. He is not omnipotent. He is not God, parent or judge. The knotty question for all therapists is how to be an expert without appearing to the patient to be all-powerful, omniscient, or presuming to know always what is right and wrong.

b. The therapist does have a special advantage in being able to study the patient's family situation as an experienced observer, while remaining outside it, above the power struggle, so to speak. Like a camera with a wide-angle lens, he can see things from the position of each person present and act as a representative of each. He sees transactions, as well as the individuals involved, and thus has a unique viewpoint.

c. Because of this, the family can place their trust in him as an "official observer," one who can report impartially on what he sees and hears. Above all, he can report on what the family cannot see and cannot report on.

13. The therapist must also see himself as a model of communication.

a. First of all, he must take care to be aware of his own prejudices and unconscious assumptions so as not to fall into the trap he warns others about, that of suiting reality to himself. His lack of fear in revealing himself may be the first experience the family has had with clear communication.

b. In addition, the way he interprets and structures the action of therapy from the start is the first step in introducing the family to new techniques in communication.

c. Here is an example of how the therapist clarifies the process of interaction for a family:

Th: (to husband) I notice your brow is wrinkled, Ralph. Does that mean you are angry at this moment?

H: I did not know that my brow was wrinkled.

Th: Sometimes a person looks or sounds in a way of which he is not aware. As far as you can tell, what were you thinking and feeling just now?

H: I was thinking over what she (his wife) said.

Th: What thing that she said were you thinking about?

H: When she said that when she was talking so loud, she wished I would tell her.

Th: What were you thinking about that?

H: I never thought about telling her. I thought she would get mad.

Th: Ah, then maybe that wrinkle meant you were puzzled because your wife was hoping you would do something and you did not know she had this hope. Do you suppose that by your wrinkled brow you were signalling that you were puzzled?

H: Yes, I guess so.

Th: As far as you know, have you ever been in that same spot before, that is, where you were puzzled by something Alice said or did?

H: Hell, yes, lots of times.

Th: Have you ever told Alice you were puzzled when you were?

W: He never says anything.

Th: (smiling, to Alice) Just a minute, Alice, let me hear what Ralph's idea is of what he does. Ralph, how do you think you have let Alice know when you are puzzled?

H: I think she knows.

Th: Well, let's see. Suppose you ask Alice if she knows.

H: This is silly.

Th: (smiling) I suppose it might seem so in this situation, because Alice is right here and certainly has heard what your question is. She knows what it is. I have the suspicion, though, that neither you nor Alice are very sure about what the other expects, and I think you have not developed ways to find out. Alice, let's go back to when I commented on Ralph's wrinkled brow. Did you happen to notice it, too?

W: (complaining) Yes, he always looks like that.

Th: What kind of a message did you get from that wrinkled brow?

W: He don't want to be here. He don't care. He never talks. Just looks at television or he isn't home.

Th: I'm curious. Do you mean that when Ralph has a wrinkled brow that you take this as Ralph's way of saying, "I don't love you, Alice. I don't care about you, Alice."?

W: (exasperated and tearfully) I don't know.

Th: Well, maybe the two of you have not yet worked out crystal-clear ways of giving your love and value messages to each other. Everyone needs crystal-clear ways of giving their value messages. (to son) What do you know, Jim, about how you give your value messages to your parents?

S: I don't know what you mean.

Th: Well, how do you let your mother, for instance, know that you like her, when you are feeling that way? Everyone feels different ways at different times. When you are feeling glad your mother is around, how do you let her know?

S: I do what she tells me to do. Work and stuff.

Th: I see, so when you do your work at home, you mean this for a message to your mother that you're glad she is around.

S: Not exactly.

Th: You mean you are giving a different message then. Well, Alice, did you take this message from Jim to be a love message? (to Jim) What do you do to give your father a message that you like him?

S: (after a pause) I can't think of nothin'.

Th: Let me put it another way. What do you know crystal-clear that you could do that would bring a smile to your father's face?

S: I could get better grades in school.

Th: Let's check this out and see if you are perceiving clearly. Do you, Alice, get a love message from Jim when he works around the house?

W: I s'pose—he doesn't do very much.

Th: So from where you sit, Alice, you don't get many love messages from Jim. Tell me, Alice, does Jim have any other ways that he might not now be thinking about that he has that say to you that he is glad you are around?

W: (softly) The other day he told me I looked nice.

Th: What about you, Ralph, does Jim perceive correctly that if he got better grades you would smile?

H: I don't imagine I will be smiling for some time.

Th: I hear that you don't think he is getting good grades, but would you smile if he did?

H: Sure, hell, I would be glad.

Th: As you think about it, how do you suppose you would show it?

W: You never know if you ever please him.

Th: We have already discovered that you and Ralph have not yet developed crystal-clear ways of showing value feelings toward one another. Maybe you, Alice, are now observing this between Jim and Ralph. What do you think, Ralph? Do you suppose it would be hard for Jim to find out when he has pleased you?

14. The therapist will not only exemplify what he means by clear communication, but he will teach his patients how to achieve it themselves.

  a. He will spell out the rules for communication accurately. In particular, he will emphasize the necessity for checking out meaning given with meaning received. He will see that the patient keeps in mind the following complicated set of mirror images:

  — Self's idea (how I see me).
  — Self's idea of other (how I see you).
  — Self's idea of other's idea of self (how I see you seeing me).
  — Self's idea of other's idea of self's idea of other (how I see you seeing me seeing you).

  Only if a person is able to check back and forth across the lines of communication, can he be sure that he has completed a clear exchange.

  b. The therapist will help the patient to be aware of messages that are incongruent, confused or covert. . . .

  c. At the same time, the therapist will show the patient how to check on invalid assumptions that are used as fact. He knows that members of dysfunctional families are afraid to question each other to find out what each really means. They seem to say to each other: "I can't let you know what I see and hear and think and feel or you will drop dead, attack or desert me." As a result, each operates from his assumptions, which he takes from the other person's manifestations and thereupon treats as fact. The therapist uses various questions to ferret out these invalid assumptions, such as:

> "What did you say? What did you hear me say?"
>
> "What did you see or hear that led you to make that conclusion?"
>
> "What message did you intend to get across?"
>
> "If I had been there, what would I have seen or heard?"
>
> "How do you know? How can you find out?"
>
> "You look calm, but how do you feel in the stomach?"

    d. Like any good teacher, the therapist will try to be crystal clear.
- He will repeat, restate and emphasize his own observations, sometimes to the point of seeming repetitious and simple. He will do the same with observations made by members of the family.
- He will also be careful to give his reasons for arriving at any conclusion. If the patient is baffled by some statement of the therapist's and does not know the reasoning behind it, this will only increase his feelings of powerlessness.

15. The therapist will be aware of the many possibilities of interaction in therapy.
    a. In the therapeutic situation, the presence of the therapist adds as many dyads (two-person systems) as there are people in the family, since he relates to each member. The therapist, like the other people present, operates as a member of various dyads but also as the observer of other dyads. These shifts of position could be confusing to him and to the family. If, for example, he has taken someone's part, he should clearly state he is doing so.
    b. The therapist clarifies the nature of interchanges made during therapy, but he has to select those that are representative since he can't possibly keep up with everything that is said. Luckily, family sequences are apt to be redundant, so one clarification may serve a number of exchanges.
    c. Here is an illustration of the way the therapist isolates and underlines each exchange.
- When the therapist states, "When you, Ralph, said you were angry, I noticed that you, Alice, had a frown on your

face," this is an example of the therapist reporting himself as a monad ("I see you, Alice; I hear you, Ralph"), and reporting to Ralph and Alice as monads (the use of the word you, followed by the specific name). Then, by the therapist's use of the word when, he establishes that there is a connection between the husband's report and the wife's report, thus validating the presence of an interaction.

— If the therapist then turns to the oldest son, Jim, and says, "What do you, Jim, make of what just happened between your mother and father?" the therapist is establishing Jim as an observer, since family members may forget that they monitor each other's behavior.

— When Jim answers, everyone knows what his perception is. If it turns out that Jim's report does not fit what either Alice or Ralph intended, then there is an opportunity to find out what was intended, what was picked up by Jim, and why he interpreted it that way.

16. Labeling an illness is a part of therapy that a therapist must approach with particular care.

   a. A therapist, when he deals with a patient, is confronting a person who has been labeled by others or by himself as having emotional, physical or social disorders. To the non-therapeutic observer, the behavior which signals the presence of a disorder is usually labeled "stupid," "crazy," "sick" or "bad."

   b. The therapist will use other labels, like "mentally defective," "underachieving," "schizophrenic," "manic-depressive," "psychosomatic," "sociopathic." These are labels used by clinicians to describe behavior which is seen to be deviant: deviant from the rest of the person's character, deviant from the expectation of others, and deviant from the context in which the person finds himself.

   c. The observations made by clinicians over the years have been brought together under a standardized labeling system called the "psychiatric nomenclature." It is a method of shorthand used by clinicians to describe deviant behavior.

   d. These labels often presuppose an exact duplication of all the individuals so labeled. Over the years, each of the labels has been given an identity, with prognosis and treatment implications based on the dimensions of that identity.

   e. If a therapist has labeled a person "schizophrenic," for instance, he may have based his prognosis of that person on his ideas about schizophrenia, rather than on an observation of a person who, among other labels like "human being," "Jim," "husband," "father," "chemist," has the label "schizophrenic."

   f. But neither the clinician or any other person has the right to treat him only in terms of the label "schizophrenic" while losing sight of him as a total human being. No label is infallible, because no diagnosis is, but by identifying the person with the label, the therapist shuts his mind to the possibility of different interpretations which different evidence might point to.

g. The therapist must say to his patient, in effect: You are behaving now with behavior which I, as a clinician, label "schizophrenia." But this label only applies at this time, in this place, and in this context. Future times, places and contexts may show something quite different.

17. Let us close this discussion of the role of the therapist with a look at some of the specific advantages family therapy will have compared to individual or group therapy.

a. In family therapy, the therapist will have a greater opportunity to observe objectively. In individual therapy, since there are only two people, the therapist is part of the interaction. It is hard for him to be impartial. In addition, he must sift out the patient's own reactions and feelings from those which might be a response to clues from the therapist himself.

b. The family therapist will be able to get firsthand knowledge of the patient in two important areas.

— By observing the individual in his family, the therapist can see where he is in terms of his present level of growth.

— By observing a child in the family group, the therapist can find out how his functioning came to be handicapped. He can see for himself how the husband and wife relate to each other and how they relate to the child.

— This kind of firsthand knowledge is not possible in individual therapy, or even in group therapy, where the individual is with members of his peer group and the kind of interaction that can be studied is limited to this single aspect.

18. As a therapist, I have found certain concepts useful, somewhat like measuring tools, in determining the nature and extent of dysfunction in a family.

a. I make an analysis of the techniques used by each member of the family for handling the presence of different-ness. A person's reaction to different-ness is an index to his ability to adapt to growth and change. It also indicates what attitudes he will have toward other members of his family, and whether he will be able to express these attitudes directly or not.

— The members of any family need to have ways to find out about and make room for their different-ness. This requires that each can report directly what he perceives about himself and the other, to himself and to the other.

— Example: Janet misses her hatpin. She must say, "I need my hatpin (clear), which I am telling you, Betty, about, (di-

rect), and it is the hatpin that I use for the only black hat I
have (specific)." Not: "Why don't you leave my hat alone?"
or "Isn't there something you want to tell me?" or going
into Betty's room and turning things upsidedown (unclear,
indirect, and unspecific).

— As I have said before, when one of the partners in a marriage is confronted with a different-ness in the other that
he did not expect, or that he did not know about, it is important that he treat this as an opportunity to explore and
to understand rather than as a signal for war.

— If the techniques for handling different-ness are based on
determining who is right (war), or pretending that the
different-ness does not exist (denial), then there is a potential for pathological behavior on the part of any member of
the family, but particularly the children.

b. I make what I call a role function analysis to find out whether
the members of a family are covertly playing roles different
from those which their position in the family demands that they
play. . . .

— If two people have entered a marriage with the hope of
extending the self, each is in effect put in charge of the
other, thus creating a kind of mutual parasitic relationship.

— This relationship will eventually be translated into something that looks like a parent-child relationship. The adults,
labeled "husband" and "wife," may in reality be functioning
as mother and son, father and daughter, or as siblings, to
the confusion of the rest of the family and, ultimately,
themselves.

— Here is an oversimplified example of the way things might
go in such a family:

Suppose Mary takes over the role of sole parent, with
Joe acting the part of her child. Joe then takes the part
of a brother to their two children, John and Patty, and
becomes a rival with them for their mother's affections.
To handle his rivalry and prove his place, he may start
drinking excessively, or he may bury himself in his
work in order to avoid coming home. Mary, deserted,
may turn to John in such a way as to make him feel he
must take his father's place. Wishing to do so but in
reality unable to, John may become delinquent, turning against his mother and choosing someone on the
outside. Or he may accept his mother's invitation,
which would be to give up being male and become
homosexual. Patty may regress or remain infantile to
keep her place. Joe may get ulcers. Mary may become
psychotic.

— These are only some of the possibilities for disturbance in a family that has become dislocated by incongruent role-playing.

c. I make a self-manifestation analysis for each member of a family. If what a person says does not fit with the way he looks, sounds and acts, or if he reports his wishes and feelings as belonging to someone else or as coming from somewhere else, I know that he will not be able to produce reliable clues for any other person interacting with him. When such behavior, which I call "manifesting incongruency," is present in the members of a family to any large degree, there will be a potential for development of pathology.

d. In order to find out how the early life of each member of a family has affected his present ways of behaving, I make what I call a model analysis. . . .

— This means that I try to discover who the models were (or are) that influenced each family member in his early life; who gave him messages about the presence and desirability of growth; who gave him the blueprint from which he learned to evaluate and act on new experience; who showed him how to become close to others.

— Because these messages have survival significance, the ways in which they are given will automatically determine the way the individual interprets later messages from other adults, who may not be survival-connected but who may be invested with survival significance, like spouses, in-laws or bosses.[3]

19. The ideas in this chapter have been discussed out of the context of ongoing therapy, where they belong. In the next three chapters, I hope to show very specifically how I, as a therapist, incorporate them into the action of therapy, from the first time I see a family to the termination of treatment.

NOTES

[1] This description of maturity emphasizes social and communication skills rather than the acquisition of knowledge and recognized achievement, which in my view derive from the first two.

[2] The communication aspects of this situation Jackson has labeled "past-present switches." Thus, the answer to the therapist's question, "How out of all the millions of people in the world did you two find each other?" may be as useful in family diagnosis as psychological testing. This question allows the spouses to describe their present relationship under cover of talking about the past. For further examples of this phenomenon, see Watzlawick's *An Anthology of Human Communication.* (256)

[3] While there are obvious connections between this theory and both the analytic concept of transference and the Sullivanian concept of parataxic distortion, there are also differences. In particular, instead of inferring from the transference the probable nature of the individual's early environment, I use the information about his past to evaluate the survival significance of his current messages.

26

Transactional Analysis: A New Method for Helping Offenders

RICHARD C. NICHOLSON

Chief Probation Officer, United States District Court, Sacramento, California

---

"I'm okay; you're okay!" If a group counselor feels this way about himself and his clients, the social transactions within the group can become straightforward and free of games. This is the position recommended by Eric Berne, M.D., author of *Transactional Analysis in Psychotherapy.** He likens the successful group therapist or counselor to a "cowboy." By that he means that the therapist should be relaxed, alert, adaptable as well as a straight shooter. Unlike the tense therapist, the "cowboy" does not believe that the members of his group will get better faster if everyone remains serious. He considers that laughter is as much an expression of feeling as is hostility: "We like laughter; our patients like laughter."[1] Another feature of Transactional Analysis is that it employs colloquial terms that are easily understood by all. Doctor Berne has introduced a new way of talking about human behavior. His terminology is simple and direct:

> Transactional Analysis because of its clearcut statements rooted in easily accessible material, because of its operational nature, and because of its specialized vocabulary (consisting of only five words: Parent, Adult, Child, Game and Script), offers an easily-learned framework for clarification.[2]

Since its development, Transactional Analysis[3] has attracted international interest. Over 1,000 professionals have received formal training in Berne's methods. He is perhaps more popularly known for his best seller, *Games People Play,* but in professional circles he is also acclaimed for such works as *Principles of Group Treatment* which serves as an excellent textbook for persons interested in the application of his method; and *The Structure and Dynamics of Organizations and Groups,* which offers a systematic framework for group treatment.

Reprinted by permission from *Federal Probation* Quarterly, September 1970, pp. 29–38.

After receiving his degree in medicine at McGill University and serving his residency at Yale's Psychiatric Clinic, Eric Berne received specialized training in psychoanalysis in the respective institutes at New York and San Francisco. Sometime later, during a session of one of his therapy groups, one of his patients commented that he felt like a little boy. Traditionally, a psychoanalyst would have given a different interpretation to such a comment, but Berne, who had previously observed the same person being quite adult, later queried, "Who's talking now, the adult man, or the little boy?"[4] Subsequent observations led him to believe that there are three "ego states" operative in all of us. Berne has colloquially called them the Parent, Adult, and Child. His conclusions were also based upon the hypotheses suggested by Wilder Penfield's study and treatment of epileptic patients.[5]

Penfield discovered that when he applied mild electric stimulation to the exposed cortex of his patients, that they would re-experience past events, usually from childhood, in as fresh and animated form as when they first happened. Apparently, our brain functions very much like a three-track, high-fidelity tape recording, that can reproduce the past events in our lives, including the interpretations that we gave them and the emotions felt at the time. Our "memory tapes" are available for replay today, and they can greatly influence our present behavior.

From Penfield's experiments Berne perceived the existence of two "ego states," one based upon the present, external, and psychological situation; the other based upon the "re-living" of occurrences going back as far as the first year of our life.[6]

PARENT, ADULT, AND CHILD

While watching and listening to his patients, Berne noticed that they would change right before his eyes. He observed changes in facial expressions, postures, gestures, voice intonations, vocabulary, and body functions (blushing, etc.). A father's face will harden when his son defies him; a person turns pale and trembles when stopped by the red light and siren of a pursuing traffic officer; an adult person shouts with child-like excitement when his slot machine hits the jackpot and the winning bell clangs. Such changes can be observed in the same person. "He changes from *what* to *what*?"[7]

According to Berne, these changes are shifts from one "ego state" to another, like the previously described patient who would feel like a small child at one time, and like an adult at another time. The shifts occur between our Parent, Adult, and Child (PAC).

The Parent

We have said that the external events that occur in a person's life are recorded in the human brain pretty much like a high-fidelity tape recording. Such events are recorded during our early years (about 0-5 years) and are, for the most part, provided by the significant persons in our lives—our own parents, or those who substitute as our parents.

In selecting the name "Parent" for these recordings, Doctor Berne was mindful of the examples that our own parents give: their advice and admonishments; their nurturence, assistance, and affection; and all of the traits that one's parents exhibit, including their prejudices. During our early years we know very little about word formations. Our ability to make realistic evaluations and judgments is therefore quite limited. We take in these "Parent" recordings or tapes just as we perceive them—without any processing based upon what is real and correct. Our future behavior is highly influenced by our "Parent" tapes. We might hear others say, "He's like his father, you know." When a drunken father lashes out at his own feelings of depression and guilt by striking the small child, or by verbally abusing him, all that the child can record is that "Daddy doesn't love me; I can't be any good," and he later may come around to feeling that persons possessing authority are also abusive and unloving. Such a "Parent" tape may sound very familiar to people in corrections.

The Child

At the same time our "Parent" tapes are being recorded, the internal events occurring in early childhood are being recorded also. These recordings are described as:

> . . . The responses of the little person to what he hears and feels. Thus, an evoked childhood recollection is not an accurate reproduction of what occurred but of what the person *saw and heard and felt and understood.*[8]

Such recordings or "Child" tapes are therefore full of misconceptions, fusions, and emotional conflicts. The reactions of the small child are mostly *feelings*. His ability to make reality judgments is limited by his incomplete knowledge of word formations. He is small, clumsy, and unable to control his body functions. Since he is constantly being corrected by the significant adults in his life, he comes to feel that he is the object of their disapproval. Our "Child" tapes play back many "not okay" feelings. Where parents have been rejecting, too demanding, or harsh, the "not okay" feelings will predominate. These negative feelings are easily evoked when we perceive signs of disapproval from others—when our friends or co-workers do not respond to our "good morning"; or when the boss is grumpy; or when we hear the police siren and fear that we have been singled out for a traffic arrest. In TA we say that such incidents "hook the Child." By that we mean there is a replay of the "not okay Child tapes."[9]

On the positive side, the Child is creative, curious, explorative, affectionate, and playful. Our "happy" Child can also be hooked, as when our "good morning" begets a favorable response. A man who is skilled at hooking the "happy Child" of others can become a good husband, father, or boss.

The Adult

When the little person begins to feel the power of movement, starts moving out, starts handling objects, and when he starts exploring his environment, he is freeing himself from his original inertia. It is at this stage of development that our Adult comes into being. As we mature, our Adult functions more and more effectively, despite the commands and blockings of our parents and despite the anxieties they have aroused in the small child. The Adult can be described as a sort of computer that processes reality data. "Mommie is wrong, school isn't all fun," or "Mommie is right, the cars in the street can hurt me."

The primary goal in Berne's treatment is to emancipate the Adult, enabling it thus to examine the Parent in order to determine whether the recordings are realistic or correct (see Figure 2). The Adult can accept or reject the "Parent" tapes depending upon their validity. The Adult may not be able to erase the "not okay" feelings uncovered in the Child, but it can shut them off. In TA the patient or client is encouraged to place his Adult in command of his personality, or to make it the executive, so to speak. With the Adult in command, we are able to activate the Parent or let out the Child when appropriate to the occasion. If we do not bring out our restraining Parent when junior threatens a tantrum, we may beget a "problem child." Our Adult rejects dictums from the Parent that tell us "The only good Indian is a dead Indian," but it accepts and employs wise sayings such as, "A stitch in time saves nine." Our Adult does not allow the Child to express sexuality in public, but it does allow its levity to come out when our duties at work become too burdensome.

THE FOUR LIFE POSITIONS

Referring to Figure 1, we see a continuum depicting a life span from the moment of conception to the age of about 5 years.

The first 9 months of our existence is the most perfect situation that a human being can experience. At biological birth the infant is pushed out and into a situation of terrifying contrast and presumably exposed to extremes of temperature, noise, light, separateness, and abandonment.[10]

Conception	Biological Birth	Psychological Birth	Social Birth (school)
(9 months)	(estrangement)		(age 5)

Figure 1

This "birth trauma" is recorded and stored in the brain cells. Soon after birth, a rescuer wraps the infant in a blanket, comforts him, and strokes him. Without this he will die—as foundling infants sometimes do from progressive emaciation. By the rescue and by receiving "strokes," the infant finds out that life on the outside is at least endurable. Depending upon the gap between biological birth and the rescue (psychological birth), the quality and frequency of stroking, the child will develop a "central emotional position to which he will automatically return for the rest of his days as a major safeguard of the major vulnerability of his life."[11]

There are four life positions:

1. *I'm not OK; you're OK:* The environment of the growing infant can be likened to that of a Lilliputian living in a land of giants. He finds himself dependent upon his giant-like parents for strokings and for feelings of being OK. The child-rearing policies of his parents, although necessary, leave him with many "not OK" feelings. He is always being corrected, and eventually finds himself in the life position of "I'm not OK; you're OK." This is the neurotic or depressed position, and is the most common one in our society. Although we can rise above it, we will find that it continues to have a profound effect upon the way we handle our everyday social transactions. All correctional workers have encountered cases in which the offender is trying to prove that, in fact, he is "not OK."

2. *I'm not OK; you're not OK:* This is the position occupied by the autistic child—the child whose early experiences denied him a timely rescue or sufficient stroking. Such a child has little will to live. Schizophrenia may be the outcome of this position.

3. *I'm OK; you're not OK:* This is a denial of position number 1, frequently adopted by a child who wants to retaliate. It is the sociopathic or psychopathic position so often observed in the incorrigibles.

4. *I'm OK; you're OK:* This position requires a statement of faith, and it is the basis for getting well. The first three positions are assumed at the preverbal stage and are based upon feelings. The fourth position results from thought, confidence in ourselves and others, and willingness to venture out of our defenses.

It is a decision that we have to make. In some respects it is like a religious conversion.[12]

The most common position is "I'm not OK; you're OK," and may be expressed by the playing of "games." Later, we will go into Berne's definition and description of games. For the moment it is important to emphasize that our "not OK" Child stays with us. Through TA a person can be enabled to collect new recordings or "tapes" through the experiencing of successful outcomes in his Adult transactions and through successes gained by arriving at proper judgments. Patience and perseverence are required to secure the position of "I'm OK; you're OK" because our previous "bad tapes" and social inadequacies cannot be overcome immediately. Our Child wants immediate results; our Adult can exercise patience. Berne's method of treatment takes time, but less time than do the traditional therapies.

STRUCTURAL ANALYSIS

Before a client can profitably participate in TA, he must first understand something about Structural Analysis. Although social transactions are complex, TA enables us to diagram such transactions, thus making them more easily understood.

1. *Ideal:* We all have a Parent, Adult, and Child, but the working relationships among these ego states may differ. Ideally, as in Figure 2, the lines or boundaries between Parent, Adult, and Child are clean-cut and relatively impermeable.

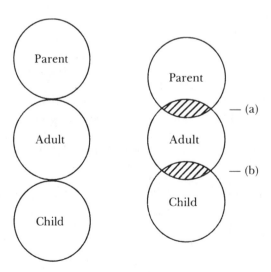

Figure 2   **Figure 3**

The Adult, although holding the executive position, is nevertheless able to admit the "examined Parent" and the "adapted Child," when appropriate. Berne's treatment aims at clearly separating the three "ego states," and at determining just what is each client's Parent, Adult, and Child. His treatment goals are easily understood by everyone. Thomas A. Harris, M.D., cites the example of a deprived and unsuccessful school dropout (a teenage girl) who indicated her understanding of PAC after the initial interview, thus: "It (PAC) means that we are all made up of three parts and we'd better keep them separated or we're in trouble."[13]

2. *Contaminations:* Instead of the ideal situation, as presented in Figure 2, we most often find that the boundaries or circles overlap each other. Such an overlap is called a contamination (see Figure 3).

The (a) overlap depicts a contamination of the Adult by a "dated and unexamined" Parent with the recorded parental data deemed to be true and accurate. A person thus contaminated suffers from prejudice. "Negroes are inferior; all Germans are mass murderers; law-enforcement officials are sadistic; court judges are stupid, prejudicial and corrupt," etc. We all have encountered persons whose prejudices are unshakeable. The only way to eliminate our prejudices is by realizing that it is no longer dangerous to disagree with one's parents, or to modify the data that one has in his "Parent."

The (b) overlap represents an Adult contaminated by the Child. When this contamination is at its worst, the Adult is seldom in control and the person is liable to suffer from delusions or hallucinations. A person who views the world as a grim, ugly place is probably seeing it as it appeared to him during childhood. A little child who lives in fear of angry, unpredictable parents can, when grown up, experience the same fear in stressful situations.[14] By decontaminating his Adult, a person becomes able to process reality data. Hallucinations develop when the boundary between the Child and Adult breaks down and the original haranguing dialogue between a child and his parents is projected outward as real. "While the voice emanates from the Parent the audience consists of the Child and sometimes the contaminated Adult as well."[15]

3. *Exclusions:* According to Berne, "an exclusion is manifested by a stereotyped, predictable attitude which is steadfastly maintained as long as possible in the face of a threatening situation. The constant Parent, the constant Adult, and the constant Child all result primarily from defensive exclusion of the two complementary aspects in each case."[16]

Figure 4 depicts the person who cannot play. He works late at the office; duty dominates his activities; he is all business. He has been so overpowered by stern, unrelenting parents that he feels secure only when his Child is completely turned off. His theme is, "Children should be seen and not heard . . . Didn't I tell you . . . grow up!" He has very little happiness recorded in his Child tapes. By freeing his Adult and firming up the boundaries between Parent and Adult, the Parent can be then examined and some of its unrealistic and harsh dictums rejected. The result: Our duty-dominated client is enabled to cut down on his office hours, listen lovingly to his children's fantasies, and start sharing his life with his family.

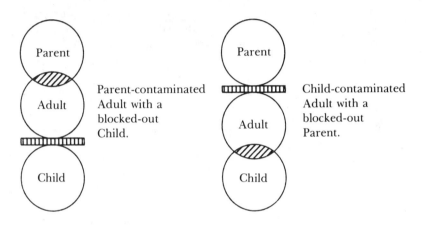

Parent-contaminated Adult with a blocked-out Child.

Child-contaminated Adult with a blocked-out Parent.

Figure 4   **Figure 5**

Figure 5 is of particular interest to correctional workers. It represents the person without a conscience, the dyssocial or sociopathic (antisocial) personality. If his parents have been frightening, brutal, indifferent to his feelings or unpredictable, he preserves himself by turning them off. From the "I'm not OK; you're OK" position, he retaliates with "I'm OK, you're not OK." By excluding the painful parent he also excludes, unfortunately, what little good was in them. Feelings of guilt, embarrassment, or remorse are noticeably absent. Treatment of such a person is admittedly difficult. According to Dr. Harris, "He may never have an operational Parent to back up his Adult, but his Adult can be strong enough to carry him through a successful life wherein he gains the approval and even the esteem of others. It is on this possibility that all our rehabilitative efforts in the field of corrections must be based."[17]

ANALYZING TRANSACTIONS

"A unit of social intercourse is called a transaction. If two or more people encounter each other . . . sooner or later one of them will speak, or give some indication of acknowledging the presence of the others. This is called a *transactional stimulus.* Another person will do or say something which is in some way related to the stimulus. This is called the *transactional response.*"[18] The response may in turn become another stimulus inviting a new response, chain fashion. The important purpose of transactional analysis is for the participating clients to determine which part of our PAC—Parent, Adult, or Child—is providing the stimulus and which is giving the response. Clues that the Parent is providing either the transactional stimulus or response include finger and head wagging; clucking and sighing; tightening of the lips, tilting the head, etc. For the Child: words signifying refusal, or wants; "mine's better," etc. For the Adult: a vocabulary indicating why, who, where, when, how. The clues for each ego state consist of differences in gestures, facial expressions, postures, voice intonations, vocabulary, and body functions (blushing, etc.).

Complementary Transactions

Figure 6 shows examples of complementary transactions.

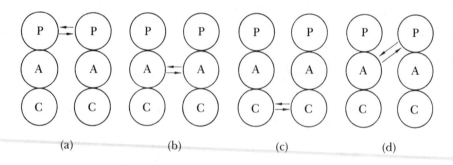

(a)   (b)   (c)   (d)

Figure 6

In example (a), we find a couple of elderly persons complaining ɔout times and morals. Their discussion is without any consideration of new data so that the Adult never enters into their conversation. They might, for example, consider the "why's" of changing times. At any rate the vectors, both stimulus and response, are Parent to Parent. This brings us to Berne's first rule of communications: *When stimulus and response on the PAC transactional diagram make parallel lines, the transaction is complementary and can go on indefinitely.*

In situation (b), Adult to Adult, we might find a person asking another for street directions. Situation (c) might be two members of a fraternity plotting initiation rights (Child to Child). We might get a situation as diagrammed in (d) if hubby were to ask wifey to help him control his cigarette habit.

Crossed Transactions

These transactions bring about trouble in our interpersonal relations.

Referring to Figure 7, Berne gives the example of a transaction between a husband and wife in which he asks: "Dear, where are my cuff links (Adult stimulus)?" A complementary response (parallel vectors) from his spouse might be, "In your top dresser drawer." But if wifey has had a rough day, storing up her resentments, she might respond with, "Why are you always picking on me?" The result is a crossed Transaction as seen in Figure 7. His stimulus is Adult to Adult; her response is Child to Parent, and the vectors cross. This brings us to Berne's second rule of communication: *When the stimulus and response on the PAC transaction diagram cross, communication stops.*

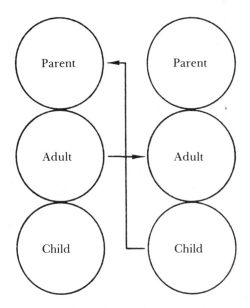

Figure 7

The husband and wife won't talk about cuff links anymore, but rather something like the game of "uproar." Or, wifey could have replied: "Why don't you put things where they belong?" As shown in Figure 8, we would then get another crossed transaction of Parent to Child, and again, the communications cease, and the games begin.

The origin of non-Adult responses is in the life position of the "not OK" Child. This can be seen when a person "reads" into another's statements, thus: "Where did you get these steaks?" says the husband. "Why, is there something wrong with them?" wifey retorts. The individual with the "not OK" Child cannot handle Adult transactions, if the

Child is in control. The primary requirement in Adult transactions is that we deal with reality.

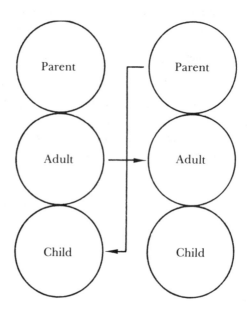

Figure 8

The "not OK" position can also be expressed in the stimulus. Figure 9 offers an example wherein hubby asks, "Where did you hide the can opener?" An attempt to get this information via Adult stimulus would be a straight, verbal question (Adult to Adult). But in our example, the husband not only wants to get information, but his Parent is also covertly saying (Parent to Child), "You're a lousy housekeeper." Whether or not we get a crossed transaction would hinge upon how the wife would respond. If she feels OK enough not to be threatened, her response would be parallel or complementary, thus: "I hid it next to the forks, darling." But if her response were to be, "Don't get smart with me," the search for the can opener terminates and the wrangling begins.

Central to the possibility of change is whether or not the Adult can be strong enough to keep the Child in control. According to Dr. Harris, "First of all a conscious effort is required, built on a conscious plan which rests on a set of values adopted by the Adult. It is said that you cannot teach navigation in the middle of a storm. Likewise, you cannot expect to carry through a successful transaction with your Adult in charge if you never thought about, or never built, any set of values which gives it purpose."[19]

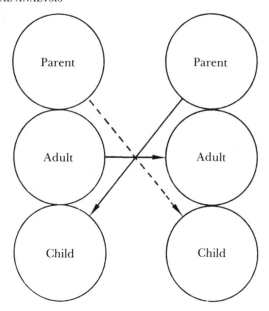

Figure 9

THE STRUCTURING OF TIME

We hear that our average life span is three score and 10 years, but today's trend is to increase this expectancy. We are frequently concerned with what to do with the smaller periods of time, next week, today, the next hour, or right now. People who do not structure their own time look to others to tell them what to do.

Berne has concluded that there are six ways of structuring time which includes all of the transactions: withdrawal; rituals; activities; pastimes; games; intimacy.

Withdrawal

This is not a transaction in a strict sense, but it always occurs in a social setting. A school boy's withdrawal into fantasies in order to escape classroom tedium is one example.

Rituals

"A ritual is a socially-programmed use of time where everybody agrees to do the same thing."[20] In rituals we risk no involvement with others, the outcome is predictable, and the activity makes us feel we are doing something that is expected. Our salutatory activities are examples, e.g., "good morning!" This is worth about one stroke. Rituals are found everywhere, at cocktail parties, at church, in courtrooms, etc.

Pastimes

Usually are in the form of "semiritualistic" discussions on common topics. Pastimes may be engaged in for their own sake, but with "not OK" individuals they are used exactly for what the term implies, i.e., a way of passing time: To sweat out an hour, a day, until it is time to retire for the night, until work or school commences, until some cure is obtained, or until death rescues them from feelings of guilt, despair, or boredom. At best, pastimes are enjoyed for their own sake, serving as a means to develop acquaintanceships and intimacy.

Berne's high sense of humor shows in his descriptions of certain pastimes, conversations that often occur at luncheons, cocktail parties, or club meetings: "General Motors" (comparing cars) and "who won" (man talk); or "morning after" (hangover); "What became of" (good old Joe).

Activity

An ordinary, comfortable way of structuring time by dealing with reality, e.g., building a house, washing a car, etc.

Games

Berne has published a book devoted solely to games. Like pastimes, his games have some amusing titles such as "NIGYSOB" (now I've got you; you S.O.B.); "If it weren't for you;" "Ain't it awful;" "Schlemiel;" and "ITHY" (I'm only trying to help you—played by social caseworkers and correctional workers). He defines games as:

> An ongoing series of complementary ulterior transactions progressing to a well-defined, predictable outcome. Descriptively, it is a recurrent set of transactions, often repetitious, superficially plausible, with a concealed motivation, or more colloquially, a series of moves with a snare, or "gimmick." Games are clearly differentiated from procedures, rituals and pastimes by two characteristics: (a) their ulterior quality, and (b) the payoff. Procedures may be successful, rituals effective and pastimes profitable, but all of them are by definition candid; they may involve contest, but not conflict, and the ending may be sensational, but it is not dramatic. Every game, on the other hand, is basically dishonest, and the outcome has a dramatic, as distinct from exciting quality.[21]

Games are played for primary and secondary gains and these are what Berne terms "payoffs" for the players. Some of these gains are the relief of tension; the avoidance of noxious situations; internal and external psychological advantages, etc.

Berne points out that most studies of criminality are unproductive and ambiguous. The reason for this, he says, is that most criminologists fail to detect that there are two basic types of criminals, a) the big-money maker whose Child does not want to be caught and who rarely is caught. This is the "professional" criminal who is careful to obliterate any evidence resulting from his crime. He calls this type the "compulsive winner." He is the untouchable for whom a fix is often made; b) the "compulsive loser" who plays the game "cops and robbers." He is usually caught; and if he does realize some profit through his criminality, it is the result of chance rather than skill.

There are many games: "Uproar" (a sexual game); "Schlemiel" (a party game); "Courtroom" (a marital game), and "I'm only trying to help you" (consulting room game), to name a few. Of interest to correctional workers are those described by Berne as "Underworld Games." One of these is "Cops and Robbers."

The latter game reflects the offender's hatred of authority, particularly the police whom he tries to outwit. In fact, the primary motive for playing "cops and robbers" is not to obtain stolen property, but rather to get caught, making it either difficult or easy for the police to catch up with him, according to the game player's individual preference. True, at the Adult level the offense is committed for material gains, but at the Child level it is the thrill of the chase, or the getaway and the cool-off that motivates the player. Berne sees the prototype for "cops and robbers" in the childhood game of hide-and-seek. When father is "it," the little boy or girl shows chagrin if caught too easily. If father plays the game well and holds off on finding the hidden boy or girl, they will give him a clue as to their whereabouts. If father gives up, the children are disappointed, for "being caught" is the actual payoff.

"Cops and robbers" is a battle of wits and yields a more satisfying payoff when each player does his best. Yet at the psychological level the offender's Adult must lose in order for his Child to win. Not being caught is actually the antithesis, for the offender is thus eliminating the Child element and turns the whole game into an Adult procedure, as professional criminals will do.

Intimacy

Consists of an accepting affection and understanding between persons that are "OK" enough to give, take, and share. From the "I'm OK; you're OK" position we come to realize that each person is unique or "something special." In intimacy our emotional expressions are spontaneous as well as appropriate, and not merely role-like responses to what is socially programmed. The "OK" person is not afraid to give strokes or to risk involvement.

METHODS OF TRANSACTIONAL ANALYSIS

The goal of TA is social control which is achieved by the freeing of the client's Adult, thus making it the executive of the personality. By consciously examining his Parent and Child, the client's Adult can then make the decision as to when his Parent or Child can be released, and when the Adult should resume its primacy. The Adult may call upon the Parent, for example, to determine whether any planned behavior is socially appropriate, ethical, and legal. Transactional Analysis lends itself easily to group treatment, primarily because, ". . . the natural function of therapy groups is transactional analysis."[22] It also has an application in one-to-one counseling. It appears particularly helpful in the treatment of offenders, because the liberated Adult in command of the personality is able to circumscribe tendencies to "act out," can learn to stand firm in the face of evil and hostile impulses, or to repress them, if necessary. With the Adult in command we become responsible for what happens to us in the future, regardless of what has happened in the past.

We are cautioned that the analysis of games and scripts (similar to life themes) is a useful therapeutic device when employed by a professional who has received clinical training in Transactional Analysis, but these techniques do not occupy as important a position in treatment as do structural and transactional analysis. For a person to "know his game" or "script" does not necessarily make positive change possible. Not only does structural and transactional analysis hold more promise for change in short-term treatment, but it also avoids the danger of depriving a client of a defense before he has come to understand his position, as well as the situation in childhood when it was first established. Unless the group leader has experienced complete training in Berne's treatment methods, he should confine his treatment techniques to structural and transactional analysis. True, the leader must be aware of what games are being played by the group members, but only for the purposes of breaking up the games, and for leading the group into the more productive activity of analyzing the group's transactions, determining whether the stimuli and responses are from the Parent, Adult, or Child. The group's training and exercises strengthen the primacy of the Adult.

TREATMENT OF OFFENDERS

Berne's methods are used in group treatment afforded to probationers and parolees in the federal probation office for the Eastern District of

California. Participants are selected on the basis of their own requests, or in cases where the supervising officer believes that a need exists for such treatment. Otherwise the selections are made without regard to sex, age, type of offense, or whether the participant is on probation or parole. A series of 12 weekly meetings is held on Tuesday evenings for an hour and a half, with the agreement that the participants can enroll for the next 12-week series. However, once the participant attends the first meeting, he is obliged to complete the series by attending 11 more meetings. There are three rather firm rules that all members must observe: (a) no fraternization with other group members; (b) during treatment sessions a member may say anything he wishes, but he cannot make any physical contact with other members, except for the handshake that is permitted at the beginning and end of each meeting; (c) a member is not obliged to answer any questions put to him by the rest of the group.

The first meeting is handled almost exclusively by the group leader who discusses the organizational aspects of the group: the goals of group treatment, the selection of the membership, and, more important, Berne's theory of Structural Analysis. A blackboard is a necessary item for the application of Berne's treatment methods. Transactions occurring within the group are thus diagrammed for explanation and study purposes. The organizational aspects of the group as each member is related to the authoritarian structure of federal corrections is also outlined on the blackboard. In line with the recommended limitations placed on the use of Berne's methods, the group is advised that TA is not group therapy but "group treatment"; that we do not explore psychological cellars, so to speak, and they are told that the aims of TA treatment are to help each member in his relationships with others, and to help him become the master over his own behavior. Stated more colloquially, "We are here to make winners out of losers." Often a specific contract is made between the group leader and a client, such as, "My contract with you is to help you get along on the job," or "to quit drinking," or "to control your frightened child," etc.

The group soon becomes familiar with the three ego states, Parent, Adult, and Child (PAC), and begins to perceive which state is active in group interactions, in themselves, as well as in other members. It is important that the group leader diagram on the blackboard some of the more important transactions.

OFFENDERS ARE UNIQUE IN GROUP TREATMENT

Berne regards therapy as a kind of contest involving four persons, the patient's Parent and Child acting as warring factions against the Adult, with the therapist holding the role of "auxiliary Adult." This situation presents even odds that the patient will do better, but if the therapist finds a triumvirate of the patient's Parent, Adult, and Child working against him, as in the treatment of sociopathic individuals, the odds are three against one that the outcome will be successful. The group leader who attempts to treat offenders, should be prepared for alliances formed against successful outcomes, since each offender group will have in it at least one sociopathic type. By seeing to it that the group becomes more and more efficient in analyzing its transactions, these "anti-get-well" alliances will eventually dissolve.

Franklin Ernst, M.D., has employed Berne's methods for over 9 years in treating groups of prisoners at the California Medical Facility. Besides discovering the "Underworld Game," "How do you get out of here," he has also observed other games or maneuvers played by inmate groups. Some members will "rat pack" another member ("the hot seat technique"), or a single member will pull a "stick-up job" using the group's time ("You better get me what I'm asking for or——").[23]

Likewise, special maneuverings and games can be observed in the group treatment of probationers and parolees, i.e., persons living in free society: "Why do we have to attend these meetings," and "What do *you* get out of this Mr. Group Leader?" (both variations of NIGYSOB); "Now let me tell *you* why I hate probation officers" (Courtroom); and, "I'm a good boy, aren't I papa?" (Santa Clause fantasy—"If I do what is expected, I'll be presented with the magic orb").

The following transactions occurred at one of our earlier meetings and are offered as a good example of how quickly the members learn how to analyze them.

Jerry, an alcoholic, comes into the meeting room, already partially occupied, before the meeting commenced. He is obviously under the influence of alcohol. Upon being introduced to Larry who wears his hair long, and adorns himself with beads, Jerry slurs out something about a "hair do" and "hippie." The group leader is smoking a cigar. Jerry asks him, "Aren't you afraid that cigar will make you sick or something?" The group leader offers Jerry a cigar. After the meeting has commenced Jerry first tells how he wrestles with his sons, how they are going to become real "he-men." He then turns to Larry:

JERRY: If my kids wore their hair long, I'd kick the s——out of them.

LARRY: Well, OK. You'd kick the s——out of 'em. What I'm concerned about is getting a job . . .

JERRY   (interrupting): Wanta job—cut your goddamn hair! Let me ask you, do you think you're cute with your long hair and beads?

LARRY: No, I just wear it this way (clears throat) . . .

JERRY   (winking at other group members, apparently to let them in on the "sport"): Tell me, bud, why do you wear your hair long?

LARRY: Why do you drink?

JERRY: Why do *I* drink . . . hmm.

LARRY: I'm not listening to you, anyway.

JERRY   (eyes narrowing, pitch of voice raising): Why aren't you listening to me?

LARRY   (tilting his head, strengthening his voice): Because you've been drinking. My mother was a lush. I don't like lushes.

JERRY   (voice higher yet): You calling me a lush?

LARRY: If you want it that way . . .

DOUG   (probably our sincerest and best motivated client): Boy, Jerry! He sure hooked your Child! You started out being the big, bullying Parent, trying to hook Larry's Child, but instead you hooked his Parent.

BARBARA (Jerry's spouse, pointing her index finger to the ceiling): That's right, Doug he *is* a bully when he's drunk—an *Irish* bully!

DOUG: OK, Barbara, but now you're being a punishing Parent.

BARBARA (voice raising, eyes moistening): OK, so I'm a Parent, but if *you* had to—Well, I am working at being an Adult. Anyhow, Larry, if you want to wear your hair long, do it. You're still OK.

The meeting ended on a friendly note, with the group giving Larry some "strokes." Jerry remained subdued and depressed.

The following transactions, occurring at a later meeting involving the same group, illustrate how the group leader may receive the "hot seat" technique. The meeting commences with a brief discussion by the group leader on the four life positions. The desirability of striving for the position, "I'm OK; you're OK" was stressed. Billy, a check-writer, recently reparoled, attempted to maneuver the group into playing a game:

BILLY: I can't buy this I'm OK, you're OK, because it's just brainwashing stuff, because *nobody's* OK. I just read where a probation officer was convicted of taking a bribe. . . .

LEADER   (interrupting): Of embezzlement.

BILLY: So what! He's a crook! They're *all* crooks! A guy comes up on a check rap in front of a crooked judge and gets 5 years. . . .

JUDY   (interrupting): Are you saying you're OK and the rest of us are not? You're perfect?

BILLY: You're damn right.

DON: Well, these federal probation officers haven't done *me* a bit of good. And those stupid bastards in the employment agencies! They're drawing their pay checks, and when you ask for help . . . what a runaround. . . .

JERRY: (referring to group leader): Mr. Nick's a probation officer and I think he's OK. He always played it straight with me . . . (I'm a good boy, aren't I, papa?)

BILLY: Oh Yeh? What *goodies* are you *getting* out of this, Mr. Nick?

GROUP
LEADER: My Adult gets a salary. My Parent is trying to do something about helping people free up the Adult and making it the boss—and protecting society; and my Child is curious about what comes out of TA.

JERRY: Don't you *resent* what Billy's saying? *I* would!

GROUP
LEADER: What's important for us to do is to analyze what part of us—Parent, Adult, Child—is doing the talking.

JUDY: I think it was Billy's Parent talking just now—and, well I guess it was my Parent telling him *he* thinks *he's* perfect (laughter).

DOUG: Well, Billy, you're *acting* like a Parent, but I picked up a lot of Child in what you *and* Don said.

DON: Child!

DOUG: Yeh, a not OK Child and a scared Child.

The discussion went on with Billy protesting that he isn't afraid of anything. The noteworthy thing coming out of this session is Billy's confirmation of his life position of "I'm OK, you're not OK" which actually represents his reversal of the position, "I'm not OK, you're OK." His unloved and frightened Child sought group support for his need to rehearse his defenses. An attempt was made to entice the group leader into playing games, but Billy's maneuver was diverted into the more productive activity of analyzing group transactions. Billy never returned.

SUMMARY

Transactional Analysis does not have all the answers and many of our group members do not profit by their participation, but those who do use it profitably have demonstrated remarkable improvement in their life positions and in their vocations, recreations, and interpersonal relationships. A former nomadic and depressive parole violator is now studying to become an IBM computer analyst; an alcoholic probationer has voluntarily committed himself for treatment in a state hospital; another probationer without trade skills is studying to become an automobile mechanic. And there are others making similar attempts at improving themselves. Transactional Analysis helps a person to become responsible for his future; to feel "OK."

NOTES

*Dr. Berne died unexpectedly July 15, 1970, from a cardiac disorder.—*The Editors.*

[1] Eric Berne, "Analyzing 'Games' and 'Scripts' in Transactional Psychotherapy," *Frontiers of Clinical Psychiatry*, October 1945, p. 1.

[2] Eric Berne, *Principles of Group Treatment* (New York: Oxford University Press, 1966), p. 214.

[3] Hereinafter to be designated as TA.

[4] Berne, *Group Treatment*, p. 2.

[5] W. Penfield, "Memory Mechanisms," *Archives of Neurology and Psychiatry* 67 (1952): 178–179.

[6] Eric Berne, *Transactional Analysis in Psychotherapy* (New York: Grove Press, 1961), p. 19.

[7] Thomas A. Harris, *I'm OK–You're OK* (New York: Harper and Row, 1969), p. 16.

[8] Ibid., p. 25.

[9] Ibid., p. 27.

[10] Ibid, pp. 37–53.

[11] Ibid., p. 42.

[12] Ibid., pp. 50–51.

[13] Ibid., pp. 97–98.

[14] Ibid., pp. 98–99.

[15] Eric Berne, *Transactional Analysis in Psychotherapy*, p. 62.

[16] Ibid., p. 44.

[17] Harris, *I'm OK*, p. 104.

[18] Eric Berne, M.D., *Games People Play* (New York: Grove Press, 1964), p. 29.

[19] Harris, *I'm OK*, pp. 94–95.

[20] Ibid., p. 116.

[21] Eric Berne, *Games People Play*, p. 48.

[22] Eric Berne, *Transactional Analysis in Psychotherapy*, pp. 90–91.

[23] Franklin H. Ernst, M.D., and William C. Keating, M.D., "Psychiatric Treatment of the California Felon," *The American Journal of Psychiatry*, April 1964.

27

Winners and Losers

MURIEL JAMES AND DOROTHY JONGEWARD

You cannot teach a man anything.
You can only help him discover it within himself.
Galileo

Each human being is born as something new, something that never existed before. He is born with what he needs to win at life. Each person in his own way can see, hear, touch, taste, and think for himself. Each has his own unique potentials—his capabilities and limitations. Each can be a significant, thinking, aware, and creatively productive person in his own right—a winner.

The words "winner" and "loser" have many meanings. When we refer to a person as a winner, we do not mean one who beats the other guy by winning over him and making him lose. To us, a winner is one who responds authentically by being credible, trustworthy, responsive, and genuine, both as an individual and as a member of a society. A loser is one who fails to respond authentically. Martin Buber expresses this idea as he retells an old story of a rabbi who on his death bed sees himself as a loser. The rabbi laments that, in the world to come, he will not be asked why he wasn't Moses; he will be asked why he wasn't himself[1].

Few people are one hundred percent winners or one hundred percent losers. It's a matter of degree. However, once a person is on the road to being a winner, his chances are greater for becoming even more so. This book is intended to facilitate the journey.

WINNERS

Winners have different potentials. Achievement is not the most important thing. Authenticity is. The authentic person experiences the reality

Born To Win: Transactional Analysis With Gestalt Experiments, pages 1–12, by Muriel James and Dorothy Jongeward, 1971, Addison-Wesley, Reading, Mass. Reprinted with permission of the publisher.

of himself by knowing himself, being himself, and becoming a credible, responsive person. He actualizes his own unprecedented uniqueness and appreciates the uniqueness of others.*

He does not dedicate his life to a concept of what he imagines he *should* be, rather he *is himself* and as such he does not use his energy putting on a performance, maintaining pretence, and manipulating others into his games. A winner can reveal himself instead of projecting images that please, provoke, or entice others. He is aware that there is a difference between being loving and acting loving, between being stupid and acting stupid, between being knowledgeable and acting knowledgeable. He does not need to hide behind a mask. He throws off unrealistic self-images of inferiority or superiority. Autonomy does not frighten a winner.

Everyone has moments of autonomy, if only fleeting. However, a winner is able to sustain his autonomy over ever-increasing periods of time. He may lose ground occasionally. He may even fail. Yet, in spite of setbacks a winner maintains a basic faith in himself.

A winner is not afraid to do his own thinking and to use his own knowledge. He can separate facts from opinion and doesn't pretend to have all the answers. He listens to others, evaluates what they say, but comes to his own conclusions. While he can admire and respect other people, he is not totally defined, demolished, bound, or awed by them.

A winner does not play "helpless" nor does he play the blaming game. Instead he assumes responsibility for his own life. He does not give others a false authority over him. He's his own boss and knows it.

A winner's timing is right. He responds appropriately to the situation. His response is appropriate when it is related to the message sent and preserves the significance, worth, well-being, and dignity of the people involved. He knows that for everything there is a season and for every activity a time.

A time to be aggressive and a time to be passive,

A time to be together and a time to be alone,

A time to fight and a time to love,

A time to work and a time to play,

A time to cry and a time to laugh,

A time to confront and a time to withdraw,

A time to speak and a time to be silent,

A time to hurry and a time to wait.

*The common pronoun "he" refers to persons of either sex except when "she" is definitely applicable.

To a winner time is precious. He doesn't kill it. He lives it here and now. Living in the now does not mean that he foolishly ignores his own past history or fails to prepare for his future. Rather, he knows his past, is aware and alive in the present, and looks forward to the future.

A winner learns to know his feelings and his limitations and is not afraid of them. He is not stopped by his own contradictions and ambivalences. He knows when he is angry and can listen when others are angry with him. He can give and receive affection. He is able to love and be loved.

A winner can be spontaneous. He does not have to respond in predetermined, rigid ways. He can change his plans when the situation calls for it. A winner has a zest for life. He enjoys work, play, food, other people, sex, and the world of nature. Without guilt he enjoys his own accomplishments. Without envy he enjoys the accomplishments of others.

Although a winner can freely enjoy himself, he can also postpone enjoyment. He can discipline himself in the present to enhance his enjoyment in the future. He is not afraid to go after what he wants but does so in appropriate ways. He does not get his security by controlling others. He does not set himself up to lose.

A winner cares about the world and its peoples. He is not isolated from the general problems of society. He is concerned, compassionate, and committed to improving the quality of life. Even in the face of national and international adversity, he does not see himself as totally powerless. He does what he can to make the world a better place.

LOSERS

Although people are born to win, they are also born helpless and totally dependent on their environment. Winners successfully make the transition from total helplessness to independence, and then to interdependence. Losers do not. Somewhere along the line they begin to avoid becoming self-responsible.

As we have noted, few people are total winners or losers. Most of them are winners in some areas of their lives and losers in others. Their winning or losing is influenced by what happens to them in childhood.

A lack of response to dependency needs, poor nutrition, brutality, unhappy relationships, disease, continuing disappointments, inadequate physical care, and traumatic events are among the many experiences that contribute to making people losers. Such experiences interrupt, deter, or prevent the normal progress toward autonomy and self-actualization. To cope with negative experiences a child learns to manipulate himself and others. These manipulative techniques are hard to give up later in life and often become set patterns. A winner works to shed them. A loser hangs on to them.

Some losers speak of themselves as successful but anxious, successful but trapped, or successful but unhappy. Others speak of themselves as totally beaten, without purpose, unable to move, half dead, or bored to death. A loser may not recognize that, for the most part, he has been building his own cage and digging his own grave, and is a bore to himself.

A loser seldom lives in the present. He destroys the present by occupying his mind with past memories or future expectations.

When the loser lives in his past, he dwells on the good old days or on his past misfortunes. Nostalgically, he either clings to the way things "used to be" or bemoans his bad luck. He feels sorry for himself and shifts the responsibility for his unsatisfactory life onto others. Blaming others and excusing himself are often part of his games. A loser who lives in the past may lament *if only:*

If only I had married some one else . . .

If only I had a different job . . .

If only I had finished school . . .

If only I had been handsome (beautiful) . . .

If only my spouse had stopped drinking . . .

If only I had been born rich . . .

If only I had had better parents . . .

When a person lives in the future he may dream of some miracle after which he can "live happily ever after." Rather than pursuing his own life, he waits—waits for the magical rescue. How wonderful life will be *when:*

When school is over . . .

When Prince Charming or the ideal woman finally comes . . .

When the kids grow up . . .

When that new job opens . . .

When the boss dies . . .

When my ship comes in . . .

In contrast to those who live with the delusion of a magical rescue, some losers live constantly under the dread of future catastrophe. They conjure up expectations of *what if:*

What if I lose my job . . .

What if I lose my mind . . .

What if something falls on me . . .

What if I break my leg . . .

What if they don't like me . . .

What if I make a mistake . . .

By continually focusing on the future, a person experiences anxiety in the present. He is anxious over what he anticipates—either real or imagined—tests, bill paying, a love affair, crisis, illness, retirement, the weather, and so forth. A person overly involved with imaginings lets the actual possibilities of the moment pass him by. He occupies his mind with material that is irrelevant to the current situation. His anxiety tunes out current reality. Consequently, he is unable to see for himself, hear for himself, feel for himself, or taste, touch, or think for himself.

Unable to bring the full potential of his senses into the immediate situation, a loser's perceptions are incorrect or incomplete. He sees himself and others through a prismlike distortion. His ability to deal effectively with the real world is hampered.

A loser spends much of his time play-acting. He pretends, manipulates, and perpetuates old roles from childhood. He invests his energy in maintaining his masks, often projecting a phony front. Karen Horney writes, "The fostering of the phony self is always at the expense of the real self, the latter being treated with disdain, at best like a poor relative".[2] To the play-acting loser, his performance is often more important than his reality.

A loser represses his capacity to express spontaneously and appropriately his full range of possible behavior. He may be unaware of other options for his life if the path he chooses goes nowhere. He is afraid to try new things. He maintains his own status quo. He is a repeater. He repeats not only his own mistakes; he often repeats those of his family and culture.

A loser has difficulty giving and receiving affection. He does not enter into intimate, honest, direct relationships with others. Instead, he tries to manipulate them into living up to his expectations and channels his energies into living up to their expectations.

When a person is being a loser, he is not using his intellect appropriately. He is misusing it by rationalizing and intellectualizing. When rationalizing, he gives excuses to make his actions seem plausible. When intellectualizing, he tries to snow others with his verbiage. Consequently, much of his potential remains dormant, unrealized, and unrecognized. Like the frog-prince in the fairy tale, he is spellbound and lives life being something he isn't meant to be.

TOOLS FOR CHANGE

When a person wants to discover and change his "losing streak," when he wants to become more like the winner he was born to be, he can use Gestalt type experiments and Transactional Analysis to make change happen. These are two new, exciting, psychological approaches to human problems. The first was given new life by Dr. Frederick Perls; the second was developed by Dr. Eric Berne.

Perls was born in Germany in 1893 and left the country when Hitler came into power. Berne was born in Montreal in 1910. Both men were trained as Freudian psychoanalysts; both broke away from the use of orthodox psychoanalysis; both found their greatest popularity and acceptance in the United States. We have studied with both Berne and Perls, and we like their methods because their methods work.

In this book we hope to show how the theory of Transactional Analysis, *supplemented* by experiments we have personally designed and others which were derived from Gestalt therapy, can be used to develop and extend a "winning streak." We believe that everyone—at least in some phase of his humanness—has the potential to be a winner: to be a real person, an alive person, an aware person.

FREDERICK PERLS AND GESTALT THERAPY

Gestalt therapy is not new. However, its current popularity has grown very rapidly since it was given new impetus and direction by Dr. Frederick Perls. *Gestalt* is a German word for which there is no exact English equivalent; it means, roughly, the forming of an organized, meaningful whole.

Perls perceives many personalities as lacking wholeness, as being fragmented. He claims people are often aware of only parts of themselves rather than of the whole self. For example, a woman may not know or want to admit that sometimes she acts like her mother; a man may not know or want to admit that sometimes he wants to cry like a baby.

The aim of Gestalt therapy is to help become whole—to help the person become aware of, admit to, reclaim, and integrate his fragmented parts. Integration helps a person make the transition from dependency to self-sufficiency; from authoritarian outer support to authentic inner support[3]. Concretely, having inner support means that a person is able to stand on his own two feet. He is no longer compelled to depend upon external support—his spouse, academic degrees, job title, therapist, bank account, and so forth—to hold him up. Instead he discovers that the capacities he needs are already within himself, and he can depend on them. According to Perls a person who refuses to do this is neurotic:

> *I call neurotic any man*
> *Who uses his potential to*
> *Manipulate the others*
> *Instead of growing up himself.*
> *He takes control, gets power-mad,*
> *And mobilizes friends and kin*
> *In places where he's impotent*
> *To use his own resources.*

He does so 'cause he cannot stand
Such tensions and frustrations
That go along with growing up.
And: taking risks is risky too
Too fearful to consider. [4]

Some of the methods common in Gestalt therapy are role-playing, exaggeration of symptoms or behavior, use of fantasy, the principle of staying with the immediate moment which is the experience of "being in the now," the use of the word "I" rather than "it" as a way to assume responsibility for behavior, learning how to talk *to* rather than *at* someone, becoming aware of bodily senses, and learning to "stay with feelings" until they are understood and integrated[5].

The most difficult method for many people to understand is Perls' specialized form of role-playing. Role-playing is not new to psychological practice. As early as 1908 Dr. Jacob Moreno was working on this method from which have emerged many forms of group encounter and treatment. He coined the word "psychodrama" in 1919 to describe how he directed people to take on the identities of others and to act out their problems from different points of view[6].

In contrast to Moreno, Perls rarely uses other people to role-play with his patient. He claims these others would "bring in *their own* fantasies, *their own* interpretations"[7]. Therefore, Perls requires the patient himself to imagine and act out all the parts. He focuses on *how* the patient is acting *now,* not on the *why* of his behavior.

While many arrangements can be used for this kind of role-playing, the chair technique is uniquely Perls'. His props are (1) the "hot-seat," a chair for the patient who chooses to "work," (2) an empty chair facing the patient onto which he projects his many selves, and (3) a box of tissues for runny noses and tearful eyes.

The "hot-seat" method was used with a teacher who described herself as friendly and helpful yet couldn't understand why she had no close friends. Although she denied any angry feelings, common expressions she used were "you'll be sorry for that" and "I feel sorry for anyone like you." Others heard this as threatening and hostile.

When this woman role-played her fragmented parts, she acted her "friendly self" from the hot-seat and imagined her "angry self" on the opposite chair. She switched chairs when she switched roles and slowly began a dialogue:

> *Hot-seats:* I don't know why I'm here. I'm always friendly and helpful.
> *Opposite chair:* You do too know why you're here. You don't have any friends.
> *Hot-seat:* I can't understand it. I'm always doing things for people.

Opposite chair: That's the trouble with you. Always being "helpful
  Hannah." You have everybody obligated to you.

In a short time the teacher's voice grew shrill and loud. When she was
in the hot seat, she struck out against the "helpful Hannah" comment.
Amazed at her own aggressiveness, she commented in disbelief, "I
never knew I could feel so angry." Although other people had seen this
aspect of her personality quite often, this was the first time she admit-
ted to her opposites of anger and helpfulness—her polarities.

Sometimes a person is aware of only *one* of his poles, as in the case
of the teacher above. Sometimes a person may be aware of both and
say, "I'm either as high as a kite or weighted down with depression," or
"I'm either angry and aggressive, or afraid and full of doubt."

A person whose personality is fragmented by polarization operates
in an either/or manner—he is either arrogant or worthless, helpless or
tyrannical, wicked or righteous. When a person is stuck at the impasse
of his own opposing forces, he is at war with himself. By using Perls'
role-playing technique these opposing forces can have it out with each
other, forgive each other, compromise, or at least come to know each
other.

In this setting a person can develop an awareness of his fragmented parts. He discovers these fragments by starting his own
dialogue and by acting out various roles, switching chairs when he
switches roles. He may be a person—himself as a child, himself now, his
mother, father, spouse, or boss. He may be a physical symptom—an
ulcer, headache, backache, sweaty palms, palpitating heart. He may
even be an object that he encounters in his dream—a piece of furniture, an animal, a window.

Role-playing with the use of the hot-seat can also be used to clarify
relationships between people. To do this one person imagines another
person in the opposite chair. He speaks to him and tells him what's
really on his mind. He then becomes the other and responds. In this
process unspoken resentments and affection often come to the surface
where they can be understood and resolved.

Various parts of a dream can also be role-played to gain self-
awareness. According to Perls, the dream is "the royal road to integration"[8].

> ... all the different parts of the dream are fragments of our per-
> sonalities. Since our aim is to make every one of us a wholesome per-
> son, which means a unified person, without conflicts what we have to
> do is put the different fragments of the dream together. We have to
> *re-own* these projected, fragmented parts of our personality, and
> *re-own* the hidden potential that appears in the dream[9].

Or, put another way, all the dream is the dreamer. Each person and
each thing in the dream is some aspect of the dreamer. By role-playing

the people in the dream, the objects in the dream, or even a dream fragment, the existential message that the dream holds can be unlocked, not by analyzing it, but by reliving it.

For example, one man had a recurring dream in which there was always a desk. When asked to imagine himself as this piece of furniture he muttered, "How silly, I'm not a desk." With a bit of encouragement he got over his stage fright and started his performance. "I am a big desk. I'm stuffed full of other peoples' things. People pile things on me, write on me, poke me with pens. They just use me and I can't move. . . ." Later he said, "That's me, all right! Just like a desk I let everybody use me, and I just sit there!"

In Gestalt therapy people gain both emotional and intellectual insight, but the methods focus on the former. Emotional awareness is that moment of self-discovery when a person says "ahah." Perls describes the "ahah" experience as ". . . what happens whenever something clicks, falls into place; each time a Gestalt closes, there is this 'ahah!' click, the shock of recognition"[10]. Intellectual insight comes with the gathering of data.

ERIC BERNE AND TRANSACTIONAL ANALYSIS

In Transactional Analysis people gain both emotional and intellectual insight, but the method focuses on the latter. It is a thinking process, often analytical, in which the person frequently concludes, "So *that's* the way it is!"

According to Dr. Berne, his theories evolved as he observed behavioral changes occurring in a patient when a new stimulus such as a word, gesture, or sound, entered his focus. These changes involved facial expressions, word intonations, sentence structure, body movements, gestures, tics, posture, and carriage. It was as though there were several different people inside the individual. At times one or the other of these inner different people seemed to be in control of his patient's total personality.

He observed that these various "selves" transacted with other people in different ways and that these transactions could be analyzed. He saw that some of the transactions had ulterior motives; the individual used them as a means of manipulating others into psychological games and rackets.* He also observed that people performed in predetermined ways—acting as if they were on stage and reading from a theatrical script. These observations led Berne to develop his unique theory called Transactional Analysis, abbreviated to TA.

Originally TA was developed as a method of psychotherapy. Transactional Analysis is preferably used in groups (as is Gestalt

---

*The analysis of games has received wide popularity in Berne's bestseller, *Games People Play*[11].

therapy). The group serves as a setting in which people can become more aware of themselves, the structure of their individual personality, how they transact with others, the games they play, and the scripts they act out. Such awareness enables persons to see themselves more clearly so that they can change what they want to change and strengthen what they want to strengthen.

Changes begin with a bilateral contract between the therapist and client. A contract may be about the alleviation of symptoms such as blushing, frigidity, or headaches. It may be about gaining control over behavior such as excessive drinking, mistreating children, failing in school. It may focus on childhood experiences which underlie current specific symptoms and behavior, experiences where the child was belittled, abandoned, overindulged, ignored, or brutalized.[12] The contractual approach preserves the self-determination of a client. It also allows a client to know when he's gotten what he came for.

TA is not only a useful tool for those in psychotherapy, it also provides a thought-provoking perspective of human behavior that most people can understand and put to use. It encourages the use of words that are simple, direct, and often colloquial instead of psychological, scientific words or jargon. For example, the major parts of the personality are called *Parent, Adult,* and *Child.*

Transactional analysis is a rational approach to understanding behavior and is based on the assumption that any individual can learn to trust himself, think for himself, make his own decisions, and express his feelings. Its principles can be applied on the job, in the home, in the classroom, in the neighborhood—wherever people deal with people.

Berne says an important goal of Transactional Analysis is "to establish the most open and authentic communication possible between the affective and intellectual components of the personality".[13] When this happens, the person is able to use both his emotions and intellect, not just one at the expense of the other. Gestalt techniques can accelerate the process particularly at the feeling level.

* * *

SUMMARY

A person who is not aware of how he acts or how he feels is impoverished. Lacking a core of confidence, he fluctuates between his conflicting inner forces. He is less than whole because he has alienated parts of himself. He may be alienated from his intellect, his emotions, his creativeness, his body feelings, or some of his behavior. When a person becomes aware and moves toward becoming a whole person, he is enriched.

A person who decides to become more of a winner than a loser allows such insights. Through them he discovers that he can rely, more and more, on his own capacities for sensing and making judgments. He continues to discover and renew himself. For him life consists not in getting more but in being more. A winner is glad to be alive!

NOTES

[1] Martin Buber, *Hasidism and Modern Man* (New York: Harper & Row, 1958), pp. 138–144.

[2] Karen Horney, *Self Analysis* (New York: W. W. Norton, 1942), p. 23.

[3] Frederick S. Perls, *Gestalt Therapy Verbatim* (Lafayette, Calif.: Real People Press, 1969), p. 29.

[4] Frederick S. Perls, *In and Out the Garbage Pail* (Lafayette, Calif.: Real People Press, 1969), n.p.

[5] Abraham Levitsky and Frederick S. Perls, "The Rules and Games of Gestalt Therapy," in Joen Fagan and Irma Lee Shepherd, eds., *Gestalt Therapy Now* (Palo Alto: Science and Behavior Books, 1970), pp. 140–149.

[6] J. L. Moreno, "The Viennese Origins of the Encounter Movement, Paving the Way for Existentialism, Group Psychotherapy, and Psychodrama," *Group Psychotherapy*, 22, No. 1–2 (1969): 7–16.

[7] Perls, *Gestalt Therapy Verbatim*, p. 121.

[8] Ibid., p. 66.

[9] Ibid., p. 67.

[10] Ibid., p. 236.

[11] Eric Berne, *Games People Play* (New York: Grove Press, 1964).

[12] Eric Berne, *Principles of Group Treatment* (New York: Oxford University Press, 1964).

[13] Ibid., p. 216.

28

Gestalt Therapy: A Behavioristic Phenomenology

ELAINE KEPNER AND LOIS BRIEN

It seems generally agreed now that human problem behavior is learned, and that psychotherapy is essentially a reeducational or learning process. Usually the use of such terms as *learning* and *behaviorism* implies that man is simply a collection of conditioned responses to environmental stimuli. We believe with Anderson (1968) that

> The behavior of human beings . . . is adequately accounted for only in terms of a radically different conception of the nature of man. Man is a creature, the only creature, with a sense of self. Given this sense of self, he is able to carry on internal dialogues with himself, and he does so during practically every waking moment [p. 1].

In this article, we shall be translating Gestalt therapy into a behavioristic-phenomenological framework. That is, we propose to consider phenomenological events as actual behaviors.

Since our only access to experience is through some form of behavior, be it verbal or nonverbal, the Gestalt therapist considers *all* that is going on in a person—what he is thinking, feeling, doing, remembering, and sensing—as the data of behavior. This does not imply that Gestalt therapy is a form of behavioristic therapy (via the model of Wolpe, Goldiamond, etc.). We use the language of behavioristic learning theory because it allows us to refer to experiential events in operational terms and provides principles that account for changes in a subject's feelings, perceptions, and actions. Whether this translation will serve its function remains to be seen. As Scriven (1964) says, "The test is to whether a vocabulary imparts a new and genuine understanding is its capacity to predict new relationships, to retrodict old ones and to show a unity where there was a previous diversity [p. 183]."

Reprinted by permission of the editor and the publisher from Elaine Kepner and Lois Brien. "Gestalt Therapy: A Behavioristic Phenomenology," in Joen Fagan and Irma Lee Shepherd (Eds.), *Gestalt Therapy Now: Theory, Technique and Application.* Palo Alto, California: Science and Behavior Books, 1970, pp. 39–46.

BEHAVIORISM AND PHENOMENOLOGY:
TWO APPROACHES TO LEARNING

A brief description of learning theory seems in order to set a background for this analysis. Learning theory is used here as a generic term designating a number of different systems developed by psychologists to account for the acquisition of knowledge and/or the emergence of new responses. Historically, psychology has approached this subject from two different views:, the tradition of associationism, which today can be referred to as *behaviorism,* and the schools of introspection, functionalism, and Gestalt psychology, which may be grouped under the heading of *phenomenology* or *existentialism.*

Neither behaviorism nor phenomenology are in themselves psychological systems. Rather, they are approaches or methods in psychology for describing and studying the crucial variables which relate to and account for behavior. All learning theories take as their major function the specification of stimulus conditions that determine behavior. Both the behaviorist and the phenomenologist consider learning to be a lawful phenomenon whose laws can be discovered. Since learning is an internal state and not directly observable, the behaviorist studies a response or performance as an indicator of learning. The phenomenologist, on the other hand, studies learning as well as other behaviors through the individual's report of sensory, perceptual, or cognitive data.

There are a number of different theories. What they share in common is a language that emphasizes operational definitions of specifiable behaviors and a concern with the role of reinforcement or reward as a determinant of behavior. The behavioristic psychologist further believes that observable behavior is the only legitimate subject matter of psychology, and the only criterion against which the outcome of any experimental procedure, including psychotherapy, can be evaluated.

The phenomenologist, on the other hand, considers all that goes on inside a person—that is, his sensations, perceptions, cognitions—in a word, his experiencing—as valid psychological data, even though these events cannot be verified but must be inferred and labeled as hypothetical constructs by another person. Thus changes in such constructs as self-concept, or self-awareness, or ego-control are acknowledged as valid psychological data and valid criteria against which the outcome of therapy can be appraised.

Contemporary behaviorism and phenomenology are showing evidences of convergent thinking. For example, several learning theorists, notably, Miller, Tolman, and Skinner, have moved away from an almost exclusive concern with the environment (that is, with objective, observable, publicly verifiable behavior) to include internal psychological events as stimuli governing or shaping behavior. Osgood proposes a two-stage model of behavior utilizing an implicit stimulus-producing response assumed to mediate between observable *S* and observable *R*, yielding: *S-r-s-R*. The *r-s* refers to a covert process and might represent, for example, a listener's meaningful reaction to something just said (*r*) and the self-stimulation or thinking that the reaction triggers (*s*), both of which might lead to some overt responding.

This model is an attempt to overcome some of the limitations of the single-stage *S-R* behavioral model, chiefly its failure to handle symbolic processes such as ideation, cognition, and meaning. In this type of paradigm, phenomenological events can be regarded as intervening variables or internal mediating responses. Skinner (1964), in a discussion of public and private events in psychology, stated: "It is particularly important that a science of behavior face the problem of privacy. An adequate science of behavior must consider events taking place within the skin of the organism, not as physiological mediators of behavior, but as part of the behavior itself [p. 84]."

Concerning this same issue of private events in psychology, Homme (1965) coined the word *coverant* as a contraction of *covert-operant*. In Homme's words, "Coverants are events the laymen call mental. These include thinking, imagining, reflecting, ruminating, relaxing, day-dreaming, fantasying, etc. Difficulties in the control of one or the other of the coverant class undoubtedly underlie a good many behavioral or personality disorders [p. 502]."

To summarize, what seems to characterize the present scene is an increasingly fruitful dialogue between behaviorism and phenomenology. What seems to be developing is a view that "Man is at once both a whole being and a collection of habits and behaviors: that man's total being can be seen as a product of the interplay between molar self and the specific acts and habits that fill in the mosaic of daily living [Truax, 1967, p. 150]."

EXPERIENCE AS BEHAVIOR

Liverant (1965) has pointed out that:

> At its most primitive level, experience (as is usually understood) is involved whenever any organism reacts to any stimulus. As a consequence of learning (i.e., as a result of an organism's interactions with his environment), these experiences are undergoing continuous alteration which in some deterministic fashion affects an arbitrarily selected (by the observer) end-state called a response. Viewed in this manner, all learning formulations deal with experience [p. 4].

Verbal reports then are the direct tie to this experience.

In Gestalt therapy we treat the phenomenology of the person —that is, his sensations, perceptions, thoughts, visualizations, etc.—as behaviors. In Skinnerian terms these could be called *internal mediating responses* or in Hommeian terms, *coverants.* We could then translate self-awareness as used in Gestalt therapy as a process by which these coverants are made observable to the subject and observer; that is, the therapist. In other words, in Gestalt therapy we make observable or visible the phenomenal world of the subject. As Perls (1951) has pointed out:

> We emphasize that in all types of activity, whether it be sensing, re-
> membering, or moving, our blind-spots and rigidities are in some as-
> pect aware and not completely buried in an inaccessible unconscious.
> What is necessary is to give whatever aspect *is* aware more attention
> and interest so that the dim figure will sharpen and become clear
> against its ground. We can, at least, be aware that there *is* a blind-spot,
> and, by working alternately on what we can see or remember and on
> the muscular manipulations by which we *make* ourselves blind, we can
> gradually dissolve the blocks to full awareness [p. 117].

In the Gestalt approach, then, work in the present, in the here and now, is designed to produce observable behavior rather than merely to lead the person to talk about what he is thinking. The questions which guide the therapist are *not,* "Why are you behaving this way," but "What are you doing?" "How are you doing it?" "What is it doing for you to behave this way?"

LEARNING, PERSONALITY THEORIES, AND PERSONALITY CHANGE STRATEGIES

As we have seen from the discussion of learning theory, learning is considered to be a relatively stable change in behavior, through prac-tice, over time. Or, to put it more simply, learning is a change in be-havior as a result of experience. As such, learning has a place in per-sonality theory and in psychotherapy.

Personality theories have two major functions: meaningfully to de-scribe a person as he is, and to explain how and why he has become this way. These explanatory concepts, as Gendlin (1964) pointed out, tell us what prevents an individual from changing or being changed by ex-perience. In other words, people somehow learn to be the way they are, and personality theories tell us something about how they got to be that way. Psychotherapy is essentially a process designed to change the indi-vidual in a meaningful way. The strategies employed in psychotherapy to effect change are usually based on a theory of personality, but the overall aim is to enable the individual to learn new ways of thinking, feeling, and behaving. To put this into a learning framework, we could say that the psychotherapy strategies differ depending on what the par-ticular personality theory sees as the crucial determinants of behavior.

For example, psychoanalytic personality theory explains behavior, particularly maladaptive or neurotic behavior, on the basis of past learnings. Psychoanalytic therapy then deals with the past, with the stimulus history of the client. Through the techniques of free association and dream interpretation, he learns to understand better how he came to be the way he is. The analysis of the transference relations with the therapist enables the client to discover how he still continues to behave as if the past existed. The discovery of reality comes about through new learning in his relationship with the nonpunitive person of the analyst.

The behavior therapists, on the other hand, focus on the actual behavior or symptom that is causing the chief problem for the client. If the therapy is based on operant principles, new and appropriate behavior is rewarded when it occurs. Old and inappropriate responses are extinguished either through punishment or nonreward.

The existential therapists consider the important determinants of behavior to lie inside the person, and thus they focus on the client's phenomenology, that is, the internal events, or his inner world of experience.

GESTALT THERAPY AND PHENOMENOLOGICAL LEARNING

The aim of Gestalt therapy is to develop more "intelligent" behavior; that is, to enable the individual to act on the basis of all possible information and to apprehend not only the relevant factors in the external field, but also relevant information from within. The individual is directed to pay attention at any given moment to what he is feeling, what he wants, and what he is doing. The goal of such direction is noninterrupted awareness. The process of increasing awareness enables the individual to discover how he interrupts his own functioning. These interruptions can be thought of as the resistances, or the evidence of resistances. What is being resisted is the awareness of the needs that organize his behavior. Awareness in the present then becomes a tool for uncovering those needs and for discovering the ways in which the individual prevents himself from experiencing the needs.

Because of the centrality of the concept of "awareness," Gestalt therapists call attention to the manner in which a person blocks or interrupts his communications, either with his internal self-system or with the interpersonal system. Awareness of the block can be facilitated by directing attention to what his body is doing, what his mind is doing, and what is or is not going on between people (*motoric, symbolic, and interpersonal* behaviors).

Motoric behavior refers to the language of the body and may be seen in how the client looks, how his voice sounds, how he is sitting, what parts of his body are moving. This is directly observable behavior, and the client's attention is directed to what he is doing. For instance, the therapist might initiate body work by saying, "Close your eyes and pay attention to your bodily sensations. Concentrate on them. What do you feel in your body? Can you stay with that?" Or the therapist might observe some movement in the client and begin there.

Focusing on a client's motoric behavior may, for example, call attention to the manner in which he is blocking his anger from awareness and from overt expression. In learning terms, the coverant, anger, is then labeled and identified as belonging to the self. Such identification makes possible a congruent and appropriate expression of the feeling.

Symbolic behavior refers to "mental events" such as thinking, imagining, daydreaming, etc. Such behavior is not directly observable by the therapist, but the client's attention may be directed toward his own phenomenology, that is, toward what he is *feeling*, chiefly by way of fantasy or actual visualization. Gestalt therapists are especially interested in the client's symbolic representations as these are the coverants that determine his overt behavior. Visualization may involve imagining a dialogue with another person or with a whole cast of characters. In working with visualization, the client is instructed to stay with the imagined situation and to let it change as it will. The therapist then deals with the client's feelings, movements, etc., in relation to the visualization as it is emerging. For example, one client, in visualizing an encounter with his father-in-law, has a fantasy about being pursued by Indians. As the fantasy develops, he is able to turn around and shoot back, thereby saving himself. The visualization was a symbolic representation of a problem; it showed his initial avoidance of it by running away, and his possible solution, namely, confronting the pursuer and asserting himself. By making these coverants overt, the client was able to discover an alternative response to avoidance.

Interpersonal behavior refers to those behaviors which bridge the psychological contact boundaries between separate organisms. The person has certain functions by means of which he contacts others, for example, seeing, hearing, touching, vocalizing, etc. If we see one of the basic purposes of therapy as being a return to contact with others, then it becomes especially important that the client become aware of how he is blocking contact and that he experiment with interpersonal behaviors that increase contact.

By experimenting, a client can discover how he keeps himself apart from others. For example, a woman who believed herself to be inferior was able to test the reality of this concept with other group members. She discovered that although she may have felt inferior to others in the group in some ways, she also felt adequate in relation to them in other ways.

Experiments in the here and now permit the client to observe, cognize and specify his coverants. Much of our behavior is under the control of these coverants. What is learned by experiencing is what governs behavior. In other words, the individual learns what it is he is doing, or not doing, that prevents him from being in contact with himself and with others. Such awareness means that he can choose to continue the behavior or to change it.

Thus we may view human problem behavior, that is, "pathology," as learned behavior and psychotherapy as essentially a reeducational process. All psychological learning theories attempt to specify the variables that determine behavior. The behaviorist is primarily concerned with and attempts to account for external events, that is, for stimuli and responses. The phenomenologist, on the other hand, assumes certain "givens" about the nature of man and is concerned with what goes on inside the person, that is, with the rich, variegated, and elusive internal world of the individual. The behavioristic phenomenologist deals with this world of personal experiencing in such a way as to make it external, overt, specifiable, and communicable.

REFERENCES

Anderson, Henry. "Toward a Sociology of Being." *Manas*, 21, no. 3 (1968).

Brien, Lois. "The Behaviorist's Approach to Learning." *Ohio Journal of Speech and Hearing*, 2 (1966): 74–79.

Deese, James. *The Psychology of Learning*. New York: McGraw-Hill, 1958.

Gendlin, Eugene T. "A Theory of Personality Change." In *Personality Change*, edited by P. Worchel and D. Byrne. New York: John Wiley & Sons, 1964.

Hill, Winifred F. *Learning*. San Francisco: Chandler Publishers, 1963.

Homme, Lloyd E. "Perspectives in Psychology: 24, Control of Coverants, the Operants of the Mind." *Psychological Record*, 15 (1965): 501–511.

Kepner, Elaine. "Application of Learning Theory to the Etiology and Treatment of Alcoholism." *Quarterly Journal of Studies on Alcohol*, 25 (1964): 279–291.

Koch, Sigmund. "Psychology and Emerging Conceptions of Knowledge as Unitary." In *Behaviorism and Phenomenology*, edited by T. W. Wann. Chicago: University of Chicago Press, 1964, pp. 1–45.

Liverant, Shephard. *Learning Theory and Clinical Psychology*. Washington, D.C.: Clearing house for Federal Scientific and Technical Information, Defense Documentation Center, AD 612–126, 1965.

May, Angel E., and Ellenberger, H. F., eds. *Existence*. New York: Basic Books, 1958.

Mednick, Sarnoff A. *Learning*. Englewood Cliffs, N.J.: Prentice-Hall, 1964.

Michael, Jack, and Meyerson, Lee. "A Behavioral Approach to Counseling and Guidance." In *Guidance: An Examination*, R. L. Mosher, et al. New York: Harcourt, Brace and World, 1965.

Osgood, C. E., and Miron, M.S., eds. *Approaches to the Study of Aphasia.* Urbana: University of Illinois Press, 1963.

Perls, Frederick, Hefferline, R. F., and Goodman, Paul. *Gestalt Therapy.* New York: Dell, 1951.

Scriven, M. "Views of Human Nature." In *Behaviorism and Phenomenology,* edited by T. W. Wann. Chicago: University of Chicago Press, 1964.

Skinner, B. F. "Behaviorism at Fifty." In *Behaviorism and Phenomenology,* edited by T. W. Wann. Chicago: University of Chicago Press, 1964.

Spence, Kenneth W. *Behavior Theory and Conditioning.* New Haven, Conn.: Yale University Press, 1956.

Truax, Charles B., and Carkhuff, Robert R. *Toward Effective Counseling and Psychotherapy: Training and Practice.* Chicago: Aldine, 1967.

29

The Tasks of The Therapist

JOEN FAGAN

All professional persons are basically problem solvers who are employed to reduce discomfort or conflict and to increase the possibilities of certain valued outcomes for the persons who request their assistance.* Therapists, specifically, are engaged by persons who are dissatisfied with their own, or another's experiencing and behaving, which may include internal experiences of anxiety, discomfort, conflict, or dissatisfaction, and external behaviors that are either inadequate or insufficient for the tasks at hand or that result in difficulties with other people. The problems presented to the therapist may be central to the person and require extensive changes, or they may be peripheral and quickly solved. Not only the problems are varied, but also therapists differ widely, both in their procedures and in their effectiveness with different kinds of persons and problems. I believe that therapists and therapeutic techniques will become increasingly specialized and increasingly effective, partially as a function of research and partially as a function of rapidly growing willingness to experiment with a variety of new techniques. However, while many changes will occur, the basic tasks of the therapist will remain similar. The purpose of this chapter is to examine the tasks or requirements of the therapeutic endeavor under five headings: patterning, control, potency, humanness, and commitment; to indicate briefly the contributions of various approaches or "schools" to each of these; and to focus on contributions from Gestalt therapy.

PATTERNING

The therapist is first of all a perceiver and constructor of patterns. As soon as he is informed of a symptom or a request for change, and

Reprinted by permission of the editor and the publisher from Joen Fagan. "The Tasks of The Therapist," in Joen Fagan and Irma Lee Shepherd (Eds.), *Gestalt Therapy Now: Theory, Techniques and Application.* Palo Alto, California: Science and Behavior Books, 1970, pp. 88–106.

*While this article deals specifically with therapists, the tasks described can be modified and extrapolated to describe any professional group.

begins listening to and observing a patient and responding to him, he begins a process that I refer to as *patterning*. While *diagnosis* is a more common term, it has the disadvantage of provoking the analogy of the medical model and implying that the purpose of the process is arriving at a specific label. A better analogy for the process of patterning is that of artistic creation, involving sometimes cognitive, sometimes perceptual and intuitive skills in interaction with the material and demands of the environment as, for example, in the creation of a mobile, in which a variety of pieces or systems are interconnected into an overall unity and balance.

As the therapist begins his contact with the patient requesting help, he has available a body of theory which is largely cognitive in nature, a background of past experience, and a number of awarenesses and personal responses derived from the ongoing interaction that have large emotional and intuitive components. From these, which may be given varying degrees of importance by a specific therapist, he begins to form an understanding of the interaction of events and systems that result in a given life style that supports a given symptom pattern. *Events* refers to the things that have happened or do happen to the patient; *systems* includes all those interlocking events that interact on a specific level of existence, such as biological systems, self-perception systems, family systems, etc. The patient is visualized as a focal point of many systems, including the cellular, historical, economic, etc. The more the therapist can specify the entire interaction, or be sensitive to the possible effects of systems he is not directly concerned with (such as the neurological), or intuit the connecting points between systems where the most strain exists, the more effective he can be in producing change. He can act on a level and at a point that promises the most positive change in symptoms or conflicts at the least cost of effort, and where the least disruptive change will occur to other systems.

An example may clarify some of the above description. A mother refers her son whose increasing stomach distress causes him frequently to stay home from school. The therapist shortly begins to accumulate information of various sorts. He learns that: the boy also has stomachaches that keep him from going to camp or from visiting relatives; the mother has few interests outside the home; the father does not like his job and also has frequent illnesses; the mother and father have intercourse very infrequently; the boy has average intelligence; the grandmother is very interested in his becoming a doctor; the other children tease him for being a sissy; his teacher is considered strict; the school system has a new superintendent who has made many changes, etc. The therapist observes that the boy waits for his mother to answer for him; that his voice is weak when he does answer; and so on through a long list of responses, observations, and experiments in which the therapist obtains some sort of assessment of the abilities of the boy and his family to respond to varying suggestions and pressures. Through these processes a picture emerges with increasing clarity. The boy, his stomach, his family, his peer group, the school, the school system, and the community come into focus with varying degrees of explicitness.

We first label our understanding of the crux of the problem and then move to intervene on one or possibly several levels, depending on our personal preference, style, and understanding. No matter how badly we do initially in spotting the interactions that are most important, there is a clear possibility that intervention on any level may sooner or later produce the changes we wish, since the systems are interlocking and a change in one system may produce changes in some or many of the other systems. (This may be paraphrased, "Everyone has a little bit of the truth.") We may start with a medical approach, choosing antispasmodics, antiemetics, or tranquilizers. We may attempt to produce primarily internal psychological changes by play therapy, hypnosis, rational-emotive procedures, or desensitization. We may attempt to set up environmental learning situations by academic coaching or by activity group therapy. We may use behavior modification by observing the ways in which the mother reinforces the boy's avoidance behavior and may work with her to change these. We may see the mother individually to help her change her perception of mothering, support her in developing outside interests, or involve her in sensitivity training. We may work with the father in exploring his frequent illnesses or in helping him to find more job satisfaction. We may select couple therapy to assist the parents in dealing with their sexual problems and developing a more satisfactory marriage. We may use family therapy to increase communication, clarify the parents' interactions with the boy, and find ways of modifying the grandmother's influence. It is also possible to arrange environmental changes, such as changing teachers or schools. We could work with the teacher or school counselor, and finally (but grandiosely) we could envision involving the school system, the community, or eventually, the country.

No matter what procedures are chosen, we will need to evaluate our results by three main criteria: how rapidly the symptom has been removed, what positive behavior has replaced it, and how little disturbance has been created in the interlocking systems. These areas of evaluation will be discussed at more length in the section on techniques that follows.

Each therapy system has its own rationale and its own ideas about personality and procedure. Techniques are designed to intervene at the place or places where the theory says the pattern can most easily be modified. All theories and techniques fail at times because no two patterns are exactly alike and the points of conflict may vary widely. However, all theories that are taken seriously have some successes since changes in any system can affect others.

The Gestalt contribution to patterning involves a de-emphasis on cognitive theory and provides extensive assistance with the therapist's own awareness. Enright . . . describes this process in detail, emphasizing the clues to underlying events and life styles that can be uncovered by awareness of the person's movements, tones, expressions, word choice, etc., and suggesting some appropriate techniques for exploration. Much of Gestalt patterning is worked out in the therapy process itself rather than by history-taking or interviewing. The meanings that result, as in dream work, are very different from the more traditional analytic interpretive approaches where certain meanings are specified in advance by theory or predicted from the patient's previous history. Of course, past events of much importance do arise from the process of exploring posture, gestures, and dreams. However, the Gestalt therapist is not interested in the historical reconstruction of the patient's life, nor in weighing the effects of various environmental forces, nor in focusing upon one specific behavior such as communication style. Rather, he is interested in a global way in the point of contact between the various systems available for observation. The interactions between a person and his body, between his words and his tone of voice, between his posture and the person he is talking to, between himself and the group he is a member of are the focal points. The Gestalt therapist does not hypothesize nor make inferences about other systems that he cannot observe, though he may ask the patient to reenact *his* perceptions of them, as in a dialogue with his father, for example. Most Gestalt procedures are designed to bear upon the point of intersection, and the nature of the other system is viewed as less important than how the patient perceives or reacts to it.

In other words, the patterning emphasis in Gestalt therapy is on the process of interaction itself, including the patient's skills in fostering and risking interaction, or blocking awareness and change. Since these are skills of importance in the intersection of any systems from the biological through the social, the Gestalt therapist sees himself as preparing the individual to interact more effectively in all aspects of life. Perls's ideas concerning a therapeutic community, which he is presently formulating, represent a possible extension of Gestalt thinking to a more extensive system.

CONTROL

No matter how clear and adequate the therapist's patterning is, he must be able immediately to exercise control or nothing else can follow. Control is defined as the therapist's being able to persuade or coerce the patient into following the procedures he has set, which may include a variety of conditions. Control is not used here with cynicism or a Svengali attitude, nor is there any implication of ignoring the value of genuine concern and liking for the patient; it simply reflects the reality that unless patients do some of the things that therapists suggest, little will happen, and that which does happen will be mostly by accident.

Whitaker (1968) makes this idea very explicit: "Therapy has to begin with a fight . . . a fight over who controls the context of therapy. . . . I want it understood that I'm in charge of what happens. I see this as the administrative battle I have to win [in Haley and Hoffman, 1968, pp. 266, 267]" (A number of other therapists have written extensively about the importance of control: Haley, 1961 a, 1961 b, 1963; Rosen, 1953). Haley and Erickson often use a paradoxical double-bind, a command so phrased that there is no way of disobeying it, or disobedience involves making admissions that are extremely damaging or revealing. These not only maintain control but often contribute to a very rapid reduction in symptoms. Rosen, Bach, and others often use group pressure as a means of control. A patient may be able to meet or defeat the therapist in a fight, but his chances against eight or ten people who are aware of what he is attempting are very slim.

Part of the importance of control is that all symptoms represent indirect ways of trying to control or force others into certain patterns of behavior. The therapist has to counter being controlled by the patient's symptom pattern and also establish the conditions he needs to work. Some of the conditions will be overt behavioral requirements, such as keeping appointments, paying, bringing other family members, etc. Other conditions will be more covert or implicit, such as the willingness to give information, attempt suggestions, or produce fantasies. While the required aspects of external behavior vary from therapist to therapist, it is essential that the conditions most important to him be met to his reasonable satisfaction. It is common knowledge that patients who initially ask for special favors or conditions, such as special appointment times or reduced fees, will be more difficult to work with; and the therapist often counters by setting up stronger-than-usual controls, such as payment at each interview or the use of a consultant.

Two of the major aspects of implicit control can be examined under the concepts of motivation and rapport. Motivation is often thought of as being related to the patient's discomfort or anxiety; the higher these are, the more the patient is willing to work. However, the degree of distress can be thought of with equal validity as the willingness of the patient to relinquish control to the therapist. Some persons who are experiencing marked distress are difficult to work with because they attribute their discomfort to others via blame. Their motivation for change is high but their willingness to surrender control is low.

Rapport is usually presented somewhat ideally as the "good feeling" and amount of positive relationship between patient and therapist; more accurately it is the therapist's ability to persuade the patient, or the patient's willingness to trust the therapist's control of the situation.

While liking for the therapist is probably necessary somewhere along the therapeutic process, and of value even initially, it is probably more important in the early stages for the patient to believe that the therapist knows what he's doing.

The techniques the therapist uses to gain and maintain control are often, though not necessarily, different from the ones he uses to produce personality or behavioral change. (All techniques, of course, depend heavily on the style of the individual.) The therapist must recognize, manifest, and counter the patient's efforts at taking control by his usual means, some of which will be represented by his symptoms, others more deviously. He must manage to avoid being put off, frightened, or bored by the psychotic; to keep from being had by the psychopath or enjoying him too much; and to avoid being too sympathetic or agreeing with the neurotic's formulations. He must be able to remain his own man while also becoming enough involved with the patient's life style to experience its problems and difficulties.

A special problem is presented by the patient who comes because of external coercion, such as court order, divorce threat, or parent's commands. The situation is such that the external agent has the control, and the therapist runs the risk of becoming his hireling, ostensibly agreeing that he and the patient will work hard to please this outside person. The therapist has, however, at least three main ploys to regain control: he can involve the referring agent, thus indicating that both the agent and the patient need help; he can disavow the external payoff ("It's no concern of mine whether you flunk out of school"); or he can go along by an initial identification with the person's goals to contrast with the agent's as, for example, in Schwartz's (1967) and Greenwald's (1967) offering to make their patients into better psychopaths.

External compliance with a threatened punishment has an internal parallel—the pseudocompliance and "improvement" labeled by analysts as "intellectual insight" or "transference cure" and by transactional analysts as playing "Greenhouse" or "Psychiatry" or "Gee, You're a Wonderful Therapist" (Berne, 1964). Perls's label is "bear-trapper," which describes the patient who, having learned something about the expectations of the therapist, goes through the motions of cooperation, then at a crucial moment refuses to comply with suggestions, thus catching the therapist off balance. Often the bear-trapper is a person with considerable underlying pathology who has much invested in demonstrating that he cannot be helped or changed, and that those who try do not have the power to force him. In this situation, regaining control is difficult since the patient has made it clear that efforts on the part of the therapist to control only indicate an admission of his failure. Renouncing control and admitting failure is one way of regaining it.

Another problem of control can be anticipated with the patient whose presenting symptoms include psychosis or potential psychosis, suicide, and the more severe varieties of "acting out." These are persons who in the past have effectively utilized the threat, "If you don't do what I want, then I'll . . . (kill myself, go crazy, embarrass you, etc.)." These are potent threats and can invoke fear and self-doubts, or may even blackmail the therapist into acting in ways that jeopardize his purpose and position. Suicide or homicide are the ultimate threats, and each of these may force the therapist into assuming more control than he wishes—which, of course, admits that the patient is in control. One of the most effective ways of neutralizing such threats is to make a clear contract initially. Szasz (1965a) informs patients that they will need to make arrangements with someone else if they require hospitalization; Goulding (1967) requires signed contracts from potentially suicidal patients in which they agree without reservation to make no suicide attempts while they are seeing him.

Another type of control only now beginning to be explored systematically is that offered by total environments, such as prisons and mental hospitals. For many years we attempted to deny that external control, other than gross loss of liberty and bare conformity with institution procedures, was either important or desirable. The success of behavior-modification procedures, which make many of the bare amenities of living dependent on certain patient behaviors, is forcing a reevaluation of the position that external control is not appropriate for persons who are unwilling or unable to utilize internal control. The painfully sincere and extensive study by Rogers and his associates (1967) in which competent and dedicated men attempted to modify the behavior of chronic schizophrenics by ignoring external control and attempting to assist the recovery of internal control by nondirective therapy resulted in almost complete futility. It is becoming increasingly evident that in patterning and control, chronic schizophrenics have obliterated almost all of the usual systems and procedures, and can be approached initially most effectively by very specific controls related to the immediate environment. Evidence is also accumulating to suggest that treatment of acute schizophrenic episodes may be approached most effectively by treatment of the total family (Langsley et al., 1968). The major implication of environmental control as represented by behavior modification is that it is needed to the extent to which the individual is unable or unwilling to assume internal control; to the extent to which internal control is possible, external control is insulting, inefficient, or a violation of civil liberties.

Control is most important in the beginning of therapy. The need for control decreases as cooperative control by patient and therapist increases because of greater ability to communicate in each other's language and the development of trust. However, at important points of change, the struggle for control will reemerge, usually on a more intense level, and the therapist should be prepared to fight this battle periodically.

Even initially, the attempt to maintain complete control is impossible and the appearance needs to be periodically renounced, first as a paradoxical way of maintaining control and secondly as a way of encouraging the patient's own assumption of responsibility and growth. (An excellent example of this is found in Simkin's chapter "Mary." . . .) However, the abandoning of control should be viewed as an occasional technique and not as a complete system, as in the early days of non-directive therapy, or in group situations (see, for example, Bion, 1961) where the leader refuses to assume a leadership role. The inevitable outcome is that the group, in order to fill the vacuum, engages in a struggle for leadership accompanied by considerable expression of anger. Since this is a systems effect, the leader cannot claim credit for having produced any special results, and the value to the participants is dubious. While the person whose electric supply is disrupted may be able to get along with candles and a fireplace, this demonstration of self-sufficiency is not what he is paying the power company to produce.

The Gestalt contribution to problems of control includes a number of responses and procedures. Initially the therapist encourages patient autonomy and minimizes struggles by telling the patient that if he has strong objections to complying with suggestions he can (has the therapist's permission to) refuse, and his refusal will be honored. However, he is told that he has to state his reason for refusal. Often, as the reason is given, it can be explored for validity ("What's so terrible about being embarrassed?") and the patient will decide to continue.

Gestalt therapists ask for a clear statement from the patient concerning what he wishes to accomplish. Proceeding from this central theme keeps the emphasis on the patient's stated wishes, not the therapist's expectations. Procedures that keep in the present and make it clear that the therapist is in sensitive awareness with what is happening also decrease resistance. (When a patient begins meeting opposition from his conflicts and the discomfort that surrounds them, he may clearly resist, but this is on a very different order from resistance of control.) The patient is often asked if he would be willing to try an experiment: an acceptance carries a mild commitment to continue, while a refusal is honored if a reason is given. The patient who freezes, draws a blank, or has nothing come to mind can be asked to verbalize his refusal more specifically or to take responsibility for it by saying, "I am making my mind blank." Another procedure is to go with the resistance ("Tell me that it's no business of mine what you're thinking") and then have the fantasied therapist answer back. The value of resistance can also be approached ("What are all the good reasons for refusing me now; what does refusing do for you that is valuable for you?").

POTENCY

To justify his hire, the therapist must be able to assist the patient to move in the direction that he wishes, that is, to accelerate and provoke change in a positive direction. We are rapidly leaving the time when the therapist, in the absence of more specific knowledge, relies on "something" in the relationship that will result in "something" happening. We are approaching the time when the therapist can specify procedures that promote rapid change in a way that the patient can experience directly and others can observe clearly. For a given patient, many of the changes that do occur are a direct or by-product of the therapeutic relationships as described in the next section on humanness. (The therapeutic relationship is both a technique and a transcendence of techniques.) However, the therapist has need at many points of techniques, procedures, experiments, gimmicks, directions, and suggestions that can overcome inertia and promote movement. The patient who asks for specific assistance should expect to receive it.

Techniques are one of the more publicized aspects of psychotherapy; everyone knows that Freudians interpret and analyze dreams, and others hypnotize, analyze transactions, give tokens, etc. With increasing speed and accuracy, we are able to remove symptoms and change behaviors such as phobias, sexual deviations, inhibitions, etc., that only a few years ago were thought to require extended treatment. The increasing power of the therapist has resurrected two old topics that have a long history: the question of therapist authenticity versus techniques and the problem of symptom substitution.

The existentialists and neo-Rogerians (Rogers, 1951; Bugental, 1965; Carkhuff and Berenson, 1967) write powerfully of the human condition and the need for genuine relationships. However, techniques are often ignored or decried as being artificial, with the implication that authenticity cannot occur in their presence. I observed one of the most highly respected existential therapists in the country leading a group that was being observed by several hundred people and videotaped as a record of his way of working. The group, composed of student volunteers, spent over forty minutes continuing to be uncomfortably aware of the audience and verbalizing their discomfort at being observed and expected to produce. The therapist periodically shared with the group his own anxiety, selfconsciousness, and fears that nothing would happen. When, at the end of the hour, a group member finally volunteered a "problem"—that he was temporarily short of money—the group responded with great relief and vast amounts of concern and sympathy. However, neither the therapist nor the group would have had to remain "stuck" had he been willing to utilize any of a number of techniques.

Gestalt techniques appropriate to the situation would have had members of the group in turn play the part of the critical audience and the stupid, helpless child, externalize their projections, take the role of critic and criticize the audience, "ham up" their own discomfort, etc. These procedures would have allowed them to further their own growth by reducing the internalized demands of others' expectations and to reclaim and modify their disowned disapproval, while at the same time they would be reducing the audience to "ground" and then could continue with whatever needs emerged as "figure." Suffering with another when the reasons for his suffering are not genuine or allowing him to continue with discomfort when this can be reduced is hardly humane.

A second therapist on the program specialized in behavior modification in groups. His techniques invoked persons in the group into becoming involved in such obviously insincere and artificial interactions that it came as no surprise to discover that he had carefully rehearsed the group members the night before. However, there is no need to think of suffering-with or artificial techniques as representing an either-or choice; rather, they are two undesirable extremes, between which lie many combinations of the values of potency and humanness.

The problem of symptom substitution has reappeared with the advent of behavior modification, and it has apparently become important for behavior modifiers to defend their procedures and their potency against questions as to the possibility of substitution of other unwished-for behavior and lack of permanency in the behavioral changes (see, for example, Calhoon, 1968). Part of the problem concerns the rapidity of the change—the extent to which rapid change is permanent or will be replaced with equivalent symptoms. The speed with which behavior can be changed with a reasonable degree of permanence depends on whether it is central or peripheral to personality structure and to what extent it intersects with other systems that can reapply pressure to keep it in force. In other words, the combination of speed and potency of behavior change depends on the number and strength of the props that hold up a given bit of behavior. Props may be the reinforcements of other people, catastrophic expectations on the part of the patients, ignorance, unchecked assumptions, etc. Some of these may be removed easily, especially if they are discomfort producing and if other systems are minimally affected. The question of symptom substitution must take into account three questions: whether the symptom is replaced by another on the same level, what positive goals have occurred, and to what extent other systems have been disrupted. Let us return to the example of the boy with the stomachache presented earlier and assume that he is given medical treatment of such potency that he ceases to have stomach complaints. However, he then develops acrophobia that just as effectively keeps him at home. The physician, concerned only with the physical system, states that there is no symptom substitution, that is, there are no other medical problems and therefore the problem is solved. However, the therapist, who views the boy's main problem as avoiding school, defines the phobia as symptom substitution and proceeds to treat him by behavior modification. As a result the boy attends school but cries all the time and fails his work. Another result might be that the boy's mother, finding that she can enjoy directly controlling passively resisting men, puts such pressure on her husband that a divorce occurs. While Freud apparently cured the phobia of Little Hans, his parents did divorce (Strean, 1967). Other therapists who define the problem as success at school or the mutual satisfaction of the entire family would see each of these attempts as evidences of inadequate, incomplete, or inept therapy. We can continue moving up the systems ladder by hypothesizing other possibilites: what if, because of the improvement in the entire family, they come into conflict with the authoritarian school system; or the father, by deciding to leave his job, contributes to the bankruptcy of the company he worked for?

There are no final nor even clear answers to this morass, but I can offer some suggestions:

1. It is not enough to specify the symptom to be removed; it is also necessary to describe what positive functioning is expected.
2. The most important interconnecting systems should be specified and attempts made to keep disruptions to a minimum.
3. If disruptions are inevitable, the therapist should specify his value choice.

The three points above need amplification and the detailing of underlying assumptions. One is that, with very few exceptions, symptoms represent a positive as well as a negative force. Most symptoms, be they medical, individual, or social, even though painful, disturbing, and time consuming, are indicative of intersections that need to be repaired lest greater damage occur. In trying to change symptoms, we must always look to the larger system to note whether the symptom is justified. (It is possible that the school system could become so destructive that to force children's attendance would be to contribute to much more serious problems than would arise from nonattendance.) Symptoms may also have positive value, such as holding a couple together.

With our powerful Western technology we change and redo large parts of our physical environment without any appreciation of the values that we are negating and without any provisions for replacing their loss. As a result we are constantly being faced with land erosion, floods, air pollution, drops in water-tables, etc. Similarly, in therapy we are creating a technology that lets us change personality faster than we know how to solidify it or provide for the fragments left behind. If we attempt to specify what is healthy in a symptom pattern, then we will know more clearly what to leave alone.

It is also important to specify the replacement behavior for symptomatic difficulties, even though this is presently somewhat utopian. Of what value is it to remove a snake phobia—what does this contribute to living in a positive sense? Or, if we remove overt homosexual behavior, is asexuality adequate, or ability to have intercourse with randomly chosen females? Or do we aim toward the formation of a sustained, personally satisfying heterosexual involvement? Most therapists would prefer to avoid the specification of positive goals, since this involves them in clear value choices and since achievement may be embarrassingly short of the goals. It is also true that most patients request the removal of symptoms rather than specifying replacement behavior, and their goals usually change during the treatment process as additional possibilities become available. However, the therapist who does not consider the question of goals in their broader aspect becomes a mere technician, or a flunky of the values of the culture and its institutional systems.

Finally, and also ideally, if we have done our jobs thoroughly, we have not markedly disrupted any other system. This is a complicated issue, and only some of the parameters can be suggested here. It is, of course, true that growth and change are both disruptive of systems. The child will leave home in the process of growing up; changes in other systems will make an institutional administrative arrangement inadequate, causing different and expanded procedures and organization, and perhaps another kind of discomfort. We therefore have to decide whether the disruption of a system is inevitable or whether it is destructive, that is, whether it creates wounds that require extensive energy to heal, energy that could be better used for expanded growth. This question is one for Solomon; however, the therapist, even with his much more limited resources, should still have at least an awareness of his role as a system disrupter. A denial of this effect ("The only thing I do is to change a person's specific behavior") can be regarded as gross myopia. For example, consider a therapist whose patients are primarily dissatisfied housewives. In his work with them, he fosters their becoming appropriately more demanding and assertive. However, the end result is frequent marital problems and divorces, as the husbands reject their wives' demands or use them as excuses for affairs, etc. Much of this could be avoided if the therapist were willing to see couples jointly (or could modify his strong rescue needs). If the goal is to make a person less dependent, then the immediate question can be raised, less dependent upon whom? It follows that the "whom" may have some responses of his own that will likely lead to strains in the family system. If the therapist is aware of these strains, he can take steps to anticipate and deal with them.

Sometimes disruption cannot be avoided. If we are able to "de-craze" a late-adolescent schizophrenic whose family refuses to be changed, then one or both parents may show psychotic symptoms themselves. (At times, one measure of change is the disruption of inter-related systems or the extent of the pressures they employ to force return to earlier states.) There are times when systems may well need to be abandoned: when the student should drop out of school or the worker quit his job. The therapist no longer has the luxury of avoiding the problem by decreeing that no decisions be made during therapy (life moves too quickly for this), nor can he ignore the fact that changes resulting from therapy inevitably create decision situations. Helping the patient with deciding in a given situation whether to run, fight, or compromise requires a full measure of the therapist's humanness. In general, I would prefer to maintain rather than to disrupt systems. However, this implies degrees of wisdom and power that are not yet consistently available.

When leaving a system is inevitable, the therapist can assist the patient with the reduction of unfinished business by having him in the therapy session confront, in directly spoken fantasy, the person(s) with his resentments, appreciations, regrets, and good-bys.

Finally, the therapist can predict for the patient as early as possible that system disruption may occur, allowing him to anticipate and have increased choice in the outcome. While the choice of end goals is basically the patient's, the therapist has the responsibility of anticipating and reminding the patient of as many choices as possible. There are unfortunately many conditions that reduce the number of options, and with a given patient, quite limited goals are often inevitable, given limited resources and rigid systems. The therapist should be able to accept these while being aware of further possibilities.

One of the major contributions of Gestalt therapy is the power of its techniques, which make possible the very rapid reaching of deep emotional levels. Since the other papers in this section ably describe these, no effort will be made to include them here. It should be noted, however, that having access to potent techniques presents a temptation to overuse them, and the therapist needs to be aware that he has other tasks of importance.

HUMANNESS

The therapist's contribution to the therapeutic process as a person and the importance of the genuineness and depth of the therapeutic relationship have been emphasized by a large number of therapists. Humanness, as it is used here, includes a variety of involvements: the therapist's concern for and caring about his patient on a personal and emotional level; his willingness to share himself and bring to the patient his own direct emotional responses and/or pertinent accounts of his own experiences; his ability to recognize in the patient gropings toward deepened authenticity, which need support and recognition; and his continued openness to his own growth, which serves as a model for the patient.

Some patients' needs are peripheral and can be adequately attended to by therapists with only brief or minimal involvement. But many—if not most—people were raised by families who, even while doing the best they could, taught them less about being human than they need to know. If a patient's problems stem from inadequate rearing, then the teaching of more adequate behavior is basically a process of rearing. This requires adequate humanness in the therapist who assumes the parenting role, since he will serve extensively as a model and will have to make many value-laden decisions. This does not rule out briefer therapeutic contacts. There is a trend among some therapists who assume long-range responsibility to suggest or arrange for patients at certain stages such adjunct experiences as sensitivity training, art therapy, structural reintegration, or marathons. There is also an increasing emphasis among some behavior modifiers to consider their assignment unfinished until more adequate behavior is substituted for the symptom that is removed.

In raising children, it is the subtle learnings, attitudes, and non-verbal messages that are perhaps the most important. As the father teaches his son to fix the sled, or the mother shops for clothes with her daughter, they communicate perceptions of the child as stupid or bright, pleasant or unpleasant, likable or disgusting, and demonstrate attitudes such as interest, endurance, and enjoyment. Factual knowledge and routine bits of information are most efficiently taught by teaching machines or their equivalents, but not tolerance or curiosity, nor the value of "wasting" time.

Patients inevitably put therapists in a parental position, that is, they see them has having the secrets of living and test them in many ways to see if they will be adequate models. I tell patients, "Basically what we are doing here is seeing if I, as I am now, could have grown up in your family as you present it to me in your person, and remain sane." The patient in rapidly alternating ways involves me with his problems to see if I can respond more adequately than his parents could, and presents me with his parent's problems to see if I can find better ways of dealing with them than he was able to. For those patients for whom therapy is and becomes a central and intense experience, external living crises become relatively less important, and reenactments of growing-up crises occupy increasing attention. They progress backward through time and present their unsolved problems in a roughly reverse temporal order. Most often the final decision to accept me totally as parent comes as the result of a crisis, often following a minor mistake I made at the same time the patient is beginning to come to grips with core problems. (A somewhat limited example is given in Fagan, 1968.) The crisis is unexpected in that I can never anticipate its presentation; in retrospect it becomes apparent that the patient sets up a situation in which I am put to the test that his parents failed most badly. The crisis

clearly measures my understanding of the patient's patterning, my
ability to control, my potency, but most of all my humanness, since a
response is unavoidable and usually must be immediate and genuine,
drawing on resources that lie far below the level of techniques. I do not
always pass the test. Sometimes when I do not, the patient tries again
later; sometimes he gives up and adopts lesser goals; sometimes he
turns to other sources of help. When I have passed, I know immediately since the patient in an unmistakable way becomes my infant
and our feelings toward each other involve a kind of adoration (for
example, Searles, 1965, Chap. 21). We work our way back up through
developmental milestones of childhood and adolescence until the patient is as well regrown as my own resources as a parent allow. [Other
descriptions of this process are given by Whitaker and Malone (1953)
as the *core phase,* and by Carkhuff and Berenson (1967) as the *downward
and upward stages* of therapy.] It is of course true that many therapists
do not and/or cannot involve their patients to this extent, and many
patients ask for assistance of a much more limited nature. However,
deep personal regrowth is still experienced by those involved as either
patients or therapists as the crux of therapy.

On a less intense and involved level, but still important, are those
crises of living on which the therapist must respond to the patient more
from this humanness than from his knowledge or techniques. These
would include a severe illness, a child killed, an important goal having
become unattainable, a deep rejection. Before or after dealing with
those aspects that are correctable, there exists the need for bearing
those parts that can only be borne. The therapist needs to know from
inside himself when his presence is the most important contribution he
can make to the healing process, and when his response as one human
being to another is more important than any therapeutic busywork.

The events of the past few years—the civil rights struggles, student
rebellions, experimental college movements, hippie communities, and
the explosive growth of sensitivity training and group experiences
—bespeak a level of hunger for new ways of experiencing, relating,
learning, governing, etc., but they also are contributing to the development of a number of people whose experimentations are producing new levels and patterns of authenticity. If therapists fall too far
behind in their own growth, they will be out of touch with an increasing proportion of the population.

The making of oneself into a whole and genuine person is probably the most difficult and painful aspect of becoming a therapist, but,
for many, it is also the most valuable and important part. Many
therapists who see authenticity as a primary task of the therapist fear
those who, having stopped short in their own struggles with growing,
substitute increased emphasis on control and potency, with a corresponding lack of regard for questions of value associated with the ability

to produce personality change. The question of who controls the controllers becomes more acute as control over behavior becomes more possible. In the name of mental health, many horribly inhumane and degrading things have been done to people (Szasz, 1965b) and will no doubt continue to be done. Those who are certain of the good that they do are more to be feared than those who are more willing to admit and struggle with their own personal limitations, to share their doubts, and to express their values.

The contributions of Gestalt therapy to the humanness of the therapist come primarily in the workshop setting, which offers therapists direct experience with their own inauthenticities and avoidances. The emphasis on experiencing rather than computing, and the fostering of here-and-now awareness, pleasure, excitement, deep emotional involvement, and direct interaction seem especially designed for therapists, many of whom tend toward obsessive and depressive styles. Experiencing and observing ways in which authenticity can be distinguished from its many imitations is a valuable contribution.

Gestalt theory confronts therapists as directly as patients with reminders of the values and pleasures of living that can get pushed aside by our occupational hazards of overemphasis on work, responsibility, accomplishment, and study. Finally, in work with patients, Gestalt techniques offer a variety of ways of allowing them a rapid, deep, and authentic experience with themselves which provides an increased knowledge of what is possible as well as allowing a quick and direct "knowing" on the part of the therapist.

COMMITMENT

A number of major and minor commitments are necessary to the therapy process. The therapist commits himself to a vocation with its attendant demands for continued growth of his own understanding and ability. He also commits himself to individual patients in his work with them. Finally, he commits himself to contributing to the field as a whole by his research, writing, training of students, etc.

Commitment, or the continuing involvement and acceptance of assumed responsibilities, requires high levels of interest and energy. Interests may be maintained in a variety of ways. There are many problems that have large cognitive components, including understanding patients and constructing patterns. There is the broader task of theory addition and construction, or the long-term satisfaction of a research program. Also involving are the deep satisfaction of seeing the growth of patients, the challenge and excitement of devising new procedures and techniques, and the steady increments of the therapist's person and powers. However, no therapist can avoid boredom, depression, and doubts related to the therapeutic process and his own procedures, either for brief moments or for extended periods. If the therapist's techniques are mechanical and boring, involving him only passively or superficially, or if the interaction required creates too much anxiety, then the therapist will either be spurred to less directly central areas such as research or, unfortunately, training.

Gestalt therapy places most emphasis on the therapist's commitment to himself in terms of enhancing his involvement and excitement in the day-to-day tasks. It also provides or suggests ways for the therapist to assist himself in exploring his own boredom and doubts when they occur. In these respects it enhances both therapist and patient interest and offers ways of getting both "unstuck" when faced with the inevitable impasses.

Some final thoughts: The five tasks described in this paper will vary in their relative importance in response to many factors; the context surrounding therapy, specific requirements and limitations, the types of problems presented, and the time sequence or stage of therapy. At times the therapist will experience conflicts between two of the tasks, for example, between control and humanness. As the emphasis shifts from task to task, to some extent the image of the therapist shifts, in a way that, with much magnification, parallels the popular stereotypes of the therapist as the mind reader who knows all, as the hypnotist who can control persons against their will, as the magician who has a collection of magic tricks, as the loving Big Daddy or Mommie, and as the faithful, patient family retainer.

In summary, many requirements are made of the therapist as he sets out to assist another person. These have been discussed under five headings: patterning, control, potency, humanness, and commitment. The therapist's response to these involves him as a complete person, including his intellectual knowledge and cognitive abilities, his interpersonal effectiveness, his emotional awareness and personal sensitivity, his values and interests, and his experience in living. Certainly one of the continued challenges and fascinations of therapy is the variety of demands that it places on the therapist and its ability to require and evoke from him an involvement and utilization of all his resources.

REFERENCES

Berne, E. *Games People Play.* New York: Grove Press, 1964.

Bion, W. R. *Experience in Groups, and other Papers.* New York: Basic Books, 1961.

Bugental, J. F. T. *The Search for Authenticity: An Existential-analytic Approach to Psychotherapy.* New York: Holt, Rinehart & Winston, 1965.

Calhoon, D. D. "Symptom Substitution and the Behavioral Therapies: A Reappraisal." *Psychological Bulletin,* 69 (1968): 149–156.

Carkhuff, R. R., and Berenson, B. G. *Beyond Counseling and Therapy.* New York: Holt, Rinehart & Winston, 1967.

Fagan, J. "Message from Mother." *Psychotherapy: Theory, Research and Practice,* 5 (1968): 21–23.

Goulding, R. Introductory Lectures in Transactional Analysis. Atlanta, Ga., 1967.

Greenwald, H. "Treatment of the Psychopath." *Voices,* 3 no. 1 (1967): 50–61.

Haley, J. "The Art of Psychoanalysis." In *Our Language and Our World,* edited by S. I. Hayakawa. New York: Harper & Brothers, 1959.

———. "Control in Brief Psychotherapy." *Archives of General Psychiatry,* 4 (1961): 139–153. (a)

———. "Control in Psychotherapy with Schizophrenics." *Archives of General Psychiatry,* 5 (1961): 340–353. (b)

———. *Strategies of Psychotherapy.* New York: Grune & Stratton, 1963.

Haley, J. and Hoffman, L. *Techniques of Family Therapy.* New York: Basic Books, 1968.

Langsley, D. G., Pittman, F. S., Machotka, P., and Flomenhaft, K. "Family Crisis Therapy—Results and Implications." *Family Process,* 7 (1968): 145–158.

Rogers, C. R. *Client-centered Therapy.* Boston: Houghton-Mifflin, 1951.

Rogers, C. R., ed. *The Therapeutic Relationship and Its Impact: A Study of Psychotherapy with Schizophrenics.* Madison, Wisc.: University of Wisconsin Press, 1967.

Rosen, J. N. *Direct Analysis: Selected Papers.* New York: Grune & Stratton, 1953.

Schwartz, L. J. "Treatment of the Adolescent Psychopath—Theory and Case Report." *Psychotherapy: Theory, Research and Practice,* 4 (1967): 133–137.

Searles, H. F. *Collected Papers on Schizophrenia and Related Subjects.* New York: International Universities Press, 1965.

Strean, H. S. "A Family Therapist Looks at 'Little Hans.'" *Family Process,* 6 (1967): 227–234.

Szasz, T. S. *The Ethics of Psychoanalysis: The Theory and Method of Autonomous Psychotherapy.* New York: Basic Books, 1965. (a)

———. *Psychiatric Justice.* New York: Macmillan, 1965. (b)

Truax, C. B., and Carkhuff, R. R. *Toward Effective Counseling and Psychotherapy: Training and Practice.* Chicago: Aldine, 1967.

Whitaker, C. A., and Malone, T. P. *The Roots of Psychotherapy.* New York: Blakiston, 1953.

30

The Probation Officer and Gestalt Therapy Techniques

ERIC H. MARCUS, M.D.

The roles of the probation officer are extremely varied, encompassing a variety of functions ranging from "policeman" to "counselor." In addition to preparing personal background investigation reports for the Court as an aid in sentencing, the bulk of probation work involves supervision of persons placed on probation by the Courts. This "supervision" varies from receiving perfunctory monthly report postcards from probationers to relatively intensive supervision (e.g. "counseling"). This paper focuses upon the counseling role of probation officers and offers specific suggestions as to probation officer-client interactions.

The variety and techniques of counseling will not be enumerated here. The "non-directive" techniques, such as the psychoanalytically oriented approaches, have been found to be relatively ineffective in modifying the personality characteristics of most probationers.

Gestalt therapy has features in common, but is not identical with either behavioral therapy or Glasser's "reality therapy." Behavioral therapy involves the mechanical deconditioning of undesirable behavior and symptoms. Reality therapy focuses on the client's interactions and stresses the development of more appropriate and socially acceptable behavior. Gestalt therapy's aims encompass more than the development of new "reflexes" or more desirable behavior patterns; the goal is the achievement of "maturity." Maturity is defined as the transition from environmental support to self-support. The client is assisted in the development of his own potential through decreasing environmental support, increasing his frustration tolerance and by debunking his phony playing of infantile and adult roles. The probationer manipulates his environment for support by acting helpless and

Reprinted, with permission of the California Probation, Parole and Correctional Association from, *Crime and Correction*, the journal of the California Probation, Parole and Correctional Association, Summer 1970, pp. 3–6.

stupid, wheedling, bribing and flattering. He is not infantile, but plays an infantile and dependent role, expecting to control the situation by submissive behavior. With maturation he is increasingly able to mobilize spontaneously his own resources in order to deal with the environment. He learns to stand on his own feet, thus becoming able to cope with his own problems as well as the exigencies of life. The mature individual is better able to cope with the situation by mobilizing his own resources. He no longer reacts with fixed responses and preconceived ideas. He doesn't cry for environmental support because he can do for himself (4).

Only a few specific techniques of Gestalt therapy will be enumerated on this paper. It should be kept in mind that the following techniques may seem trite, but the reader is urged to experiment with them before rejecting them out of hand.

As mentioned above, the objective of having the probationer assume responsibility for his actions is of utmost importance. The following techniques are specifically focused upon this goal.

The psychoanalytic heritage with its concern for psychodynamics, emphasizes the "why" of human behavior. An increasingly larger number of psychotherapists have found that "why" questions merely lead to "because" answers and a repetitious why-because cycle. The result is a prolonged, therapeutically fruitless experience with a client, resulting mostly in rationalizations and intellectualizations. By forbidding "why" questions and allowing only "how" and "what" questions, the probation officer will find that the client's responses are *descriptive* rather than merely *explanatory*. "Most people most of the time don't really know 'what' they're doing fully, and it is a considerable therapeutic contribution if the client can achieve a vivid and ongoing awareness of his moment-to-moment behavior and surroundings. In a sense, the achievement of such full awareness is all that therapy need do; when a person feels fully and vividly what he is doing, his concern about 'why' usually fades away. If he does remain interested, he is in a good position to work it out for himself." (1)

The proclivity of probationers to talk *about* other individuals in relation to their own "helpless" role is well-known. One technique designed to eliminate the tedious and fruitless narrations of clients is to have the client talk "to" whichever individual he has been talking about. An extra empty chair serves adequately to symbolize the missing person. Role reversal, i.e., having the probationer change chairs and speak for the missing person, provides invaluable insights and growth experiences for the client. This simple psychodramatic technique helps the client become aware of his projections and, thereby, assists him in confronting the task of overcoming his endless manipulations in convincing the probation officer of his being a "victim of circumstance."

The typical probationer is usually considered to be a "character disorder" rather than a "neurotic." Impulsive, "acting out" behavior is of course, what has resulted in his being placed on probation. The client's unawareness of his tensions and anxieties results in self-destructive behavior. A hallmark of Gestalt therapy is the development of self-awareness. Awareness, of course, can only take place within a "here and now" framework rather than by means of a discussion about past or future events or experiences. The client is frequently asked, "What do you experience?" The total range of experience is focused upon, viz., thoughts, emotions, physical sensations, posture, etc. It quickly becomes apparent that the probationer has blocked off awareness of almost all sensation. If he is aware of anxiety, he is usually unaware of how the anxiety is affecting *him*. Increasing his awareness of the latter contributes to a diminution of his tensions and anxieties with the consequent lessening of his need for "acting out."

The probationer's propensity for asking questions should be given careful consideration. Neither answering all questions uncritically nor responding to each question with a non-directive, "Why do you ask?" contributes to the individual's maturity. The former, allows him to maintain his dependency and immaturity and the latter, allows him an opportunity to rationalize. Instead, Gestalt therapy proposes that the therapist ask the client to, "Change your question into a statement." Much more meaningful growth-producing transactions will then occur.

The probationer's proclivity for not assuming responsibility for his own actions is exemplified in his frequent use of projection. By not recognizing his own projections, he constantly is able to justify his behavior and attitudes. One technique is to have the client precede any statement indicating a projection by the words, "I imagine that." With constant repetition, he soon realizes that there is a difference between the thoughts and attitudes people hold *toward* him and the thoughts and attitudes he *imagines* people hold.

Self-awareness is enhanced by focusing upon the client's body movements and gestures. No attempts are made to interpret any bodily movement, but rather have the client exaggerate the motion in order to increase his awareness of it. For example, the client may deny feeling tense and yet constantly shake his foot. Requesting that he exaggerate his foot's movement often results in a diminution of his tension.

The development of the client's ability to assume responsibility for his behavior, life style and well-being is enhanced by preventing him from using generalizations in his speech, such as "we," "you," or "one." Whenever these words appear in his speech, he is urged to substitute the word "X."

The above described techniques are only a fraction of the Gestalt techniques developed and found clinically efficacious. The reader is referred elsewhere for elaboration of the above techniques as well as descriptions of additional techniques (1, 2, 5).

Probation officers have been most enthusiastic in their receptivity to Gestalt methods and many have already utilized them with their clients. I hope that personnel in other areas of correctional work, such as parole agents and institutional counselors, will experiment with these techniques.

REFERENCES

1. Enright, John B., "Techniques of Gestalt Therapy." In *Gestalt Therapy Now.* Science and Behavior Books, Inc., 1969.
2. Levitsky, Abraham, "The Rules and Games of Gestalt Therapy." In *Gestalt Therapy Now.* Science and Behavior Books, Inc., 1969.
3. Perls, Frederick S., et al, *Gestalt Therapy.* New York: Dell, 1965 (paperback reprint of 1951 edition published by Julian Press).
4. Perls, Frederick S., *Gestalt Therapy in Human Potentialities.* In "Explorations in Human Potentialities." Otto, Charles C Thomas, 1966.
5. Simkin, James S., "Introduction to Gestalt Therapy." Paper.

31

Reality Therapy: Helping People Help Themselves

RICHARD L. RACHIN

Chief, Bureau of Group Treatment, Florida Division of Youth
Services; Editor, *Journal of Drug Issues*

Efforts to redirect the behavior of persons who violate laws,
customs, and morals are often unsuccessful, perhaps because
we tend to view behavior different from our own as evidence of
mental illness of some kind or degree. We ignore legal, cultural, and other idiosyncratic determinants of who may be
"okay" today and who may be in trouble tomorrow, and instead
seek pathological explanations for nonconforming behavior.
Many people have been harmed by our insistence that human
behavior is understandable and thereby treatable only in terms
of mental health or mental illness, a dogma that has compart-
mentalized, isolated, and stigmatized those who, for one reason
or another, act unconventionally. This paper explores a more
humanistic, economic, and societally productive alternative for
changing behavior and considers its application and availability
to offender groups in particular. Reality therapy departs radically from the conventional treatment orthodoxy. The conceptual differences between the two approaches as well as the
basic steps for practicing reality therapy are also outlined and
discussed.

The realities of mental-health operations, said Anthony Graziano two
years ago, "seldom match the idealism with which they are described in
the rhetoric."

> Our professional rhetoric is powerfully reinforcing when it enables us
> to obscure our own doubts and to disguise our own shortcomings. We
> seldom actually do what we say we are really doing. Sustained by their
> own deception, individual clinicians believe they are performing noble

Reprinted, with permission of the National Council on Crime and Delinquency, from
Crime and Delinquency, January 1974, pp. 45–53.

functions in essentially bureaucratic, unsympathetic, and doubtfully effective agencies.[1]

Graziano was not saying anything new. This same message has been delivered, with increasing volume, since the early fifties. Only recently, however, have the efficacy and ethical underpinning of classical treatment procedures been openly attacked.[2] Today it seems almost fashionable to expose, if not castigate, psychoanalysts for defects of character and purpose—faults which they have always shared with the rest of us.[3]

While psychotherapy, particularly of the psychoanalytic type, has never proven to be more effective or dependable than less pretentious kinds of help, orthodox practitioners tend to be as defensive as shamans in examining this incongruity. With certain notable exceptions, there is a remarkable absence of discussion among psychotherapists concerning the efficacy of their treatment techniques in spite of the paucity of evidence mustered to support the belief that psychotherapy is more effective than other treatment procedures.

The influence of mental health practitioners is largely responsible for acceptance of the view that socially disapproved behavior is evidence of emotional illness. Too often the label becomes a self-fulfilling prophecy building impenetrable barriers between *them* (those labeled) and the rest of us.

People in trouble, whether they are patients in mental institutions, drug dependents, or kids who play truant, often are not in a position where they can choose to be treated or not be treated. Public agencies armed with clinical evaluations make the choice for them. The recipient of such public largesse and his family have had little to say about rejecting or terminating treatment, even when the service seems to endanger his health and well-being.[4] Explanations designed to justify these practices are patronizing and lack the evidence that would support continuing them.

Ponder Graziano's theme that American mental health practitioners seem more concerned about improving their status and enhancing their power base than they are about treating. Clinical services have not been freely available to persons needing such care—especially in correction, where both the quality and the quantity of clinical personnel have left something to be desired. Considering juvenile correction alone, the President's Crime Commission reported that, of the 21,000 persons employed during 1965 in 220 state-operated juvenile facilities, only 1,154 were treatment staff. While the accepted national standard required one psychiatrist for every 150 juvenile inmates, the actual ratio in American institutions for children was 1:910. Forty-six psychiatrists (over half of them concentrated in five states) were then listed as the treatment backbone of juvenile correction.[5] As Donald Cressey observed, "The trap is this: We subscribe to a theory of rehabilitation that can be implemented only by highly educated, 'professionally trained' persons, and then scream that there are not enough of these persons to man our correctional agencies and institutions."[6]

DISSATISFACTION WITH THE MEDICAL MODEL

The following are some of the reasons for the accelerating development of alternatives to traditional, medically based approaches to helping troubled people:

1. "The recidivism rate for offenders," writes Seymour Halleck, "remains depressingly high and the number of psychiatrists interested in treating the delinquent remains shamefully low."[7] Publicity given to crime and the problems of our criminal justice system has not led to any significant increase in the number of clinicians devoting themselves to correction.

2. Even if there were enough conventionally prepared clinicians available, it is doubtful that government would be able or willing to assume the cost of their employment. Psychiatric attention is expensive and psychiatry's patients in the correctional system have never been high on the list of public priorities.

3. Important class, cultural, and racial barriers between those treating and those being treated have hindered the development of rapport and effective treatment programs. This problem has been magnified by our dependence on institutional care and the location of most of the institutions in rural areas, where staff recruitment beyond the surrounding communities (when attempted) is usually unsuccessful. Generally, in a state with a relatively large urban population, few of the staff—but, conversely, a disproportionately large part of the inmate population—are members of city-dwelling minority groups.

4. Research has not demonstrated that people receiving conventional treatment are any better off than those not receiving treatment. While this may be disturbing to advocates of the status quo, it is well to recall Jerome Frank's words: "Comparison of the effects of psychotherapy and placebos on a group of psychiatric outpatients suggests certain symptoms may be relieved equally well by both forms of treatment and raises the possibility that one of the features accounting for some of the success of all forms of psychotherapy is their ability to arouse the patient's expectation of help."[8] We are witnessing an accelerating growth of more humane, socially accountable therapies in which people with problems depend on other people with similar problems for help. The influence that human beings have on one another has long been noted, but has not been applied in practice.[9]

Although middle-class values and standards provide no valid measure for assessing mental health or mental illness, this yardstick has been customarily employed to measure deviation and the need for correctional care, especially in juvenile courts. Fortunately, simply economics has forced a re-examination of the traditional treatment orthodoxy. We have finally come to question the concept of mental illness as behavior that deviates from an established norm and its concept of cure as intervention by professionally trained mental health practitioners.

There should be little argument about the pervasive long-term ineffectiveness of most "treatment" programs. Although poorly trained staff, crumbling and inadequate physical plants, skimpy budgets, and overcrowding contribute to their futility, it is doubtful that unlimited resources alone would make it possible to rehabilitate significantly more offenders. Many private child-care agencies with budgets and per capita costs several times those of their public counterparts have discovered this when they become involved with court-referred children —even though they have been highly selective when deciding which court-committed children they will accept. A major reason for the poor results may be that many of the ways in which most well-adjusted adults once behaved are now viewed as symptomatic of underlying pathology. Two important circumstances are usually overlooked: (1) usually behavior brought to the attention of the courts and other official agencies is disproportionately that of poor and minority group children; (2) as George Vold observed, "in a delinquency area, delinquency is the normal response of the normal individual. . . . The nondelinquent is really the 'problem case,' the nonconformist whose behavior needs to be accounted for."[10]

The imprimatur of the court clinician is usually sufficient to dispose of children whose true feelings and needs are probably better known to their peers than to anyone coming into contact with the child for the first time. As Martin Silver found, "The detection of a 'proclivity to bad behavior' is facilitated by the court's 'treatment' process." Silver goes on to quote Dick Gregory: "Being black is not needing a psychiatrist to tell you what's bugging you."[11]

Offenders who have proved to be poor candidates for traditional treatment approaches in many cases seem responsive to peer group "here and now" therapies. As Carl Rogers expressed it, "It makes me realize what incredible potential for helping resides in the ordinary untrained person, if only he feels the freedom to use it."[12] The medical model for understanding and treating essentially psychosocial, ethical, or legal deviations makes it, as Szasz suggests, "logically absurd to expect that it will help solve problems whose very existence has been defined and established on nonmedical grounds."[13]

Nevertheless, when available in correction and more than just in name, diagnostic and treatment services essentially remain cast from the same orthodox mold. Vested interests and ignorance combine to apply a method of treatment that even Freud himself was to disavow in later life.[14] Ironically, proposals made to improve treatment services are usually accompanied by pleas for more psychiatrists, clinical psychologists, and psychiatric social workers. The influence which mental health practitioners have had on the design and delivery of treatment services seems accounted for not by any greater success in helping people but by seemingly convincing arguments disparaging alternative approaches. Put to the test, conventional treatment practices based upon the mental health/mental illness model have been as unsuccessful with offender groups as they often have been unavailable. Operating in the penumbra of the clinician and frequently in awe of him, legislators and correctional administrators have clung tenaciously to procedures about which they understand little and feel the need to understand less. And this problem has not been restricted to correction.

The development of less costly, more effective, and readily attainable treatment alternatives can be traced to three conditions: first, a quest for involvement, understanding, and clear communication by significant numbers of people—a need which could hardly be met by the small coterie of conventional mental health practitioners; second, voluntary patients' dissatisfaction with the time and expense required for treatment; and third, a crescendo of criticism directed by practitioners and researchers at a treatment methodology that has never been validated.[15]

William Glasser shared this concern. Near the completion of his psychiatric training he began to doubt much of what he had been taught. "Only a very few questioned the basic tenets of conventional psychiatry. One of these few was my last teacher, Dr. G. L. Harrington. When I hesitatingly expressed my own concern, he reached across the desk, shook my hand and said 'join the club.' "[16]

REALITY THERAPY

Glasser's theories departed radically from classical procedures. He postulated that, regardless of the symptom—be it drug use, fear of heights, suspicion that others may be plotting against one, or whatever—the problem could be traced in all instances to an inability to fulfill two basic needs:

> Psychiatry must be concerned with two basic psychological needs: *the need to love and be loved and the need to feel that we are worthwhile to ourselves and to others.*[17]

Glasser believed that the severity of the symptom reflected the degree to which the person was failing to meet these needs. No matter how bizarre or irrational the behavior seems to be, it always has meaning to the person: a rather ineffective but nevertheless necessary attempt to satisfy these basic needs.

Regardless of behavior, people who are not meeting their needs refuse to acknowledge the reality of the world in which they live. This becomes more apparent with each successive failure to gain relatedness and respect. Reality therapy mobilizes its efforts toward helping a person accept reality and aims to help him meet his needs within its confines.

We fulfill our needs by being involved with other people. Involvement, of course, means a great deal more than simply being with other people. It is a reciprocal relationship of care and concern. Most people usually experience this relationship with parents, spouses, close friends, or others. When there is no involvement with at least one other human being, reality begins to be denied and the ability to meet one's needs suffers accordingly.

Glasser points out that advice given to a person who needs help is of little value. People who deny the reality of the world around them cannot be expected to respond to exhortations to do better or to behave. Involvement means having a relationship with another person who can both model and mirror reality. The reality therapist presumes that people who are experiencing difficulty in living are having difficulty meeting their needs within the confines of the "real world." To help someone adopt a more successful life style, the reality therapist must first become involved with him. Involvement is the reality therapist's expression of genuine care and concern. It is the key to his success in influencing behavior. Involvement does not come easily. The therapist must be patient and determined not to reject the person because of aberrance or misbehavior.

REALITY AND TRADITIONAL THERAPY COMPARED

Reality therapy rejects the classical system whereby problem-ridden people are viewed as mentally ill and their behavior is labeled according to a complex and extensive classification scheme. Instead of the terms "mental health" and "mental illness," reality therapy refers to behavior as "responsible" or "irresponsible." The extensive, ambiguous, and unreliable diagnostic scheme on which conventional practitioners depend is discarded. As diagnostician the reality therapist simply determines whether the person is meeting his needs in a manner that does not interfere with others meeting theirs. If he is, he is acting responsibly; if he isn't, he is acting irresponsibly.

Conventional procedures lead the patient back through a maze of old experiences in search of the origin of his problem, because, the analyst assumes, the patient will be unable to deal with the present until he understands how the problem began in the elusive link in the past. Reality therapy concentrates on the present, on the "here and now" rather than the "there and then." Nothing can change the past, no matter how sad or unfortunate it may have been. The past does not influence present behavior any more than the person permits it to. The focus of the reality therapist, therefore, is on present behavior, about which something can be done.

Conventional therapy emphasizes the process during which the patient relives significant occurrences in his past and projects his past wishes, thoughts, and feelings onto the therapist; through interpretation of these past events the therapist helps the patient understand his present inadequate behavior. In contrast, reality therapy rejects the need for insight into one's past; the reality therapist relates to the person as he is and does not relive the past. The conventional practitioner seeks to uncover unconscious conflicts and motivations and to help the patient gain insight into these mental processes; he de-emphasizes conscious problems while helping the patient understand his unconscious through dreams, free associations, and analysis of the transference. The reality therapist insists that the person examine his conscious self and behavior; conceding that efforts to understand motivation or other complex mental processes may be interesting, he doubts that the results merit the time spent to obtain them: it has yet to be demonstrated, he argues, that these pursuits have anything to do with helping the person.

Conventional practice makes no ethical judgments and frees the patient of moral responsibility for his actions; it views the patient as being under the influence of a psychic illness which makes him incapable of controlling his behavior. In reality therapy the patient is forced to face the consequences of his behavior: Was it right or wrong? What were the results for him?

Finally, the conventionally schooled practitioner insists that his role remain inexplicit, almost ambiguous, to the patient; he does not take an active part in helping him find a more productive way to live. Although the reality therapist does not take over for the person, he helps him —even teaches him when necessary—to learn better ways to meet his needs.

FOURTEEN STEPS

The reality therapist follows certain steps in attaining involvement and influencing responsible, realistic behavior. Responsibility, the basic concept of reality therapy, is defined simply as the ability to meet one's needs without depriving others of the ability to meet theirs. Realistic behavior occurs when one considers and compares the immediate and remote consequences of his actions.

Step 1: *Personalizes.*—The reality therapist becomes emotionally involved. He carefully models responsibility and does not practice something other than he preaches. He is a warm, tough, interested, and sensitive human being who genuinely gives a damn—and demonstrates it.

Step 2: *Reveals Self.*—He has frailties as well as strengths and does not need to project an image of omniscience or omnipotence. If he is asked personal questions he sees nothing wrong with responding.

Step 3: *Concentrates on the "Here and Now."*—He is concerned only with behavior that can be tested by reality. The only problems or issues that can be confronted are those occurring in the present. Permitting the person to dwell on the past is a waste of time. He does not allow the person to use the unfavorable past as a justification of irresponsible action in the present.

Step 4: *Emphasizes Behavior.*—Unlike attitudes or motives, behavior can be observed. The reality therapist is not interested in uncovering underlying motivations or drives; rather, he concentrates on helping the person act in a manner that will help him meet his needs responsibly. Although the person may be convinced that new behavior will not attain responsible ends, the reality therapist insists that he try.

Step 5: *Rarely Asks Why.*—He is concerned with helping the person understand what he is doing, what he has accomplished, what he is learning from his behavior, and whether he could do better than he is doing now. Asking the person the reasons for his actions implies that they make a difference. The reality therapist takes a posture that irresponsible behavior is just that, regardless of the reasons. He is not interested in time-consuming and often counterproductive explanations for self-defeating behavior. Rather, he conveys to the person that more responsible behavior will be expected.

Step 6: *Helps the Person Evaluate His Behavior.*—He is persistent in guiding the person to explore his actions for signs of irresponsible, unrealistic behavior. He does not permit the person to deny the importance of difficult things he would like to do. He repeatedly asks the person what his current behavior is accomplishing and whether it is meeting his needs.

Step 7: *Helps Him Develop a Better Plan for Future Behavior.*—By questioning *what* the person is doing now and *what* he can do differently, he conveys his belief in the person's ability to behave responsibly. If the person cannot develop his own plan for future action, the reality therapist will help him develop one. Once the plan is worked out, a contract is drawn up and signed by the person and the reality therapist.

It is a minimum plan for behaving differently in matters in which the person admits he has acted irresponsibly. If the contract is broken, a new one is designed and agreed upon. If a contract is honored, a new one with tasks more closely attuned to the person's ability is designed. Plans are made for the contract to be reviewed periodically.

Step 8: *Rejects Excuses.*—He does not encourage searching for reasons to justify irresponsible behavior: to do so would support a belief that the person has acceptable reasons for not doing what he had agreed was within his capabilities. Excuses do not improve a situation; they do not help a person to see the need for an honest, scrutinizing examination of his behavior. Excuses only delay improvement.

Step 9: *Offers No Tears of Sympathy.*—Sympathy does little more than convey the therapist's lack of confidence in the person's ability to act more responsibly. The reality therapist does not become inveigled into listening to long sad stories about a person's past. The past cannot justify present irresponsible behavior. The therapist has a relationship with the person which is based upon genuine care and concern; sympathizing with a person's misery or inability to act in a more productive and need-fulfilling manner will do nothing to improve his ability to lead a responsible life. The therapist must convey to the person that he cares enough about him that, if need be, he will try to force him to act more responsibly.

Step 10: *Praises and Approves Responsible Behavior.*—People need recognition and esteem for their positive accomplishments. However, the reality therapist should not become unduly excited about a person's success in grappling with problems that he previously avoided or handled poorly. But just as a person's irresponsible behavior is recognized when he is asked what he plans to do about it, so should his responsible behavior be recognized.

Step 11: *Believes People Are Capable of Changing Their Behavior.*—Positive expectations do much to enhance the chances of a person's adopting a more productive life style regardless of how many times he may have failed in the past. Negative expectations, on the other hand, serve to undermine progress. It is easier to do things well when others are encouraging and optimistic.

Step 12: *Tries to Work in Groups.*—People are most responsive to the influence and pressure of their peers. It is much easier to express oneself with a group of peers than it is to relate to a therapist alone. People are also more likely to be open and honest with a peer group. Problems one often imagines are unique are quickly discovered by group members to be similar to the difficulties others also are encountering. Group involvement itself is immediate and helpful grist for observation and discussion. Learning experiences derived from interaction in treatment groups carry over to personal group encounters.

Step 13: *Does Not Give Up.*—The reality therapist rejects the idea that anyone is unable to learn how to live a more productive and responsible life. There are instances when a person may be unwilling to do anything about his life, but this does not mean that, given another opportunity, he will not work to change it. Failure need not be documented in a detailed case record. Case records too often become little more than repetitive and largely subjective harbingers of failure. Sometimes professionals seem more involved with records than with the people the records pretend to describe. The reality therapist does not let historical material interfere with his becoming involved with people or prevent him from beginning afresh.

Step 14: *Does Not Label People.*—He does not believe that elaborate diagnostic rituals aid involvement or help the person. Behavior is simply described as responsible or irresponsible. The therapist does not classify people as sick, disturbed, or emotionally disabled.

The principles of reality therapy are common sense interwoven with a firm belief in the dignity of man and his ability to improve his lot. Its value is twofold: it is a means by which people can help one another, and it is a treatment technique, applicable regardless of symptomatology. It is simple to learn albeit somewhat difficult for the novice to practice. Experience, not extensive theoretical grooming, is the key to accomplishment.

Correctional clients who have proven least amenable to conventional treatment methods respond well to reality therapy. That its employment involves only a fraction of the time as well as the cost required by traditional (and not more effective) psychoanalytically oriented treatment modalities only further underscores its value. Until research can demonstrate its relative effectiveness and permanence, these reasons alone make its utilization well worth a try.

NOTES

[1] Anthony M. Graziano, "Stimulus/Response: In the Mental-Health Industry, Illness Is Our Most Important Product," *Psychology Today*, January 1972, p. 17.

[2] *Los Angeles Times*, June 26, 1972, p. 3.

[3] Phyllis Chester, "The Sensuous Psychiatrists," *New York*, June 19, 1972, pp. 52–61.

[4] Frontal lobotomy, electric shock, and insulin therapy to relieve anxiety were far from being the most humane procedures. See Percival Bailey, "The Great Psychiatric Revolution," *American Journal of Psychiatry*, 113, (1956): 387–406. Those who have complete confidence in the new wonder drugs should see Richard Elman's "All the Thorazine You Can Drink at Bellevue," *New York*, Nov. 22, 1971, pp. 40–46; also, *New York Times*, July 15, 1972, p. 7.

[5] President's Commission on Law Enforcement and Administration of Justice, *Task Force Report: Corrections* (Washington, D.C.: Government Printing Office, 1967), p. 145.

[6] Donald R. Cressey, remarks on "The Division of Correctional Labor," in *Manpower and Training for Corrections*, Proceedings of an Arden House Conference, June 24–26, 1964, p. 56.

[7] Seymour L. Halleck, "The Criminal's Problem with Psychiatry," *Morality and Mental Health*, eds. O. Hobart Mowrer et al. (Chicago: Rand McNally, 1967), p. 86.

[8] Jerome D. Frank, *Persuasion and Healing* (New York: Schocken Books, 1964), p. 74. See also R. G. Appel et al., "Prognosis in Psychiatry," *A.M.A. Arch. Neurol. Psychiat.*, 70, (1953): 459–68; O. H. Mowrer, *The Crisis in Psychiatry and Religion* (Princeton, N.J.: Van Nostrand, 1961), p. 121; Hans D. Eysenck, *The Effects of Psychotherapy* (New York: International Science Press, 1966), p. 121.

[9] J. Dejerine and E. Gauckler, *The Psychoneuroses and Their Treatment* (Philadelphia: J. B. Lippincott, 1913), p. 17.

[10] F. Lovell Bixby and Lloyd W. McCorkle, "Discussion of Guided Group Interaction and Correctional Work," *American Sociological Review*, August 1951, p. 460.

[11] Martin T. Silver, "The New York City Family Court: A Law Guardian's Overview," *Crime and Delinquency*, January 1972, p. 95.

[12] Carl Rogers, *Carl Rogers on Encounter Groups* (New York: Harper & Row, 1970), p. 58.

[13] Thomas S. Szasz, "The Myth of Mental Illness," *American Psychologist*, 15, (1960).

[14] J. Wortis, *Fragments of an Analysis with Freud* (New York: Simon and Schuster, 1954), p. 57.

[15] Eysenck, *Effects of Psychotherapy*, p. 94; quotes D. H. Malan, the Senior Hospital Medical Officer at London's Tavistock Clinic, the locus of orthodox psychoanalysis in England: "There is not the slightest indication from the published figures that psychotherapy has any value at all."

[16] William M. Glasser, *Reality Therapy: A New Approach to Psychiatry* (New York: Harper and Row, 1965), p. xxiii.

[17] Ibid., p. 9.

32
Reality Therapy

ROBERT J. WICKS

Marketing fur parkas in the equatorial city of Entebbe would undoubtedly be futile. No matter how enterprising a clothing jobber might be, if he didn't take climatic conditions into account he would be doomed to failure. In selling coats, as in almost any pursuit involving human beings, the practitioner must suit his approach to his target population as well as to his own theories if it is to be effective.

Psychologists' recognition of this simple principle is evidenced by the variety of therapeutic approaches now in use. Although all these approaches have achieved at least limited success with at least one form of behavioral problem, most techniques have had more impact on one type of personality disorder than on others. For example, the behavioristic method now appears to be more effective with sociopaths than is lengthy, in-depth psychoanalysis.

Since correctional psychologists come from a variety of backgrounds and have dealt with nearly every conceivable psychological problem, we can assume that every widely accepted therapeutic philosophy has probably been tried out in a penal setting at some time. We will limit our discussion to those major techniques that seem to be most successful in correctional institutions today. (This excludes behaviorism. ...) These methods are reality therapy, Transactional Analysis, the therapeutic community, and guided group interaction. Of the four, one technique in particular has received increasing attention in the western part of the United States and in Great Britain. It is referred to as *reality therapy*.

REALITY THERAPY

Freud could not be ignored in his time. His revolutionary theories and striking personality wouldn't allow it. Today theorists are still reacting to his work, and going beyond it with their own.

Theories of personality are multiplying like the plague. The diseases can take the form of types or traits, factors or fields, canalizations or cathexes. Unlike most epidemics, however, this one is allowed to rage unchecked. It almost seems to be more fun for the doctor to get the bug himself than to try to discover what caused the victim to die. The prognosis in such cases must be deemed, in the vernacular, guarded.[1]

Two of the practitioners who have found Freudian psychoanalytic procedures ineffective and who can be included among those who have contracted "the bug" are Los Angeles psychiatrists William Glasser and G. L. Harrington. Together they have contributed significantly to the development of reality therapy. Unlike many other bugs, though, this one may have curative effects, especially in the correctional field. The success claimed by the Ventura School for Girls of the California Youth Authority, where reality therapy is applied, offers support for a positive appraisal of it.

Mentally Ill?

In reality therapy, the therapist becomes personally involved with the patient in an effort to get him to face life and accept responsibility. According to proponents of reality therapy, people who have serious problems dealing with life, such as those classed as neurotic or psychotic, are not *mentally ill* in the conventional sense of the term. Instead, such persons lack a sense of responsibility and are unable to fulfill their basic needs. The type and severity of their problems depend upon how they are dealing with reality. If therapy is to succeed, it must teach these people to fulfill their needs within the confines of reality. In other words, reality therapy is founded on the theory that every human being has social needs that must be met, such as the need to love and be loved and the need to feel that he is unique and important. When a person is unable to meet these needs through normal social contacts, he often resorts to unrealistic, and sometimes antisocial, means to fulfill them.

Reality Therapy versus Conventional Psychiatry

To understand why Dr. Glasser says reality therapy differs from the conventional "camp," one must be familiar with how he sees conventional therapy. In summary, Dr. Glasser believes "conventional therapists" hold the following tenets:

1. *Mentally ill* individuals exist, and should be categorized and treated accordingly.
2. The psychological roots (in the past) of a problem must be known if treatment is to be effective.

3. Transference and insight are necessary. (Transference refers to the situation in which a patient transfers attitudes he has, or had, toward people in his past life to the therapist.)
4. The patient must become aware of his unconscious forces.
5. Morality is an issue to be avoided.
6. The patient must understand what his problems are and how they affect him before he can adopt proper behavior patterns—not vice versa.
7. The therapist should be impersonal and objective and avoid becoming involved with the patient.[2]

Glasser defines the differences between conventional and reality therapy, then, as follows:

1. Because we do not accept the concept of mental illness, the patient cannot become involved with us as a mentally ill person who has no responsibility for his behavior.
2. Working in the present and toward the future, we do not get involved with the patient's history because we can neither change what happened to him nor accept the fact that he is limited by his past.
3. We relate to patients as ourselves, not as transference figures.
4. We do not look for unconscious conflicts or the reasons for them. A patient cannot become involved with us by excusing his behavior on the basis of unconscious motivations.
5. We emphasize the morality of behavior. We face the issue of right and wrong which we believe solidifies the involvement, in contrast to conventional psychiatrists who do not make the distinction between right and wrong, feeling it would be detrimental to attaining the transference relationship they seek.
6. We teach patients better ways to fulfill their needs. The proper involvement will not be maintained unless the patient is helped to find more satisfactory patterns of behavior. Conventional therapists do not feel that teaching better behavior is part of therapy.[3]

Application

Reality therapy is designed to be a learning experience for the patient. It involves three steps. First, the patient must form an honest personal relationship with his therapist. This can be extremely difficult, especially with a young, sensitive first offender. (By virtue of his needing assistance, the patient is assumed to have had difficulties with interpersonal relationships in the past.) Next, the therapist must indicate to the patient that he understands, but does not condone, his irresponsible behavior. The patient's behavior is rejected, but he himself is accepted. Finally, the therapist teaches the patient better ways to fulfill his needs within the framework of reality (society as it exists).

Reality therapy deals directly with the patient's conscious, immediate situation. Accordingly, the therapist begins by outlining for the patient some tentative goals for treatment, and explaining how reality therapy works. Timing is of the essence in this approach. The psychiatrist must see the patient when he is ready for treatment; a patient who is put on a waiting list may be in trouble again by the time he is eventually treated.[4]

A reality therapy program was developed at Western State Hospital in Washington to provide the control, re-education, and community reintegration necessary for the rehabilitation of sexual offenders. The subjects for this study were picked on the basis of their motivation to change. Treatment included vigorous self-examination, intensive involvement with others, and constant demands for honest and responsible behavior. Small patient groups chose their own leaders and were held accountable for their own custody and treatment. The staff's role was to establish standards and expectations, teach, guide, and provide supplementary administrative and clinical services. When an offender showed responsible behavior in his relationships with other offenders and his family, and during psychotherapy, work and recreational activities, he was recommended for conditional release. Although the study has not been followed up in depth, hospital records indicate only an 8.9 percent re-arrest rate from 1958 to 1968, which suggests that the program was successful.[5]

Case Study

In the study done at Western State Hospital, one of the conclusions psychiatrists reached was that the reality therapy approach would probably be useful with alcoholics and drug addicts. The following case illustrates how reality therapy worked with one young, embittered offender who had been involved with drugs.

John was a black, unemployed 17-year-old, convicted of armed robbery in New York, where he had lived for most of his life. Records of his background showed that he came from an inadequate home—his mother was often absent, his father was an alcoholic. John left school to work for a trucking firm when he was 16. Before his conviction, he had previously been arrested three times for possession of marijuana and "works" (hypodermic needle and other drug paraphernalia).

When John first entered therapy, he spent a good deal of time detailing his disadvantaged background and berating the society around him for the way it had perpetuated his poverty and continued to reject him. He also verbally attacked the therapist for being part of the system. He condemned the therapist as rich, condescending, un-feeling, and prejudiced to try to force him to become angry and reject him as others had done in the past.

In response to John's attempts to stir him to anger, the psychologist showed no negative emotion. Instead, he allowed the con-finee to release his feelings of hostility freely. When John calmed down, the therapist discussed with him the tentative goals they had mentioned during the initial session.

After seven sessions, John started to show some trust for the psychologist and began to believe in him as a person, not just as a pro-fessional assigned to help him. However, many years of being rejected by family and friends had made him quite wary of becoming attached to anyone for fear of being hurt and abandoned. Consequently, during the eighth session he tested the therapist again by telling him he didn't want to come any more. He claimed he preferred to stay in the cell-block.

John clearly expected the therapist to react to this announcement emotionally, since he had spent considerable time with him and seemed to have achieved some success. It thus came as a surprise to John when the therapist simply replied to the challenge with a question: "How will staying in the block and leaving therapy help you?"

After being confronted this way with the real consequences of his request to end therapy, John tried once more to see if he could put off the psychologist by telling him unpleasant, degrading things he had done in the past. John related in vivid terms some of the things he had done to get money for drugs. The following is one such story:

> Once I went into a small candy store and asked for something I knew the owner would have to go into the back room to get. While the owner was out of the store, I reached over and took the money from the Heart Association canister standing next to the cash register. A college student walking into the store caught me, but I got away by grabbing a compass and stabbing him in the hand when he tried to stop me.

When he finished telling this melodramatic story, John looked for at least a nonverbal expression of disgust on the face of the therapist. He was caught off guard, though, for the psychologist did not grimace, but said in a frank manner, "Now that you've told me these things, am I supposed to think ill of you?" And he smiled.

After this episode John seemed to realize that he could really count on the therapist. The first phase of therapy had substantially been completed; the relationship between John and the therapist was cemented.

As therapy continued, the psychologist drew John's attention to the unsuccessful results of his irresponsible behavior. Slowly, but steadily, they worked together to formulate a concrete, detailed plan for the future. They also discussed the excuses he had used for failure in the past and how they would threaten him in the future since he could employ them easily as a "cop-out."

A year after he was released from prison, John sent a letter to the psychologist (a rare occurrence in itself), saying,

> . . . I'm not working two jobs anymore. I got promoted in one and the money I make is enough to pay the rent on my apartment in the Village. Man, is it ever good to be out of [there].
> . . . I start school in the Fall. The forms are filled out and the fee paid—you see I take care of all the details now, so I won't back out.
> . . . Everything's not rosey, but I got a couple of girls and . . . I know it's going to get better.[6]

Impact of Reality Therapy

Reality therapy, then, seems to be an effective way of treating some types of offenders. It has other advantages as well: For example, it offers paraprofessionals a wider role in the therapeutic setting. Since the theory behind reality therapy is not as complex as in conventional psychoanalysis, trained paraprofessionals can easily learn to help treat patients. And as other personnel besides clinical psychologists and psychiatrists take part in therapy, more patients can be treated. Another consequence of using reality therapy might be better continuity between prison treatment and parole supervision. Both the reality therapist and the parole officer believe that the criminal must be held responsible for the consequences of his behavior, and that he must learn to see his behavior in terms of right and wrong. An offender who has accepted these concepts in therapy within the institution might well adjust more easily to parole and the street environment.[7]

Criticisms of Reality Therapy

Although reality therapy shows strong promise as a method of treating offenders, it has been criticized as well as praised. One reviewer of Glasser's book, *Reality Therapy*, felt that the stress on the therapist's values might encourage authoritarian and paternalistic attitudes in therapeutic practice.[8] Primarily, despite claims by Glasser that it is unique, reality therapy still has much in common with other therapies currently in use. Accordingly, some observers contend that it is unlikely to be significantly more effective than other similar methods of treatment.

Furthermore, although reality therapy is not as complex and time-consuming as psychoanalysis, the psychologist or paraprofessional who uses it will still need extensive training. And even its so-called "short-term" approach may take over a year to be effective with some patients.

However, though some critics warn against or disregard reality therapy as a technique, it is already being used extensively in today's penal settings. Thus, it is essential for those interested and involved in the fields of correctional psychology and penology to be familiar with this form of treatment.

NOTES

[1] Gerald S. Blum, *Psychoanalytic Theories of Personality* (New York: McGraw-Hill, 1953), p. vii.

[2] William Glasser, *Reality Therapy* (New York: Harper & Row, 1965), pp. 42–44.

[3] Excerpts from pp. 44–45 in *Reality Therapy* by William Glasser, M.D. Copyright © 1965 by William Glasser, M.D. Reprinted by permission of Harper & Row, Publishers, Inc.

[4] Benjamin I. Coleman, "Reality Therapy with Offenders: Practice," and Melitta Schmideberg, "Reality Therapy with Offenders: Principle," *International Journal of Offender Therapy*, 14, no. 1 (1970).

[5] George J. MacDonald, Robinson Williams, and H. R. Nichols, "Treatment of the Sex Offender," Western State Hospital, Fort Steilacoom, Washington, 1968.

[6] "John" was a patient treated by the author. . . .

[7] John R. Ackerman, "Reality therapy approach to probation and parole supervision," *Probation and Parole*, 1969, 1(1), pp. 15–17.

[8] Rodney G. Loper, "Essay Review: Glasser's Reality Therapy," *National Catholic Guidance Conference Journal*, 12, no. 4 (1968); 287-288.

VI

CONCLUSION

33

Sorting From The Treatment Maze

EDWARD E. PEOPLES

After being exposed to a wide variety of different counseling methods, either in training or in the literature, caseworkers frequently respond in one of four ways. Some say that the very existence of so many different approaches shows that no one has the real answer, so they will wait until *the* counseling technique is discovered. Others feign confusion, and say that they can be more effective on their own by "communicating" with their clients as people (whatever that means). Both of these responses are cop-outs that justify the caseworker doing nothing. They ring of crisis nonintervention, an avoidance technique of the fearful or the incompetent.

A third avoidance response comes from the caseworker who locks himself up with one theory of behavior. He picks the counseling model derived from *his* theory, clings to it like a blanket, and attempts to apply it in every situation as if it were mana. Often he has more problems, and is more afraid of change, than any offender on his caseload.

The mature response comes from the caseworker who suspends judgment on the "rightness" or "wrongness" of all methods, learns as much as he can about all theories and their application, and is selective in matching his approach in counseling to the client and the nature of the situation. He seeks to become equally skillful with each method, or blends the relevant ingredients of several methods together into an eclectic approach.

Actually, there are more similarities than differences among the many strategies used in counseling. And, where there are differences, they are more often complementary than in conflict. This concluding chapter presents those similarities and differences, and suggests ways of implementing them in various combinations.

CLASSIFICATION

Preliminary efforts must focus on some process of classification. The perspective, orientation, needs, problems or motives of the offender

366

must be placed in some framework of understanding relative to the nature of the treatment model to be used.

The two formal classification techniques presented in the text are I-Level and FIRO. Some individuals see implications of a labeling theory, which is abhorrent to them, and reject these techniques out of hand. To them, an individual cannot be defined by letters (as an I something, subtype x) or by a set of numbers (as in FIRO). The uniqueness of the individual is as sacred to them as mom and apple pie are to others. This reaction, a blend of rigid thinking and emotional distortion, is unfortunate. Caseworkers (and students) quick to reject these concepts usually have little knowledge or understanding of them.

Of course, each individual is a unique being. Nevertheless, individuals do share many things in common: political persuasions; moral values; religious beliefs; cultural, racial and family heritages; and much more, even down to sharing a commitment to the principles of a fraternal lodge. We can categorize people by their identification in these areas and can make some general statements about them. Such stereotyping, guided by wisdom, can save a lot of time. Compare your own image of an Irish Catholic Democrat with an English Protestant Republican Mason. Even with that brief description of each, you can make some general observations about all individuals of each type, recognizing the vast array of differences among individuals within each category.

In I-Level, individuals are recognized as unique, but also as sharing common stages of development. Remember, it is the individual's stage of development, his integration level that is being classified by I-Level, not the individual himself. Within each stage of development, individuals do share a common orientation to their environment, common general perceptions of themselves and others, and a common orientation about internalized values. One merely needs to enter a dorm full of I2AA's and then a dorm full of I3MP's to recognize the commonalities shared by each type and the differences between them. Or attempt family counseling with I3 parents and I4 children—the parents have absolutely no ability to comprehend abstract concepts yet the children do, and the children's perception of their environment is far beyond their parents in scope; one appreciates the frustration of trying to bring them together in some common understanding.

It is not suggested that every client be classified by I-Level and then be treated as if he were absolutely fixed as type X. However, it is suggested that the I-Level interview process be performed with each client, and that an interpretive evaluation be written up and placed in the case file as *one* basis, not *the* basis, of further evaluation and treatment. Remember that the I-Level interview process itself forces the caseworker to listen to the client describe his world and where he is coming from on his terms, rather than on terms imposed by the caseworker.

Much of the information gained as a result of an I-Level evaluation may be complemented by an analysis of the client's FIRO profile. For example, the I4NX's "poor-me" posture will be projected in his lo/hi behavior scores in each need-area. The I3 will show a lo/med score in Control behavior because he is a follower seeking reassurance. However, the CFM usually projects a lo/hi in Inclusion behavior with a hi/lo in Inclusion feeling, while the MP has more balanced Inclusion and Affection scores. The I4 CI, or psychopath, will project hi/lo scores in all behavior need areas, mirrored by lo/hi feeling scores. As an aside, the mature offender, whose orientation reflects paranoid thinking, usually projects hi/lo behavior Control scores as his only significant need. Combined with the I-Level analysis, the FIRO profile evaluation adds depth and scope in understanding who the client is and where he is coming from.

If conjoint family therapy is the counselor's choice for treatment intervention, an analysis of the family's FIRO profile can be extremely valuable. In the conjoint model the marital relationship is the key to a healthy family. The reciprocal compatability between the husband's and wife's scores, then, is the first area of concern in FIRO. The second relates to the concept of the Identified Patient (IP). FIRO is based on a learning theory which postulates that individuals learn how to socialize, how to be assertive and responsible, and how to relate on a one-to-one basis by the way they were taught at home.[1]

In this process of being taught, children also learn to identify with the roles expected of them as male or female.[2] This may reflect a cultural bias, but in a healthy environment, boys identify with their father and girls with their mother. In the FIRO profile of dysfunctional family, the IP shows a lack of such identification as compared with other children in the home. An effective way to blend FIRO with conjoint in treatment is to discuss the FIRO profiles openly with the family and point out these areas of incompatability and conflict.

I-Level can also be a valuable source of information in deciding whether or not to use conjoint. Usually, the I4NX or NA will be the IP and his identification as the sick one in the family will come through loud and clear on the taped interview. However, each of these subtypes respond differently to intervention. The NA is crying out for help in rejecting his IP status and participates vigorously in rearranging the homeostasis of the family. The NX, on the other hand, has much more of an investment in his own sickness, and will experience extreme discomfort with conjoint intervention.

Classification by I-Level and FIRO can also provide the basis for treatment with Transactional Analysis, Behavior Modification, Contract

Counseling, Reality Therapy, or with any other model. In Reality Therapy, for example, the client's behavior and feeling needs, and his method of operating in his environment are exposed and can be dealt with openly. Using Behavior Modification the FIRO profile, which is considered dysfunctional by both client and counselor, can be changed with new and rewarding learning experiences. Behavior Modification can be more effective with certain I-Level types than with others.

If TA is the counselor's choice for treatment, parental scripting and injunctions are often vividly projected with FIRO, or in the I-Level interview.[3] Consider the combination of lo/lo scores in all behavior areas with lo/hi scores in the feeling areas. This individual is saying "I'm Not OK—You're Not OK." Or the individual with the opposite scores, hi/hi in Inclusion and Affection behavior and high expressed feeling scores. He is saying "I'm O.K. if . . . ," and his compulsive need to relate and interact helps to meet that *if* qualifier. Another obvious FIRO score related to scripting is the hi/lo score in Control behavior with lo/lo scores in Inclusion and Affection, combined with lo/hi scores in Control feelings. He is saying "I'm OK—You're Not OK" but his OKness is qualified by "as long as I am responsible, achieve, and win."

In I-Level interviews, one can hear the "I'm Not OK—You're OK" script of the I4NX usually accompanied by the parental injunction "Don't be." In the I4 CI, one can hear the "I'm OK—You're Not OK" position clearly taken. This position is also reflected in the I3 CFC type, but modified by the "We're OK" of the gang. By analyzing the client's orientation on I-Level and/or FIRO, other TA life positions and parental injunctions will become evident to the counselor who develops the skills necessary to make connections.

A third classification technique introduced recently relates specifically to TA. It combines material taken from the workbook *Winning With People*[4] and a short questionnaire called the Miniscript Checklist designed by Hedges Capers, L.H.D., and Taibi Kahler, Ph.D.[5] Responses provide descriptive information on an individual's TA life script and the parental injunctions which enforce it. Used together, the checklist and the workbook give insight and direction for TA counseling and are particularly useful with groups.

TREATMENT

In correctional counseling, a variety of treatment methods can be blended together, or one specific approach can be taken alone. The choice depends on the nature of the behavior involved, the counseling environment, and the goals of treatment. FIRO lends itself well as a basis for classifying almost any individual. Although its use in treatment is described in chapter 18, some additional observations seem appropriate here.

A form of Behavior Modification, Assertive Therapy, can be planned around the FIRO-behavior orientation that the client wants to change. Basically, Assertive Therapy calls for the client to behave in ways, or participate in activities, which he wants but which are uncomfortable for him. With each forced experience he feels less discomfort and less anxiety until he reaches the point of comfort and, in fact, pleasure from the experience. Take, for example, the client who has lo/lo, or lo/hi scores in Inclusion behavior. The first scores indicate that the person has not learned how to socialize or how to anticipiate rejection, and avoids people as a defense against being hurt. The second scores indicate that, during his early socialization period, he was often discounted, made to feel the fool before others, and put on exhibition. He wants unqualified acceptance; however, he lacks the social skills for initiating his own involvement. He checks out others to determine if the group is safe, then moves in slowly with a constant eye open for cues of rejection. A simple form of Assertive Therapy would be to join a toastmaster's club, or to run for school offices, or to participate in school or civic activities.

FIRO facilitates family or marriage group counseling that has a sensitivity or encounter orientation. In fact, one of the leading figures in the encounter group movement is William C. Schutz (FIRO). In his bestselling book *Joy*,[6] Schutz describes in detail a number of group exercises designed to move people through the Inclusion, Control and Affection processes to the point where meaningful communications can occur.

Some counselors use these exercises from *Joy* to bring the group together, as it were, and then proceed with TA, or TA and Gestalt for the actual counseling. Blending TA with Gestalt was introduced in chapter 27, by James and Jongeward; they state in the Preface of *Born to Win:*

> Transactional Analysis gives a person a rational method for analyzing and understanding behavior; gestalt therapy gives a person a useful method for discovering the fragmented parts of his personality, integrating them, and developing a core of self-confidence. Both methods are concerned with discovering and fostering awareness, self-responsibility, and genuineness. Both methods are concerned with what is happening *now.*[7]

One of the fundamental goals of counseling is to move the client from environmental support to self-support—to help him achieve self-responsibility. TA with Gestalt certainly is one approach that gives direction in making this move. TA alone is considered by many counselors equally effective, and it is widely used in corrections at the county, state, and federal levels. In fact, the application of TA knows no age limit,[8] nor does it preclude from counseling individuals of seemingly low I.Q. or maturity level.

However, a preliminary report from the California Youth Authority indicates that youths respond differently to TA counseling at different stages of maturity. The report, an overview of the Youth Center Research Projects, presents a description of research conducted between 1968 and 1972 on the comparative effectiveness of transactional analysis vs. behavior modification on the rehabilitation of institutionalized delinquents. Committed youths were classified by I-Level, then randomly assigned to one of two institutions, O. H. Close School (TA) and Karl Holton School (Beh. Mod.). Generally, the more mature delinquents participated more actively in both treatment programs. However, upon release from the institution, some of the youths who had been in the TA program had a much more positive attitude about themselves, their future, and their ability to be responsible than did those treated with Behavior Modification. This was especially true for the I_3 CFM and MP, whereas the I_2AP and I_3 CFC seemed to gain more from Behavior Modification. This was also true in some behavior areas for the I_4 NX and NA. The opposite results were anticipated: that the I_4's would show greater gains from TA and the I_3's from Behavior Modification. The evidence also indicates that, after one year's parole, the recidivist rate for delinquents in both experimental programs was less than those released from both institutions prior to implementing the treatment programs, and less than those youths paroled from other Youth Authority institutions.[9]

To many, TA and Behavior Modification seem like two distinctly different approaches. A closer look suggests that they are similar in several ways. Both are concerned with changing behavior in the here and now; both focus on making the client assume the responsibility for his own decisions; and both attempt to move the client from environmental support to self-support (as does Gestalt). One difference might be that TA helps the individual to feel better about himself so that he will have less need to behave inappropriately, and behavior modification focuses on helping him to behave appropriately, and in the end he will feel better about himself by internalizing the direction given by his new learning experiences.

Similar parallels can be drawn between these methods and reality therapy. As Rachins indicates, reality therapy is concerned with present behavior. It focuses on helping the client evaluate his behavior, as does TA and Gestalt, and rejects the use of excuses, as TA rejects the use of excuses and games. It also approves (rewards) responsible (appropriate) behavior. The similarities are almost endless, and often it is only the idiosyncratic jargon that differentiates them.

Conjoint family therapy also has many parallels with the other treatment models. The "mature person" for Satir seems to correspond to the responsible adult in TA. The dynamics of communication seem amazingly similar. In fact, TA and conjoint seem to use different terms to describe the same phenomena, to compare the dysfunctional with the functional human.

There are differences among all the counseling methods: different theoretical tenets; different words to express concepts and terms; and different mechanics to implement the various strategies. However, when considered in a broad perspective, these differences are almost inconsequential. Perhaps the real difference lies in the counselor—he understands some methods better than others and, because of his personal style and emotional comfort level, he can apply some methods better than others. Perhaps, in the end, zero does equal zero.

The significant point to emphasize is *do something*. Shelve the paper work, forget the coffee, get out of the office—and counsel. Risk a little involvement with the human beings on your caseload. Learn, teach and grow with them in experiencing the most vital quicksilver of all, human behavior.

NOTES

[1] Schutz, William C., *The Interpersonal Underworld* (Palo Alto, Ca.: Science and Behavior Books, 1966), pp. 18–33.

[2] Ibid., pp. 81–102.

[3] For additional reading on TA scripting and injunctions, see Steiner, Claude, *Games Alcoholics Play* (New York: Ballantine Books 1971); and Berne, Eric, *What Do You Say after You Say Hello?* (New York: Bantum Books, 1973).

[4] James, Muriel, and Dorothy Jongeward, *Winning With People: Group Exercises in Transactional Analysis* (Reading, Mass.: Addison-Wesley, 1973). Pages 6, 7, 24, 25, 105, and 106 are particularly useful during the initial classification process; the balance of the workbook makes an excellent source for self-evaluation by the client and for group treatment.

[5] At the time of this writing, the source of this questionnaire and the location of these individuals is not known. They are somewhere in the Southern California area. However, the author has participated in groups using the Checklist and has found it to be most effective, especially when combined with the above-cited workbook.

[6] Schutz, William C., *Joy* (New York: Grove Press, 1967).

[7] Reprinted, with permission of the publisher, from *Born to Win: Transactional Analysis with Gestalt Experiments* (Reading, Mass.: Addison-Wesley, 1971), p. ix.

[8] Two excellent books for TA counseling with the very young are *TA for Tots* and *TA for Kids* by Alvyn M. Freed, Ph.D., a psychologist. They may be purchased directly from him at a nominal cost (391 Munroe Street, Sacramento, Ca. 95825). Two pamphlets, for juveniles and parents, are *Introduce Yourself to Transactional Analysis* and *Introduce Your Marriage to Transactional Analysis* by Paul McCormick and Leonard Campos, published by the San Joaquin TA Institute, and distributed by Transactional Pubs, 3155 College Ave., Berkeley, Ca. 94705.

[9] Copies may be obtained from the California Youth Authority.

DATE DUE